Adaptive Strategies and Population Ecology of Northern Grouse

STATE OF ALASKA
DEPARTMENT OF FISH AND GAME
DIVISION OF WILDLIFE CONSERVATION
P.O. BOX 3-2000
JUNEAU, ALASKA 99802-2000

STATE OF ALASKA
DIVISION OF WILDLIFE CONSERVATION
P.O. BOX 3-2000

Adaptive Strategies and Population Ecology of Northern Grouse

Volume II. Theory and Synthesis

Arthur T. Bergerud
and Michael W. Gratson, Editors

A Wildlife Management Institute-sponsored Book
Published by the
University of Minnesota Press   Minneapolis

Published by the University of Minnesota Press
2037 University Avenue Southeast, Minneapolis MN 55414.
Published simultaneously in Canada
by Fitzhenry & Whiteside Limited, Markham.
Printed in the United States of America.

Library of Congress Cataloging-in-Publication Data

Adaptive strategies and population ecology of northern grouse.
   "A Wildlife Management Institute sponsored book."
   Includes bibliographies and index.
   1. Grouse. 2. Bird populations. 3. Adaptation
(Biology) I. Bergerud, A. T. II. Gratson, Michael W.
QL696.G285A33   1987   598'.616   86-19248
ISBN 0-8166-1469-5
ISBN 0-8166-1470-9 (pbk.: v. 1)
ISBN 0-8166-1471-7 (pbk.: v. 2)

The University of Minnesota
is an equal-opportunity
educator and employer.

Contents

STEPPE GROUSE

Chapter 5. Spatial Patterns, Movements, and Cover Selection by Sharp-tailed Grouse
M. W. Gratson

TUNDRA GROUSE

Part II

Theory and Synthesis

12

A Genetic Explanation for Ten-Year Cycles of Grouse

R. E. Page and A. T. Bergerud

12.1 Introduction

With the exception of a few specific cases, there is still no general answer to the question "Why do populations of animals cease growing and not continue to increase without limit?" (Pielou 1977, Krebs 1978b). Population ecology as science has no universal paradigm under which it operates (Kuhn 1962, Lakatos & Musgrave 1965).

Dennis Chitty (1958) proposed an encompassing theory, that all animals have the ability to self-regulate their population levels below resource limits. The theory was intuitively appealing, but initially was not sufficiently precise to provide much direction for research programs, or to allow falsification by empirical testing. Pitelka (1958, p. 247) criticized the concept on the basis that "it may be a strain on Occam's razor to suggest genetical hypotheses regarding such fluctuations as long as more directly ecological explanations can be invoked and tested." Since then, no "directly ecological" theory has emerged, yet the entire field of sociobiology has arisen with its explanations of behavioral traits based on just such genetical hypotheses (Wilson 1975).

Chitty's theories developed further and became more rigidly specified as Chitty's Polymorphic Behavioural Hypothesis (Chitty 1967), henceforth abbreviated to CPBH. Briefly, CPBH states that at low densities passive individuals that can tolerate crowding are selectively favored, allowing population buildup and increased density. At high densities, more aggressive, less viable individuals are favored. Interference or spacing behavior results in lower breeding density

424   R. E. PAGE AND A. T. BERGERUD

and causes a population decline. The theory was developed to explain changes in abundance of animals that undergo regular periodic fluctuations, commonly called "cycles" (Elton 1942, Keith 1963). It would benefit the reader to be familiar with the review presented by Krebs (1978a). In the present paper, a study is detailed in which the logical consistency and falsifiability of the Chitty Hypothesis were investigated, leading to the definition of the central core of the hypothesis. The results were mathematically represented and simulated with empirical data from willow ptarmigan (*Lagopus lagopus*).

Chitty first suggested that the theory could be "falsified . . . by proving that there are no significant differences between expanding, stationary, and declining populations in the distributions of the properties of the individuals" (Chitty 1960, p. 99). Such a situation would in fact be a disproof, but it could never be expected to be realized. Only in the impossible situation where variations among individuals were totally irrelevant to fitness and were nonadaptive would changes in density not cause genotypic changes in density-dependent and frequency-dependent alleles (Wright 1968, Roughgarden 1971, Smouse 1976, Poulsen 1979). "Differences in the properties of individuals" would always be present. The existence of these genotypic changes with density changes does not distinguish genetic viability as either cause or effect.

To the present, testability has been enhanced but no absolute disproofs of CPBH have yet been conceived. Continual experimentation, particularly on microtine rodents, did not seem to significantly support or refute the theory (Krebs & Myers 1974), despite the fact that Chitty himself believed strongly in the Popperian view of a sophisticated falsificationist approach to science (Popper 1959, 1965, Lakatos & Musgrave 1965, Koertge 1979) and favored attempts to falsify the theory. The situation was that envisioned by Lakatos (1965) wherein the central theory forms a core surrounded by a belt of testable hypotheses. Empirical data do not necessarily impinge on the core theory itself, but if the belt is sufficiently riddled by falsified hypotheses, the belt collapses and the central theory is rejected. All tests of CPBH to date have been in the very outer fringe of the belt, owing to the great conceptual leap of inferring changes in the genotype from changes in the behavioral phenotype at a population level.

There have been no recent advances in our understanding of CPBH. Many of Chitty's supporters have become disillusioned and have moved on to other studies, or are lending support to Keith's Hypothesis for cycling in snowshoe hare (*Lepus americanus*) (Keith & Windberg 1978). For these reasons, it appeared relevant to attempt a mathematical simulation of CPBH to determine which of the potential factors involved were truly necessary to explain cyclic populations (Krebs et al. 1973, Krebs & Myers 1974). To mathematically model the theory, it was necessary to closely investigate its structure and explicitly define its basic assumptions. By so doing, hypotheses close to the core were developed. The majority of this discussion deals with cycling animals where CPBH has been most extensively debated. Our emphasis is on grouse, particularly ptarmigan.

12.2 Defining the assumptions

The Chitty Hypothesis has been couched in semantic terms that are vague and empirically imprecise. Chitty never did concisely define his theory himself. Some problems are obvious. We know that behavior is under genetic control, but how susceptible is it to environmental and other influences? What did Chitty mean by quality? What is viability? Does intrinsic mean strictly genetic? There are even a few logical inconsistencies.

The most serious logical fallacy is that at high population levels a genotype would be favored that produces "individuals in a declining population that are intrinsically less viable than their predecessors." (Chitty 1960, p. 99). If viability and fitness are synonymous, by its very definition selection could not favor less-fit individuals. The existence of this paradox in the field data of voles is an artifact of the data-collection methodology and will be seen as caused by the confusion of population parameters of the total population with that of the breeding population in the selective arguments.

We would paraphrase Chitty's definition of CPBH for cycling small mammals as follows: At low densities, individuals of low aggressive levels tolerate crowding such that population densities increase to the point where highly aggressive individuals are favored and the population declines. Within this definition are three inherent assumptions that are crucial to CPBH:

(1) Level of aggression of an individual is primarily genetically determined.

(2) Net population fecundity is inversely related to population level of aggression.

(3) Aggressive individuals are more successful in breeding competition at high densities.

Assumption 1 is explicitly stated by Chitty and must necessarily be met to consider a genetic explanation for these fluctuations.

Assumption 2 has not been specifically identified previously. Only three methods are available to force population growth to cease and become negative at high densities. Either mortality increases, dispersal increases, or fecundity decreases (Pielou 1977). Measured mortality rates often do increase in the decline phase, but this condition is not necessary. Disappearance from the study site has often been confused with mortality. Overwinter mortality rates are relatively constant for one 10-year cycle in ptarmigan (Bergerud 1970a). Dispersal has been identified as a major population-regulation factor (Wynne-Edwards 1962) and was thought to be critical in voles, but the number of dispersers is greatest during the increase phase and drops significantly before the population begins to decline (Myers & Krebs 1971). There is usually no major dispersal in ptarmigan populations (Bergerud 1970, Myrberget 1972). Dispersal is not necessary to explain the decline.

The only method remaining to cause the decline is a decrease in population fecundity. Yet litter sizes in voles and clutch sizes in ptarmigan are not correlated with changes in density (Zedja 1966, Bergerud 1970a, Keller & Krebs 1970, Weeden & Theberge 1972). The critical factor causing population declines from peak densities must be lack of recruitment to the breeding population. Given that aggression is correlated with population density (Moss & Watson 1980, Moss et al. 1984), assumption 2 is necessary.

Assumption 3 is also implicit and necessary. Aggressives are at a selective advantage at high densities. For their fitness to be higher at high densities, they must pass more genes to the succeeding generations than must passives. They must either breed more often, or produce more offspring from each breeding. But given assumption 2, fecundity is lower; therefore, the option of producing more offspring is not available. Aggressives must breed more often than passives at high densities. For all intents, ptarmigan have only a single breeding period per year. Thus, aggressives must increase their fitness by dominating breeding competition such that some passives are excluded from successful recruitment.

Are these three assumptions all that are necessary to explain cyclic fluctuations in abundance of animals? The criteria by which science accepts or rejects scientific explanations are the subject of continual philosophical debate (Lakatos 1965, Salmon 1979, Romesburg 1981). Predictive value, simplicity and goodness-of-fit to empirical data are all valid criteria by which to judge the worth of a theory; but unless we invoke the "Psychology of Research" (Kuhn 1965), resistance to falsification is the strongest, single criterion scientists possess (Popper 1959, Lakatos 1965, Koertge 1979). If a simple computer simulation incorporating only these three conditions could produce population fluctuations indistinguishable from real-world behavior, it would be strong evidence that CPBH is valid. Most important, the simulation could also help generate empirical falsification tests.

To be represented mathematically, the assumptions must be more precise. It is necessary to restate assumption 2 in terms of individual selection. Given assumption 1, learning and accumulative population stress can be ignored. Thus, net fecundity is inversely related to parental level of aggression on an individual basis. Assumption 3 was generalized so that aggressives were always more successful in breeding competition, regardless of density.

It was then possible to rigidly specify the assumptions so that they could be modeled. The parameters of aggressive level (i.e., success in breeding competition) and fecundity were specific to the genotype and constant over density changes.

12.3 The model

The final form of the assumptions is:

(1) Level of aggression is solely genetically determined by simple Mendelian selection of two alleles at one locus.

(2) Recruitment is inversely related to female parental level of aggression (female genotype).

(3) Aggressives are completely successful in breeding competition.

The difficult simulation step was to formulate a competitive breeding system that was realistic. Willow ptarmigan proved ideal to simulate from this standpoint. Their breeding system is fairly well known because they are highly visible and breed in open habitats. Territories are required to attract a mate and both sexes are territorial. Males and females arrive in the breeding grounds separately and compete independently for territories (Chap. 10, Weeden 1959b, Hannon 1982).

The simulation began in the spring, representing a finite breeding area in which territorial competition occurred. The most aggressive individuals arrived first and established territories. Other birds arrived in order of aggression and established territories until all had territories, or there was no area left. In the latter case, birds without territory joined a "waiting" flock. Packing of territories was perfect. Aggressive individuals also occupied larger territories with the result that a relatively small number of aggressive birds could dominate breeding. The process was repeated independently for females.

All individuals with territories mated randomly. Fecundities were relative to female genotype, such that clutch sizes were equal, but passive birds had the greatest brood survival to 2 months. From fall to spring, survival rates were applied to arrive at the new breeding population. Juveniles were considered as capable of breeding as adults (Hannon & Smith 1984). The flow chart of the model is shown for one breeding period (Fig. 12.1).

Initially, population information was stored in a matrix comprising two sexes by three genotypes by five age classes to investigate age-structure and sex-ratio effects. Gene flow was modeled by matrix manipulation. A compressed model was developed later, using equations of gene flow and considering only females.

The model was run on an Apple II, 48K microcomputer in BASIC. Most of the more than 75,000 simulated years of runs were conducted on the Apple, but a FORTRAN IV version of an IBM 4341 provided graphical output.

12.4 Parameters of the simulation

Whenever possible, population parameters are from Bergerud (1970a) for willow ptarmigan in Newfoundland. Most of the parameters necessary for the simulation differ between genotypes and could not be extracted from a single population statistic. Bergerud recognized nonnormality and bimodality in his data, and presented distributions for hatching dates and brood sizes.

Clutch sizes are invariant with genotype, density, and period of the cycle, averaging 10.2 ± 0.3 in Newfoundland. A clutch size of ten was used in the simulation.

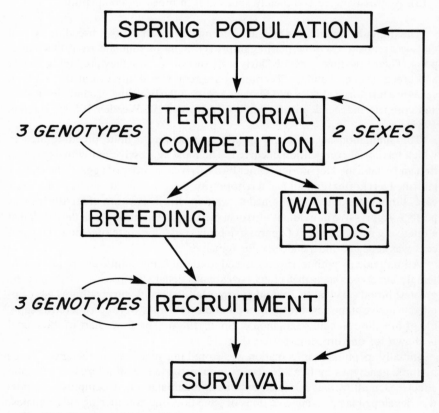

Fig. 12.1. Flowchart of the model for grouse.

Survival of chicks until August does not follow a normal distribution between broods. We considered that three distributions occur with means of 9, 6 and 4 (Fig. 12.2; from Bergerud 1970a). These were the parameters used for August brood sizes for passive, heterozygous, and aggressive genotypes, respectively.

A survival rate of 0.3 was applied to the adult population and to juveniles after August, consistent with results of Newfoundland banding studies.

The only parameter remaining is territory size. No published information was available on this aspect that would allow the separation of genotypes. Maps of

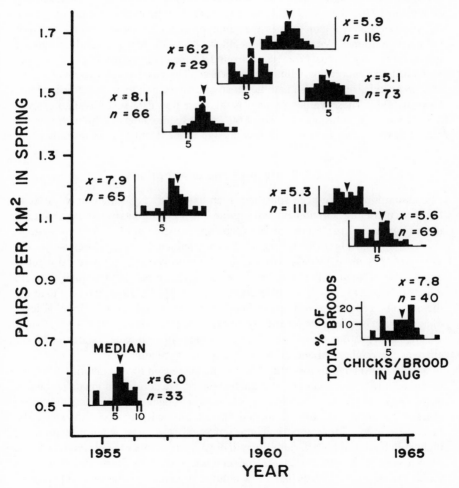

Fig. 12.2. Brood size distributions for Newfoundland ptarmigan over one cycle period (from Bergerud 1970a).

territories of willow ptarmigan for three years for the Chilkat Pass in northern British Columbia were provided by Dave Mossop (see Fig. 10.19). Two basic territory sizes were apparent, with a ratio of smallest to largest of 1:6. A range this wide may be an exaggeration of the actual genotypic means, but in the simulation, territory size was the integrator of all possible aggressive interactions, so this range was used. Similar results have been found elsewhere (Pedersen 1984).

In addition, stochastic variation in brood survival was added to represent the effects of weather. It has been noticed that brood survival is lower in decline years given the same weather conditions (Jenkins et al. 1963, Bergerud 1970a, Jenkins & Watson 1970). This was interpreted to mean that the aggressive genotype had lower brood survival than the passive genotype under the same, adverse environmental conditions. We simulated weather effects by using a random-number generator to vary August brood sizes around the mean for the particular genotype, with variances increasing with aggressiveness. The passive genotype had a variance in brood sizes of 10%, and the most aggressive genotype had a brood variance of 60%. These values seemed to fit what few data were available, even though variance in brood survival of 60% may seem somewhat high. It was the only way to get chicks/hen ratios low enough in the decline phase to fit the data.

12.5 Realism of the assumptions

The assumptions have been specified in an extremely rigid manner in order to facilitate modeling. Obviously, assumption 1 is not completely realistic, as it denies any effects of the environment. Tests of the degree of heritability of aggressiveness in ptarmigan have recently been conducted. Aggressiveness in red grouse (L. l. scoticus) chicks was slightly better correlated with parental level of aggression of their father than with learning, maternal (nonparental), or sib effects (Moss et al. 1982b, cf. also Boag & Alway 1981). Though trying to avoid the obvious, red grouse workers in Scotland are inevitably concluding that level of aggression is primarily genetically determined (Moss et al. 1984, 1985). Moss and Watson (1980, p. 116) in speaking of changes in dominance, state that "these changes were inherited and could well have been genetic."

Jacobs (1981) has discovered what may be the reason for the inability of workers to quantify the heritability of these behaviors. He defined an innateness index as the apparent degree of heritability of a measured behavior and found that spontaneous variation, i.e., environmental fluctuations, will significantly reduce the innateness index. Most important, the reduction is greatest when heritability is high. A behavior of high heritability will not appear so in a variable environment.

Working with blue grouse (Dendragapus obscurus), Bergerud (Chap. 2) found that aggressive birds had a low amount of genetic variation and produced only aggressive offspring, whereas passive birds produced offspring exhibiting the full range of aggressive behaviors. This observation is interesting because it indicates that the environment may have very little effect in reducing the aggressive level of an individual that is genetically determined to be aggressive, but may increase aggressiveness in passive birds. Most emphasis by experimenters has been placed upon the means of increasing aggression in passive individuals rather than the reverse.

Correlations between genotype and aggression have been identified in other birds. In their breeding displays, male ruffs (*Philomachus pugnax*) on the breeding grounds showed two distinctly different levels of aggression that are believed to be under genetic control (Hogen-Warburg 1966). Similarly, the distribution of territory sizes in male Arctic skuas (*Catharacta skua*) was not normal but clustered around a large and a small peak. Males with large territories ranked higher in tests of aggression and arrived on the breeding ground earlier, consistent with the model structure. In addition, aggressive males were melanistic, showing a pattern consistent with two alleles at one locus (O'Donald 1977). Testosterone is important in the production of melanin (Wydoski 1964), so the correlation between dark pigmentation and aggressiveness may not be spurious.

It has been shown in many animals that aggression is affected by androgen levels (Allee et al. 1939, Watson 1970, Gandelman & Svare 1974, Dixson 1980, Wagner et al. 1979, Watson & Parr 1981). Androgen production provides the mechanism for aggressive levels to be determined by a simple Mendelian system of inheritance. If a gene significantly increased androgen production, the behaviors hypothesized here could be realized.

With the expression of this gene for androgen production in both sexes, assumption 2 takes on new realism. A female exhibiting high levels of aggression probably would be a poorer mother. The female would incubate for shorter periods of time. Constant movement would increase nest detection by predators (Erikstad et al. 1981). Once eggs were hatched, an aggressive female would not brood as often or as steadily. This would explain greater susceptibility to bad weather of broods from aggressive mothers. Other mechanisms could be theorized by which increased female aggressiveness would lower chick survival and net fecundity.

Female birds require high levels of testosterone for laying eggs and building nests, but levels must decrease to allow incubation (Silver et al. 1979). Female California quail (*Lophortyx californicus*) injected with testosterone stopped incubating (Collias 1950). An interesting case for the effect of testosterone on mothering occurs naturally in the Wilson's phalarope (*Steganopus tricolor*), in which incubation is undertaken by the male. Ovaries of female Wilson's phalaropes produce more testosterone than the testes of the males. Females do not incubate (Johns & Pfeiffer 1963).

In a test of the genetic control of behavior, chickens could fairly easily be artificially selected for breeding behaviors (McCollom et al. 1974). Even in these highly manipulated birds, breeding behavior was strongly controlled genetically (Craig et al. 1965).

Finally, androgens stimulate RNA coding and could thus cause expression of genetically coded sexual behavior that would not otherwise be exhibited (O'Malley 1977, Beyer et al. 1979). Male ptarmigan must hold territories to attract females (Hjorth 1970), and territory size is correlated with level of aggression (Watson 1964, 1970, Watson & Parr 1981). Females chose males with larger territories and thus either directly or indirectly chose more aggressive males (Chap. 13, O'Donald 1977, Weatherhead & Robertson 1981). The model uses this principle at the limit, where any aggressive male will be chosen over any passive male, fulfilling Assumption 3.

12.6 Results

12.6.1 Basic factors

The simulation was judged successful when a region was found of high-amplitude, regular limit cycles of a 10-year period. The realistic parameters already outlined produced such cycles. The amplitude of the strictly deterministic model was increased by the weather effects introduced by the addition of variance to brood survival (Fig. 12.3). Cycle period then varied from 8 to 14 years, with a cycle missed every few hundred years.

If the passive allele (designated as A) is considered partly dominant over the aggressive allele (B), an intermediate heterozygote would result as indicated by the Newfoundland brood-size distributions. Phase maps of the flow between the two alleles illustrate the genetic properties of the model (Fig. 12.4). Note that in the increase phase, at the top of the graph, gene A increases rapidly with a slow buildup of gene B at the peak. Gene A decreases rapidly, then gene B decreases in frequency to begin the cycle again. Buildup of gene B in the population occurs through the production of sufficient homozygous aggressives by reproduction of heterozygotes in the peak year to force a decline for many years thereafter.

Changes in the breeding population are more dramatic than in the population as a whole. Cycles are driven by aggressive breeders, but variation in number of these birds is low. The effect of aggressives on passives is pronounced. Even though gene A is more abundant in the population, passives are excluded from breeding in the decline phase.

The stability properties of this model have not yet been fully explored. There appears to be an unstable equilibrium point in the cyclic cases that exists outside the normal range of the model (Fig. 12.5). A very simple but less realistic series

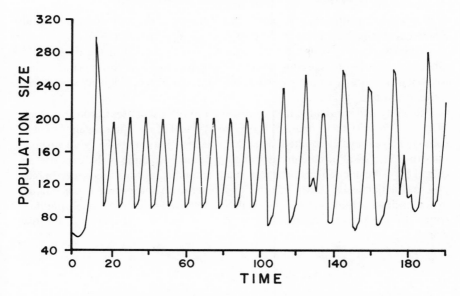

Fig. 12.3. Influence of weather effects on regularity of cycling. Weather imposed at year 100.

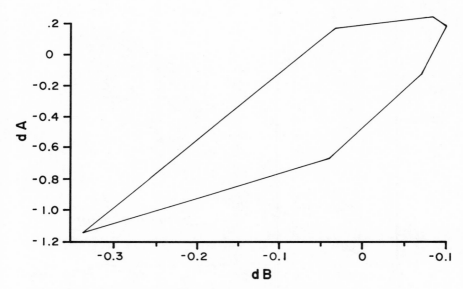

Fig. 12.4. Phase map of changes in frequency of the two model alleles.

of differential equations has been solved for the same problem and may lead to a better mathematical understanding of this situation (Hung 1982).

Territory size of the aggressive birds was six times that of the passives. A difference of three times produced a stable, polymorphic equilibrium (Fig. 12.6). Reducing variance in brood sizes because of weather effects predictably produced lower amplitude cycles.

Fecundity and survival values were varied to represent other grouse species. With survival of 0.4 and smaller brood sizes, typical of rock ptarmigan (*Lagopus mutus*), 14-year cycles resulted, as in that species (Watson 1965). With survival rates of 0.7, typical of blue grouse, cycling ceased, as in the real-world species (Fig. 12.7). Weather effects produced small eruptions, as sometimes seen in blue grouse (Redfield *et al*. 1970). Effects of a forest fire on blue grouse was simulated by increasing the limit on territory available, followed by a decay in this parameter representing successional changes. Model behavior was typical of the real world.

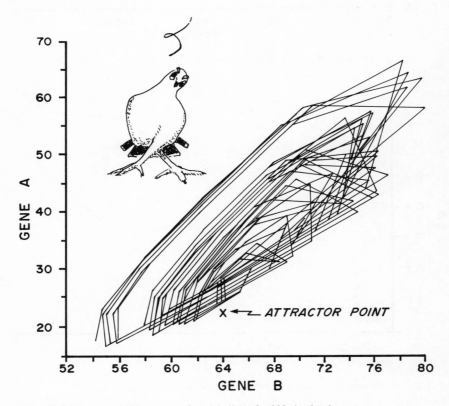

Fig. 12.5. Phase map of frequency of model alleles for 200 simulated years.

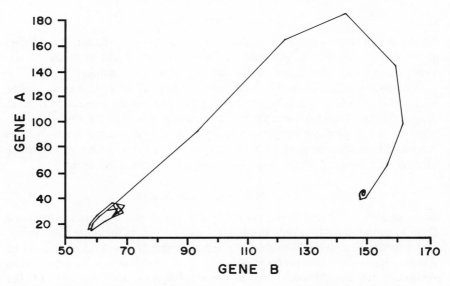

Fig. 12.6. Effect on model cycling of reducing territory size of homozygous aggressives by half. A stable polymorphic equilibrium is achieved.

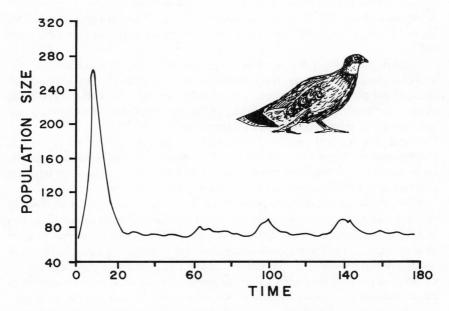

Fig. 12.7. Simulated blue grouse population. First increase caused by initial conditions.

12.6.2 Other factors

Model output appeared realistic in the simple case, but other factors were incorporated to see whether realism could be increased, and effectively to test the importance of these other factors to the theory and to cyclic animals.

Dispersal was represented by killing off the surplus or waiting birds. There was a slight increase in amplitude owing to the greater time required to recover from a decline. Passives initiate increases and they form the majority of the surplus. Similarly, predator switching was represented by increasing mortality rates from one year after the peak for various numbers of years. Although amplitude slightly increased, again no significant change in behavior occurred.

12.6.3 Realism of the results

Is the surplus necessary? In this simple model, yes. If passives are not excluded from breeding, a polymorphic equilibrium will persist. In the more heterogeneous, real world, a parallel situation can be envisioned. If there is an area of prime habitat, aggressives will preferentially occupy it. Passives will be relegated to secondary habitats. At some level, as the population expands outward from the primary centers, habitat quality will be low enough that net recruitment for the individuals in that habitat will become negative (Wolff 1980). The effect of birds that breed beyond this limit on the breeders in the prime habitat is effectively the same as if they did not breed at all. The continuum of habitat types from positive to negative recruitment has been identified in Chilkat Pass, British Columbia, by Dave Mossop (Chap. 10), but it does not exist in all years (see also Pedersen 1984).

Intraspecific strife is not necessary to prevent breeding. In a hierarchical system of resource partitioning, it is advantageous for an individual to determine its hierarchical position and if success is unlikely, to disperse with the hope that chances are better elsewhere (Lomnicki 1978). The absence of overt fighting cannot be used as indication of lack of aggression.

Wiger has reached similar conclusions for the mechanisms of cycling in *Clethrionomys* (Wiger 1982). He believes that dominant females must occupy the limited number of breeding territories and identifies the relationship between population size and recruitment in his assumptions 1, 2, and 3.

Changes in total population parameters of the model are similar to those in the real world. Genetic makeup of the model surplus is similar to the dispersers in natural populations of voles (Myers & Krebs 1971). Changes in the variance of aggressiveness of the population replicate that found for red grouse (Moss & Watson 1980). There is a considerable volume of confirming evidence for the theory, but because the theory cannot be proved, this evidence serves mainly to attract the interest of other scientists. The test record of a theory, or its resistance to falsification, is critical. What falsification tests of CPBH are suggested by the model?

12.6.4 Falsification tests

(1) The aggressiveness of an individual should not change with the stage of the cycle.

(2) The fecundity of an individual should not change with the stage of the cycle.

(3) Some passive individuals should fail to breed successfully after peak years, even though they may have bred successfully before.

(4) Removal of predators should not stop cycling (except see 8).

(5) Addition of food should not stop cycling.

(6) Extreme removal of food should stop cycling, if it severely reduces fecundity.

(7) Removal of aggressive individuals in the peak years should maintain high population levels.

(8) Increasing survival rates (i.e., to 60% for willow ptarmigan) should stop cycling.

12.7 Conclusions

More work is required to determine the underlying mechanisms that produce auto-correlations between aggressiveness and fecundity. Androgens may not provide the complete answer. The essence of CPBH is in the behavioral and reproductive success of individuals. More attention should be focused on individual differences and less on population parameters. We are convinced that Dennis Chitty found the key to cycling animals. It is hoped that this paper will open the lock.

12.8 Summary

Chitty's Polymorphic Behavioural Hypothesis (Chitty 1967) was logically reduced to three main assumptions that were mathematically modeled:

(1) Level of aggression is genetically determined by simple Mendelian selection.

(2) Recruitment is inversely related to female parental level of aggression.

(3) Aggressives are completely successful in breeding competition.

The model utilized data from willow ptarmigan populations, but was generalized to other grouse species. Simulation results were indistinguishable from the behavior of real-world grouse populations, lending support to Chitty's hypothesis as the explanation of cycles. Eight tests that would falsify the model were identified.

13

Mating Systems in Grouse

A. T. Bergerud

13.1 Introduction

The evolution of mating systems can be best understood by determining the fitness costs and benefits of various reproductive options available to individual males and females (Wittenberger 1979), within the framework of sexual selection and parental investment theory (Darwin 1871, Trivers 1972). Such an approach permits the environmental constraints impinging on the options to be identified, leading to an integrated theory (Wittenberger 1979).

Mating-system theory is well advanced in the study of birds, and the grouse (Tetraonidae) has received special emphasis (Wiley 1974, Wittenberger 1978, Bradbury 1981, Oring 1982). It is especially intriguing that all three ptarmigan species — white-tailed ptarmigan (*Lagopus leucurus*), rock ptarmigan (*L. mutus*), and willow ptarmigan (*L. lagopus*) — are monogamous; the six remaining North American grouse are polygynous. The most general explanation for monogamy in birds is that the male is needed for parental care (Lack 1968). But monogamous ptarmigan, like the polygynous grouse, are cursorial and nidifugous; males are not needed to feed the young. Removal of this constraint provides the potential for polygyny, provided that environmental conditions permit males to capitalize on this polygyny potential (Emlen & Oring 1977).

Also of interest is that forest grouse, blue grouse (*Dendragapus obscurus*), ruffed grouse (*Bonasa umbellus*), and spruce grouse (*Dendragapus canadensis*) have adopted a system of dispersed polygyny where males display solitary and do not guard resources needed by the female, and where females come to the males for breeding. In contrast the steppe grouse, sage grouse (*Centrocercus urophasianus*), prairie chickens (*Tympanuchus cupido*), and sharp-tailed grouse (*Tympanuchus phasianellus*) have a system of males displaying at a communal arena (a lek). These males display a clumped polygyny system. Thus, each mating system—monogamy, dispersed polygyny, and clumped polygyny—has evolved in a different biome—tundra, forest, or steppe. The theme of this chapter is that there are different predation pressures in these three biomes and that this predation is the prime mover in the evolution of the diverse mating systems.

13.2 The monogamy model

First I present a paradigm for the prolonged pair bond (monogamy) in ptarmigan integrating the following environmental variables: (1) few nest predators, (2) effective avian predators of adults, (3) open habitats with good visibility, and (4) long daylight hours. These factors, I suggest, have selected for the antipredator strategies of mutually exclusive, *small* prelaying ranges of females, and selection by females of males that are conspicuous in behavior and plumage and that have large territories with good nesting cover (Fig. 13.1). Conspicuous males should deflect predation pressure away from females, and females should select for a prolonged pair bond and male vigilance to reduce their risk from the effective avian predators.

13.2.1 Size of the prelaying range

I define the prelaying range of females as that space a female travels on the *breeding range* after leaving winter flocks or the forest cover used in winter and before laying her first egg. Female ptarmigan, unlike other grouse, settle in the territories of males (Weeden 1959b, Jenkins et al. 1963).

In the Bergerud and Mossop (1985) model these prelaying movements represent a nest-searching range, wherein females examine nesting cover and may evaluate the frequency of nest predators. Predation of nests accounts for most of the loss of young and potential fitness in ptarmigan and other grouse (Chap. 15). The choice of where a female places her nest to minimize detection by predators and thus hatch her eggs is the single most important decision within her control. One option in decision making is to acquire additional information before deciding among options (Wittenberger 1979).

Prelaying ranges of monogamous ptarmigan are smaller than those of the polygynous grouse. Bradbury's (1981) review presents the home range of ptarmigan females before egg-laying as varying from 0.2 to 13 ha. The prelaying ranges of females of the forest polygynous species—ruffed grouse, blue grouse, and spruce grouse—were listed as 10–50 ha, a tenfold increase; the prelaying ranges of grouse of the steppe, which mate at leks—prairie chickens, sharp-tailed grouse, and sage grouse—were over 200 ha, or another tenfold increase.

The differences in home-range size among the three grouse groups (tundra-ptarmigan, forest, and steppe) can be explained by the fact that ranges are posi-

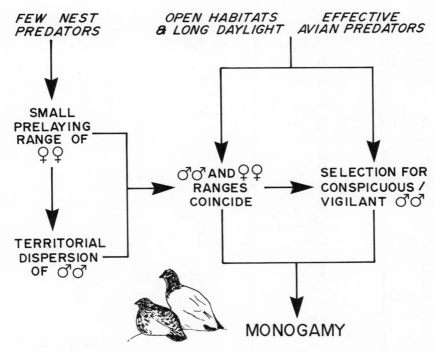

Fig. 13.1. Proposed model (Bergerud & Mossop 1985) for the evolution of monogamy in ptarmigan.

tively correlated with the abundance of nest predators and negatively correlated with loss of nests by predators and the percentage of nests preyed on (Fig. 13.2). The correlation between the size of the prelaying ranges and nesting success for the 9 grouse species is r = −0.792 (see Fig. 16.2). Cursorial, ground-nesting birds should space their nests to reduce the risk of predation (Lack 1968). Nesting success of females declines in several groups of birds as densities increase—in ducks (Weller 1979, Livezey 1981), grouse (Bump et al. 1947, Boag et al. 1979), Phasianidae (Potts 1980), and in shorebirds and passerines (Horn 1968, Krebs 1971, Andersson & Wiklund 1978, Page et al. 1983).

Reduced predation risk to nests should mean that ptarmigan are prepared to accept or to search for small prelaying ranges—nests can be relatively closely spaced and still hatch successfully. The more southern, forest and steppe grouse should search larger areas and invest more effort in the nest location because of increased contact with predators and greater importance of predation in their fitness.

Ptarmigan live in the alpine-tundra biome where nest predators are scarce. The only common predators of ptarmigan are foxes (*Vulpes vulpes, Alopex lagopus*),

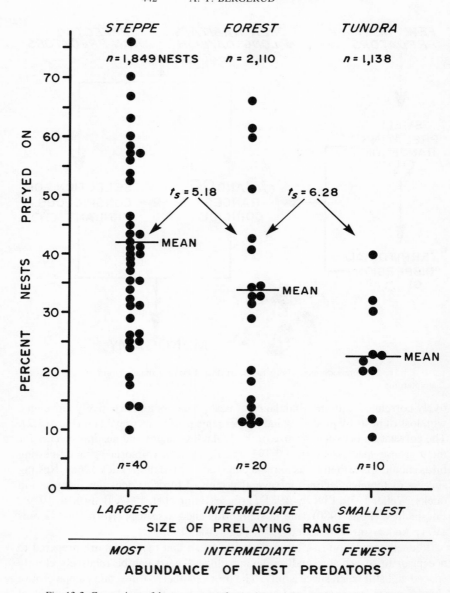

Fig. 13.2. Comparison of the percentage of nests destroyed by predators for steppe, forest, and tundra grouse. Each dot equals one study value, calculated by dividing nests destroyed by total nests found. *Sources*: *Steppe*—Gross 1930, Hamerstrom 1941, Keller et al. 1941, Lehmann 1941, Allred 1942, Schwartz 1945, Batterson & Morse 1948, Grange 1948, Hart et al. 1950, Patterson 1952, Baker 1953, Nelson 1955, Yeatter 1963, Gill 1965, Brown 1966b, 1967, 1968b, Silvy 1968, Bernhoft 1969, Klebenow 1969, Artmann 1970, Christen-

weasels (*Mustela erminea*), and crows and ravens (*Corvus* spp.) (Dixon 1927, Olstad 1932, Kristoffersen 1937, Weeden 1965, Bergerud 1970a, Giesen et al.
1980). At Chilkat Pass, British Columbia, we estimated that fewer than five mammalian predators/km^2 were present. Jones and Theberge (1982) radio-tracked
foxes at Chilkat Pass and reported that home ranges were larger there than for
red foxes in more temperate regions. Arctic foxes and weasels also exist at low
densities in the Arctic (Riewe 1975).

A generalization is that the number of mammal species in North America
decreases with increasing latitude (Fleming 1973, Wilson 1974, McCoy & Connor 1980). The polygynous grouse species that nest south of Arctic ptarmigan
have more kinds of nest predators, and at higher densities. The forest grouse species may encounter any of six to seven genera of common nest predators. One
estimate for ruffed grouse, based on an intensive predator removal, was ten pred-
ators/km^2 (Bump et al. 1947). The steppe grouse that inhabit grasslands and sagebrush (*Artemisia* spp.) may have to contend with nine genera of predators, which
may reach densities of 15/km^2 (Balser et al. 1968, Chesness et al. 1968, Beasom
1974) or more if snakes and ground squirrels (*Spermophilus* spp.) are included.

The percentage of nests destroyed by predators is correlated with latitude.
South of latitude 40°, 45 ± 2.7% (± SE) (*n* = 11 studies) of the grouse nests
were destroyed by predators. Between 40° and 46° north latitude, 36 ± 4.0%
(*n* = 18 studies) were destroyed and in the north above 46°, 26 ± 3.4% (*n* =
21 studies) of the grouse nests were lost to predation (see Fig. 15.7). Nesting success of passerines follows the same south-to-north sequence, and Ricklefs (1969)
attributed the continuum to reduced predation. The percentage of nests destroyed
by predators is significantly less for ptarmigan than for more southern, forest or
steppe grouse (Chap. 15); it is likely that some of this improvement results from
males assisting nesting hens (a circular argument) but much of it is due to the
reduced abundance of predators.

The small size of the prelaying ranges of ptarmigan, listed by Bradbury
(1981), was based on the size of the territory that monogamous females shared
with males in spring. Females of the polygynous grouse have prelaying ranges
noncoincidental with the display territories of males; hence, their prelayng

son 1970, May 1970, Bowen 1971, Pepper 1972, Schiller 1973, Horak 1974, Wallestad &
Pyrah 1974, Rice & Carter 1975, 1976, 1977, Kohn 1976, Ramharter 1976, Sisson 1976,
Horkel et al. 1978, Riley 1978, Petersen 1979, 1980, Sell 1979, Svedarsky 1979, Vance &
Westemeier 1979. *Forest*—Fisher 1939, Bump et al. 1947, Grange 1948, Tanner 1948, Fallis
& Hope 1950, Hardy 1950, Bendell 1955a, Kupa 1966, Neave & Wright 1969, Barrett 1970,
Mossop 1971, Ellison 1974, Haas 1974, Maxson 1974, Zwickel 1975, Zwickel & Carveth
1978, Hoffmann 1979, Sopuck 1979, Robinson 1980, Keppie 1982, Rusch et al. 1984, pers.
comm. *Tundra*—Kristoffersen 1937, Choate 1963a, Watson 1965, Bergerud 1970a, Gardarsson 1971, Weeden & Theberge 1972, pers. comm., Giesen et al. 1980, Hannon 1982, Myrberget 1983, pers. comm.

ranges are probably associated with female preferences, as distinct from territorial boundaries defended by males.

However, evidence indicates that female ptarmigan have a distinct affinity for prelaying ranges apart from the ones they acquire from joining males defending territories. Females commonly return to previous ranges, even if the prior mate is absent, and defend space (Choate 1963a,b, Watson & Jenkins 1964, Schmidt 1969, MacDonald 1970, Hannon 1982, 1983). Females may also desert apparent mates and move elsewhere (Schmidt 1969, Chap. 8). Females appear to assess the quality of the male's territory and sometimes visit several male territories before settling (Watson & Jenkins 1964). When males are removed from territories in experiments or by predators, the females remain (Gardarsson 1971, Chap. 9, Hannon 1983). If removals are done early in the season, new males may join the females (Hannon 1983, Table 10.10), or if no replacements are available, existing males can enlarge their territories to encompass more female ranges (Fig. 9.6). Again, the ranges of females appear centered on the nest sites and do not commonly adjoin, as do male territories (Jenkins et al. 1963, cf. Hannon 1983, p. 815). Hannon (1983) has documented that females defend prelaying ranges even in the absence of males. I feel that suitable habitat for nesting is an important component of female philopatry, and is distinct from an affiliation with the male.

13.2.2 Dispersion of males

Bradbury (1981) has recently presented a tightly argued hypothesis that the spacing pattern of female grouse dictates the spacing pattern of males. If females have small home ranges, or are prepared to accept a small space resource, males can show a dispersed, uniform spacing pattern. Uniform spacing (territoriality) can be selected for only if resources are economical to defend (Brown 1964). The fitness of ptarmigan males will be enhanced if they disperse and defend the space and nest-cover resources sought by females; as a consequence more males will have the opportunity to breed. When males are clustered, as in the lek species, commonly less than 25% do most of the breeding (Kruijt & Hogan 1967, Wiley 1973b, Table 7.10). Ptarmigan males show a uniform spacing pattern in the spring and commonly over 70% of the males are paired (Jenkins et al. 1963, Watson 1965, Braun & Rogers 1971, Fig. 10.19). The resource that Bergerud and Mossop (1985) believe males defend is the territorial space (which must include nest cover) within which females will select nest sites.

Given that males are uniformly spaced, the prelaying ranges of females still do not, theoretically, need to coincide with the territorial boundaries of males. A female could select a nest site within one territory but still range through the territories of several males. We believe that the concomitant overlap between male and female ranges results from the vulnerability of ptarmigan in the spring to avian predators. Our model suggests that a female needs a male (mate) to act as a sentinel and deflect predators during the nest-searching period and while she lays and incubates her eggs.

13.2.3 Effective avian predators

Adult rock and willow ptarmigan are hunted by red foxes, golden eagles (*Aquila chrysaetos*), gyrfalcons, (*Falco rusticolus*), and in some regions, goshawks (*Accipiter gentilis*) and peregrine falcons (*Falco peregrinus*). The most effective predator is the gyrfalcon. The range of the gyrfalcon coincides with the range of rock ptarmigan throughout the Holarctic region except in Newfoundland, Japan, and Scotland. The distribution of gyrfalcons overlaps 80% of the range of willow ptarmigan, and 40% of the distribution of white-tailed ptarmigan. The percentage of ptarmigan in the diet of some gyrfalcon populations has been reported as: over 89% in Norway, 66% in Finland, over 73% in Iceland, 90% in Alaska, and 100% in the Yukon (Hagen 1952a, Cade 1960, Bengston 1971, Pulliainen 1975a, Langvatn 1977, and pers. files). Thus many gyrfalcon populations depend on ptarmigan, the only common terrestrial, nonmigratory bird in the Arctic.

Gyrfalcons nest in April (Fig. 13.3), when the north is still gripped in winter and before migratory birds return or hibernating ground squirrels (*Spermophilus parryii*) emerge. Gyrfalcons require ptarmigan for food during breeding — if ptarmigan are low in numbers the falcons cease breeding (Cade 1960, Barichello and Mossop 1983). The unusually early timing of the spring nesting behavior of gyrfalcons (Platt & Tull 1976) is due to the vulnerability of ptarmigan to gyrfalcon predation at that time.

Ptarmigan, especially yearlings, are vulnerable to predation in the spring when they disperse from winter cover to contest for territorial space. Large numbers of birds have been found in the spring that were recently killed by raptors (Weeden 1965, Mercer 1967, Chap. 10). Darwin (1871) noted that when the snow has disappeared that this ptarmigan is known to suffer greatly from birds of prey before it has acquired its summer dress. There are several reasons for this mortality. First, the birds are partly white but substrates are becoming brown. Second, males, and to a lesser extent females, are conspicuous because they prospect in unfamiliar habitats. Third, these birds are dispersing and are no longer able to use flocking as an antipredator strategy (Gardarsson 1971, Chaps. 9, 10). Fourth, they are no longer able to roost in snow burrows and escape detection by avian predators (Chap. 10). And last, summer leaves are not yet available to use as cover.

The female ptarmigan faces a major survival problem by molting her white plumage for pigmented summer plumage. Frequently there are only 2 weeks between the time that most of the ground is covered with snow and when she must be in brown plumage to be cryptic while nesting. Spring phenology is unpredictable, snow cover is patchy, and spring snowstorms are frequent. Further, she must prospect for nest sites on brown substrates while molting her white plumage.

The control of nesting cover by males necessitates that females arriving later must localize for nesting in the vicinity of male territories. But by selecting the territory of a particular male she can have his undivided association to deflect predation pressure away from her. Also his territory provides the space so that the nest is far from others. Using the male is the female's primary tactic against effective raptors, and the male's mutually exclusive space enables the female to space her nest away from others to reduce the risk of destruction by nest predators.

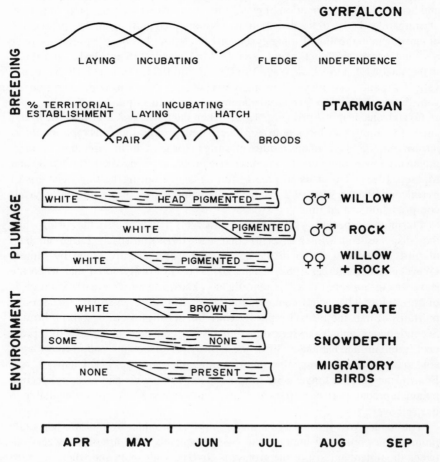

Fig. 13.3. Comparison of annual breeding cycle of gyrfalcons with annual breeding cycle and vulnerability of ptarmigan, as expressed by plumage and behavior contrasts and presence of alternative prey (migratory birds).

The males of both rock and willow ptarmigan become conspicuous in the spring at the very time that females molt and become cryptic. Huxley (1938) was possibly the first to state that the conspicuous males deflected predation pressure away from females. The male rock ptarmigan delays the molting of white feathers for a month after the female molts in several populations exposed to gyrfalcon predation (Salomonsen 1939). The male's white body is conspicuous on brown "lookouts." The male willow ptarmigan molts his white winter feathers on his head, neck, and breast sequentially to take on a conspicuous breeding plumage of a reddish brown head, neck, and breast, and white feathers on the body, which have been retained (Stokkan 1979a,b). This two-toned, solid-color combination makes him equally conspicuous on snow or against bare ground. The females of both species molt their white feathers nonsequentially — newly acquired, pigmented feathers are scattered among the white, a salt-and-pepper stage that is cryptic.

13.2.4 Conspicuousness of males

I compared the behaviors and plumages of paired, male willow ptarmigan with those of their females at Chilkat Pass, British Columbia, 15–23 May 1981, to investigate the hypothesis that males deflect predation from females. Two habitats were available in the study area, one with emergent willow (*Salix* spp.) stems, many with retained dried leaves, of which 90% was covered with snow, and one of dwarf birch (*Betula glandulosa*) on hilltops that was totally devoid of snow cover (i.e., 100% brown substrate).

All the ptarmigan pairs ($n = 93$) were in or adjacent to the willow habitat. The females averaged 69% brown plumage on their heads and 35% brown plumage on their backs (Fig. 13.4). Brown feathers were scattered among the white, and the patches of brown approximated the size of the retained, dead willow leaves. These females were cryptic, matching the willow stems and leaves and the snow beneath. The males, by contrast, averaged 96% pigmented feathers on their heads and necks and 10% on their backs. When the male was on snow his reddish brown head was visible, and when he was on the brown patches under willows his white body was in contrast. Of the pairs in which the males were motionless and silent, we saw the male before the female in 62 of 68 pairs (Table 13.1). Nonadvertising males were first seen at an average distance of 56.6 ± 3.8 m.

Males were conspicuous also because they were more often in the open than females and they frequented elevated lookouts. Females were usually under willows and in the denser parts of the vegetation stand (Table 13.1). The mean distance between males and females was 6.6 ± 0.7 m ($n = 61$).

One can argue that the birds sought willow habitats over birch because the former is a preferred food (Bryant & Kuropat 1980). However, birch is also nutritious (Gardarsson & Moss 1970). Willow could be the preferred habitat at Chilkat Pass because it provided a cryptic combination, white and brown, and provided

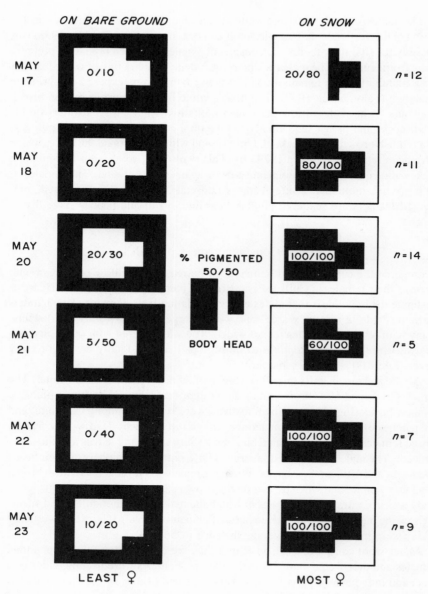

Fig. 13.4. Comparison of the sequence of molt in the most nonpigmented female and the most pigmented female observed each day. Size of the female model is reduced when there is white plumage on a snow background and pigmented plumage against a bare background. For example, on 23 May the female with the least pigment had brown feathers on only 10% of the body (90% was white) and brown on 20% of the head and white on 80%; the most pigmented female that day was all brown (100/100).

Table 13.1. Conspicuousness of males and females in pairs of willow ptarmigan observed at Chilkat Pass, B.C., May 1981

Bird	n	Male (%)	Female (%)
First seen (no calling)	68 pairs	62 (91%)	6 (9%)
In open when first seen	79 pairs	65 (82%)	14 (18%)
In willow when first seen	93 pairs	21 (23%)	72 (77%)
Body in full view—no vegetation across body during encounter	93 pairs	85 (91%)	8 (9%)
Mean number of willow stems counted crossing the body ($\pm$ SE)	11 males & 26 females	3.4 $\pm$ 0.99	7.8 $\pm$ 1.14
Bird higher in elevation	51 pairs	46 (92%)	5 (8%)

more escape cover. Predation risk should be an important component in modifying optimal foraging with respect to nutrition (Chaps. 4, 10).

When I approached a pair, the male made himself more conspicuous by giving warning calls, moving more into the open, and running on the snow ahead of the observer. The female, by contrast, crouched down and remained silent and motionless. Of the cocks in 87 pairs: 51% of the males walked in front of the observer calling, away from the female (decoy behavior); 21% flushed after the female flew; 14% walked after the female on the ground; 10% flushed but circled back, calling to the female; and only 5% flushed and left the female. My closest approach to the males in 84 pairs was 13.6 $\pm$ 0.9 m and to the females was 8.5 $\pm$ 0.6 m ($P < 0.05$). The mean distance of approach to single males was 23 $\pm$ 3.2 m ($P < 0.05$). Clearly the tactic of paired cocks was to remain near the female with a ground approach and to be available to attract attention to themselves.

I observed rock ptarmigan at Bathurst Inlet, Northwest Territories, in June 1981 and 1982. Fourteen paired males flushed only after the female of each flushed, at an average of 16.4 $\pm$ 2.7 m, whereas 14 males without females flew at 54.2 $\pm$ 8.8 m ($P < 0.05$). Males with females often made diversionary walks away from females and fanned their black tails. The white bodies of the males were in bold contrast to the brown substrates when they were on rock lookouts, and their black tails were in contrast when they were on snow.

Again at Bathurst Inlet in June 1982, I saw six male willow ptarmigan on the ground an average of 84 $\pm$ 1.2 m away, but in all six observations the females were not seen until they flew later. Males flushed at 64 $\pm$ 0.7 m ($n = 13$), whereas females flew at 15 $\pm$ 0.3 m ($n = 7$). In this location willow cover was less than 0.5 m tall. The males made distraction flights and flew away from the females when I flushed them at a mean distance of 64 m. Only when I approached where the male had been first seen was the female flushed.

Mossop secured further evidence of male deflection behavior when he flew a gyrfalcon over a pair of willow ptarmigan in June 1982 on the Dempster Highway, in the Yukon. The female flushed before the male, and the male flew behind and *above* the female. Mossop then repeated the experiments over undisturbed pairs of willow and rock ptarmigan by flying a kite model of a gyrfalcon. In all trials ($n = 15$) the willow ptarmigan males called and the females crouched. In four trials the female later flushed but flew low. The male then flushed and flew behind and higher than the female, where he would have been the first of the pair to be overtaken by a raptor coming from above. These birds did not attempt to outfly the kite. Rather, the female plunged first into dense willow cover and the male continued past her, before seeking cover. The males of rock ptarmigan pairs ($n = 6$) also flew higher than the females, but the pairs flew out of sight. Mossop and I have flushed many rock ptarmigan when we have been in helicopters, and their tactic seems to be to try to outfly the raptor (helicopter). Male rock ptarmigan seek higher vantage points in the level tundra in areas largely devoid of escape cover. They may possibly depend on a long lead time to escape raptors in habitats largely devoid of cover; they would be conspicuous if they simply crouched when on brown lookouts.

Willow ptarmigan males remain with their hens during incubation and assist in raising the broods. I observed males with 38 broods on Brunette Island, Newfoundland, in 1979. Again, males were more conspicuous than females in defense of the brood (Table 13.2). When the hunting dog pointed at a hidden brood it was normally the male rather than the female that first emerged from vegetation cover, called first, flew first, or "led" away on the ground. Females most often remained crouched, hidden, and silent until the chicks were closely approached or until a chick was captured and gave distress calls. In these instances I suggest the male was attempting to attract attention away from the hidden chicks and female.

These observations confirm that male ptarmigan act as both sentinels and decoys for their females. These observations are supported by the views of others (Weeden 1959b, Watson & Jenkins 1964, Schmidt 1969, MacDonald 1970, Watson 1972, Giesen & Braun 1979a, Hannon 1984). The vigilance of the male

Table 13.2. Comparison of behaviors of male and female willow ptarmigan in pairs with chicks on Brunette Island, Newfoundland, June and July 1979

Behavior	Broods in sample	Total male (%)	Total female (%)
Called first	21	17 (81%)	4 (19%)
Seen first in distractive behavior	36	30 (83%)	6 (17%)
Flew first	37	32 (86%)	5 (14%)
Mean distance (m) from observer when flushed ($\pm$ SE)	38	9.8 $\pm$ 1.09	6.5 $\pm$ 0.92

would be especially effective in the Arctic when all predation in May and June must occur in daylight.

13.2.5 Mortality of males

The conspicuous behavior of males in attracting the attention of raptors away from females has a mortality trade-off. The annual mortality rate of adult rock ptarmigan males in Iceland was 65%, whereas on average only 47% of the females died ($n = 1,724$, $t = 7.645$, $P < 0.01$) (data from Gardarsson 1971). The annual mortality rates of rock ptarmigan adults in Alaska also hunted by gyrfalcons were 63% for males and 54% for females, ($n = 1,008$, $t = 2.239$, $P < 0.01$) (data from Weeden & Theberge 1972, and pers. comm.). Three ptarmigan populations exposed to gyrfalcon predation averaged $49 \pm 1.2\%$ males, and six populations without gyrfalcons averaged $57 \pm 1.0\%$ males ($P < 0.05$) (Choate 1963a, Jenkins et al. 1963, Watson 1965, Weeden 1965, Mercer 1967, Bergerud 1970a, Gardarsson 1971). During an 8-year study of rock ptarmigan, Gardarsson (1971, Chap. 9) recorded a 33% mortality rate of cocks in May and June on Hrisey Island, Iceland; he estimated that few females died during the same period ($< 10\%$). He observed gyrfalcons taking nine territorial males. Others have remarked on the tendency of gyrfalcons to selectively take males in the spring (Wayne & Jolly 1958, Cade 1960).

13.3 Female choice in the model

13.3.1 Differences among species

According to sexual-selection theory, females should generally select males on the basis of phenotypic traits that reflect genetic quality (Fisher 1958); but females also should select males on the basis of quality of the territories that males defend (Orians 1969). At present the relative merits of female choice for male quality versus territory quality are debated (Searcy & Yasukawa 1981, Weatherhead & Robertson 1981, Wittenberger 1981b, Kirkpatrick 1985). One problem with the view that females select male quality (aggressiveness) to have "sexy sons" and more grandchildren is that a father's fitness should have nearly zero predictive value for offspring fitness (Falconer 1960, review Cade 1984). I propose that the benefits for female ptarmigan selecting aggressive males relate to the immediate survival of the female and her current progeny, and thus avoid the "lek-paradox" (Borgia 1979, Taylor & Williams 1982) and "sexy-son" controversy.

I can agree with Weatherhead and Robertson (1981) that female choice should involve both territory quality and male quality. Female ptarmigan must have both a safe nest site and an aggressive, vigilant male to maximize fitness. The relative importance of these two components of fitness should depend on the relative abundance of predators of adults with that of predators of nests, both between species and between populations.

The white-tailed ptarmigan has the lowest nesting success of the three ptarmigan species and the highest adult survival (Table 13.3); also, males live significantly longer than females (Braun 1969). The willow ptarmigan has the highest nesting success of the ptarmigan and the shortest life span (Table 13.3). The rock ptarmigan is intermediate between the other two species. If the risk of raptor predation compared with that of nest predation influences a female's decision of territory versus male quality, white-tailed females should be the most involved of the three species with territory quality (nest sites), because of high nest losses, and be the least selective with respect to male quality (raptor predation). In contrast, willow ptarmigan females should be the most selective of the three species for male quality and least selective for territory quality.

A greater investment by female white-tailed ptarmigan in nest sites than in male deflection behavior is suggested by the following: (1) the observations of paired females deserting their mates (Schmidt 1969, Chap. 8); (2) failure of white-tailed ptarmigan females to travel with the male in defense of boundaries (Schmidt 1969, Chap. 8)—a component of aggressiveness in female ptarmigan if male vigilance is important should be to prevent sharing her male with other females; and (3) the characteristic of female white-tailed ptarmigan to show fidelity to successful nest sites but sometimes switch males between years (Schmidt 1969, Chap. 8).

Male white-tailed ptarmigan in Colorado and Montana invest less in partners than do willow or rock ptarmigan males in the Arctic. Males in these two white-tailed ptarmigan populations travel with their females only during courtship and egg-laying (Table 13.3); they desert their females during incubation, when the chance of a female renesting ceases. Because of the long life span of males in these two populations, males can afford to invest less in reproduction of the current season than in that of the future. The two other ptarmigan that inhabit high-risk, Arctic environments and have high mortality rates and reduced longevity cannot.

Thus, in white-tailed ptarmigan, males and females invest less in each other than do the other two species. Monogamy can be explained as a by-product of the fact that the best nesting habitat is within the territory of the male. Further, the synchronous and brief nesting season and a breeding sex ratio in favor of males reduce the male's opportunity for polygamy (Emlen & Oring 1977).

Female rock ptarmigan appear more aggressive than female white-tailed ptarmigan but less aggressive than female willow ptarmigan (Schmidt 1969, Watson 1972, Hannon 1983, 1984). Female rock ptarmigan do not actually defend territorial boundaries (Watson 1972), as do willow ptarmigan females (Hannon 1982), but they do aggressively interact with other females (Watson 1972). Also,

Table 13.3. Comparison of the abundance of predators, life-history parameters, and reproduction investments among the three ptarmigan species.

Ecological parameters	White-tailed	Rock	Willow
Abundance of predators			
Predators of nest	Most	Intermediate	Least
Predators of adults	Least	Intermediate	Most
Nest location	Edge of territory	Intermediate	More central
Life history parameters			
Clutch size	5.5	8.2	9.1
Nesting success (%)	64	73	78
Annual adult mortality (%)	39	57	68
Investments			
Male vigilance and decoy behavior	F(N)	F N (Y)[a]	F N Y
Female agrressiveness to other females	Least	Intermediate	Most
Hypothesis of choice male vs. territory	Territory most	Intermediate	Male Most

[a] F = for female prior to nesting, N = for female during nesting. Y = for female with young, parentheses indicate that it was seen occasionally in some populations – after Wittenberger (1978).

Sources: Nest location: Weeden 1959b, Choate 1963a, Schmidt 1969, Gardarsson 1971; *Clutch size*: Choate 1963a, Giesen *et al.* 1980; *Nesting success*: Weeden 1959b, Choate 1963a, Watson 1965, Bergerud 1970a, Braun & Rogers 1971, Weeden & Theberge 1972, Watson & O'Hare 1979; *Annual adult mortality*: Choate 1963a, Watson 1965, Braun 1969, Bergerud 1970a, Weeden & Theberge 1972, Myrberget 1976, Hannon & Smith 1984; *Male vigilance*: Wittenberger 1978; *Female aggressiveness*: Watson & Jenkins 1964, Schmidt 1969, Watson 1972, Hannon 1982, 1984.

rock ptarmigan hens sing less frequently than do those of willow ptarmigan (Watson 1972).

In rock ptarmigan the investment of females in males is more than in white-tailed ptarmigan and less than in willow ptarmigan. The male provides vigilance and decoy behavior for the female during courtship, egg-laying, and incubation (Table 13.3), but his defense of territorial boundaries is less intense than that of willow ptarmigan. A few males defend the female and chicks when the latter first hatch (Watson 1972). Female willow ptarmigan select aggressive males with large territories in both Scotland and Chilkat Pass populations (Jenkins et al. 1963, Hannon 1983, Chap. 10).

In willow ptarmigan males defend outer boundaries of territories to maximize space and thereby attract females that are ready to nest (Fig. 13.5); these territories are generally contiguous (Chap. 10). Males with small territories commonly go without females. However, it is difficult to decide whether a female selects against a male's lack of aggressiveness and vigilance or the small area of nesting space he controls.

The male willow ptarmigan remains with the hen through nesting and brood-rearing periods, unlike male rock and white-tailed ptarmigan. When the willow ptarmigan hen is on the nest, the cock remains nearby in diurnal cover commonly overlooking the nest (Figs. 13.5, 13.6). Males at Chilkat Pass were commonly only 50 m from the nest (Hannon 1982). Hannon removed males from territories in each of 3 years. In 1 of 3 years the females that were without male assistance during incubation showed reduced nesting success compared with hens that could rely on male vigilance and decoy behavior. In addition, the distraction behavior of males accompanying broods is intense (Table 13.2, Mercer 1967). Willow ptarmigan broods use dense, tall willow and birch cover, whereas rock ptarmigan broods use low shrub cover; white-tailed ptarmigan females with broods go to rocky habitats with good visibility (Weeden 1959b, Schmidt 1969, Fig. 8.9). Ptarmigan chicks exposed to the low, Arctic-alpine temperatures commonly require brooding in inclement weather over 80% of the time during their first 2 weeks of life (Theberge & West 1973, Pedersen & Steen 1979). Brooding rock and white-tailed ptarmigan females can observe approaching predators, whereas female willow ptarmigan and their broods, in dense cover, would face increased risks in the absence of male vigilance when the females brooded the chicks.

13.3.2 Female choice of conspicuous plumage

The conspicuous plumage of male willow and rock ptarmigan during the breeding season cannot be explained by sexual selection for these plumages in the absence of differential natural-selection pressure by predators. The white plumage of male rock ptarmigan represents the retention of winter plumage and is in place before spring pairing. Male willow ptarmigan establish territories in March and April, competition begins while they are still in winter garb, and many pair before acquiring their bright, pigmented plumage. In Scotland and Newfoundland, where gyrfalcons are not present, male rock ptarmigan molt their winter plumage synchronously with females (Watson 1973, and pers. observations). Similarly, in white-tailed ptarmigan populations not exposed to serious raptor predation, the spring molt is reasonably synchronous and both sexes are equally cryptic (Braun & Rogers 1971).

The aggressive, conspicuous behavior of males in the spring has a physiological basis in testosterone levels. Males that were implanted with testosterone became more aggressive and increased the size of their territories (MacDonald 1970, Watson 1970, Watson & Parr 1981). A rise in testosterone level is known to *initiate* the molt of white plumage to conspicuous breeding plumage in willow

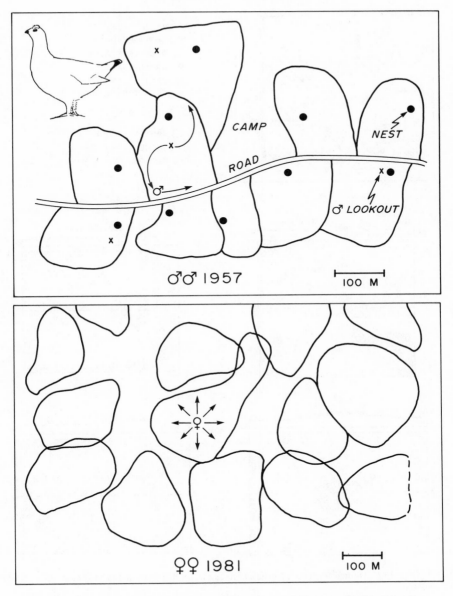

Fig. 13.5. *Top*: territories of male willow ptarmigan at Chilkat Pass, British Columbia, in 1957 (adapted from Weeden 1959b). Males defend outer boundaries to maximize space and attract females ready to nest. *Bottom*: territories of females at Chilkat Pass in 1981 (adapted from Hannon 1982). Females defend space surrounding their nests within male territories (not shown), and female territories commonly do not abut.

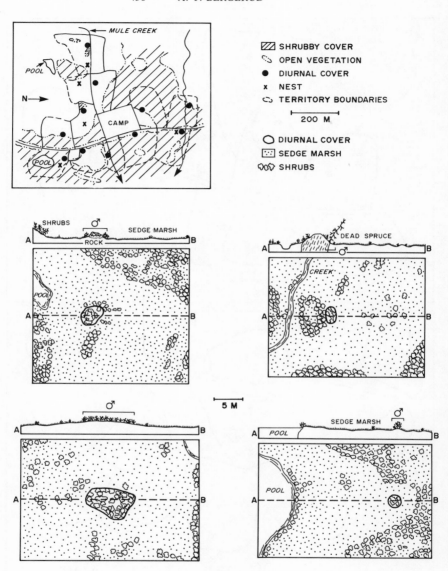

Fig. 13.6. Diurnal lookouts of male ptarmigan at Chilkat Pass in 1957 (from Weeden 1959b).

ptarmigan (Stokkan 1979b), but in rock ptarmigan male testosterone levels *inhibit* the molt of white plumage (MacDonald 1970). Thus males of both species become more in contrast to their backgrounds as they become more aggressive. If females choose aggressive males on the basis of either behavior or the large territories males may possess, they will in turn select males with the most conspicuous plumage.

By choosing a large territory a female also secures an aggressive male (Watson & Miller 1971) with conspicuous plumage. A male that is vigilant in watching for other males would have the necessary behavioral requisites for sentinel duty. But if he repeatedly flew to boundaries for defense, the female would need to accompany him before incubation to benefit from his vigilance for predators.

13.4 Food shortage and monogamy

Wittenberger (1978) hypothesized that ptarmigan were monogamous because of a food shortage. He felt that males provided two contributions to female nesting success: (1) they defended territories that provided females with exclusive foraging areas and (2) they provided vigilance for predators, which allowed females to devote more time to feeding. He postulated that ptarmigan were faced with a food shortage because of the diverse nature of their diet. He argued that the promiscuous grouse had greater food supplies because of their monophagous food habits, depending on the leaves of dominant shrub or tree species.

But ptarmigan are just as monophagous as grouse in food preferences. The dominant winter and spring foods of ptarmigan throughout the Holarctic region are the buds, leaves, and twigs of either birch (*Betula* spp.) or willow (*Salix* spp.). In some populations birds eat mostly birch, in others mostly willow. Usually one of these plant genera accounts for over 85% of the diet preceding the growing season (Watson 1964, West & Meng 1966, Weeden 1969, Bergerud & Mercer 1972, May & Braun 1972, Moss 1973). Red grouse (*L. l. scoticus*), a subspecies of willow ptarmigan, eat mostly heather (*Calluna vulgaris*). Even southern ptarmigan populations, in which birds do not eat willow and birch, forage mostly on two to three species of common shrubs (Watson 1964, Bergerud & Mercer 1972). Also, in some populations ptarmigan females gain weight during the winter and spring (May 1975, Fig. 10.26). The low in the weight cycle for ptarmigan females, like other grouse, occurs during incubation (Fig. 16.11).

Abundance of food was quantified in two studies when cyclic ptarmigan populations were at "highs"; neither population showed a food shortage (Gardarsson 1971, Figs. 9.9, 10.4). In both study areas birds spent only a small portion of their time each day feeding. If ptarmigan face local food shortage, this should be in midwinter when snow is deep and daylight is limited. There should be no food shortage in spring, when days are long and more plants are exposed by snowmelt. Also, all ptarmigan nest before the appearance of new growth in the spring. If food was a problem, they could delay nesting, as survival is high for late-hatched young (Bergerud 1970a, Parker 1981).

Williams et al. (1980) quantified the activities of large numbers of male and female willow ptarmigan just before incubation. Males stood and watched 72% of the time, whereas females stood or crouched 47% of the time. Males fed 12% of the time and females 30%. These females could not have faced a food problem if they fed only 30% of the time and stood inactive 47% of the time.

Female ptarmigan have the smallest prelaying ranges of any of the grouse. A monogamous red grouse (willow ptarmigan) female apparently can find sufficient heather for her well-being in an area only 1/1,000 the size of that traveled by a monophagous sage grouse hen. If food was in short supply for monogamous ptarmigan, their preincubation ranges should be larger than that of promiscuous species — not the reverse (Bradbury 1981).

Wittenberger (1978, p. 131) also stressed male vigilance, and stated: "It would be interesting to know whether monogamy is associated with more open habitats because food availability is generally low, because predation vulnerability is generally high, or because of other factors. I can find no data to test these hypotheses." The data presented here support the predation-vulnerability hypothesis.

13.5 The female view of the pair bond

Female ptarmigan should prefer to be monogamous and not share their male with another female. By being the sole occupant of a male's territory, she also has his space in which to select good nesting cover; the uniform spacing of male territories means that nests will be far apart (Fig. 13.5), unless a hen nests on a perimeter and the adjacent female does also. Generally, females select males with the largest territories (Jenkins et al. 1963, Hannon 1982, Chap. 10). The hypothesis that the sizes of territories are related to food quality has not been demonstrated (Lance 1978b, Miller & Watson 1978).

Vigilance and deflection behavior of males should be unshareable with other females. A female first travels with the male while she looks for a nest site. I watched a female that was oblivious to danger scraping a nest; her watchful mate spotted a gyrfalcon, called, and the female crouched and remained motionless. Two females could not travel with a single male as inconspicuously as one. Females are often not in the same stage of molt (Fig. 13.4). The inconspicuousness of a pigmented female prospecting on bare substrates would be compromised by white or partly white females also looking in brown substrates. The conspicuous male remains apart from the prospecting female, where he watches for her; predators attracted to him would overlook the cryptic female nearby.

Females also benefit from male vigilance by going to males when off the nest. These brief feeding bouts should be vigorous (Anglestam 1983) and vigilance should be helpful. Two females would have difficulty visiting the male simultaneously, and three birds should be more conspicuous than two.

Weeden (1959b) documented that when the female was absent, willow ptarmigan males selected diurnal cover that provided a vantage point and that had overhead cover. It would be difficult for a male to select a site that would provide an open view and cover, and yet also be in view of two widely spaced nests. This is especially true because females would select their sites at different times. Males that left their vantage point with one female could not watch for the second female that remained on her eggs.

In polygynous willow ptarmigan trios, Hannon (1982) documented that the male generally left their territories with the first brood that hatched. Again, it would be impossible for a male to provide distraction and deflection displays for two separate broods. Gang broods do not form in ptarmigan until chicks are able to fly.

Actually, females that share the same male with another female are infrequent in ptarmigan. Three examples of one male and two females in one territory are: 22 of 296 (7%) female rock ptarmigan in Scotland (Watson 1965), 16 of 243 (7%) female white-tailed ptarmigan in Colorado (Braun & Rogers 1971), and 5 of 57 (9%) at Chilkat Pass (Hannon 1982). Some females may attempt to return to previous nesting areas regardless of sharing if nesting losses in the population are high and they enjoyed previous nesting success. A possible tactic may be that the second hen in some of these trios joined the male after the first hen was incubating and no longer defending her nesting space (Fig. 10.21).

Conceivably, the polygyny threshold could be exceeded in some large territories—two females might both be in good nesting cover and farther apart than if the second hen selected another male with a small territory. But even in a dense, red grouse population in Scotland, one female of each polygynous pair had low reproductive success (Miller & Watson 1978):

most successful bigamous hen—4.3 young/female, $n = 9$
least successful bigamous hen—0.4 young/female, $n = 9$
monogamous (control) hens—4.1 young/female, $n = 40$

One of the bigamous hens died, three disappeared, three raised no young, and two fledged two chicks each. These results are consistent with the view that vigilance and decoy behavior are important components of female fitness and that this male quality is not shareable.

The hypothesis that explains monogamy from the female's point of view is Wittenberger and Tilson's (1980, p. 200) hypothesis No. 2, "Monogamy should evolve in territorial species if pairing with an [available] unmated male is always better than pairing with an already mated male."

13.6 The male view of the pair bond

Males should attempt to be opportunistically polygynous. Hannon (1982) showed that males attempted to prevent their hens from attacking stuffed, dummy females. Miller and Watson (1978) documented that polygynous males enjoyed a higher breeding success (more young in autumn) than monogamous males, even though bigamous females produced fewer chicks/female than did monogamous females.

If a male is to deflect predators and incur risk, he should fertilize females as soon as possible. Females faced with effective raptors should be amenable to breeding after the nest-site decision — early breeding should help keep the male monogamous to protect his investment. In contrast, in those ptarmigan populations where raptor risk is low but nest predation is relatively high, females should invest more time in the nest-site decision and withhold mating if male vigilance and deflection behavior are less crucial than the nest-location decision.

After a male has mated, he should be more concerned with vigilance and deflection. If his female dies he has little chance for a second female, because of the shortage of females and because the best territories for attracting females are taken. Further, his breeding chances decline as the season advances because females become progressively tied to their nest site and are reluctant to shift (cf. Hannon 1983).

Males should evaluate the trade-offs between survival and mating opportunities in deciding whether to display vigilant and deflective behavior. A male may opt for a safer life-style and try for future breedings, or invest heavily in his current female with the inherent risks. The effective, breeding sex ratio is the key variable in the decision. His wisdom is measured in descendants.

Consider two options: a low-risk option where the female is on her own after mating, and a high-risk option of continued male vigilance and deflection behavior. I calculated a pair of recurrence relations to generate descendants in year n to year $n + 1$ where:

$M_n(F_n) =$ the number of male (female) descendants alive in nth year
$q_m(q_f) =$ male (female) annual mortality rates
$\gamma =$ male mating success
$s =$ the number of juveniles per nest (each sex) that survive till 12 months;

Then:

$M_n + 1 = (\gamma s + (1 - q_m)) M_n + sF_n$ and
$F_n + 1 = \gamma sM_n + (s + 1 - q_f) F_n$

Now taking $M_0 = 1$, $F_0 = 0$, the number of surviving descendants in any year may be determined recursively. Assumptions in the equation generally met are:

no inbreeding (approximated for small n), juvenile males and females have similar mortality rates, and all living females breed.

For the low-risk option I used the values from white-tailed ptarmigan studied in Colorado by Braun (1969), Schmidt (1969, Chap. 8) and Braun and Rogers (1971). Their populations live south of gyrfalcons and the birds have low mortality rates. In effect males take little risk because there are few raptors and the high, foggy mountains are safe habitats. The risk to females from raptors is also small, but females have a higher mortality rate than males because they have contact with more ground predators. I equated this higher breeding mortality of females with the higher losses of females in northern populations because of raptors, *if* the males in these northern populations would choose the low-risk option. Hence, we feel the 57:43 ($n = 564$) sex ratio of this Colorado population is an approximation of the differential sex ratio and mortality that might result if the low-risk option was chosen by males coexisting with gyrfalcons (cf. Hannon 1984).

Values for the Colorado white-tailed ptarmigan population are: $\gamma = 0.73$, $q_m = 0.31$, $q_f = 0.46$ and s = 0.44. The total numbers of descendants of a male in this population with the low-risk option are $n = 1$ to $n = 5$: 1.3, 1.8, 2.5, 3.4, and 4.6.

At the other end of the risk continuum is the dangerous environment inhabitated by rock ptarmigan in Iceland. The sex ratio of adults there was 47:53 ($n = 5,009$) (Gardarsson 1971, Chap. 9). Using Gardarsson (1971) the values are: $\gamma = 1.00$, $q_m = 0.65$, $q_f = 0.47$, $\sigma = 1.93$, and s = 0.72. The numbers of descendants $n = 1$ to $n = 5$ are: 1.8, 3.3, 6.3, 11.8, and 22.3.

The high-risk option in Iceland resulted in far more descendants for the male than the low-risk option, 22.3 versus 4.6, in $n = 5$. Males that risk their lives in dangerous environments can expect to have more descendants than males that face low-risk situations, because of more-balanced sex ratios in the high-risk situation and hence increased breeding opportunities for their male offspring. The territorial system of males and the selection by females of males that have large territories mean that a significant proportion of males do not breed in a monogamous system when the mortality rate of females is higher than males.

Monogamy from the male viewpoint results from Wittenberger and Tilson's (1980, p. 200) hypothesis no. 4, "Monogamy should evolve even though the polygyny threshold is exceeded if aggression by mated females prevents males from acquiring additional mates."

13.7 Dispersed polygyny

It is not a long step from white-tailed ptarmigan, which are almost polygynous, to forest grouse, in which males display a dispersed system of advertising sites and each male travels to a few display posts. Female forest grouse search a preincubation range about the same size as that of white-tailed females (Table 14.2) (nest predation is similar, Table 15.2), and male forest grouse can be spaced at densities similar to those of whitetails (Fig. 8.7, 14.12).

Nor is there a long stride from the dispersed distribution of forest grouse males to the clumped distribution of polygynous males at communal display grounds (leks). Many authors have commented on the clumping of forest grouse males (Blackford 1963, Gullion 1967, Anderson 1973, Herzog 1977, McNicoll 1978, Little 1978, Lewis 1985, Figs. 2.16, 13.7, 14.12). One can see how a cluster of males might benefit from the "you first" principle relative to predation. I have noted that when a blue grouse hooter became silent when a raptor passed over, so did other males out of sight. McNicoll (1978) noted that blue grouse males sang in social groups. This could be "stimulus-pooling" or, simply, keeping up with the competition.

The major difference between the mating systems of forest grouse (Fig. 13.8) and ptarmigan (Fig. 13.1) is that male forest grouse remain stationary, with females coming to them (Fig. 14.6), and do not accompany females or defend territorial boundaries (Fig. 14.7). Since the preincubation ranges of females are

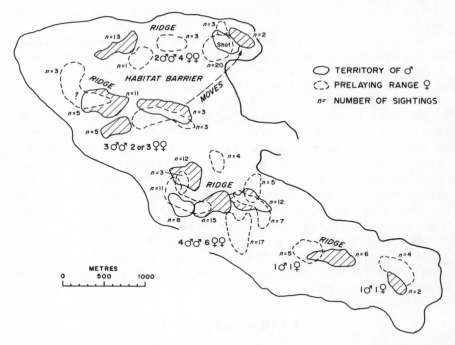

Fig. 13.7. Distribution of male territories and the prelaying ranges of females on Stuart Island, Washington, in 1976. The males are clumped on ridges. The females are spaced and generally closer to one male than to any other male. One male moved to be closer to females when another male was shot.

relatively small (Table 14.2), it is conceivable that, energetically, males could defend the nesting habitat leading to monogamy (Fig. 13.1). Males could travel boundaries and use song to repel other males despite the concealing canopy. At least for spruce and blue grouse, mobile males could remain safe by using advertising posts in conifer cover. The ruffed grouse male might be at a disadvantage if he left his secure drumming log for less safe sites.

Unlike that of ptarmigan on the tundra, vigilance of male forest grouse would not be helpful to females because of the short sighting distances in forest canopies (Fig. 13.8). Still, if the female and male traveled as a pair, which is the case for hazel grouse (*Tetrastes bonasa*) (Hjorth 1970), the male could deflect predation from the female, perhaps at a greater mortality price than that of male ptarmigan. However, two birds would be more conspicuous to ground predators than would one. Further, the female can still benefit from a nearby male that is advertising. He may attract raptors, and when he silenced, the female could be forewarned.

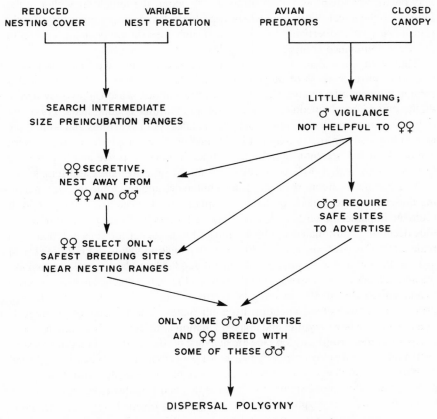

Fig. 13.8. Proposed model for the evolution of dispersed polygyny in forest grouse.

Females dictate the dispersal pattern of males (Bradbury 1981). Female forest grouse wish to remain secretive, spaced away from other nesting females and advertising males who would display to them. Hence females should mate only with males who behave predictably, do not follow them, and stay away from nesting habitats. The nests of forest grouse are away from males (Bump et al. 1947, Lance 1970, Herzog 1977) and are more frequent between male territories (Ellison 1973). There should be a compromise of being away from males yet not so far that a female must trespass across the range of another female to reach the male (Fig. 13.7). If another female is between her and a male, a second male might be able to move between the ranges of the two females and succeed in breeding (Fig. 14.12).

The second requirement of a forest female may be to breed with an appropriately placed male only if his display site is relatively safe. The display sites of males are known to predators, and ambush is possible. The safety of a new site may be an "unknown" and other things being equal, the female may choose the familiar to the novel. Since females show philopatry to nesting ranges they should revisit last year's advertising locations, and such sites should be at a premium in the ideal-dominance competition of males.

Thus with immediate survival and nesting success at stake, there is a continuum of attractiveness of display sites and males to females. Yearling males cannot compete effectively. They were not present last season, they may arrive on the range later than adults; and they are less familiar to adult hens. Polygyny in forest grouse results because nearly all females, both yearlings and adults, try to nest but yearling males may not be in the effective competition. Hence there can be about 1.4 breeding females to each adult male in spruce and blue grouse in populations with a 30% turnover and a 50:50 ratio of males and females.

Yearling males are more cryptic than adult males and resemble females in having duller plumage. One hypothesis to explain this delayed acquisition of adult plumage in passerine birds is that yearling males benefit by mimicry of females, thus deceiving adult males and being allowed to prospect for sites and mates on male territories (Rohwer et at. 1980). This explanation would not hold for forest grouse. Forest grouse do not have distinct defended boundaries, and nondisplaying adults commonly trespass. I have observed four adult blue grouse males come to a taped female call. Prospecting as a female mimic carries the penalty for the yearling of unwelcomed attention by adult males. The femalelike plumage is presumably the most cryptic, and this explanation is sufficient to explain the lookalikes. In ruffed grouse, which face the heaviest predation in the breeding season, even adult males display cryptic female color patterns and cannot be distinguished by plumage. However, the convergence of male and female color patterns in ruffed grouse does not explain why both males and females have ruffs that can be conspicuous. The cryptic color of yearling males results from the polygynous mating system. Since yearlings have a reduced chance of breeding, they should not compromise their safety for more conspicuous plumage until it is needed for successful breeding as adults (Selander 1972).

13.8 Clumped polygyny

There is not a great deal of difference between a trio of blue grouse males singing together in a montane habitat and a like number of prairie chickens or sharptails advertising at a communal arena at a forest interface. Blue grouse males are partly repulsed because they stay in trees or at other safe sites. The smallest groups of prairie chickens and sharptails also occur where forest meets steppe and the horizon and predator approaches are obscured by canopies (Amman 1957, Svedarsky et al. 1982). Mossop (pers. comm.) reports that displaying northern sharptails in the Yukon dance in small groups in forest clearings frequented by goshawks. The cocks appear nervous as daylight builds and leave early. We might expect that displays and group size would be tempered and more ephemeral with reduced sighting distances at forest edges. The dispersal continuum of polygynous males grades with a continuum in habitat visibility and safety.

A number of hypotheses have been proposed to explain a lek mating system. First we can think of hypotheses that relate to the advantage for males: (1) the *stimulation-conspicuousness hypothesis*—males display collectively to attract more females (Lack 1939, Hjorth 1970); (2) the *mutual benefit hypothesis*—males benefit by traveling in flocks for foraging and predator vigilance (DeVos 1979). The advantages to females of leks might include: (1) the *mate comparison hypothesis*—females can compare between males at a lek and select superior males (Bradbury 1981); (2) the *male vigilance hypothesis*—females benefit from communal groups because males are vigilant and detect approaching predators (Wittenberger 1981a); and (3) the *least costly male hypothesis*—females select the least costly male that must be at communal arenas (Wrangham 1980).

The male benefit hypotheses should not be valid. The average male does not benefit from a system where males contest for females at a lek. In contrast to a monogamous system where most males have breeding rights if the sex ratio is balanced, in clumped polygyny, extremely few males do the breeding (Table 7.9) and sexual selection is intense. Steppe males cannot defend economically the large preincubation ranges searched by females (Fig. 16.2) and thus force females into a prolonged pair bond as in ptarmigan.

Communal polygyny must be explained in terms of female fitness. The least costly male model is the most parsimonious of the female hypotheses. With the exception of Partridge's (1980) study of mate choice in fruit flies (*Drosophila* spp.), there is precious little evidence that females select "good genes." The least costly male hypothesis avoids the problems of the lek paradox (Taylor & Williams 1982) and the sexy-son and handicap arguments (Kirkpatrick 1985, 1986), and is consistent with the synthesis of this book, of the primary importance of successful nesting in fitness and demography.

In my model (Fig. 13.9), females must search large preincubation ranges of 80–800 ha (Fig. 16.2) to locate safe sites, given the high density of nest predators (Fig. 15.8). In addition, the heterogeneity of nesting cover and variation between years should increase searching ranges. Also, nesting females should avoid the habitats visited by males when the cocks are away from the lek feeding (cf. Rothenmaier 1979, Chap. 5).

The ranges of steppe grouse are not large because females have food problems (Bradbury 1981, Oring 1982). If food was a problem, the ranges hens search during laying should be as large or greater than those of prelaying, but they are considerably smaller (Tables 6.9, 14.2). Again, when females are away from the nest during incubation they commonly repeat-visit certain locales where other hens may also be feeding. Feeding bouts are vigorous, birds stuff themselves with limited movements and quickly return to their nests. The smallest preincubation range of any grouse is that of willow ptarmigan (Table 14.2); willow ptarmigan in Scotland (red grouse) can live in only 5 ha of a monoculture of heather (*Calluna vulgaris*) yet eat only a fraction of the green heather growth—2–3% (Savory 1978). In addition, hens are unlikely to run short of food because they can lengthen their guts in response to poor food (Moss 1983). Food variability is not the explanation for difference in the size of prelaying ranges of the grouse species facing different pressures from predation in selection of nest sites (Fig. 16.2).

Females of the steppe species must be especially secretive in the vicinity of the nest both because of mammal predators and because the open horizon permits egg-robbing by corvids (Bowen 1971, Autenrieth 1981, Gratson pers. comm.). Females cannot afford to have males display near nests or follow them when they return to nesting habitats. Nor is male vigilance helpful since corvids could orient their search near waiting males. Several nest predators of the steppe are nocturnal; vigilance could not assist hens, and the presence of the male would facilitate nest-searching when it was dark and hens could not take evasive action.

Steppe females nest away from leks, approximately halfway between adjacent arenas (Fig. 13.10, 13.11). The lek of copulation or banding is commonly not the lek nearest the nest site (Fig. 13.10). Females thus can bypass the displaying males if such activity compromises the nest location. Such withholding of privileges would force males away from nesting ranges. The farther females travel to mate with males the more the males must be clumped (Fig. 13.12). Female choice is then a major force in the location of arenas and the total males present.

An alternative explanation to predation for the locations of nests away from leks is that there is more space in ever-increasing concentric circles around an arena (Fig. 13.11). This space argument does not explain why the mean and mode distances of nests from leks are midway between display grounds (Fig. 13.10).

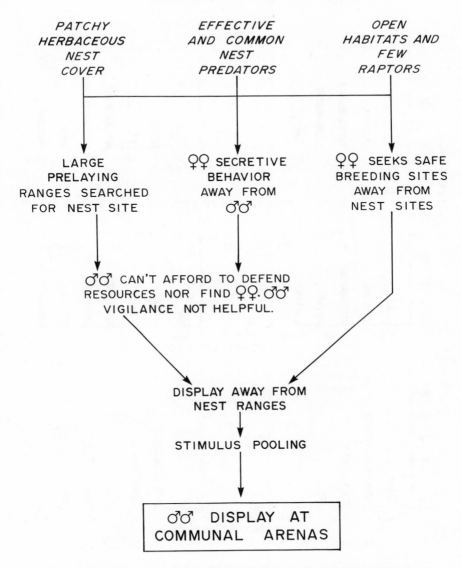

Fig. 13.9. Proposed model for the evolution of clumped polygyny (a lek mating system) in steppe grouse.

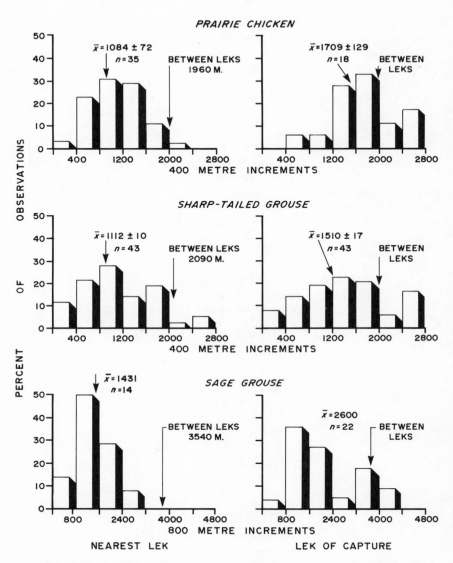

Fig. 13.10. Distribution of the distances between nests of steppe grouse and leks, using nests found by radiotelemetry. Mean distance was the average that nests were from the nearest lek, or the lek of capture. The distance between leks indicates the mean distance between leks in that population. Nests are spaced away from leks and the lek of capture is often not the nearest lek to the nest. (Data from Bernhoft 1969, Christenson 1970, Wallestad & Pyrah 1974, Kohn 1976, Svedarsky 1979).

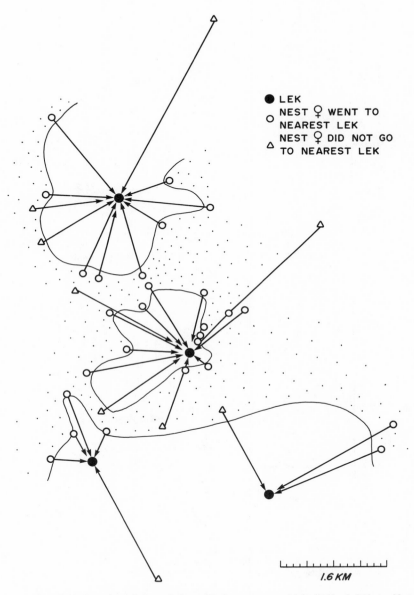

Fig. 13.11. Location of nests of sharp-tailed grouse around leks in North Dakota. Note the space adjacent to leks where few females nested. *Sources*: Bernhoft 1969, Christenson 1970, Kohn 1976.

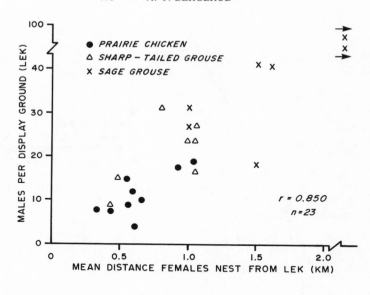

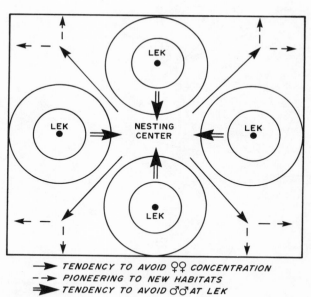

Fig. 13.12. *Top*: Males must be more clumped if females come long distances to breed. *Bottom*: Females should search for nest sites at maximum distances between leks. If the density of females in the center becomes too high, yearling females should move out beyond the leks to nest. Female progeny from yearling hens might pioneer even farther afield for nest sites.

The space argument would predict that the frequency of nests from the lek of copulation would continue to increase as one approached an adjacent lek that was somewhat near the lek of copulation compared to the overall mean distance between leks. This relationship did not hold for sharptails in North Dakota (Fig. 13.11).

Actually, females return to the breeding range and search for nest sites between leks (Fig. 5.6), before going to males to breed (Fig. 5.6). By being choosy, a female can pick a lek sufficiently far so as not to attract males yet not so far that she must expose herself to extensive travel. Whether the stimulus pooling by males plays a part in her decision remains to be tested. Generally, leks with more males also attract more females, but cause and effect are not clear.

If a population is stable in numbers females should concentrate their search between leks (Fig. 13.12) and males should establish some leks outside the preferred nesting habitat (Fig. 6.4, cf. Westemeier 1971a), in low cover where they can see ground predators. But if the population is increasing, a point should be reached when females, avoiding both males and other females, become too concentrated in the center; then some females, probably yearlings, should move past the nearest leks and localize away from the female concentration. Yearling nests should be closer to leks than should those of adults (Table 6.4), and they should have reduced nesting success (Table 15.4). Returning progeny from the yearling hens could then pioneer even farther out into new nesting habitats (Fig. 13.12). Ultimately some yearling males should move beyond the outer females and form a new lek. The sequence may be one of leapfrog, females then males then females, moving past each other in their distributions, but males should avoid the best nesting cover for display purposes.

13.9 Summary

The three North American ptarmigan species are monogamous, whereas the other six North American grouse are polygynous. In the Arctic there are few nest predators, which means that ptarmigan females should be more prepared to nest nearer each other than polygynous grouse, which lose more nests to predators. Hence ptarmigan females search relatively small prelaying ranges for nest sites. The small space requirement of females allows males to economically defend with territorial behavior the nesting resource (cover and space) that females will later seek, and require, and thus the fitness of a male is determined by the quality of the nesting resource he controls that results in selection by females. In the Arctic the open habitat, continuous daylight, and presence of effective avian predators have resulted in females also selecting conspicuous, vigilant males in a prolonged pair bond. These males reduce predation risk to females by deflecting predators away from females during nest searching and egg-laying in all three species, and from hens with chicks in willow ptarmigan.

It is suggested that the grouse represent a continuum in mating systems between the most monogamous willow ptarmigan to the most polygynous sage grouse. This continuum of monogamy to polygyny is graded with an increase in the size of the preincubation range and increasing nest predation. In general, females must select the least costly male relative to predation pressure. By withholding breeding opportunities, females can dictate the distribution of males, resulting in dispersed, solitary males in forest cover and clumped males (lek system) in open steppe habitats.

14

Survival and Breeding Strategies of Grouse

A. T. Bergerud and M. W. Gratson

14.1 Introduction

The first rule of natural selection is not to maximize reproduction, but to stay alive. Grouse must choose activities that maximize survival before they can proceed to those that maximize lifetime reproduction. The solution to these two fitness problems, to live and to breed, depends upon the evolution of satisfactory life-history strategies and tactics through the survival of fit individuals. A strategy may be defined as "a set of rules that determines which of several alternative behavioral tactics is employed to solve a particular problem or to achieve a particular goal," and a tactic as "a behavior pattern within a a species repertoire that can potentially be employed in a specified context to achieve a particular goal" (Wittenberger 1981a, p. 622).

An emerging realization from sociobiology is that many aspects of animal behavior can be predicted on the basis of a few environmental variables (Wilson 1975, Wittenberger 1981a). For grouse, the problem for both sexes is that of living and reproducing within the constraints imposed by vegetative cover and natural predators. Grouse have successfully adapted to the weather and food regimes of their habitats. Their demographic challenge is that of keeping abreast with coevolving predator populations. If we can understand the strategies of individuals, we will be in a better position to understand the demography of populations. For the individual, the goal is fitness, the strategy is survival to reproduction, and the tactics are the behavioral options chosen for success.

Behavioral options differ between the sexes. The male's primary concern is to advertise successfully for females. Breeding is only one of several problems for the female; probably the most critical is determining where to nest. She has the sole responsibility of rearing the chicks; only the willow ptarmigan (*Lagopus lagopus*) male assists in care of the young. Thus, the female's investment is much larger than that of the male's (Trivers 1972), and her behavior is moderated by a large number of environmental constraints. It may often facilitate our understanding to consider the two sexes as separate species, because their investments are so disparate (Trivers 1972). This chapter formulates some general predictive hypotheses explaining the tactics that shape overall survival and breeding strategies of male and female North American grouse. It emphasizes the environmental constraints imposed by habitats and their predators, and the relationships of these to evolved tactics.

14.2 Male advertising strategies

A male's fitness depends upon his ability to breed with females. However, the cost of advertising his presence to females is increased vulnerability and conspicuousness to predators. The male's personal hazard must be weighed against his chances for success. He should advertise when he will influence the female's mate-choice decision to the greatest degree, and at safe times and places that are conducive to attracting females.

14.2.1 Advertising displays

The major advertising tactic of the male is the use of acoustical displays (wing, tail, vocal, etc.; see descriptions in Hjorth 1970) that carry long distances. Many biologists attribute both female-attraction and male-repulsion functions to these long-range sounds, but we believe that the latter—acoustical display as an "enforcer" of territorial boundaries—has been overemphasized. Rather, we suggest that the principal role of these signals is to advertise location, a continuous reminder to females (and as a consequence, other males) that "I am here and available." Depending on their interest, receivers of the signals can approach or avoid the male's location. Individuals can recognize neighbors by their songs (Falls & McNicholl 1979, Sparling 1981). From the perspective of the male sender, the display is primarily directed at the other sex.

When blue grouse (*Dendragapus obscurus*) males approach experimental arenas (Chaps. 1, 2), they commonly stop in view of the female dummy, spread their feathers in display, and hoot. If another male appears, the hooting male ceases calling, suddenly becomes "sleek" and horizontal, and often growls. Similarly, if a male observes himself in a mirror he becomes sleek and attacks his image, but once he steps out of the sight of his reflection his feathers spread again, the esophageal air sac is reinflated, and he hoots. Bergerud has frequently attracted blue grouse males outside their normal advertising range with tape-recorded calls of females, and these birds hooted beyond their boundaries. Also, yearling males commonly approach female test arenas where there are already hooting adults. Because blue grouse males cannot distinguish the sex of conspecifics by plumage, beyond a few meters (McNicholl 1978, Jamieson 1982), these yearlings have little chance of being recognized and the sound of the hooting male does not deter them from investigating female calls within the range of the older bird. Once adult and yearling males are close (1–3 m), however, the advertising adult may assume a threat posture and may displace the yearling (Jamieson 1982).

Similar to blue grouse, male spruce grouse (*Dendragapus canadensis*) switch from vigorous sequences of display and loud wing-claps when alone to a sleek and horizontal appearance when faced with another male (MacDonald 1968). Again, once the intruding male departs, the resident returns to advertising wing-claps. Observing ruffed grouse (*Bonasa umbellus*), Archibald (1976b) has shown that in a displaying duel between two males each attempted to outdo the other in advertising his presence to females, not in intimidating his rival. Even Bergerud's rooster at home is not intimidated in his infinite predawn duel with the despot next door, and his repetitious efforts do not flag when no hens appear.

Like the long-range acoustical signals of the forest grouse, those of the prairie chicken (*Tympanuchus cupido*) and sharp-tailed grouse (*Tympanuchus phasianellus*)—"booming", and "cooing"—are female-oriented (Kermott & Oring 1975, Sparling 1981), and are in marked contrast to the more muted sounds and sleek postures that these grouse use in contesting site dominance (cf. Hjorth 1970).

A male must assess the risk that results from advertising in relation to the expected gain in breeding success. He can minimize this risk by advertising from a safe site (see also section 14.2.6). His site selection is not "ideal free" in the sense of Fretwell (Fretwell & Lucas 1969, Fretwell 1972), because other males compete for those preferred sites that are safe and that attract females. If the perceived cost of display at an inferior site exceeds the expected benefits, a male may choose not to advertise and instead may wait for the vacancy of a preferred site arising from a competitor's death. Nonadvertising *adult* males have been documented for blue grouse (Lewis & Zwickel 1980), ruffed grouse (Little 1978), and white-tailed ptarmigan (*Lagopus leucurus*) (Choate 1963a), and reported in the spruce (Olpinski 1980) and sharp-tailed grouse (Moyles & Boag 1981, Giesen pers. comm.). These nonadvertising males are not necessarily doomed to die, as argued for red grouse (*Lagopus l. scoticus*) (Jenkins et al. 1967, Watson 1985), but may actually enjoy increased longevity by remaining inconspicuous (Lewis & Zwickel 1982). Nor should the disappearance of nonadvertising males be attributed to death (cf. Rusch & Keith 1971b); such males may have assessed their display options and moved elsewhere. Silence should be considered a survival tactic and should occur when and where the perceived cost of advertisement exceeds the expected gain.

14.2.2. Fidelity as an advertising tactic

Fidelity to an advertising site is both a survival and a reproductive tactic of male grouse. The advertising location of males is their focal point of activity through-out much of the year. Ruffed grouse cocks remain near the logs where they adver-tise for females not only in the spring, but all year long. The mean annual distance of 24 males from their logs in Minnesota was only 98 m (Eng 1959), and the mean annual capture-recovery distance for drumming males in Alberta was 79 m (Rusch & Keith 1971b). The ruffed grouse is rather unique in having a "fine-grained" mixture (i.e., small patches relatively close to each other) of food and escape cover near female nesting coverts. Thus, the drumming male has the op-portunity to be relatively sedentary. Similarly, blue grouse males may remain near their advertising locations except during winter (Bendell & Elliott 1967, Chap. 2). Even in winter, the ranges of male spruce grouse in some areas include their spring advertising sites (Ellison 1973, Herzog 1977a, Herzog & Boag 1978). Male sharp-tailed grouse and prairie chickens visit their leks throughout the year except in July and August, when males are molting and females have broods (Hamerstrom & Hamerstrom 1949, 1951, Amman 1957, Chap. 5). Sage grouse (*Centrocercus urophasianus*) cocks commonly begin displaying in mid-winter and do not abandon their leks until late June (Chap. 7). Ptarmigan frequent their territories from March through June, and if weather permits and there is competition with juvenile males, they are on station again in the fall (Mercer 1967). Red grouse set up their territories in September, abandoning them for win-ter flocking only when weather interferes (Jenkins et al. 1963). Male fidelity en-hances site ownership and emphasizes the established male's reliable presence and location to females.

After the original investment, the adult male appears "locked-in" to the site he has chosen. He usually remains faithful to it even if the habitat deteriorates and the population declines (Bendell & Elliott 1967, Gullion 1967, Chap. 2). Only 4 of the 231 ruffed grouse males shifted activity centers between years (Little 1978). That these birds lived to return speaks well of the safety of the sites. Proba-bly such males also were successful with females and can expect continued suc-cess. With few exceptions, adult males of the forest and tundra species return to their advertising location of the previous year (Hale & Dorney 1963, Bendell & Elliott 1967, Gullion & Marshall 1968, McNicholl 1978, Lewis & Zwickel 1981, Pedersen et al. 1983, Steen et al. 1985, Unander & Steen 1985, Chaps. 8, 9). The only blue grouse male that shifted advertising sites on Stuart Island, British Columbia (Chap. 2), moved from one site where Bergerud never located a female to a site where he observed three hens (Fig. 13.7).

The lek species also show fidelity to previous advertising sites. The last surviv-ing heath hen was a male that returned to its lek on Martha's Vineyard, Mas-sachusetts, for 4 years after the last male companion had vanished (Gross 1928).

There were only six recorded switches in advertising leks among 21 banded cocks observed at least two springs in Wisconsin (Hamerstrom & Hamerstrom 1949). Occasionally, however, all birds on a lek will shift to a new location (e.g., Chap. 5), and we have enticed sharp-tailed grouse leks and individuals from other leks to new locations where we had placed groups of female decoys (Gratson unpubl. data). In fact, short movements from year to year are common. The degree of fidelity to these advertising sites should depend upon the stability of adjacent, female nesting habitats, and if females are not encountered nearby, males should shift. If nesting habitats change, so will lek locations.

The fidelity and continued presence of males at display sites are tactics for holding a location that has proved successful in attracting females. Also, to the extent that males are familiar with such sites, fidelity should confer a degree of safety that would not otherwise be present. The resident must be on hand also when the new generation prospects for sites, as his presence asserts his holding power.

14.2.3 Advertising in the fall

The male of several species advertises his location again in the fall. This appears timed to the dispersal of juvenile males from broods. In Minnesota and Wisconsin, juvenile ruffed grouse males leave broods and start to disperse in September (Eng 1959, Godfrey & Marshall 1969, Rodgers 1980), and some are drumming in October (Eng 1959, Gullion 1967). A correlation between the weight of droppings on logs (peak 16 October) and dispersal of 4-month-old males (Eng 1959) indicates that adults are more frequently present at advertising sites when juveniles start prospecting for sites.

The display postures and calls of male sharp-tailed grouse in the fall appear oriented more toward other males than females (Kermott 1982). At this time of year juvenile males are attempting to establish sites (Moyles & Boag 1981, Kermott 1982, Chap. 5) but females are uncommon visitors to leks. Kermott (1982) hypothesized that the resumption of display in the fall was primarily for the adult male to reassert ownership in the face of new competition.

If this hypothesis is valid, adult males should *not* advertise in the fall except in those species or populations in which juvenile males *do* compete for sites at that time. There is good support for this (Fig. 14.1). Blue grouse and sage grouse do not advertise in the fall; white-tailed ptarmigan advertise only briefly. Juvenile male blue grouse depart from the summer range in July and migrate with females to winter ranges (Lance 1967, Sopuck 1979). They first prospect for advertising sites as yearlings the following spring, but few or none hold territories. Adult males do not leave their advertising ranges in the late summer until the yearlings have left (McNicholl 1978, Sopuck 1979). Sage grouse yearlings do not generally visit leks until late spring, after most of the females have copulated with adult

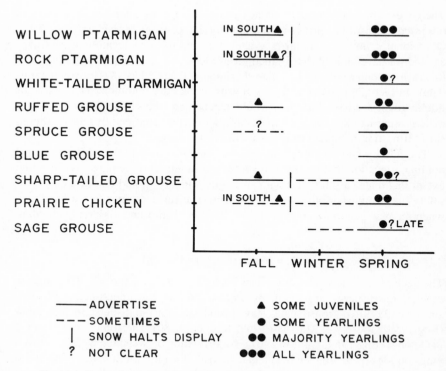

Fig. 14.1. Comparison among the nine North American grouse of when males first advertise for females and whether fall display occurs.

males and left to nest (Dalke et al. 1963, Eng 1963, Hartzler 1972, Petersen 1980). At this time, yearlings have achieved only 86% of the weight of adults (Beck & Braun 1978). The yearlings of this new generation are probably not as sexually mature as juveniles their first autumn, having attained only 75% of their adult weight by October (Patterson 1952). White-tailed ptarmigan hatch later than other grouse, in July (Braun & Roger, 1971). Winter, however, arrives earlier in the mountains than at lower altitudes, in September and October. Juveniles would thus have only 8 weeks on the breeding range before migrating downslope; under these conditions there is no time for competition in the fall.

This hypothesis of fall display in the face of competition from juveniles gains additional support from data within species. Juvenile male willow ptarmigan compete for display sites in the fall on Newfoundland, at latitude 47°N (Mercer 1967), but in northern Norway, at 69°N, they do not and adults do not display in the fall (Chap. 11). In northern Norway, migration occurs before the juveniles are mature. At lower latitudes in Norway, however, adults resume display in the fall (Phillips & Aalerud 1980, Pedersen et al. 1983), and we predict that juveniles at these sites should prospect in the fall. Pedersen et al. (1983) reported more call-ing by adults in September 1981 following high chick survival than in 1980 and 1982 when production was lower and there was less competition with juvenile males. It is interesting that in the Capercaillie (*Tetrao urogallus*), a European spe-cies and the largest and most dimorphic grouse, yearlings do not seek territories until their *second* fall or later (Hjorth 1970, Wegge & Larsen 1987). And, in this species there is fall advertisement by adults.

In summary, in those species and populations in which it occurs, fall display appears to be a tactic whereby adult males familiarize the new generation with their ownership of advertising locations in anticipation of joint competition for females in the coming spring. All the grouse of North America that do not adver-tise in the fall have in common a life-history schedule in which the new generation does not compete for sites at that time. Early winter conditions or a comparatively slow development to physical and sexual maturity, or both, can preclude the op-portunity for juvenile males to seek advertising posts in the fall.

14.2.4 Tactics of daily advertising

Male grouse usually advertise in the early morning and again in the evening; ex-cept during the height of breeding there is little midday display (Fig. 14.2). They generally begin at or just before first light, although ruffed grouse may drum on moonlit nights (Archibald 1976b). The morning display is so precise in willow ptarmigan that one can predict the commencement of becking on Newfoundland within a few minutes (Bergerud & Mercer 1966). Most cocks began within a min-ute or so of the first bird to display, similar to the short intervals reported for ruffed (Aubin 1970, 1972, Archibald 1976b) and blue grouse (McNicholl 1978). In the lekking species, males generally go to the lek in a flock from their night roosts and begin calling almost as soon as they disperse to their advertising loca-tions. With these species, too, one can predict the arrival of the first cocks and enter a blind at the edge of the lek just a few minutes before they are expected.

It is common for males to begin their displays earlier in the morning, in rela-tion to sunrise, during the peak of the breeding season. Steppe grouse males may even roost overnight at the lek for an early start (Hamerstrom & Hamerstrom 1949, Hartzler 1972, Emmons 1980). Both sharp-tailed grouse and prairie chickens arrive on the lek earlier on those days when females appear for breeding (Evans 1961, Sparling 1979). Sharp-tailed grouse shifted arrival times one-half hour earlier on 20 April 1976, but prairie chickens in the same area in Minnesota shifted to earlier times on 30 April the same year. In 1975 and 1977 no abrupt shifts were noted; sharp-tailed grouse cocks arrived at the lek only gradually earlier, consistent with the pattern of female visits in those years (Sparling 1979). Hjorth (1968) felt that the later arrival times of male blackcock (*Tetrao tetrix*) early in the breeding season could relate to the contrast of the bird on snow; he showed an abrupt switch to earlier arrival times about mid-late April when the

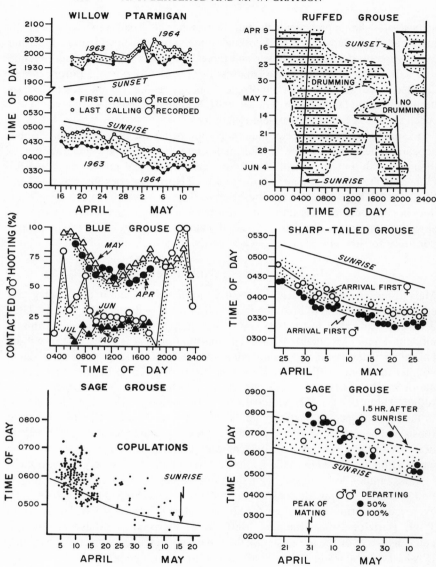

Fig. 14.2. The crepuscular nature of advertising by males and time of copulation by females. *Top left*: willow ptarmigan males on Brunette Island (Bergerud & Mercer 1966). *Top right*: drumming by ruffed grouse males in Minnesota (Archibald 1976). *Middle left*: diurnal hooting frequencies of blue grouse males on Vancouver Island (McNicholl 1978). *Middle right*: morning arrival of sharp-tailed grouse males and females on a lek in Alberta (Evans 1961). *Bottom left*: copulatons by sage grouse in Montana (Hartzler 1972). *Bottom right*: departures by sage grouse males from a lek in Wyoming (Rothenmaier 1979).

snow melted (see also Hjorth 1970). From the data for sharp-tailed grouse and prairie chickens (Sparling 1979), however, a more general explanation than the cryptic hypothesis is that the earlier arrival of cocks is the result of increased competition, heightened by the expectation of visiting hens, and the necessary condition of being in position to advertise and demonstrate site fidelity before the arrival of females.

Although daily variations occur, depending partly upon the likelihood of breeding females, a general explanation for the restriction of advertising by males to crepuscular periods is that this is an antipredator tactic of both male and female grouse. Recently, Sparling (1979, 1983) questioned this hypothesis and proposed that prairie grouse display in the early and late daylight hours, when wind velocity and thermal turbulence are often reduced, to maximize signal transmission. However, we believe that this is of secondary importance to the steppe grouse, and that this hypothesis is insufficient to explain the crepuscular displays in the forest and tundra species. With Sparling's hypothesis one might expect that birds would prolong their advertising on calm days and cease advertising early if wind velocities were high. However, birds on leks stay longer on cloudy days and vigorously display even in windy weather during the peak of breeding (Hamerstrom & Hamerstrom 1973). Also, ptarmigan frequently display all day in foggy weather, when sound transmission would be reduced, and at times on windy days. Cool, calm days do occur in the Arctic, yet ptarmigan do not advertise late into the day under these conditions. Visibility is a more consistent environmental variable acting to constrain when grouse display than are velocity and turbulence of air currents.

Curtailment of morning display and visits by females also seem to vary more with predator risk than with signal transmission quality. Morning display ceases about the time important diurnal predators become active. Ptarmigan at Chilkat Pass, British Columbia, stop displaying 2 hours after sunrise (Chap. 10), before the increased hunting activity of gyrfalcons (*Falco rusticolus*). Sharp-tailed grouse in the Yukon cease vigorous display before the arrival of goshawks (*Accipiter gentilis*) (Mossop pers. comm.). Steppe grouse appear more watchful as the morning progresses. Sage grouse commonly remain on the lek until approximately 1.5 hours after sunrise (Emmons 1980), at which time eagles (*Aquila chrysaetos*) can use the thermal currents (Hartzler 1974). Eagles frequently flush sage grouse males that stay later in the day and these grouse do not return even if the weather is favorable for signal transmission.

On Vancouver Island, British Columbia, blue grouse males commonly hoot until midmorning, whereas ruffed grouse in the same valley may stop drumming within 2 hours after sunrise. Blue grouse males have a much lower, annual mortality rate than ruffed grouse (Fig. 15.4) and appear generally more secure against predators than other grouse species. The longer daily display period of this species (Fig. 14.2, Stewart 1967) is consistent with these observations and supports the view that the daily timing of advertisement is tuned to predator risk rather than signal transmission. The safety hypothesis predicts that birds relatively safe from diurnal predators will display longer into the day than those more seriously exposed to predation. Sharp-tailed grouse in Nebraska can be expected to display longer than the same species living with goshawks in the Yukon; and ruffed grouse at Cedar Creek, Minnesota (Meslow 1966), should display later into the day than ruffed grouse at Cloquet, Minnesota, where goshawks are again an effective predator (Gullion 1967).

Commencement of the evening display period is less precise. Blue grouse commonly begin hooting by 1600 hours (McNicholl 1978), whereas ruffed grouse may not start in until 1700–1800 hours (Fig. 14.2). The open-country sage grouse start even later, approximately sunset (Hartzler 1974). Gratson (Chap. 5) noted that sharp-tailed grouse in three relic populations displayed in the afternoon and evening only at the largest leks, an observation one might not expect if the timing of advertisement depended on maximizing signal transmission. On Moresby Island, British Columbia, some blue grouse males start to hoot a half-hour or more before the majority, perhaps stimulated by the presence of a nearby female. There is a sharp peak of activity just before dark when male blue grouse leave their relatively safe and usual display sites to make noisy landings on open spots and roads. Aerial chases, hoots, and whoots usually follow, and when they do the latter confirm that a female is being actively courted on the ground (Stirling & Bendell 1970, cf. Jamieson 1982). When darkness falls, the activity abruptly ceases (cf. Stewart 1967).

The male, in deciding to advertise or not, must weigh the potential cost of his conspicuousness—a greater vulnerability to predators—with the anticipated advantages of greater access to females now or in the future. In the polygamous grouse most females visit the display sites of males for the short period in which there is just enough light to see (Fig. 14.2). The female risks conspicuousness only when predator risk is minimal, whereas the male, in attempting to influence her decision, must risk his life much more often. We can hypothesize that males with safer sites will display longer than those without; that yearlings, which generally display at sites of higher risk and with probably less success with females, will advertise less than adults; and that the display effort should be maximized when females are near and receptive. The crepuscular nature of male advertisement is most consistent with the view that it serves as an antipredator tactic. The advertising period of the male is sandwiched between diurnal and nocturnal predation periods, a time in which the female is prepared to risk increased conspicuousness in order to breed.

14.2.5 Advertising near females

An exciting hypothesis is that advertising males space themselves to maximize encounters with females (Bradbury 1981, Oring 1982). It follows from this hypothesis that males should attempt to display near areas where females will later nest. This is the converse of conventional theory, which postulates that the advertising male is the basic spacing unit around which the females locate themselves. The idea of a "sphere of influence," referring to nests located around leks (Hamerstrom 1939, Schwartz 1945), and the concept of the "nesting radius of sage grouse leks" (Braun et al. 1977) are two such hypotheses. This new hypothesis also is in contradiction with the older view that forest grouse select habitats on the basis of the availability of desirable cover for males (Gullion 1967, 1970a,b,c).

It is perhaps natural for most grouse biologists to assume that males are the basic spacing unit. Grouse are commonly counted in the spring by first locating the advertising males and biologists usually search for nests by first locating display areas. Furthermore, males arrive at the breeding ground before the females. However, if males evolutionarily track females and can recognize desired habitats for nesting, male competition for sites near these nesting areas would favor the early and synchronous return of males in order to compete for females attracted to these areas.

Several lines of evidence indicate that males of the steppe grouse species form their leks near nesting females. First, we know that these males show a wide tolerance range in the "cover" that is chosen; they frequently display on roads, at airports, at cattle salt licks, and on plowed fields, oil pads, or pipeline rights-of-way (Schwartz 1945, Hamerstrom et al. 1957, Lutz 1979, Horkel & Silvy 1980). The sites are open, usually slightly elevated, yet there are many areas that meet these requirements and are not selected. Second, invariably leks *are* located near nesting habitats (Fig. 14.3), and males frequently travel long distances from them to feed (Wallestad & Schladweiler 1974, Chap. 5). Also, the number of males per lek is commonly correlated with the abundance of nesting cover (Fig. 14.3, Hamerstrom et al. 1957, Brown 1967, Westemeier 1971b, Pepper 1972). It is also not unusual for lek locations to change from one year to the next (e.g., Kirsh et al. 1973, Kohn 1976, Chap. 5). Henderson and Jackson (1967) reported the following for sharp-tailed grouse: 104 grounds (leks) were active 4 years or less; 73 grounds were active 5 years or longer; 38 grounds were active 10 years or longer; 14 grounds were active 15 years or longer; and only three of the 178 grounds were active all 21 years of the study. Field workers have been impressed with the permanence of leks without mentioning the permanence of surrounding nest cover.

If the hypothesis that males distribute themselves in relation to females is tenable, males should change display locations if females shift. Svedarsky (1979, Chap. 6) showed that females nested mostly southeast of a lek (Fig. 6.4); there was no "radius" of dispersal. Males at this lek declined in number from 1977 to 1978, from 16 to 6, and a new lek appeared closer to the nesting females. Gratson (1983, Chap. 5), also documented that a new, sharp-tailed grouse lek appeared

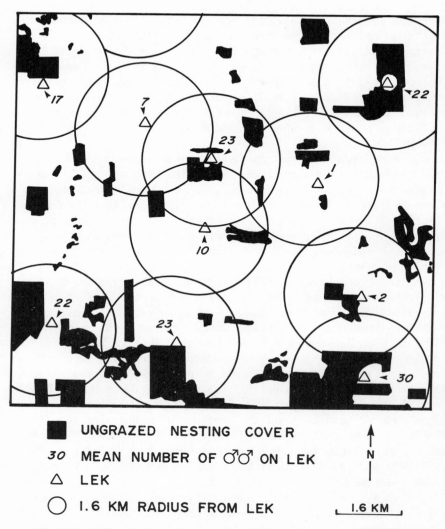

■ UNGRAZED NESTING COVER

30 MEAN NUMBER OF ♂♂ ON LEK

△ LEK

◯ 1.6 KM RADIUS FROM LEK

N

1.6 KM

Fig. 14.3. Number of sharp-tailed grouse males at leks in Saskatchewan was correlated with abundance of nesting cover found within 1.6 km (Adapted from Pepper 1972).

in the midst of female ranges. Shifts in locations of other leks on his study area also appeared to occur to areas that hens frequented. Wallestad (1975a) documented that the removal of sagebrush (*Artemisia* ssp.) used for nesting resulted in a 63 % decline in the number of males on an adjacent strutting ground, and Autenrieth (1969, pers. comm.) found that a lek where sagebrush was killed would continue to be used if the sage in the surrounding habitats used by females remained intact. Sharp-tailed grouse in Montana established new leks and the mean number of males per lek increased when the surrounding nest cover improved, but when grassland cover declined many leks were deserted (Fig. 14.4). We know that prairie grouse males themselves do not require tall grass on the lek; in fact, both sharp-tailed grouse and prairie chickens commonly abandon leks in tall cover to establish leks in recently burned or plowed areas nearby (Anderson 1969, Horak 1974, Cannon & Knopf 1979, Sexton & Gillespie 1979). Both Kirsch et al. (1973, pers. comm.) and Westemeier (1973) have experimented with creating new nesting cover for prairie grouse. Females preceded males in using the new sites by a year or so and may have become familiar with the newly seeded grassland as a result of taking broods there when the vegetation was still sparse (cf. Fig. 16.19).

In an interesting experiment, Rippin removed all the sharp-tailed grouse cocks from a lek. The next year a new arena appeared 400 m from the old location (Rippin & Boag 1974a). Nesting cover had not been altered. New birds chose the same general area for display, but because the previous owners died, the precise location of the lek changed somewhat. There are a number of examples in the literature of slight, finely tuned shifts in the precise location of display areas that likely are the result of cover factors affecting the vulnerability of displaying males themselves, such as increased plant growth, floods, or disturbance by domestic animals (Horak 1974). However, if the powerful magnet of nearby females remains, the males will not be far away.

An experiment with prairie chickens provides further evidence that females are the basic spacing unit in prairie grouse. In 1976, hand-reared prairie chickens of both sexes were held in pens while male and female, wild prairie chickens were released (Toepfer 1976, pers. comm.). Some males displayed immediately adjacent to the captive birds, and 15 others established a lek not more than 1.6 km away. We suggest that the males remained nearby because of the captive females, and not because of the captive males. Most of the wild hens dispersed long distances, only two of seven that were radio-marked remained nearby. The following year there were 16 displaying males, but in a second release of wild females, only three of ten that were radio-marked remained nearby. Many of the females traveled extensive distances, up to 56 km, before radio contact was lost. The experiment suggested that males would remain if there were some females present, and that adult females were not sufficiently attracted by the presence of a nearby, active lek for nesting. There are a number of examples of experiments in which biologists have attempted to relocate leks by placing stuffed or silhouetted male decoys, accompanied by male calls, at alternate locations (Eng et al. 1979, Tate et al. 1979, Gratson & Anderson unpubl. data). These efforts have largely failed because, we believe, males will not vacate proven display grounds near nesting females. Females, however, are more flexible, and their relatively large, preincubation range reflects the opportunity to explore newly created, nesting habitats.

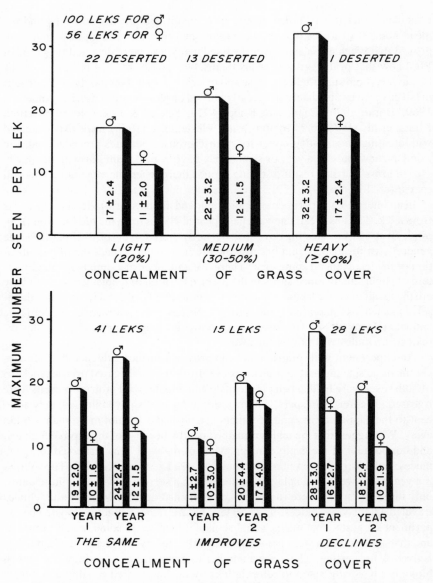

Fig. 14.4. *Top*: Abundance of male and female sharp-tailed grouse at leks and desertion of leks between years with cover constant in relation to abundance of concealing nest vegetation measured within a 4.8-km radius of each lek. Light cover (20%) indicates the mean height of grass is sufficient to conceal 20% of the body of a grouse. *Bottom*: Changes in the numbers of males and females at leks were correlated with changes in the abundance of surrounding nest cover between years. (Adapted from Brown 1966a, 1968a,b.)

If females shift or colonize new nesting areas, males will not be far behind in establishing a new lek nearby. This is what we see when we establish groups of dummy females 100–200 m away from established sharp-tailed grouse leks and watch some or all of the males shift and reestablish new territories at the dummy locations (Gratson unpubl. data).

Males of the forest species also appear to select advertising sites at places where they will encounter females. Eighty-four percent of the ruffed grouse males at Cloquet, Minnesota, advertised on upland sites, where 96% of 113 females nested (Eng 1959, Kupa 1966, Gullion 1967). Farther south, at Cedar Creek, Minnesota, 84% of 31 males chose lowland sites at which to drum (Meslow 1966); here, in contrast to Cloquet, many females nested in the lowlands (Maxson 1978). Gullion and Marshall (1968) noted that some advertising sites are used continuously over several years, despite the fact that individual occupants are often killed by goshawks (cf. Boag 1976b). They termed such sites "traps." These traps have in common the characteristic that they are near the nesting areas of females (Fig. 14.5). Males are apparently prepared to frequent dangerous advertising sites if they can expect to encounter more females there than they might at "safer" locations.

Blue grouse males also prefer some advertising sites to others. These were termed permanent and transient sites by Lewis (1979, 1982, Lewis & Zwickel 1981). Although on Vancouver Island, nesting females were evenly distributed in areas adjacent to both types of sites (half as many permanent sites and about half as many females nested nearby), more females were seen near the permanent advertising sites than near the transient ones, though there were fewer permanent sites (Table 14.1). Here, males apparently preferred the permanent sites, regardless of the distribution of nesting females. However, because the permanent sites were farther from sites of equivalent elevation, females may have been more readily attracted to males there than at the transient sites. Males also lived longer at the permanent than transient sites, and females could have benefited if these sites were safer. The higher frequency of females near the permanent sites most likely explains the males' persistent use of them.

Earlier, (Chap. 2), Bergerud recounted the way in which blue grouse males, introduced to Moresby Island, British Columbia, dispersed before they established advertising locations (Fig. 2.4). This dispersal probably occurred before females nested. Many of the females that were introduced failed to nest in 1971 and 1972 and even attempted to leave the island, despite the fact that most of the males were already localized and advertising. The remaining females nested primarily in the center of the island, away from the most aggressive and conspicuous males, but in later years five of these aggressive males shifted their ranges inland, toward the nesting hens (Fig. 2.4).

Males of all the forest grouse commonly display from different sites within their advertising ranges. Blue grouse males averaged seven sites at Comox Burn

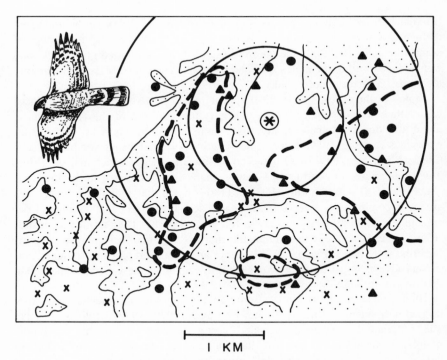

I KM

ADVERTISEMENT SITES

☐ UPLAND   ⦂⦂ LOWLAND

⊂⊐⊐ ♀♀ NESTING AREA

▲ INTERMITTENT, SHORT SURVIVAL
● PERSISTENT, SHORT SURVIVAL
✕ PERSISTENT, LONG SURVIVAL
⊛ GOSHAWK NEST

Fig. 14.5. Locations of advertising sites of ruffed grouse males at Cloquet, Minnesota. Many of the advertising sites classified as persistent and short survival (i.e., persistently used by short-lived males) were near habitats used by nesting hens and within 2 km of nesting goshawks. (Adapted from Eng & Gullion 1962, Kupa 1966.)

(McNicholl 1978) and five sites at Moresby Island (Bergerud & Hemus 1975). Gullion (1967) reported that 44% of 168 ruffed grouse males that he studied shifted drumming locations within their activity centers. Multiple display sites in activity centers have also been recorded in Alberta (Boag 1976a). Male blue and

Table 14.1. Survival and replacement of male blue grouse at permanent and transient advertising
sites, elevation of sites, and abundance of females nearby
(Lewis 1979, 1981, Lewis & Zwickel 1981)

Parameter	Permanent sites	Transient sites
Number of sites 1969–78	41	82
% of sites where new males replaced removed males	82 (11)[a]	36 (11)
Total male replacements[b]	20	4
Mean survival of males (years)	4.3	2.6
Distance (m) to nearest area of equivalent elevation	143	60
Nesting females nearby	39	74
Total females seen near sites (average per site)	444 (10.8)	301 (3.7)[c]

[a] Number of sites in parentheses.
[b] Up to 3 males were removed from some permanent sites.
[c] 301 females seen in years when sites occupied.

spruce grouse often advance and change advertising locations when tape-recorded female calls are played back to them (MacDonald 1968, Bergerud & Hemus 1975). We suggest that most of the natural shifts between display sites, possibly even between logs that lay at different angles, are made in order to move nearer to females or to enhance signal transmission aimed in the direction of a female, not to repel other males (cf. Archibald 1974). Another tactic of some ruffed grouse males is that of displaying at the border between open and dense habitats (Eng 1959, Meslow 1966, Little 1978). Such males may encounter more females than those in dense canopies, because females often prefer open canopy cover with greater ground-nesting vegetation (Maxson 1978). Displaying males that advertise in such fringe areas often suffer a higher mortality rate than those in more dense cover (Little 1978, Gullion 1984b), and probably compromise safety for increased contact with females.

The female's nesting-site decision is a critical fitness choice; the breeding site is of secondary impact. The female appears to be the basic spacing unit in grouse, and the male selects display sites to capitalize on her range selections.

14.2.6 Selection of safe advertising sites

A secondary consideration in the choice of a display site by a male, after that of localizing near females, is that the site should allow amplification of his advertising signal but not expose him unduly to predation. The advertising locations of males are inevitably known to females and predators alike.

The spruce grouse male appears secure during advertisement in many populations. The dense stands of conifers in which males commonly display (Stoneberg 1967, McLachlin 1970, Anderson 1973) should make navigation by large owls and goshawks difficult. Tree densities adjacent to advertising sites range from 3,800 to 12,400 stems/ha (Stoneberg 1967, Haas 1974, Boag et al. 1979, Hedberg 1980). In contrast, stem densities in the nesting ranges of Cooper's hawks (*Accipiter cooperii*) range from 276 to 1,728 trees/ha and in those of goshawks 273 to 750 trees/ha (Titus & Mosher 1981, Reynolds et al. 1982). The dense forests used by spruce grouse should hamper the grouse hunting success of accipiters, an explanation that is compatible with the mortality rate for males of less than 35% in several populations (Stoneberg 1967, Anderson, 1973, Boag et al. 1979).

Spruce grouse males have perfected their advertising displays to minimize vulnerability and maximize signal amplification. The male commonly perches on a low, protective limb of a conifer, approximately 1–2 m from the ground, and drops to the forest floor, clapping his wings (Anderson 1973). He remains on the exposed, open forest floor only momentarily before flying back up to protective cover where he once again produces his wing-beat signal. The sound, upon landing on the ground, is broadcast beneath the attenuating conifer foliage, but he is exposed for only a short time (Fig. 14.6).

Blue grouse males are also secure in some populations, when they, too, select thick conifer cover in which to display (Martinka 1972). Males in many populations, however, display in open conifer forests (Bendell & Elliott 1966, 1967). They frequently choose lone trees on hills and knobs where their signal is unobstructed. On rocky hilltops, where there is little understory vegetation, they can see and court females. The males on Moresby Island, British Columbia, displayed in tall conifers, 20 to 30 m high, and perched close to the base of the trunk and several meters below the exposed top of the tree. A male's position next to the trunk while vocalizing created the effect of ventriloquism, and we often nad to search for 15 minutes or more before spotting the bird. When raptors flew over, the bird became silent and crouched – the trunk and conifer branch provided effective concealment. These birds were safe but could also look for females.

Ruffed grouse range from Georgia to Alaska, in habitats varying from oak (*Quercus* spp.) to birch (*Betula* spp.), aspen (*Populus* spp.), and fir (*Abies* spp.), which are coinhabited by different arrays of predators. The assessment of costs and benefits associated with drumming locations by a male in any region must consider both predation risk and the need to be conspicuous and to amplify his signal to attract females. Males suffer high mortality in northern Minnesota and Michigan, which are within the breeding range of goshawks, especially if their activity centers are near this raptor's nests (Eng & Gullion 1962, Fig. 14.5). Here, where goshawks are prevalent, males commonly display at less exposed sites, often at the base of hills (99 of 139 males) or in lowlands (18 of 19 males) (Berner & Gysel 1969).

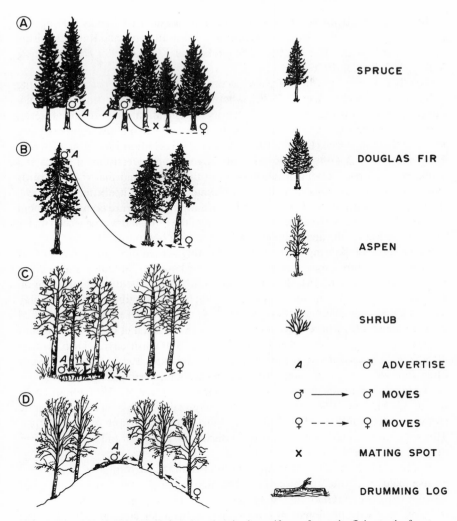

SPRUCE

DOUGLAS FIR

ASPEN

SHRUB

A   ♂ ADVERTISE

♂ ⟶ ♂ MOVES

♀ ----➤ ♀ MOVES

× MATING SPOT

DRUMMING LOG

Fig. 14.6. (*A*) Spruce grouse males advertise in coniferous forests by flying to the forest floor using wing-claps and flying back to a lower limb with another clap. They are vulnerable to predators only briefly when on the ground. Males can leave their advertising sites and meet females and remain relatively safe because of adequate cover. (*B*) Male blue grouse advertise at safe locations high in conifers, but near a protective trunk, which baffles the sound; by moving around the trunk they can direct the sound. Like spruce grouse, they can meet females away from their protective advertisement locations because of conifer cover. (*C*) Ruffed grouse males advertise on logs in a protective shield of shrub cover. Females must come closer to the male than in blue and spruce grouse because of the males' vulnerability in dediduous forests. (*D*) Ruffed grouse living south of goshawks often display on hilltops with less protective cover than where northern grouse advertise. Theoretically, these southern grouse should be able to leave their advertisement sites and meet females, unlike northern birds.

Ruffed grouse that live south of the breeding range of goshawks may opt for more conspicuous sites. Grouse in Tennessee, Iowa, Indiana, and Kentucky drum on exposed hilltops (Hardy 1950, Muehrcke and Kirkpatrick 1970, Porath & Vohs 1972, Taylor 1976a).

Another tactic in northern areas is to drum in dense forest patches of young pole-size trees (Kubisiak et al. 1980), where owls and goshawks can probably not hunt as effectively because of the high density of vegetation. In more open forests, shrubs are needed near the log to deflect predators but also allow good visibility to detect their approach (Dorney 1959, Palmer 1963, Gullion 1967, Boag 1976a). Boag and Sumanik (1969) removed shrub cover from advertisement stages and found reduced recruitment of newcomers to those sites and that resident birds switched to alternate logs in their activity centers. The log itself may serve as a deflector if the bird has sufficient warning; drumming stages are commonly about the same height above the ground as the height of the bird, and we have seen males hop off the log at our approach and remain hidden behind it.

In addition to choosing a site with a deflecting screen through which there is some visibility, birds appear to select locations where it is difficult for a predator to approach undetected (Meslow 1966, Gullion 1967). The drumming stage on a log is usually away from the ends, or if the log has obstructing roots, the display stage may be near that end (Meslow 1966). Gullion (1967) reported that ruffed grouse choose sites where they can see at least 18 m, and that males avoid drumming sites near pines and other low-visibility and ambush cover. Display sites also have an unobstructed avenue of escape (Edminster 1947). Departure most often follows a set route, suggesting familiarity with surrounding cover.

Although few males die *at* advertising logs (e.g., three of 358, Gullion 1963; one of 37, Meslow 1966), the remains of many males have been found close by (Meslow 1966, Gullion 1967, Gullion & Marshall 1968, Rusch & Keith 1971). This suggests that predation risk is higher during the approach and departure from display sites than on the logs themselves.

Because the drumming stage appears safer than the surrounding area, ruffed grouse males may often be more immobile than other grouse at the approach of females (Fig. 14.6) (Gladfelter & McBurney 1971). Blue grouse males, by contrast, move toward the female as soon as she has been detected, allowing her less choice in selection of both the male and the precise courtship area.

The conspicuousness of the ruffed grouse is also affected by snow cover; a brown bird running or flying from his log against white snow should be vulnerable. The start of the ruffed grouse's drumming season correlates closely with the disappearance of snow. For example, at Cedar Creek, Minnesota, in 1970, snow disappeared rapidly on 7 and 8 April, and males started drumming on 9 April (Archibald 1976b). At Rochester, Alberta, the ground was 50% free of snow on 4 April 1966, 1 May 1967, and 23 March 1968; drumming was first heard 6 April 1966, 30 April

1967, and 24 March 1968 (Rusch & Keith 1971b). Petraborg et al. (1953) considered the disappearance of snow the main environmental stimulus for the start of spring drumming. In northern Minnesota, spruce grouse males began to display 1 May, 1970 and snow disappeared on 3 May; the next year the snow disappeared 21 April and males advertised on 22 April (Anderson 1973). Blue grouse show a gradual increase in spring advertising. We have heard blue grouse males hooting when the weather was warm in March, 6–8 weeks before actual breeding, and lek grouse begin to visit the lek in mid-March or earlier, a full month before breeding (Hartzler 1972, Sparling 1979, Svedarsky 1979, Emmons 1980). In contrast, the less secure ruffed grouse commonly begins displaying only 2 weeks before females are ready to breed (Aubin 1970, Archibald 1973).

Males of the lek species select locations where their signal will be amplified and where they can observe the approach of predators. They appear secure on their open leks (Berger et al. 1963, Hamerstrom et al. 1965, Hartzler 1974, Sparling & Svedarsky 1978), although predators are doubtlessly aware of these locations. Horak (1974) observed an instance in which prairie chickens displayed in a sown grainfield, but when the grain reached a height of 38 cm in each of 2 years, the birds deserted the lek. Anderson (1969) moved trees 200 m closer to a prairie chicken lek, and the birds abandoned the ground. Such trees would block the view of the horizon, and provide cover for an ambushing raptor during the early-morning arrival of the birds. In another experiment, when fire reduced nearby cover, prairie chickens shifted their lek from 38-cm grass to the newly burned site, apparently because the new one provided better visibility (Anderson 1969).

Occasionally, one can find the leks of both prairie chickens and sharp-tailed grouse in relatively tall grass, shrub, or even tree cover (Svedarsky 1979, Mossop pers. comm., Hamerstrom pers. comm., pers. obs.). Apparently sharp-tailed grouse will tolerate taller grass and shrub vegetation than prairie chickens, e.g., 0.5–0.75 m compared with 0.4 m (Ammann 1957, Sparling 1979), and more tree cover.

Young males commonly display on the edges of leks. Although the frequency of ambush is apparently low at these display grounds, some males are killed (Hartzler 1972, Gratson unpubl. data). The yearlings of all the nonmonogamous species, both forest and steppe grouse, usually must settle for second-best sites in terms of security, if they wish to advertise. The decision by these yearlings to display or not must consider the risk of predation relative to the possibility of breeding females. Yearling sharp-tailed grouse and prairie chickens often breed. Ruffed grouse yearlings may advertise, but the risks are high (Gullion 1966, Gullion & Marshall 1968). For the forest grouse the risks are commonly higher than the expected reproductive benefits, and many yearlings forgo advertising (Herzog 1977a, Little 1978, Sopuck 1979, Gullion 1981).

14.3 Advertising tactics of yearling males

Breeding opportunities for yearling males of the ptarmigan, which are generally monogamous, differ from those of the polygynous grouse. Yearling rock and willow ptarmigan males commonly obtain females by occupying nesting habitat needed by females and then advertising (Chap. 13). In two white-tailed ptarmigan populations, in which males predominated, many yearlings neither competed for space with adults nor advertised. On the other hand, in five willow or rock ptarmigan populations in which males also predominated, the yearlings did display (Jenkins et al. 1963, Watson 1965, Mercer 1967, Bergerud 1970a, Unander & Steen 1985). In these latter populations, females selected those males defending the largest territories, and territory size in two of these studies was positively correlated with male aggressiveness (Watson 1964, 1965, Watson & Miller 1971). Yearlings were sometimes as aggressive as adults and secured both territories and females (see also Pedersen 1984, Steen et al. 1985).

Yearlings of the polygynous grouse show all levels of participation in advertising. Possibly 75% of the ruffed grouse yearlings in some northern populations advertise (Little 1978, Gullion 1981), whereas generally less than 30% of the blue and spruce grouse yearlings, at 11 months of age, display (Herzog 1977a, Sopuck 1979). Yearlings of the steppe grouse illustrate yet another pattern. The majority of these apparently attend leks; changes in lek counts show a correlation with fall age ratios of the previous year (Chap. 15). However, these yearling males often visit a number of leks or advertise alone or in twos and threes at female locations (Brown 1966b, Emmons & Braun 1984, Gratson unpubl. data). The repertoire of yearling behavior can be explained as the various tactics yearling males have adopted to enhance their lifetime fitness, given that male-male competition results in adults generally occupying the most-advantageous advertising locations; researchers are only beginning to investigate and understand this variation.

The most generally favored hypothesis regarding nonbreeding, yearling males is that of sexual selection, i.e., that females select the more vigorous or experienced adults rather than naive yearlings (Wittenberger 1978). An alternative to this idea proposes that yearling males do not breed because they are sexually immature, and that sexual development is delayed so that body size can increase. Males of large size presumably benefit because of reduced mortality. Adult males with improved longevity in an absence of yearling competition should be more successful in breeding, and lifetime fitness is presumably enhanced through delayed sexual maturity (bimaturism) (Wiley 1974). These competing hypotheses may be tested by removing the adult males from a population. The hypothesis of sexual selection is supported if the yearling males breed; the hypothesis of sexual bimaturism is supported if the yearling males do not breed and if the females remain unproductive and/or move elsewhere.

Removal experiments have clearly shown that yearling males *do* take part in breeding (Bendell 1972, Zwickel 1972, Keppie pers. comm.) when females no longer have the option of choosing adult males. Wittenberger (1978) also showed that the proportion of males in grouse populations decreased as sexual dimorphism increased, whereas the bimaturism hypothesis predicts the reverse—i.e., that the proportion of males in the population will increase, due to increased longevity, when there is a greater disparity between the sizes of males and females.

Most devastating to the bimaturism hypothesis has been the recent finding that large, adult sage grouse males have a shorter life expectancy than either the immature males or females, which are smaller (Braun 1979). The sage grouse is the best example of deferred maturity coupled with dimorphism in North American grouse and the best evidence against the bimaturism hypothesis. The theory of sexual selection, on the other hand, predicts that large body size, although a positive influence on intraspecific competition and mate choice, may have the disadvantage of increased conspicuousness and vulnerability to predation (Darwin 1871), consistent with the sage grouse data.

Yearling males are physiologically capable of breeding; even the slowly maturing, sage grouse males produce viable sperm their first spring (Eng 1963). Athough a yearling male does not have a free choice, he has the option of weighing the increased predation risk always associated with advertising with his chances of attracting females that probably prefer adults, for a variety of reasons. Inexperienced yearlings lack both knowledge and access to the principally adult-held sites, which are relatively secure and well-frequented by females. One tactic may be to refrain from advertising and to remain inconspicuous in the first breeding year, while becoming more familiar with the distribution of females and the security of the various sites. It is not an ideal-free tactic; if a yearling could be assured of breeding, he should change tactics and advertise. This is precisely what happens when adult males are experimentally removed, and yearlings have access to safe sites and females. However, yearling males of polygynous species, because of their smaller size and inexperience generally, cannot compete with adults; to make the best of a bad situation, they adopt a conditional strategy (Dawkins 1980) that generally yields reduced results (e.g., Rubenstein 1980, Howard 1984, review Dominey 1984).

14.3.1 Early prospecting by juvenile males

Natural selection should favor early sexual maturity in males if this enhances their reproductive fitness. Young males in some populations begin advertising in their first September and October. Ruffed grouse are probably the most precocious, some drum at 4 months of age (Eng 1959, Gullion 1967). Juvenile spruce grouse in Michigan have been reported prospecting for advertising sites (Robinson 1980), and young sharp-tailed grouse have been observed displaying in their first fall (Hamerstrom & Hamerstrom 1951, Kermott 1982, Chap. 5). On Brunette Island, Mercer and Bergerud counted a total of 75 territorial males in three springs and 115 males in October, 6 months later; at least 40 were juveniles (Bergerud & Mercer 1966, Mercer 1967). In Scotland, juvenile red grouse males are very active in contesting advertising territories in their first fall (Jenkins et al. 1963, Lance 1978a). Watson (1965) noted that rock ptarmigan also displayed during their first fall in Scotland. In most instances noted above, with the exception of red grouse, the percentages of juveniles that displayed in fall were small. These early birds may be early-hatched young, slightly ahead of other members of their cohort in physiological development (Gullion 1967, Moyles & Boag 1981).

Blue and sage grouse juveniles do not display in their first year. These two grouse species are the largest and the most sexually size-dimorphic in North America. The first-year growth rate in both species is such that yearling males in the fall are considerably smaller than adult males (Patterson 1952, Redfield 1978), and even at 12 months, sperm production by a yearling is less than that of adults (Eng 1963, Hannon et al. 1979).

Generally, not as many juveniles in more northern populations display in the fall as in more southern populations of the same species. Juvenile red grouse advertise in the fall in Scotland, as do willow ptarmigan in Maritime Newfoundland, but ptarmigan in the Arctic and northern Norway do not. Juvenile prairie chickens visit leks and display in Missouri and Oklahoma (Schwartz 1945, Copelin 1963), but fewer do so or do so less frequently in Wisconsin (Hamerstrom 1939). Ellison (1967) noted only one juvenile spruce grouse male displaying in a sample of 101 sites in Alaska. All the ruffed grouse males in Kentucky occupied logs in the fall, but in northern Minnesota, 46% of 140 waited until spring to occupy and display in sites unoccupied the previous fall (Hardy 1950, Little 1978). A juvenile bird apparently must reach a certain point in sexual development in order to advertise. In northern habitats birds hatch slightly later and the departures for winter ranges begin earlier in autumn. The north-south continuum in the proportion of juveniles that display appears to reflect the reduced development and times between birth and the onset of snow cover in northern areas; the increased conspicuousness that results from snow apparently precludes the option for fall display from being profitable.

14.3.2 Advertising in spring

The percentage of yearling males that advertise at 10 months of age in the tundra in spring varies from nearly 100% in willow and rock ptarmigan populations, to possibly only a few percent in some white-tailed ptarmigan populations. Choate (1960, 1963a) located only one of 15 tagged, yearling white-tailed ptarmigan displaying. In the same population one 2-year-old male waited until his third year to advertise.

The so-called silent males among the forest grouse are primarily yearlings. The percentage of silent males varies among populations and from one year to the next (Gullion 1981). Over a ten-year period the percentage of nonadvertising ruffed grouse varied from 0% to 38% in Alberta (Rusch et al. 1984, pers. comm.). Silent males varied from 3% to 37% of total males for ruffed grouse over a 7-year period in Minnesota (Gullion 1966b, 1981). On Moresby Island, British Columbia, there were four advertising and approximately eight silent yearling blue grouse in 1971. Near Campbell River, Vancouver Island, Bendell and Elliott (1967) reported that 26% of the 57 yearling blue grouse advertised, whereas at Comox Burn practically all yearlings and many 2-year-old males failed to advertise (Lewis & Zwickel 1981). Herzog (1977a) radio-tracked spruce grouse yearlings in Alberta and found that two of six localized and advertised, two localized but they did not display, and two showed large ranges and did not advertise.

Males of the forest grouse defend advertising sites and not space. There are no clearly defined boundaries (Aubin 1970, Anderson 1973, Archibald 1976a), and adjacent advertising ranges seldom have a common boundary (Fig. 14.7; cf. McNicholl 1978, Bendell & Zwickel 1978, Herzog & Boag (1978). Yearling males do have the option to display and may squeeze in between other males. On Moresby Island, two males repeatedly and simultaneously advertised from the same tree—perhaps an extreme, but clearly a useful example. We should question the idea that yearling males may be social outcasts and are prevented from breeding by other males. All evidence suggests that an equally likely explanation is that the yearlings themselves decide whether or not to display, and that this "decision" is made on the basis of their expectation of success and the risks incurred.

The percentage of male steppe grouse that do not advertise has not been thoroughly documented. Most radio-tracked males in many studies have been captured on leks and were already displaying. A sample of 1,039 banded, male prairie chickens trapped in the winter showed a juvenile:adult ratio of 1.3:1, whereas the ratio of yearlings to adults on leks was 1.7:1 ($n = 626$) (Hamerstrom & Hamerstrom 1973), suggesting most yearlings showed up on leks. Hamerstrom reported (1981) that of 80 immature males banded in winter 1955–56, 23 were never seen again, and 13 were seen but not on a lek. Brown found fewer yearlings on leks (1.7 yearling/adult, $n = 586$) than on winter ranges and fewer than in samples provided by hunters in the fall (Brown 1966b, 1967, 1968b). Removal experiments with sharp-tailed grouse also suggest that some yearlings had not localized until they were 18 months old (Moyles & Boag 1981). When adult prairie grouse were removed from leks they were replaced by yearlings (Robel 1970, Rippin & Boag 1974a). These may have been nondisplaying birds or birds that shifted from other arenas or that displayed alone. Yearling sage grouse males that were radio-tracked visited an average of 3.9 leks before localizing at one display ground (Emmons 1980). Thus, yearlings are mobile and often move between leks as they prospect for potential advertising sites.

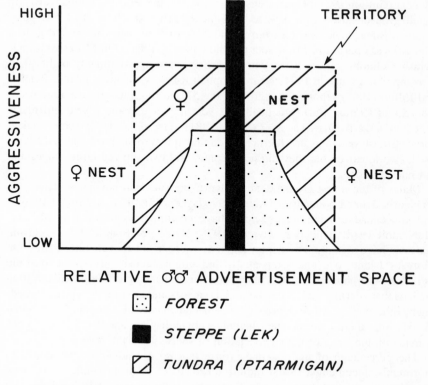

Fig. 14.7. Males of the steppe species advertise and defend small territories with precise boundaries on leks. Physical fighting is common. Tundra grouse defend much larger territories, within which females nest. Males commonly patrol boundaries, "walk the line," and engage in aerial chases and fighting. Forest grouse advertise at one to several locations within a home range, and the intensity of the male's aggressiveness to other males decreases with increasing distance from the display site. Trespassing by yearlings is common, and fighting is infrequent.

The steppe grouse suffer little predation when advertising; display grounds are safe because of good visibility and experienced adults are present. The cost of advertising should thus be low, but the immediate, expected breeding benefits are also low for yearlings because of female preferences for more vigorous and experienced males. However, a yearling's lifetime fitness may depend on his seniority at a lek (Moyles & Boag 1981, Kermott 1982). These yearlings probably spend some time deciding where to display, but theoretically a higher percentage of them should make an early decision and advertise than should the forest grouse, in which sexual selection is less intense and probably more of the total population of adult males have an opportunity to breed females.

14.3.3 Tactics for securing an advertising site

Yearling males, unlike most adults that have established sites, are not committed to specific advertising spots. Yearlings can be expected to spend considerable time prospecting. They can be opportunistic and move to newly created habitats, such as logged areas, as do blue grouse (Redfield 1972), or regenerated grasslands, as do prairie grouse (Westemeier 1973). Although opportunities for sites exist, there is uncertainty of predation risks and attractiveness to females of such areas. It appears that, except for red grouse in Scotland (Lance 1978a), yearling males only rarely attempt the tactic of vigorously contesting advertising sites with established adults. Occasionally, however, exceptional yearlings do oust older birds. Bergerud observed a yearling, male blue grouse approach a dummy female, dominate the 5-year-old resident, and mount the stuffed hen. Also, Kermott (1982) observed a banded, yearling sharp-tailed grouse secure a central location on a lek.

If females prefer adults, one tactic for yearling males is to acquire knowledge of female locations and potential advertising sites. While prospecting he should remain inconspicuous and thus relatively safe from predation.

Yearling blue grouse have elaborate tactics for securing advertising sites. This has recently been documented by radio-tracking young males at Comox Burn, on Vancouver Island, and on Hardwicke Island, just off Vancouver Island (Sopuck 1979, Jamieson 1982). Yearling males return from the winter range at the same time as females. Adult males precede both yearlings and females (Bendell & Elliott 1967, Bendell et al. 1972). There should be little advantage for yearlings to return before female occupancy, because they could not assess the distribution of females. Early in April when yearling females search large ranges for nest sites, yearling males are also wide-ranging (Hannon 1978, Sopuck 1979, Hannon et al. 1982). Ranges of these males have averaged 28.5 $\pm$ 5.2 ha ($n = 30$) (Sopuck 1979). After females localized near their future nest sites (approximately 6 May), yearling males also reduced their ranges (mean = 11.9 $\pm$ 6.9 ha, Sopuck 1979). These yearlings traveled through an average of 4.4 ranges of advertising adult males (Sopuck 1979). Sopuck recognized a wide-ranging, yearling phenotype ($n = 13$) and a more localized, yearling phenotype ($n = 17$).

Jamieson (1983) and Jamieson & Zwickel (1983) delved further into these patterns and found that a wide-ranging phenotype in their study area visited the vicinity of one to four advertising males (Fig. 14.8). These males visited areas an average of 57 $\pm$ 1.9 m from the nearest adult males. Small-ranging males showed restricted ranges and localized at vacant, but formerly occupied, advertising sites, but did not advertise. These vacant sites averaged 75 $\pm$ 2.3 m ($n = 7$) from the nearest male. Both Sopuck (1979) and Jamieson (1982) also identified a third yearling phenotype: birds of this kind ranged very widely and appeared attracted neither to a vacant site nor to the sites of currently advertising males.

Movement patterns of yearling males in these two studies suggest a basic strategy of assessing where females frequent, and then locating potential advertising sites in the vicinity. Wide-ranging males should be near the advertising sites of two to three adult males and a similar number of females (cf. Hannon 1978). Between breeding seasons, one of the adult males and one of the females should die (i.e., 33%) (Zwickel et al. 1983). The wide-ranging yearling, now an adult, can shift his activity center and advertise within the range that he learned as a yearling, in relation to the new realignment of surviving males and nesting females (Fig. 14.8). In contrast, the small-ranging yearling has his spot for next year assured, but he is committed and cannot make major adjustments later to maximize the new arrangements of males and females. The male that ranges widely could be characterized as remaining inconspicuous and tolerant to densities of surrounding males. The small-ranging male is not as secretive and could be termed density-intolerant—he preferred a vacant site, and one that was farther from the nearest, other displaying males. The bird that ranged very widely (the third phenotype) had seemingly no site attachment and followed a pattern that would allow him to colonize newly created habitats in his second year.

The three phenotypes recognized in blue grouse may also occur in spruce grouse. Again, radio-telemetry studies suggest three movement options. Herzog (1977a) found two yearlings that selected unoccupied sites and advertised; their ranges were small and similar to those of adults—approximately 1 ha. Two other yearlings ranged over areas of 6.6 ha and 2.3 ha, spent more time nearer adults, and did not advertise. Herzog's evidence of a very wide-ranging type consisted of two yearlings that moved over 10.5 and 14.8 ha and showed little site attachment. The three phenotypes described in each of the three studies (Herzog 1977a, Sopuck 1979, Jamieson 1982) appear to encompass three different tactics for the dispersal of males to advertise for females.

Ruffed grouse males show two of the site-prospecting tactics of blue and spruce grouse. Wide-ranging yearlings that prospect near many adult males (Bump et al. 1947, Marshall 1965, Godfrey & Marshall 1969), and yearlings that localized at unoccupied sites (Little 1978), have been documented. Unlike blue grouse, however, ruffed grouse may begin their activities as juvenile birds in September and October (Eng 1959).

The proportion of males that opt to search widely near other males and the proportion that localize at unoccupied sites can be estimated for one population in central Minnesota (Little 1978). Little found that during 4 years 55 yearlings took advertising sites in the spring after the sites became vacant following the disappearance of resident adults over the winter. Conversely, 28 yearlings drummed in the spring at activity centers not occupied the previous fall when these males had probably visited the areas. In addition to these yearlings were birds that did not advertise (silent males), even though the population was declining and sites formerly occupied were continuously becoming vacant. When these birds became adults 21 took over the locations of drummers that died and 26 established

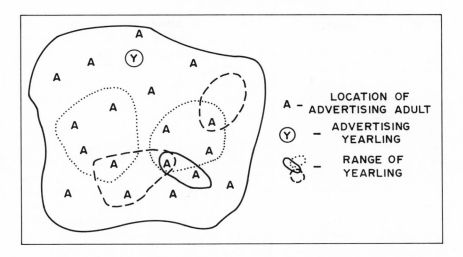

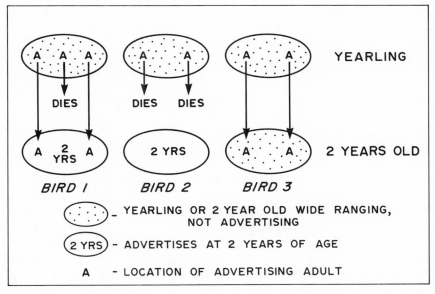

Fig. 14.8. *Top*: Yearling blue grouse males commonly prospect for future advertising sites in the vicinity of one to four advertising adults. One of six yearlings established a display site and advertised. *Bottom*: One yearling that prospected near the sites of three adults occupied one of the sites the following year when the adult was dead (*bird 1*). Another yearling advertised the following year after both males that he had visited the year before had died (*bird 2*). A third yearling remained silent as an adult when both the males he prospected near as a yearling reoccupied their sites the following year (*bird 3*). (Adapted from Sopuck 1979, Jamieson 1982, Jamieson & Zwickel 1983.)

new advertising centers (Little 1978). If these additional advertising adults represent new drummers, and not birds switching locations, the ratio of males using the tactic of ranging widely near adults (density-tolerant) to those ranging over smaller areas at unoccupied sites (density-intolerant) was 1:0.71 (76:54).

Steppe grouse yearlings can establish and advertise at new leks, or elect to display at established leks with adults. Some yearling, sharp-tailed grouse males visit the periphery of display grounds in September; at first they mostly watch and crouch (Moyles & Boag 1981). These younger birds often arrive later and leave earlier in the morning than adults (Kermott 1982). Slightly later in the season some yearlings display, but back down and walk away when adults approach. Finally, they are no longer challenged and display in peripheral positions, and in time they in turn chase newer birds that arrive. Birds that succeed are those that are both faithful to the lek and persistent (Moyles & Boag 1981, Kermott 1982). The birds that Moyles and Boag observed in Alberta continued to visit display grounds on clear and warm days throughout the winter. Most young joined the establishment between September and December, but some did not take up positions until April.

Both studies showed that birds generally worked their way toward the center position of the lek as older, interior birds disappeared (see also Rippin & Boag 1974b). On average, the sooner a yearling begins to display, the earlier he should become an inside bird; generally the more central males on a lek do the majority of breeding (Robel 1966, Hartzler 1972, Wiley 1973b, Sparling 1979, Kermott 1982, Chap. 7). Also, joining early would allow yearlings the opportunity to learn female preferences. Early persistence at established leks could advance seniority and improve fitness. This tactic is analogous to the approach used by some forest grouse yearlings of visiting advertising adults and waiting for vacancies.

Other yearlings in steppe species follow the option of forming original leks. New leks commonly appear when populations are expanding (Brown 1967, Kohn 1976, Svedarsky 1979, Cannon & Knopf 1981). Because adults seldom change locations (Hartzler 1972, Hamerstrom & Hamerstrom 1973, Hamerstrom 1981), unless there are extreme shifts in the distribution of females, a new lek should usually be formed by yearlings. The establishment of new prairie chicken and sharp-tailed grouse leks by yearlings has been observed (Robel 1964, Rippin & Boag 1974a). Robel (1964) observed seven yearling males arrive at a lek and leave together. The only banded birds seen at three new, sharp-tailed grouse leks in Montana were yearlings, and on another lek that increased from four to 16 males, ten males were yearlings (Brown 1967).

Some daily counts at leks reveal more males early in the season, before most females arrive (Artmann 1970, Bowen 1971). In other populations the peak male count generally coincides with female attendance (Hamerstrom & Hamerstrom 1973, Svedarsky 1979). In the former populations, numbers were increasing – the early, high counts could reflect yearling males prospecting at display sites early in the season, but later leaving to settle on other leks (Brown 1966b), or establish new ones (Gratson unpubl. data).

The emphasis in the literature on yearlings initially displaying at established leks is that of a new bird trying to compete with his seniors and be "admitted to the club" (Moyles & Boag 1981, Kermott 1982). However, how can an adult prevent a yearling on the edge of a lek from becoming established? The yearling need only move farther away if challenged. Another interpretation is that the yearling is evaluating his options, and based upon the likelihood of breeding females at that lek, he will make a decision whether to display there or elsewhere. The intensity of intrasexual competition would be only one aspect of this decision. Possibly some males display alone in their first year, and if they are unsuccessful because females ignore them, in their second year they establish themselves at a lek. If they follow this scenario, however, they will have lost the advantages that might accrue to yearlings that establish themselves at a lek by their first spring. Yearlings that establish new leks would probably be favored if a population was expanding and females were moving to new ranges. Yearlings that opt to go to established leks should have an advantage if a population is declining and only the established leks are visited by females.

Yearling steppe grouse males should assess the distribution of females as part of a decision to select an advertising site. This hypothesis is consistent with the observation that there were fewer males at sharp-tailed grouse leks in Montana where the surrounding, residual nest cover declined between years (Brown 1967, Fig. 14.4), and leks had more males when there was tall nesting cover in surrounding areas. A change in the number of cocks on leks between years should result primarily from variable recruitment of yearlings. In Montana, there were larger percentages of yearlings at leks near dense, tall nesting cover than at leks with low- or medium-quality nest cover nearby (Fig. 14.9). Also, a greater number of females visited leks that were near dense nesting cover. The ratio of adult males to females was 1:2, compared with a ratio of approximately 1:1 at leks near low- and medium-quality nesting cover (Fig. 14.9). Thus, leks chosen by yearlings offered improved opportunities for yearlings to breed. Brown (1966b) indicated that 22% of 106 banded yearlings had central positions on leks (cf. Hjorth 1970). Also, at two leks there was high mortality of males, yet they continued to attract yearlings (Brown 1966b). A higher proportion of females (35%) visited these leks than others (Brown 1967), similar to the large number of visits of blue grouse females to persistent advertising locations (Table 14.1). All the evidence presented above is consistent with the idea that yearlings assess the distribution of females and that this assessment is part of their site-selection process.

14.4 Female nesting strategies

The most important reproductive decision a female must make is where to locate her nest. Grouse commonly lose 50% of their clutches (Hickey 1955, Table

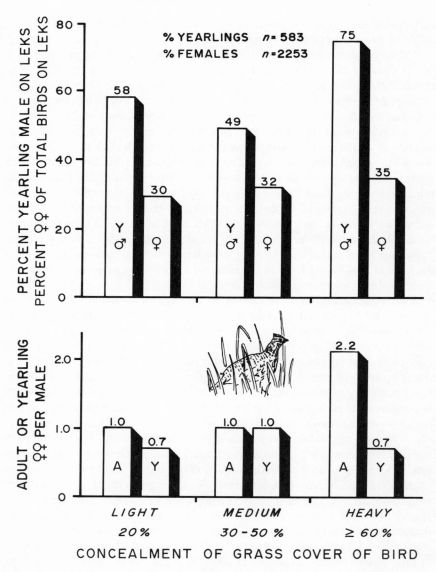

Fig. 14.9. *Top:* Yearling sharp-tailed grouse males were more common on leks that had heavy grass cover within a radius of 4.8 km. On such leks a higher proportion of females was observed than on leks surrounded by less grass cover. Yearling males, by selecting leks with more visiting females, should have a better opportunity to breed in the same or future years. *Bottom:* The ratio of females to adult males was 2.2 females/adult male compared with 0.7 female/yearling male on leks when the surrounding grass cover was at least 60%. (Adapted from Brown 1966a, 1968a,b.)

15.2). A female's potential or realized loss in fitness is greater from this single factor than from any other. A short life expectancy allows but a few opportunities to perfect nesting options. When her clutch hatches, the female may lose chicks because of inherent weakness, inclement weather, food shortages, and predation. These losses are less predictable and more beyond her control than nest losses. Selection should result in major behavioral tactics developing in populations and species to positively affect the nesting outcome.

The female's decision should relate primarily to where the nest should be located to avoid detection by predators. It may be difficult to select the nest site to maximize future chick survival by nesting near favorable brood-rearing habitat. Nests hatch 35–45 days after the female's commitment to a site by depositing eggs. During this interval there are rapid increases in plant growth and changes in abundance of invertebrates; what may have been assessed as optimal habitat for chicks in May might no longer be the best place in June and July. That broods commonly make long movements after hatch (see section 14.6.1) suggests that the female's first concern is to have a successful nest, using the available options in April and May.

The importance of the nest location decision argues that a female should begin to search for a site as soon as such action would be rewarding (Brewer & Harrison 1975). She could prospect broadly at first and fine-tune her decision later when she has a maximum choice of locations following snowmelt in spring, and when the most current information on the concealment value of cover becomes available. Some juvenile males seek advertising sites in the fall (section 14.3.1), and it is possible that females might also start their assessment of potential nesting sites then if there is adequate time before winter weather persists (cf. Weise & Meyer 1979). Herzog (1977a) reported that female spruce grouse were beginning to space themselves in November. Ruffed grouse females have a tendency to nest where they were found the previous fall (Eng 1959). In the most southern grouse, Attwater's prairie chicken, females have the largest range in November and December (Silvy & Lutz 1978). Prospecting may already have begun.

As a generalization, yearling females are less successful nesting than adults in all the grouse except ptarmigan (Table 15.4). The improved nesting success of the six other grouse species between the first and later years supports the view that experience provides knowledge on how better to proceed.

The nesting strategy in grouse may include the following tactics: (1) Females should research areas to ascertain the abundance of predators and the general availability of suitable nest sites. (2) Females should attempt to nest at the time and place of maximum cover, yet still allow for the option of renesting if necessary. (3) Hens should remain inconspicuous and avoid other females near nest sites. (4) If a female was successful last season, she should show philopatry; if she was unsuccessful and the responsible factor is likely to recur, she should shift nesting areas. (5) Females should abandon current clutches and try again elsewhere if the certainty of a current loss outweighs the unpredictability of the loss of a future effort.

14.4.1 Assessing predator abundance and nesting sites

The prelaying ranges of females—the area traveled between the time they leave winter ranges and flocks and the time of egg-laying—are generally largest for grouse in steppe environments and smallest for the tundra species (Table 14.2). The size of these ranges is inversely related to nesting success and is larger where there are many predators (Fig. 16.2). The steppe grouse must contend with about 13 groups of predators. Some of these can occur at high densities, such as ground squirrels (*Citellus* spp.) and skunks (*Mephitis* spp.). Other predators are extremely mobile, searching large areas, such as magpies (*Pica pica*), corvids (*Corvus* spp.), and coyotes (*Canis latrans*). Forest grouse have approximately nine groups of predators in the conifer and deciduous forests of North America, whereas ptarmigan have the fewest kinds and numbers of nest predators. We propose the hypothesis that the prelaying range of the female reflects her movements while prospecting for nest sites; she may assess both the number and distribution of predators, the availability of nesting cover, and the spacing of other nesting females that may add to her conspicuousness. If she frequently encounters a predator, she should range farther and in other directions.

Few data are available to directly evaluate the prediction that females are able to evaluate the distribution of predators. Seldom have researchers radio-tracked predator and prey simultaneously. We do know that females may move considerable distances after losing nests (Christenson 1970, Robel et al. 1970a, Schiller 1973, Svedarsky 1979, Chap. 6). Svedarsky found that prairie chickens preferred seeded habitats of redtop (*Agrostis* spp.) and brome grass (*Bromus* spp.) and that nesting success was higher in planted habitats than in more diversified, native vegetation. These planted grasslands had less litter than native communities and possibly attracted fewer invertebrates and voles (*Microtus* spp.), upon which skunks and foxes (*Vulpes vulpes*) prey. Sharp-tailed grouse also had reduced nesting success when there was more litter (Schiller 1973). Prairie chickens in Illinois selected grasslands that were burned 2–4 years previously over unburned sites; densities were 0.41 nests/ha compared with 0.27 nests/ha in unburned sods (Westemeier 1972). Nest success of prairie chickens is commonly higher in burned than in unburned habitats (Lehmann 1941, Kirsch & Kruse 1973), despite the often reduced density of the cover. Fewer predators may search in burned habitats with reduced faunal diversity. Maxson (1978) found that six of seven ruffed grouse nests located near water were successful, whereas overall nesting success was only 59%. Attwater's prairie chickens commonly lose nests from flooding because of the selection of lowland sites, but if such wet areas hinder some predators, the expected success could be greater than at alternative sites.

Many predators hunt in predictable patterns (Curio 1976). Also, areas near dens may be searched almost daily (cf. Sargeant 1972). Grouse may be able to respond to these patterns and correlated patterns of particular habitats.

The hypothesis that the size of the prelaying range relates to a nest-site decision is consistent with the finding that yearlings generally travel over a greater range than adults and narrow their search pattern as the time of egg-laying approaches (Herzog 1977a, Hannon 1978, Sopuck 1979). Adults, with more experience, can quickly avoid large patches of unsuitable habitat. Yearlings are less familiar with habitats and, at least for blue and spruce grouse, avoid areas occupied by adults.

The sizes of prelaying ranges vary among species within steppe and tundra grouse (Table 14.2), and potentially should vary within the forest group. Sizes of prelaying ranges of all nine species are positively correlated with the loss of nests to predators (Fig. 16.2). The different abundances and kinds of predators in the habitats of grouse species within groups may be a factor contributing to this, but the distribution and morphology of specific nesting cover should also affect nesting success and sizes of prelaying ranges. Generally, heterogeneity of vegetative cover increases in time and space in climatic regions that receive reduced rainfall (Wiens 1974). Plant cover in such arid regions is more unpredictable (Wiens 1976, Knapp 1984). Grouse in drier environments may thus need to search larger areas than those in areas with more precipitation.

Of the species in steppe environments, the sage grouse is the largest and most conspicuous of the three lek species. Females search for nest sites in dry habitats under sagebrush canopies (Patterson 1952, Klebenow 1969, Wallestad & Pyrah 1974, Petersen 1980). These steppe habitats, unlike the grasslands, are largely devoid of dense, herbaceous growth to hide nests from a horizontal view. It is relatively easy for field workers, and presumably predators, to find nests, even though large areas must be searched. The sage grouse should take the longest time and cover the largest area in the site-evaluation process. We can also expect prairie chicken and sharp-tailed grouse females to search larger areas for nest sites in places like Kansas and Montana, where the climate is generally dry and unpredictable (Knapp 1984), than in Minnesota and Wisconsin, where nest cover should be more homogenous in distribution (Table 14.2).

Of the forest grouse, the blue grouse is the largest, and usually nests in more open habitat than spruce or ruffed grouse (Bump et al. 1947, Kupa 1966, Zwickel 1975, Sopuck 1979, Redmond et al. 1982). Blue grouse generally should range over areas larger than spruce or ruffed grouse. Blue grouse on Vancouver Island had ranges similar in size to those reported for ruffed and spruce grouse in mainland, interior populations (Table 14.2). However, these estimates may not be representative of other blue grouse populations, because the data from Vancouver Island are from the dense populations at Comox Burn, where there are generally few nest predators. The ruffed grouse is smaller than the blue grouse and frequents deciduous woodlands with more herbaceous ground cover. This cover ad-

Table 14.2. Average ranges (ha $\pm$ SE) of female grouse during

Grouse groups and species	Prelaying		
	Yearling		Adult
Forest			
Spruce grouse	14.4 $\pm$ 2.9 (10)		4.1 $\pm$ 0.6 (10)
	18.5 $\pm$ 4.6 (7)		
	13.5 $\pm$ 4.2 (3)		
Ruffed grouse		6.4 (3)[f]	
		12.1 (9)	
	—		—
Blue grouse	12.0 $\pm$ 8.8 (27)		4.6 $\pm$ 2.7 (10)
	16.6 $\pm$ 1.2 (4)		6.3 $\pm$ 3.2 (5)
	16.1 $\pm$ 2.5 (18)		6.6 $\pm$ 1.3 (7)
Steppe			
Sharp-tailed grouse		464 $\pm$ 145 (3)	
	—		—
	—		—
	—		—
	—		—
Prairie chicken	34 $\pm$ 15 (2)		14 (1)
		82 $\pm$ 16 (5)	
		85 $\pm$ 37 (7)	
		194 $\pm$ 97 (2)	
		182 $\pm$ 17 (2)	
Sage grouse		882 (7)	
	—		—
	—		—
	—		—
Tundra			
White tailed ptarmigan		14.4 $\pm$ 2.9 (7)	
		5.2 $\pm$ 0.3 (92)	
		5.4 $\pm$ 0.4 (33)	
		20.9 (90)	
Willow ptarmigan		2.3 (86)	
		5.1 $\pm$ 0.3 (11)	
	2.9 $\pm$ 0.4 (33)		3.2 $\pm$ 0.3 (43)
	2.7 $\pm$ 0.1 (30)		2.9 $\pm$ 0.2 (28)
	5.6 (27)		7.2 (47)

[a] Estimates as reported or as calculated from sources listed below; in some instances SE could not be computed.

[b] For ptarmigan this estimate is the size of male territories.

[c] Chicks less than 2 weeks old.

[d] Chicks at least 2 weeks old.

[e] Early and late combined.

[f] Yearlings and adults combined.

Sources: Spruce grouse — Alberta, Herzog 1977a; Minnesota, Haas 1974; Alaska, Ellison 1973. *Ruffed grouse* — Minnesota, Archibald 1975; Minnesota, Maxson 1974; Minnesota, Godfrey 1975. *Blue grouse* — British Columbia, Sopuck 1979; British Columbia, Hannon 1978; British Columbia,

different phases of the breeding cycle.[a] Number of females in parentheses.

Laying and incubation	Brood-rearing	
	Early[c]	Late[d]
4.2 ± 1.0 (10)	29.0 ± 4.8 (6)[e]	
–	8.0 ± 1.5 (3)	19.8 ± 4.2 (11)
–	42.1 ± 17.0 (8)	
1.9 ± 0.5 (3)	–	–
8.4 ± 0.6 (8)	4.9 ± 0.6 (8)	15.9 ± 2.7 (4)
–	12.8 ± 2.7 (4)	
–	14.0 (8)	
4.1 (9)	–	–
–	45.3 ± 26.6 (7)	
14 ± 5 (6)	48 ± 36 (4)	55 ± 20 (3)
–	10 ± 4 (6)	44 ± 7 (5)
–	11 (9)	94 (5)
–	54 ± 12 (9)	
–	19 ± 3 (8)	108 ± 35 (7)
31 (9)	67 (10)	
31 ± 6 (11)	18 ± 4 (9)	11 ± 2 (4)
42 ± 57 (13)	115 ± 106 (8)	59 ± 46 (7)
–	–	–
–	134 ± 72 (10)	
–	–	–
–	127 ± 30 (3)	
–	56 ± 15 (3)	
–	86 (13)	
–	–	–
–	–	–
–	–	–
–	–	–
–	27 ± 5.4 (18)	
–	7.3 ± 3.4 (15)	14.3 ± 7.9 (15)
–	65.8 (12)	
–	–	–
–	–	–

Armleder 1980; British Columbia, Ash 1979; British Columbia, Hines 1986a; Montana, Mussehl & Schladweiler 1969. *Sharp-tailed grouse*—Wisconsin, Gratson 1983, Chap. 5; Wisconsin, Ramharter 1976; Minnesota, Schiller 1973; Minnesota, Artmann 1970; North Dakota, Christenson 1970. *Prairie Chicken*—Texas, Sell 1979; Minnesota, Svedarsky 1979; Texas, Silvy & Lutz 1978; Missouri, Arthaud 1968; Kansas, Robel et al. 1970a; Texas, Taylor & Guthery 1980. *Sage grouse*—Idaho, Connelly 1982; Idaho, Autenrieth 1981; Wyoming, Berry & Eng 1984; Montana, Wallestad 1971. *White-tailed ptarmigan*—Colorado, Schmidt 1969. *Rock ptarmigan*—Iceland, Gardarsson 1971; Scotland, Watson 1965; Svalbard, Unander & Steen 1985. *Willow ptarmigan*—Scotland, Miller & Watson 1978; British Columbia, Mossop pers. comm; British Columbia, Hannon & Smith 1984; British Columbia, Weeden 1959b; Norway, Erikstad 1985a; Norway, Pedersen 1984.

vantage for nesting suggests to us that ruffed grouse females should range over smaller areas than blue grouse.

An alternative hypothesis for the differences in the size of prelaying ranges of grouse is that birds with larger body size will have a wider variety of foods but will take only the highest quality items; this selectivity will lead to larger home ranges. Further, a shift to a monoculture diet such as sagebrush leads to greater selectivity for plant parts and phenological stages, and thus to wide-ranging foraging patterns (Bradbury 1981).

However, all the grouse are largely monophagous regardless of the size of their ranges or their body sizes (Robinson 1969, Gardarsson & Moss 1970, Pendergast & Boag 1970, Wallestad et al. 1975, Ellison 1976, Herzog 1978, Williams et al. 1980, Chaps. 4, 9, 10). No one has shown differences in quality of food in relation to range sizes. The red grouse, with the smallest prelaying range, has one of the most monophagous and poorest diets (Moss & Hanssen 1980). Birds occasionally die from starvation (Jenkins et al. 1963). Blue and spruce grouse eat needles of generally lower nutritional quality than do ruffed grouse that utilize high-quality buds (Huff 1970), but the ranges of all three species are roughly similar in size (Table 14.2). Blue grouse are twice the size of spruce grouse yet they eat similar foods and their ranges are of comparable size. The suggested correlations among body size, food quality, and home range size are not convincing.

Another alternative to the hypothesis that the first priority of females is a safe nesting site is that in the spring females move from winter habitats to male advertising locations for breeding, and *then* they search for their nest site. This model had the important implication that the male location may be the focus of the female's search for a nest location. But this sequence does not provide enough time for a yearling female to adequately assess potential nest sites, because females generally deposit their first egg within a few days of breeding with males (Brander 1967, Christenson 1970, Svedarsky 1979, Chap. 6). The problem is not so acute for returning adult females, especially if they were successful the previous year; they may "know" where they are going. However, most returning adults and generally all yearling females should prospect for nest sites *before* selecting males.

Radio-telemetry studies of forest grouse have verified that females do select nesting sites before breeding. Four yearling, blue grouse females localized on their nest ranges 13 ± 0.8 days before the egg-laying period, and five adults localized 12 ± 3.8 days before laying eggs (Hannon 1978). Female spruce grouse visited males just before laying eggs but had established their nesting areas in mutually exclusive ranges several weeks before they began laying eggs (Herzog 1977a). Particularly good data are available for ruffed grouse at Cedar Creek, Minnesota. One female visited her future nest site 15, 19, and 23 April and laid her first egg on the 24th; a second female visited her site 13, 16, 17, 24, 26, and

27 April and laid her first egg on the 28th; and the last female visited her site on 25, 26, 27 and 29 April, and on 1, 2, 4, 5, 7, and 8 May, and laid her first egg on 9 May (Maxson 1974, 1977). Edminster (1954) had said much earlier that ruffed grouse lay their first egg a week after they make the nest, and Brander (1967) had shown that females laid eggs 1–7 days *after* visiting several males. These females had to have selected their nest sites before they visited males.

Steppe grouse often travel a long and relatively straight course toward the nest site after leaving the lek following breeding; this suggests a goal-oriented movement. Some hens return to areas where they had successfully nested previously (Berry & Eng 1985, Chap. 6, Gratson unpubl. data). The time is too short between copulation and deposition of the first egg for these females to adequately select sites after breeding (1–3 days for sharp-tailed grouse, Schiller 1973; and 3–5 days in prairie chickens, Chap. 6). An interesting twist to the pattern can be seen in sage grouse: yearling females average 9.5 days between breeding and egg-laying and adults dally a mean of 7.6 days (Petersen 1980). But Petersen found that most radio-tracked hens took only a day to localize after leaving the lek. One hen took 2 days to travel the 11 km from the lek to her nest area. Petersen (1980, p. 156) suggested that "this small amount of variability could possibly be due to most hens having chosen the nest location prior to breeding." Thus, these female sage grouse arrived an average of 8 days in advance of laying their first egg at the nest site. What does the female do during this period? Predation on nests is extensive in sage grouse (Table 15.2), hens are large, and herbaceous cover is lacking at the nest site. It may be that a sage grouse hen delays her commitment to a precise nest location, until just before sperm viability begins to decrease (see Eng 1963), so that a last-minute and very local assessment of predator activity and vegetation suitability can be made. In summary, the assessment strategy of nest-site selection should require more time where predators are mobile, abundant, and of many kinds. Increased heterogeneity of suitable nest cover in time and space, such as in steppe environments, should also result in more time invested. A reasonable tactic of a female would be to put some distance between herself and an area of high risk. If the potential of nest loss is high, birds should increase the probability of success by increased effort and selectivity in selecting nest sites.

14.4.2 Timing and inconspicuousness

Another tactic should be to nest at a time that provides a hen the option to renest if she loses her first clutch (cf. Cartwright 1944). Grouse could nest in June and July when there is maximum, new plant growth. Rather, they nest earlier and do not initially use the new, annual vegetation. Sage grouse nest under sagebrush, ptarmigan under Krumholz or ericaceous shrubs; forest grouse have little herbaceous cover in shady forests, but nest at the base of trees. Prairie grouse seek residual cover from the previous year, but later there is new plant growth for renesting (Christenson 1970, Schiller 1973). All the grouse normally have over-head vegetation that provides some cover from corvids, which rely on vision, but the dense, low cover for concealment from mammalian predators seems inadequate since a number of ground predators depend more on scent than vision.

A universal tactic should be to nest when there is a maximum amount of nesting habitat that predators must search to find nests. Hens should start their search for nest sites as soon as snow cover has disappeared. Some of the most secure sites could be in depressions and shrub thickets, which may lose their snow cover last. Also, brown females would be conspicuous if snow cover was complete. Byrkjedal (1980) placed dummy clutches in the field in May when bare patches were small and in the same scrapes in June when snow was gone. Predators (mostly foxes) found more nests in May, when their search areas were smaller, than in June when more of the area was brown and they had to search larger areas.

The timing of breeding and nesting commonly varies a maximum of 2 weeks in grouse populations (Table 14.3). Birds nest earlier in years when there is little snow in March and April and later when snow lingers in April (Fig. 14.10). In Minnesota, spruce grouse bred 2 weeks later in 1970, when 61 cm of snow fell in mid-April than in 1969 (Haas 1974). Spruce grouse in Alberta nested later in 1967 than in 3 other years; the delay followed a winter of much snowfall and deep snow on the ground (McCourt 1969). Ruffed grouse in the same area also delayed nesting. Peaks in drumming frequency of ruffed grouse males are correlated with the number of female visits, and females begin to lay eggs shortly after breeding (Brander 1965, Kupa 1966, Maxson 1974). Aubin (1970, p. 27) said of one year that "the entire study area was blanketed by approximately two inches of snow until the 7th of May. This appears to be responsible for the delay in peak drumming until May 17" (the normal date for 4 years was 3–4 May). In British Columbia, blue grouse breed approximately a week later each year at Tsolum Main than at Comox Burn, corresponding with the later disappearance of snow at the former site (Zwickel 1977).

The relationship between breeding and nesting and the disappearance of snow cover also holds for the steppe and tundra grouse. The mean date of nesting by prairie grouse in North Dakota is correlated with snowfall in April and May ($r = 0.531$, $n = 16$ years, data from Kobriger pers. comm.). Sharp-tailed grouse severely curtailed advertising and nesting 10 April–4 May in North Dakota in 1970, when 66 cm of snow fell (Christenson 1970). The date of peak numbers of breeding prairie chickens in Wisconsin and the date of nesting by females in Minnesota are both correlated with spring snow conditions (Fig. 14.10, Table 14.4). Sage grouse in Colorado nested later in 1979, after a winter of deep and persistent snow, than in 1978 after a mild winter (mean nesting date of 16 versus 1 April, respectively, Emmons 1980). Patterson (1952) suggested that sage grouse wait on the range for the snow to recede before breeding.

Table 14.3. Variation among years in breeding or hatching nests

Grouse groups and species	No. of years	Hatching date			Difference (days)
		Mean[a]	Earliest	Latest	
Forest					
Spruce grouse					
Alberta[a]	13	30 June	20 June	8 July	18
Blue grouse					
Vancouver Island[b]	12	18 June	7–8 June	~ 1 July	10
Ruffed grouse					
Central B.C.	12	11 June	6 June	17 June	11
Central Alberta	6	10 June	5 June	21 June	16
Steppe					
Sharp-tailed grouse					
North Dakota	22	20 June	14 June	26 June	12
Prairie chicken[c]					
Wisconsin	14	23 April	14 April	28 April	14
Sage grouse					
Montana	10	13 June	7 June	21 June	14
Tundra					
White-tailed ptarmigan					
Colorado	12	19 July	5 July	26 July	21
Rock ptarmigan					
Alaska	9	22 June	18 June	1 July	13
Willow ptarmigan					
Norway	21	23 June	18 June	2 July	14

[a] Mean or median date reported.
[b] Zwickel & Bendell (1967) and Zwickel (1977) present hatch by weeks; values in table are only approximate.
[c] Represents peak numbers of copulations.
Sources: Spruce Grouse — Smyth & Boag 1984; *Blue grouse* — Zwickel & Bendell 1967, Mossop 1971, Zwickel 1977; *Ruffed grouse* — Central B.C., Davies & Bergerud, Chap. 3; Central Alberta Rusch et al. 1984, pers. comm; *Sharp-tailed grouse* — Kobriger pers. comm; *Prairie chicken* — Hamerstrom & Hamerstrom 1973; *Sage grouse* — Wallestad & Watts 1972; *White-tailed ptarmigan* — Gieson et al. 1980; *Rock ptarmigan* — Weeden & Theberge pers. comm; *Willow ptarmigan* — Myrberget Chap. 11.

Ptarmigan also breed later in years of late springs (Watson 1965, Mercer 1967, Bergerud 1970a, Fig. 14.10). Indeed, the generalization appears to apply to all northern grouse. There is a synchronization of the disappearance of snow and the start of nest searching in grouse. This synchronization allows females maximum residual cover in which to select nest sites, reduced conspicuousness, and results in maximum space that predators must search.

An alternative hypothesis to explain the close synchronization between spring weather and nesting dates is that in years with an early disappearance of snow,

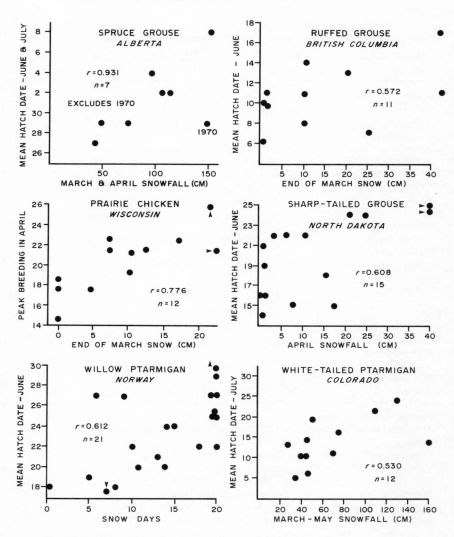

Fig. 14.10. Annual dates of nesting are correlated with disappearance of snow cover. All snow statistics shown above were gathered at government weather stations, often at some distance from the study areas. (Data from McCourt 1969, Hamerstrom & Hamerstrom 1973, Giesen et al. 1980, Davies & Bergerud Chap. 3, Myrberget Chap. 11, Keppie pers. comm., Kobriger pers. comm.)

females can begin feeding on new plant growth and develop eggs sooner than in a later year (Lack 1968). Contrary to this hypothesis is a lack of correlation between the appearance of spring plants and the date of nesting in grouse. In the

Table 14.4 Breeding and nesting by prairie chicken hens in Minnesota in relation to spring weather and weight of hens (adapted from Svedarsky 1979)

Parameters	Late spring (1975)	Intermediate spring (1976)	Early spring (1977)
Mean date went to lek for breeding	15 May (5)[a]	30 April (12)	19 April (12)
Mean date of first egg	15 May (8)	29 April (10)	1 May (7)
Clutch size (first nests)	13.3 ± 0.56 (6)	13.5 ± 0.43 (10)	14.0 ± 0.62 (7)
Weight when captured on lek (g)	934 ± 12 (5)	944 ± 21 (6)	856 ± 14 (7)
April minimum temperature (°C)[b]	−16.1	−3.9	8.9
April mean temperature (°C)	2.3	8.3	9.5
End-of-March snow depth (cm)	18	0	0
March snowfall (cm)	35	31	10

[a] Number of hens in parentheses.
[b] Weather data from Crookston, Minnesota.

far south, by the time the birds nest, growing seasons are well under way for the Attwater's prairie chicken in Texas and for ruffed grouse in Georgia and Kentucky. As one moves north, there is progressively less time between the start of new plant growth and the egg-laying period. Ruffed grouse in central Alberta hatch about 7 June (Rusch et al. 1984, pers. comm.), and the growth of green plants begins about 25 April. Here egg-laying is concomitant with new plant growth and too late to affect the prelaying weight and condition of the hen. Similarly, willow ptarmigan in Newfoundland hatch their chicks the last week of June, but egg-laying begins in mid-May at the time mean temperatures first reach values needed for plant growth. Rock ptarmigan in Scotland start laying just as new plant growth is initiated (Watson 1965), and ptarmigan in the high Arctic must lay eggs before the start of the growing season (cf. MacDonald 1970). Most populations show variations in the timing of nesting, but plant growth in many places is relatively constant. In many other places birds must nest before the growing season starts, thereby precluding any variability in herbaceous plant nutrition affecting laying hens.

Also in contradiction to the nutrition hypothesis is that weights of females in a series of springs are either constant or vary with winter nutrition, and do not reflect gross availability of spring foods. The average dates first eggs were laid by prairie chickens in Minnesota, from 1975 to 1977, were 15 May, 29 April, and 1 May (Svedarsky 1979, Table 14.4). Neither the date of copulation nor the start of egg-laying covary with the weight of females captured at breeding leks (Table 14.4); thus, hens that were heavier did not begin sooner. The mean hatching date of ruffed grouse in central Minnesota was 23 April in 1971 and 28 April in 1972 ($P < 0.01$), whereas on average females were lighter in the earlier year (517.4 ± 19.0 g versus 544.3 ± 14.9 g, $P < 0.01$) (Maxson 1974). March and April weights of Wisconsin prairie chickens also showed no correlation with copulation peaks, (Hamerstrom & Hamerstrom 1973, Hamerstrom pers. comm., Figs 14.10, 16.10).

Yet another hypothesis states that the start of breeding in ptarmigan is correlated with numbers. As breeding density increases, nesting is progressively later (Moss et al. 1974). However, we find no significant correlation between the density of birds and date of hatch in Scotland's red grouse ($r = 0.139$, $n = 9$; Jenkins et al. 1963), rock ptarmigan in Alaska ($r = -0.199$; $n = 9$; Weeden & Theberge 1972, pers. comm.), nor for willow ptarmigan on Brunette Island, Newfoundland ($r = -0.752$, $n = 4$; Mercer, 1967), or for Newfoundland as a whole ($r = 0.230$; $n = 5$; Bergerud 1970a). Earlier, Watson (1965) had said that rock ptarmigan hens nest earlier in warm Mays and also that breeding was delayed by an unusually late disappearance of snow (e.g., 1951) and by heavy snowfalls in April and May.

A final hypothesis proposed to explain variability in nesting dates is that females nest at a time that ensures a maximum abundance of insect food when the young hatch (Lack 1954). Several studies have shown that the number of young per adult in summer and fall is higher after early-nesting springs than after late ones (Jenkins et al. 1963, Marcstrom & Hoglund 1980, Chap. 11). One possible factor is that clutches are larger in early years. We found no studies that documented a peak in insect abundance coinciding with hatching, but two studies of blue and spruce grouse have shown that insect numbers do not necessarily align with peak dates of hatching (Elliot 1979, Armleder 1980).

Evidence also indicates that late-hatched young may survive as well as young that hatch early (Bergerud 1970b, Parker 1981b). Eggs may be larger in late years in willow ptarmigan (Myrberget 1977, Parker 1981b, but see Erikstad et al. 1985). Yearlings generally nest slightly later than adults and have fewer chicks, but differences in brood size can be explained on the basis of clutch size (Zwickel et al. 1977, Keppie 1982); the chicks of yearlings survive as well as those of adults. A major problem for chicks at hatch is their inability to thermoregulate. Early-hatched young face colder temperatures and require more brooding time, leaving less time for feeding (Erikstad & Spidso 1982, Erikstad & Andersen 1983). Later-hatched young have been shown to grow faster than early-hatched young in blue grouse (Redfield 1978), spruce grouse (Quinn & Keppie 1981), and willow ptarmigan (Myrberget 1977).

Females initiate egg-laying approximately 40 days before their eggs should hatch. The environment during laying is brown; temperatures are variable and there are no environmental clues that would clearly relate to the predictability and abundance of insects more than a month later. The considerable variation in chick survival in the first 14 days of life may be balanced by the advantages of nesting early; females can be expected to improve their fitness by experience, and nesting early permits sufficient time to use this experience in a second attempt, if necessary. The timing of the entire nesting sequence relates, in our view, to successfully hatching the nest, and only secondarily to chick survival. The female has more control of the nesting decision and less control of the more unpredictable mortality factors that operate after her chicks hatch.

14.4.3 Spacing and other behaviors to remain inconspicuous

Females may reduce the likelihood of their nests being discovered by remaining motionless and in place as predators pass nearby, by performing distraction displays at appropriate times, and by spacing away from conspecifics. Also, females should remain away from the nest site when feeding (cf. Lance 1984, p. 79).

We all recognize that females are cryptic; they have a general "female coloration pattern" (Hjorth 1970). Females do have contrasting colors that they usually keep concealed. The black ruff, the black rectrices under brown coverts, and the white shoulder spots of ruffed grouse are examples (Hjorth 1970, Lumsden 1970). Females commonly walk lower to the ground than males, and in general behave in ways that emphasize inconspicuousness (cf. Bendell & Elliott 1967). A female's behavior should be most inconspicuous near the nest unless she is discovered and displays to distract attention away from it. In general, female grouse come and go secretly to their nests, and travel some distance before they fly. They often "sneak" back after landing. Females nesting without overhead canopies move to and from the nest most frequently in the crepuscular hours when light intensity is low and few diurnal predators are about. Females use a host of tactics that we believe help to prevent the nest from being discovered (Table 14.5). Giesen & Braun (1979a) reported that white-tailed ptarmigan most frequently left the nest during foggy weather. Sage grouse females may wander farther from the nest on darker days than on bright ones (Petersen 1980). Generally, females "sit tight" during the late stage of incubation, and risk their own safety to keep the eggs concealed. In black and white photographs of the nests of ruffed grouse, sage grouse, and prairie chickens, the eggs are much more conspicuous when the hens are absent (Bump et al. 1947, Patterson 1952) than when they are incubating (e.g., Gross 1930, Schwartz 1944, Hamerstrom et al. 1957). But early in the nesting period, when females are possibly still prepared to renest, females may favor their own safety and sneak or fly from nests when predators are still at long distances (see also section 14.4.6). Between these extremes females may perform distraction behaviors near nest sites to decoy predators away. However, field workers seldom disturb nesting females and there is little information on the quality or variability of tactics, or of the environmental constraints that affect a female's options. For example, Gross (1930) reported that female prairie chickens seldom used broken-wing displays, but Schwartz (1945) reported that they performed decoy behavior; Svedarsky (pers. comm.) thought prairie chicken females mostly flew away or 'sat tight." In Manitoba, Gratson has observed some sharp-tailed grouse hens decoy humans away from nests by wing-dragging and tail-flicking behaviors and by clucking, but most simply flew away.

One possible consideration in assessing the potential cost of distraction in relation to the alternative — sitting tight — is the stage of chick development. Predators may prefer protein-rich egg yolk and albumen in lieu of bone and feathers of partly developed chicks. Foxes prefer eggs, and Sargeant (pers. comm.) has ob-

Table 14.5. Behavior of nesting grouse hens[a]

Spruce grouse: May or may not cover eggs with vegetation during laying phase; few feathers in nest bowl; feeds 20–200 m from nest; deposits eggs at 1315, 1700, 1100, 1200, 1305, 1630 hours; during incubation phase feeds about 32–83 m away, walks a few paces from nest and flies; feeds rapidly and deposits "clocker" droppings while feeding in trees, or < 10 m from nest, flies back to nest site and walks last meter to nest bowl; reported feeding times were 15.2 min/bout 3–6 × /day, 16 min/bout 2–3 × /day and 53 min/bout 1–3 × day, between 0600–1015 hours and 1715–2025 hours (McCourt et al. 1973, Haas 1974, Herzog 1978, Keppie & Herzog 1978, Robinson 1980).

Blue grouse: During incubation phase in AM may walk to feed, walk back, fly to feed, fly back, or a combination; in PM consistently flies both ways after walking away from or landing a meter from the nest (Lance 1967).

Ruffed grouse: Female lays eggs at all times of daylight — 0530–1600 hours; spends several hours laying eggs; eggs left uncovered; during incubation phase feeds 15–30 min/bout 1–3 × /day, 0400–2100 hours; 88% of absences in AM before 1000 hours and 75% PM absences after 1700 hours; yearlings spend longer time feeding than adults (Bump et al. 1947, Kupa 1966, Barrett 1970, Maxson 1977).

Willow ptarmigan: Lays eggs < 10 min. after arriving at nest; covers eggs with vegetation before leaving; during incubation conceals white primaries; rarely accumulates feathers in nest bowl; clocker droppings away from nest, where it feeds in male's territory; female scans before leaving and does not cover eggs; walks 20–40 cm, flies to feeding area; 53% of feeding absences between 0600 and 1800 hours and 48% between 1800 and 0600 hours; averages 52.5 min/bout 3 × /day (Weeden 1965, Pulliainen 1978, Bergerud pers. files).

Rock ptarmigan: Early laying phase, covers eggs completely; during incubation phase no covering; feeds between 2200 and 0200 hours in "dusky hours of Arctic night"; averages 24.1 min/feeding bout; returns by walking and flying partway, feeds quickly with head and tail low,

served a fox burrow *under* an incubating duck to steal her eggs! The food value of the eggs should further decrease as incubation progresses. Predators may search more for, or more easily locate, nests during egg-laying than when most females are incubating. Their preference for eggs over flesh may be one of the factors that has allowed sitting tight to be an option. If a grouse can feign death, like a mallard (Sargeant & Eberhardt 1975), a female may still escape even when discovered (Sargeant pers. comm.).

The risk of distraction may also vary with different kinds of predators, their experience, and the vegetative cover. Ptarmigan often give distraction displays at the feet of feeding caribou. Here there is no risk to the female herself, but egg destruction is a real possibility. To fly or sneak off is not an option. Gross (1930) recorded a prairie chicken using the broken-wing display on a domestic cow, yet the same female sat tight as a local farmer passed by. It is conceivable that females

Table 14.5. continued

concealing white underparts, then repeats "run-feed" closer to nest; at the last minute runs and settles on clutch; eats white feathers in nest bowl; will perform distraction displays—hissing, "trembling," and dragging lower wings and tail (Weeden 1965, MacDonald 1970, Watson 1972).

White-tailed ptarmigan; Deposits eggs 0830–1630 hours; lays eggs immediately upon reaching bowl, then becomes inactive until leaving nest; feeds in male's territory 100–300 m away from nest; eggs completely covered with vegetation while absent; during incubation phase feeds mostly before sunrise and after sunset 300 m from nest; deposits clocker droppings at feeding; may swallow white feathers at nest; 4 of 8 times left nest during daylight when there was fog, rain, or snow; distraction—hissing while exposing white carpal patches and "advance-retreat" behavior (Schmidt 1969, Giesen & Braun 1970a, Giesen et al. 1980, Chap. 8).

Sharp-tailed grouse: During incubation leaves nest to feed 20–45 min/bout 1–2 ×/day 0800–1200 hours and 1600–1900 hours; feeds < 200 m from nest—mostly 1 or 2 directions away from nest site; eggs uncovered during incubation phase (Hart et al. 1950, Schiller 1973, Gratson 1983).

Prairie chicken: Some hens cover eggs during laying phase; lays eggs 0800–1400 hours; incubating hens average 38 min/bout off the nest feeding in AM and 50 min in PM, departing 0500–0800 hours and 1630–2230 hours; eggs uncovered during incubation phase; distraction displays include "broken-wing" and flying slowly away and circling back to nest; walks in crouched position away from nest a few meters after surveying area, hesitates, then flies to feeding site; flies back and stops 15–30 m away before stealthily approaching nest and settling on eggs (Gross 1930, Lehmann 1941, Schwartz 1945, Silvy 1968, Bowen 1971, Svedarsky 1979).

Sage grouse: Feeding sites of incubation hens 0.3 km from nest; feeds before sunrise and after sunset, averages 15–30 min/bout 1–2 ×/day; often goes through the sagebrush to exit the nest (Patterson 1952, Nelson 1955, Peterson 1980, Autenrieth 1981).

[a] Data are unavailable on all behaviors for each species.

may be able to distinguish foxes from skunks, and hunting, "sharp-set" hawks from resting, recently fed ones and adjust their strategy of inconspicuousness. One reason why some ruffed grouse females nest in vegetation edges (Bump et al. 1947) may not only be to have a safe exit, but to be able to assess the identity and character of any approaching danger. A bird nesting where there is little cover at ground level, or a sage grouse under a sagebrush, may have to sit tight and take a greater risk than a prairie chicken in the center of a grass tussock, where the bird can sneak away or appear at a distance with decoy antics. We have not even scratched the surface of the variability of and the factors that influence female decision-making in preventing her nest from being discovered.

Female willow ptarmigan are in a unique position because the male helps with distraction behavior. However, males stay away from the nest in diurnal cover when not helping (Fig. 13.6, Weeden 1959b). Pulliainen (1978) reported that males never came closer than 10 m when the female was incubating. Females do appear to benefit from the presence of males. The mean nesting success of females that had males compared with a group in which some had no male (males removed) was 79% ($n = 66$) and 68% ($n = 56$) respectively (Hannon 1982). Mossop observed at Chilkat Pass, British Columbia, that when there was a dense population, male ptarmigan were usually obvious visually and also called when females were nesting and he disturbed them. By contrast, in a sparse population in Newfoundland in the 1960s, males were seldom seen; however, they were more obvious in one year (1962) when the population was dense and aggressive (Mercer 1967). When populations are dense, territories are small and wandering intruders pass closer to nesting females than when populations are sparse and females are farther apart. Foxes may be habituated to the constant decoy behavior of male ptarmigan. Possibly a factor that we do not appreciate is that males running on the ground or "walking in circles" (Watson & Jenkins 1964) may leave a maze of scent trails that masks the route of the female when she leaves the nest. What is clear is that female willow ptarmigan have a high nesting success to which the male may contribute significantly.

A major tactic of females of the promiscuous species should be to avoid males during nesting (Brown 1964, Crook 1965, Wittenberger 1978, Chap. 5) (Figs. 14.11, 14.12). Males are conspicuous and can be expected to display if they encounter females. The separation between females and males is clearly apparent in forest grouse. The nests of spruce grouse are generally between or away from the location of advertising males (Ellison 1971, 1973, Herzog & Boag 1978, Nugent & Boag 1982, Fig. 14.12). Forty-seven percent of 484 ruffed grouse nests were more than 125 m from drumming males (Bump et al. 1947). Nesting ranges of female blue grouse on Stuart Island, British Columbia, in 1976 showed little overlap with male ranges (Fig. 13.7, Bergerud & Butler 1985). When Lewis (1984) removed territorial, blue grouse males he found that females increased

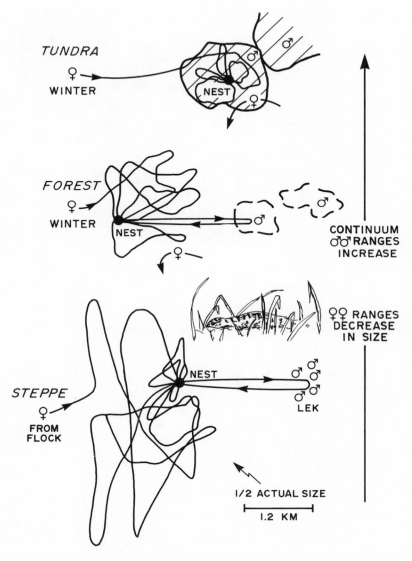

Fig. 14.11. Sizes of advertising ranges of males increase from steppe to forest to tundra; sizes of prelaying ranges of females decrease steppe to forest to tundra. Females of polygynous species visit males for breeding but nest away from these conspicuous males and on the edges of their prelaying ranges. Nesting forest grouse females also avoid other females. Females of the monogamous ptarmigan exclude other females, and possibly their males, from the immediate vicinities of their nests.

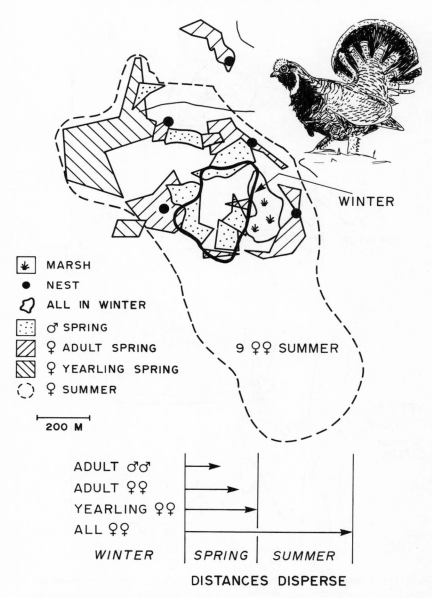

Fig. 14.12. Spruce grouse wintered in a small area of "winter" cover. In spring, yearling females moved farthest from the cover and spaced themselves away from adult females and advertising males; adult females moved away from advertising males; males moved the least distance from their winter cover. Spring prelaying ranges of females were mutually spaced, and nests were commonly located on the edges of their ranges. Females with broods traveled over wider, overlapping ranges in the summer. (Adapted from Herzog 1977a).

their ranges—here is experimental evidence that females will avoid the ranges of males.

The mean distance of nests from males of the lek species is most commonly equal to half the distance between leks (Fig. 13.10) (Christensen 1970, Schiller 1973, Wallestad & Pyrah 1974, Chaps. 5, 6). Females also appear to avoid the locations used by males when the latter are feeding away from leks (Chap. 5). In several grouse species, e.g., in sharp-tailed grouse, prairie chickens, and ruffed grouse (Hamerstrom 1939, Hjorth 1970), males probably cannot easily recognize females by morphology. In other species, such as blue grouse, they probably cannot recognize females until they are only a few meters away (e.g., Jamieson 1982). This sexual indistinguishability permits females to escape the attention of males unless they reveal their identity by postures or calls.

It should increase female and nest inconspicuousness to also avoid other females, and to have nests dispersed (Tinbergen et al. 1967). Dispersed nests should suffer lower predation rates by crows than clumped nests (e.g., Sugden & Beyersbergen 1986). This dispersion has been documented in forest grouse but not in steppe grouse. In both spruce and blue grouse, nesting ranges of females may be mutually exclusive and female aggressiveness and territoriality have been documented (Lance 1967, 1970, Stirling 1968, Herzog & Boag 1977, 1978, Hannon 1978, Nugent & Boag 1982, Bergerud & Butler 1985, but see Hines 1986a). The spacing of ruffed grouse females has not been determined; no one has tagged all or most of the individuals in a prescribed space. Females have, however, appeared evenly spaced as they flushed on walking transects (Rusch & Keith 1971a) and "ranges of adjacent hens usually had little overlap suggesting some spacing mechanism" (Maxson 1978, p. 65).

The spacing of steppe grouse females is not yet clear. Females are commonly seen together, especially in sage grouse. Nests of sage grouse and of prairie chickens are often found near each other in optimum habitats (Schwartz 1945, Baker 1953, Gill 1965, Klebenow 1968, 1969, Stewart 1975). For example, in 1903 a large prairie fire exposed many prairie chicken nests. These nests were clumped around sloughs and some were 15–20 m apart (cf. Johnson 1964). Does such clumping result from the loss of nesting habitats or is it a naturally-evolved behavior to utilize patchy, heterogeneous environments? The habitats in 1903 should have been relatively pristine.

Females of the lek species search prelaying ranges that are too large for females to defend. They are also in open habitats where the predation risks associated with overt, aggressive behavior may be higher than in forest habitats. Still, they could, through mutual avoidance, disperse themselves.

Indirect evidence of spacing can be seen in a comparison of prairie chicken populations in Minnesota, where recently they expanded their range, compared to those in Wisconsin, where habitat was mostly unsuitable surrounding relic populations. In Minnesota, as total numbers increased, the mean number of males per lek and lek density remained relatively constant (Fig. 16.1); as the population increased new leks were formed and spaced away from other leks. If male prairie chickens form leks in areas to be near females, as we argue earlier, then this should mean there is a limit to the number of females within a given space and that females space themselves, thus expanding into new habitats. In Wisconsin, however, the mean number of males per lek was correlated with the total male count ($r = 0.757$, $n = 22$; Hamerstrom & Hamerstrom 1973). There, females were "packed into" more restricted and less variable acreage of habitat and spacing was reduced.

Alternatively, under some as yet unknown conditions clumping may be the most inconspicuousness pattern for females and nests. A clumped distribution, where nests within a cluster are close but there are long distances between clumps, might reduce the probability of discovery by predators where space is extensive. Dummy nests in a clumped dispersion in Attwater's chicken habitat were preyed on less than nests in a dispersed pattern (Horkel et al. 1978). Horkel et al. (1978) argued that the rare patches of nests may preclude the formation of a "searching image" (Tinbergen et al. 1967, Croze 1970, Krebs 1973).

All female grouse are less mobile while laying eggs and incubating (Table 14.2). Reduced ranges should help them to avoid conspecifics and predators. The ranges of nesting, female spruce grouse overlap less with displaying males than with yearling males (9% versus 42% overlap), and they overlap on average only 6% with other nesting females (Herzog & Boag 1978, Fig. 14.12). The locations of advertising males would be predictable, but because yearling males move unobtrusively they would be more difficult to avoid.

14.4.4 Avoiding nest ambush

Females may often be faced with the decision of whether to flush from a predator and have the eggs located, or to sit tight and risk being killed. If females can select nest sites with reduced risk to themselves, they can afford to remain on the nest longer and give greater preference to the concealment of the eggs. The female herself provides the best camouflage of the clutch.

One behavior that should reduce risk to the female on the nest is for her to range on only one side of the nest during egg-laying and incubation periods. Clocker droppings and ground scent would then be restricted to this route. Because adjacent, female nest ranges seldom overlap, at least in forest grouse, it is unlikely that another female would travel near the side that the resident hen does not visit. Predators could pass near the nest on at least one side with a reduced probability of detecting the female's or her neighbor's scent.

With the exception of willow ptarmigan all grouse appear to nest most often on the outside perimeter of their nesting ranges (cf. Herzog & Boag 1978, Hannon 1978, Chaps. 5, 6, 8, 9). Pheasants (*Phasianus colchicus*) also show this tactic (Dumke & Pils 1979). Female willow ptarmigan commonly locate their nests within the center of the male's territory (Weeden 1959b, Erikstad 1978, Hannon 1982, Erikstad 1985a,b, Chap. 13, but see Steen et al. 1985). The ptarmigan cock stays with the female during nesting and prevents other males (and thus other females) from coming near the nest. If communal foraging areas occur, they are at the edges of territories (Pedersen et al. 1983). Thus, all the grouse have tactics of reducing activity near the nest.

Forest grouse commonly reinforce their edge position by having a backstop—a tree or stump adjacent to and behind the nest (i.e., females face away from it). Bump et al. (1947) indicated that 52% of 1,158 ruffed grouse nests were at the base of trees, 15% at the base of stumps, 14% under bushes, and 14% beside logs or rocks. Haas (1974) reported 8 of 11 spruce grouse nests at the base of trees, and Redmond et al. (1982) found 88% of 104 nests within 10 cm of a conifer. Similarly, Bendell and Elliot (1967) reported that most blue grouse hens nested under logs, near stumps, or beside small conifers. These backstops permit the female to focus her attention outward, to that part of her range with which she is familiar, and where she is most likely to be detected because of scent. If she is detected from behind, the predator can not spring directly on the hen because of the obstructing backstop.

By being next to a tree or shrub, grouse also benefit by having maximum overhead cover to prevent detection by raptors and corvids (Sugden & Beyersbergen 1986). What predator other than a squirrel would travel a search route that went from tree to tree? If tree squirrels are a potential problem, as are red squirrels (*Tamiasciurus hudsonicus*), the tactic may cost the hen an occasional egg. Nesting next to vertical stems has the additional advantage of deflecting wind currents, allowing the hen to nest in a wind shadow. If the nest is on the lee side of the backstop, predators that hunt by scent would less frequently detect the hen.

Sage grouse nest under sagebrush and sharp-tailed grouse commonly nest under bushes if available (Patterson 1952, Artmann 1970, Schiller 1973). Ptarmigan nest beneath prostrate conifers and shrubs, and white-tailed ptarmigan often nest beside rocks. Only the prairie chicken usually nests without benefit of either shrub, tree, or some backstop (e.g., Svedarsky 1979). Twenty-three of 35 prairie chicken nests in Wisconsin had no backstop or overhead shrub cover, based on photographs taked by F. J. Schmidt (University of Wisconsin files). Shrubs and rocks should often prevent a successful ambush, but in grassland habitats where shrubs are rare, prairie chicken hens and sharp-tailed grouse hens should avoid nesting under lone shrubs and instead attempt to become lost in a "sea of grass" (cf. photographs in Hamerstrom et al. 1957, pp. 19, 39). In one study of prairie chickens a worker marked nests with poles and found that corvids sat on the conspicuous marks and found the nests (Bowen 1971). Authenrieth (1981) marked sage grouse nests with conspicuous flags, and ravens (*Corvus corax*) investigated the objects and found the nests.

The lack of backstops in grassland habitats has cost some prairie chicken females their lives (Table 14.6). Hens apparently hesitate to flush until the very last moment, and without cover that helps deflect predators they are often killed. Except for sharp-tailed grouse and prairie chickens the frequency of ambushed grouse hens is generally less than 1% (Table 14.6).

14.4.5 Philopatry of nesting females

Females that nested successfully generally should return to the same area the next year to attempt to nest. The safety of the site has been proven, and the uncertainty

Table 14.6. Percentages of grouse hens killed on the nest and that abandon their nests

Type of grouse	% die on nest[a] (n)		% abandon nest[b] (n)	
	All studies[c]	Telemetry	All studies[c]	Telemetry
Forest				
Spruce grouse	0.0 (0/58)	0.0 (0/53)	4.1 (6 /148)	2.0 (2/102)
Blue grouse	0.0 (0/92)	0.0 (0/33)	10.6 (27/256)	4.6 (3/65)
Ruffed grouse	0.3 (4/1,598)	0.0 (0/23)	1.0 (17/1,629)	2.1 (2/97)
Steppe				
Sage grouse	0.4 (1/281)	0.0 (0/14)	13.9 (71/510)	16.1 (9/56)
Prairie chicken	9.1 (11/121)	7.8 (5/64)	7.3 (64/876)	9.9 (14/142)
Sharp-tailed grouse	1.3 (2/159)	4.3 (2/47)	7.8 (24/308)	6.7 (10/150)
Tundra				
White-tailed ptarmigan	0.0 (0/72)	–	2.9 (2 /70)	–
Rock ptarmigan	4.7 (2/43)	–	3.1 (3 /96)	–
Willow ptarmigan	0.0 (0/115)	–	10.0 (12/115)	–

[a] Number that reportedly are killed on the nest ÷ total hens observed for which there is sufficient information to determine their fates, × 100.

[b] Number that reportedly abandon nests of undamaged eggs ÷ total hens (nests) observed for which there is sufficient evidence that an author reported abandonment if it occurred, × 100.

[c] Sources: *Spruce grouse* – Ellison 1974, Hass 1974, Keppie & Herzog 1978, Robinson 1980, Keppie 1982; *Blue grouse* – Zwickel & Lance 1965, Mossop 1971, Weber 1975, Zwickel & Carveth 1978, Sopuck 1979; *Ruffed grouse* – Bump *et al.* 1947, Grange 1948, Kupa 1966, Neave 1967, Barrett 1970, Maxson 1974; *Sage grouse* – Batterson & Morse 1948, Patterson 1952, Gill 1965, Klebenow 1969, May 1970, Wallestad & Pyrah 1974, Petersen 1980; *Prairie chicken* – Gross 1930, Hamerstrom 1939, Lehmann 1941, Schwartz 1945, Grange 1948, Baker 1953, Ammann 1957, Yeatter 1963, Silvy 1968, Bowen 1971, Horak 1974, Rice & Carter 1975, 1976, 1977, Sisson 1976, Horkel *et al.* 1978, Riley 1978, Sell 1979,Svedarsky 1979, Vance & Westemeier 1979; *Sharp-tailed grouse* – Gross 1930, Hamerstrom 1939, Grange 1948, Ammann 1957, Brown 1966b, 1967, 1968b, Bernhoft 1969, Artmann 1970, Christenson 1970, Pepper 1972, Schiller 1973, Rice & Carter 1975, 1976, 1977, Kohn 1976, Ramharter 1976, Sisson 1976; *White-tailed ptarmigan* – Choate 1963b, Schmidt 1969, Giesen *et al.* 1980; *Rock ptarmigan* – Watson 1965, Weeden & Theberge 1972, pers. comm. 1982; *Willow ptarmigan* – Bergerud 1970a, Hannon 1982.

associated with new sites should impart a greater risk. If, however, females encounter current, unfavorable information, such as low vegetation suitability and
high predator activity, about the old site when they return in spring, they may
elect to move. Philopatry of hens has been documented for all the grouse groups
(Choate 1963a, Berry & Eng 1985, Chaps. 6, 8). What remains to be determined
are its general frequency, variability, and factors that influence it. Adult hens
usually move shorter distances between wintering areas and breeding ranges than
do juvenile females and return earlier (Table 14.7). This difference suggests less
searching in spring by returning adults than by naive yearlings. Adults have invested time in learning an area — this experience should be incorporated into their
nesting strategy.

Although successful hens should show philopatry, it is less clear if unsuccessful hens should again invest in the same site if unsuccessful. If failure was a result
of weather, flooding, burning, or filching of eggs, a suitable stimulus to shift may
be lacking (see also section 14.4.6). These factors are also unpredictable in their
recurrence, and a hen may be "betting" for the site when she returns after an unsuccessful year. But if nest loss is associated with a strenuous encounter with a
predator, the female may reduce her current risk by changing areas.

It is conceivable that the distance a female moves between nesting efforts from
one year to the next may relate to the mobility of the predators that caused the
nest failure. For example, red-winged blackbird (*Agelaius phoeniceus*) females
move farther when they lose their clutches to magpies than when mice take their
eggs (L. Rotterman pers. comm.). Many of the subtleties of philopatry as a tactic
need to be clarified.

14.4.6 Nest abandonment and renesting

Females should abandon their current clutch if disturbed and try again if the certainty of a current loss outweighs the unpredictability of the loss of a future effort
(Fig. 14.13). Abandonment may occur during laying or incubation phases.
Dawkins and Carlisle (1976) argue that the decision to abandon the nest and
renest should depend more on future prospects than on the loss of current investment. Nest abandonment in grouse decreases as investment increases throughout
the nesting schedule. Eleven of 12 (92%) blue grouse females deserted their nests
following human disturbance when they had three or fewer eggs, whereas only
9 of 22 (41%) deserted when the number of eggs was from four to seven (Zwickel
& Carveth 1978). A female whose clutch is near hatching has almost succeeded
and the probability of success, even if disturbed, may still outweigh starting over.
The probability of further disturbance and the severity of the encounter should
also be considered in the female's decision on whether to abandon her current investment. We believe that grouse may nest earlier than is optimal for early chick
survival in order not to prohibit the opportunity to try again — abandonment

Table 14.7. Movements of banded grouse,

Grouse groups and species	Movement type
Forest	
Spruce grouse	summer to winter
	summer to summer
	summer to fall
	winter to spring
Ruffed grouse	winter to spring
	summer to winter
	summer to fall
	summer to fall
	summer to fall
Blue grouse	summer to fall
	summer to fall
	summer to spring
	summer to winter
Steppe	
Sharp-tailed grouse	winter to fall
	winter to fall
	winter to spring
Prairie chicken	winter to spring
	fall to spring
	spring to fall
Sage grouse	summer to fall
	spring to winter
Tundra[d]	
White-tailed ptarmigan	summer to fall
	summer to winter
	winter to summer
	summer to winter
Willow ptarmigan	summer to fall

[a] Refers to distance moved; A = adult, Y = yearling, J = juvenile, B = brooding, NB = non-brooding.
[b] Mean ± 1 SE (n) of each sex and age class for which a trend is shown; in some instances SE could not be computed.
[c] Approximate; computed from reference given.
[d] No estimates were located for rock ptarmigan.

emphasizing trends of sex and age classes

Trend[a]	Distances (km)[b]
A♂ < A♀	1.7 ± 0.5 (4); 5.0 ± 1.0 (9)
J♂ < J♀	1.6 ± 0.5 (14); 3.2 ± 0.5 (12)
A < J	0.9 (9); 3.2 (13)[c]
A♂ < J♂ < A♀ < J♀	0.8 ± 0.2 (19); 1.8 ± 0.9 (9);
	2.2 ± 0.4 (46); 2.3 ± 0.5 (19)
♂ < ♀	0.3 (15); 1.9 (6)[c]
A♂ < A♀ < J♂ < J♀	0.1 (11); 0.5 (15); 0.7 (82); 1.2 (40)[c]
A♂ < A♀ < J	0.6 ± 0.1 (36); 1.0 ± 0.3 (11); 1.8 ± 0.1 (125)
J♂ < J♀	2.7 ± 1.1 (3); 2.9 ± 0.5 (3)
J♂ < J♀	0.4 (50); 2.9 (43)[c]
Y♂ < NB♀ < B♀	4.4 ± 0.9 (10); 5.4 ± 1.2 (11); 13.9 (1)
J♂ < J♀	6.7 ± 3.8 (6); 13.7 ± 4.2 (12)
J♂ < J♀	0.9 (24); 1.4 (42)
Y♂ = Y♀, < A♀ &	0.3 (17); 0.3 (16); 0.5 (21); 0.7 (24)
< A♂ < J♂ < J♀	1.9 (34); 2.3 (76)
A♂ < J♂ < A♀ < J♀	6.9 ± 0.8 (34); 9.1 ± 0.8 (87);
	10.6 ± 1.8 (32); 21.6 ± 3.7 (80)
A♂ < J♂ < J♀ < A♀	4.2 ± 0.3 (9); 6.1 ± 0.7 (33);
	13.6 ± 1.8 (42); 15.8 ± 3.9 (18)
J♂ < A♂ < A♀ < J♀	1.2 ± 0.3 (5); 2.2 ± 0.5 (5);
	2.8 ± 0.6 (3); 48.5 (1)
A♂ < J♂ < A♀ < J♀	2.7 (297); 3.7 (369); 4.7 (98); 7.9 (125)[c]
J♂ < J♀	1.2 ± 0.3 (27); 4.1 ± 1.3 (5)
A♂ < Y♀	3.4 ± 1.1 (4); 8.8 ± 2.2 (9)
A♂ < A♀	6.1 ± 1.1 (8); 8.1 ± 2.1 (12)
	9.4 (68); 17.5 (10)[c]
J♂ < J♀	2.3 ± 0.2 (53); 3.0 ± 0.2 (68)[c]
♂ < ♀	3.5 ± 0.4 (6); 5.1 ± 0.4 (9)[c]
A♂ < J♂ < A♀	2.4 ± 0.5 (14); 3.8 ± 0.7 (18);
	6.2 ± 0.8 (28); 10.4 ± 0.9 (39)[c]
A♂ < J♂ < J♀ < A♀	1.5 ± 0.4 (4); 3.8 ± 1.2 (2); 6.0 (1);
	6.4 ± 0.5 (5)
J♂ < A♀ < A♂ < J♀	1.3 (17); 1.4 (9); 2.2 (14)[c] 3.4 (15)

Sources: *Forest grouse* — Herzog & Keppie 1980, Robinson 1980, Ellison 1973, Schroeder 1985, Hale & Dorney 1963, Dorney & Kabat 1960, Godfrey & Marshall 1969, Rusch & Keith 1971b, Sopuck 1979, Zwickel et al. 1968, Hines 1986a,b; *Steppe grouse* — Robel et al. 1972, Sisson 1976, Hamerstrom & Hamerstrom 1973, Copelin 1963, Campbell 1972, May 1970, Beck 1975; *Tundra grouse* — Giesen 1977, Hoffman & Braun 1975, Herzog 1980, Bergerud 1970a.

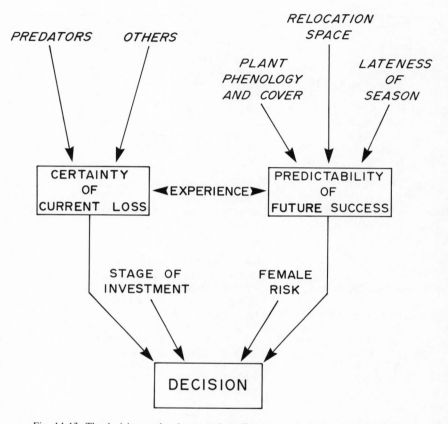

Fig. 14.13. The decision to abandon a nesting effort is hypothesized to be influenced by the certainity of a current loss as perceived by experience and moderated by stage of invest-ment and female risk. Renesting is a tactic in which the decision is hypothesized to be based on predictability of future success, which is moderated by plant cover, relocation space, and lateness of the season.

should be considered a tactic to remove some of the uncertainty of success. Aban-donment and renesting can correct for an initial error in nest location or unpre-dictable circumstances.

With the exception of willow ptarmigan and possibly blue grouse, nest aban-donment is higher for steppe grouse than for the other groups (Table 14.6). The sage grouse hen has little concealing, herbaceous growth in sagebrush nesting habitats, but has a backstop and is rarely ambushed. If predators are active near her nest the probability of eventual discovery is high—the eggs are not concealed during egg-laying. She also has a large preincubation range and can move to familiar locations far-removed from the initial nest site. Abandonment and moving may be a better tactic than awaiting almost certain loss. Because prairie chickens and many sharp-tailed grouse do not have backstops or overhead cover to prevent ambush, they should frequently abandon the nest, rather than wait and later be killed on the nest (Table 14.6). They too can move to renesting locations within their large prelaying ranges (Table 14.2). On the prairies and savannas, new June plant growth may provide more cover for second nests of prairie grouse than residual cover did for the initial nests (Schiller 1973).

Nest abandonment is generally less frequent in forest grouse than in steppe grouse (Table 14.6). For these species there is less nest predation and females are seldom killed on the nest. Thus, the probable costs of staying are lower than for steppe grouse. Forest grouse also have small preincubation ranges, and it is more difficult to put distance between themselves and imposing risks while remaining in a familiar habitat.

In tundra grouse the frequency of nest abandonment varies. Nesting efforts varied during a 10-year cycle of abundance of willow ptarmigan in Newfoundland (Bergerud 1970a). Nine of 41 hens abandoned clutches in 1962, preceding a population decline, but few deserted their nests in other years (2 of 24). In the monogamous ptarmigan, nesting females benefit from male vigilance and decoy behavior. Thus, an assessment of the potential trade-off when abandoning a current clutch should include consideration of what males may do. In white-tailed and rock ptarmigan, cocks may abandon females during nesting. After abandonment, renesting attempts could thus lose the benefits of a vigilant male. Also, there are fewer predators of nests in the arctic than in the more southern latitudes (Fig. 15.7), and nesting success is higher. Abandonment in ptarmigan probably results more often from weather factors than from predator disturbances.

Few data exist to determine if nest abandonment varies with the age, and thus the experience of the female. An adult should normally have more experience with predators than a yearling, but she may also have strong site tenacity because of prior nesting success. Yearlings have less experience with predators but probably abandon more readily. One prediction is that an adult nesting in a new site will have a higher probability of abandoning her nest than an adult showing philopatry at a site where she was previously successful.

Renesting is a major tactic that quickly incorporates knowledge from an initial failure in order to succeed in the same season before hen mortality intercedes. A major theme of Chapter 15 is that predation of nests is density-dependent. Grouse may increase nesting success with second attempts because nesting densities are lower, as noted for passerine birds (Nolan 1963). Gratson (unpubl. data) has found that dummy nests in July were significantly more successful than were dummy clutches placed out in May and June at the peak of nesting by grouse and ducks (see also Sugden & Beyersbergen 1986). Another consideration is that late renesting birds could be out of synchrony with denning mammals like foxes, which may switch later to more abundant but less nutritious foods.

The decision to renest in the same year may be influenced by the life expectancy of the female. To postpone until the next year depends on the gamble of her being alive. Grouse with long life expectancies should renest less often than those with short life expectancies. The usual timing of death should also affect the decision. Females in some populations die primarily during the nesting and brood-rearing periods (e.g., Maxson 1974, Svedarsky 1979, Angelstam 1984). Females in other populations may face more dangers during the winter (Chap. 4, Huempfner pers. comm.) or in early spring (Mercer 1967). A prairie chicken may have a better probability of being successful later in the season than to postpone her attempt until next year on the chance that she will still be alive; but a female spruce grouse in Alberta might profit more by waiting until the following year, as her probability of overwinter survival is fairly high (Keppie 1979). Blue grouse on Vancouver Island, spruce grouse in Alberta and Minnesota, and white-tailed ptarmigan in Colorado generally show long life expectancies and low renesting frequencies (Sopuck 1979, Haas 1974, Giesen & Braun 1976, Giesen et al. 1980, Keppie 1982, Sopuck & Zwickel 1983, Chap. 16). Sharp-tailed grouse in North Dakota, Minnesota and Manitoba; prairie chickens in Wisconsin and Minnesota; and willow ptarmigan in Norway and Newfoundland show short life expectancies, and frequently renest (Bergerud 1970a, Christenson 1970, calculated from Hamerstrom & Hamerstrom 1973, Schiller 1973, Erikstad 1978, Svedarsky 1979, Parker 1981b). But there are many exceptions; short-lived ruffed grouse in Minnesota and New York seldom renest, nor do rock ptarmigan in Alaska or short-lived spruce grouse in Alaska (Bump et al. 1947, Ellison 1974, Maxson 1974, Weeden & Theberge 1972, Weeden & Theberge unpubl. data).

Steppe grouse should generally renest more frequently than forest grouse, for reasons similar to those explaining abandonment (Fig. 14.13). Forest grouse have small preincubation ranges and rather constant vegetative cover; they can use neither distance nor a major increase in cover to improve their second attempt. Steppe grouse have large prelaying areas from which to choose a second nest site, and new herbaceous growth to conceal eggs has appeared during the laying period.

Early grouse workers, such as Hamerstrom (1939) and Ammann (1957), felt that renesting frequencies were low in prairie grouse, but they probably missed renesting attempts without the aid of radio telemetry. Schiller (1973) reported that one sharp-tailed grouse hen moved 19 km between first and second attempts. This renesting hen would surely have been missed had she not been radio-tagged. Gratson has observed that third nesting attempts are common for sharp-tailed grouse radio-tagged in Manitoba, and fourth attempts do occur.

In ptarmigan, the sorting out of renesting tendencies, like abandonment proclivities, are confounded by cyclic changes in breeding behavior. Ptarmigan in Newfoundland readily renested when the population was increasing from a cyclic low, but had reduced renesting in 1962 before the crash (Bergerud 1970a). There was little renesting in rock ptarmigan in 3 of 10 years of low initial failure in 1962, 1963, 1964 (Table 15.3, Weeden pers. comm.). Two studies suggested that late-hatched young of second nests had good survival rates until fall (Bergerud 1970a, Parker 1981b). Still, it seems intuitive that the smaller juveniles of late-hatched clutches would be vulnerable to the effective avian predators of the Arctic. In Newfoundland, late-hatched young were extremely vulnerable to hunting (Bergerud & Huxter 1969b).

14.5 The strategy of selecting a male for breeding

The higher parental investment of females than males in the reproductive process should result in female rather than male choice of mates (Bateman 1948, Maynard-Smith 1958, Trivers 1972, Bateson 1983). We argue that the mate-selection decision is not as critical as the nest-location decision to a female grouse, but if she can show discretion without compromising her nest decision, she should select a male that best enhances her fitness prospects. Females normally mate with only one male, but males of the steppe species may breed more than one female (Hamerstrom & Hamerstrom 1955, Robel 1966, Wiley 1974); commonly only very few of the males mate with most of the females and some males obtain no copulations at all (Table 7.9). Even in the forest grouse, because many yearling males do not breed, some adult males will breed more than one female. Males localize and advertise before mating; clearly it is the female that moves in and closes the distance between the male and herself and makes the choice. Her mate-choice decision in the nonmonogamous species should be based on: (1) assuring fertilization, (2) maximizing expected survival during courtship and coitus, and (3) maintaining an inconspicuous nest site. In addition, in monogamous ptarmigan, the female should select vigilant males who satisfactorily control nesting sites (Chap. 13). Whether or not it is theoretically possible that the female also or solely selects mates on the basis of a correlate of high genotypic quality and thereby possibly improves the fitness of progeny is currently under contention (e.g., Borgia 1979, Weatherhead & Robertson 1979, Lande 1981, Wittenberger 1981b, Kirkpatrick 1982, 1985, 1986, Taylor & Williams 1982, Bateson 1983, Heisler 1985).

Females of the three forest grouse should prefer to remain inconspicuous during breeding. Visibility is restricted under canopies, reducing the distance at which birds can detect predators. The female will be at a disadvantage during copulation because ambush is possible and frequently there is little undergrowth in which to hide. Males display at relatively safe sites, but their locations are probably known to predators; and they are frequently killed adjacent to display stages. A female's inconspicuousness is lost once the male recognizes her as a female and begins courtship.

A female may use many tactics to maintain her inconspicuousness. If a hen travels to a distant male, she will often trespass in other females' ranges. If discovered she may lose her conspicuousness by the aggressive actions of a resident female (Hannon 1978, Herzog & Boag 1978, Bergerud & Butler 1985). If the females' ranges she must pass through are unfamiliar this should also increase her risk. Unless there are additional costs a female may often simply choose nearby males.

Male and female blue grouse on Stuart Island, British Columbia, and spruce grouse at Gorge Creek, Alberta, were spaced such that there was one male considerably closer to each female than were other males (Bergerud & Butler 1985, Fig. 14.12). At Gorge Creek, Alberta, nine yearling, spruce grouse females were on average 303 $\pm$ 60 m from the nearest male, compared with 177 $\pm$ 53 m for 11 adult females (from Herzog 1977a). Yearlings there may have had to pass near adult females to reach males, but adult females generally had at least one male nearby that could be reached without conspicuous encounters with other females.

The three forest grouse vary in the distance the two sexes will travel for mating (Fig. 14.6). If the male ruffed grouse will not leave his safe advertising log, the female must go to him (Allen 1934, Barrett 1970). Thus, at least for ruffed grouse, it is possible that the female may not pick the spot of coitus. In contrast, female blue grouse may lead males considerable distances on the ground. Such females may have more control than the ruffed grouse female in selecting safe sites for breeding.

Female forest grouse select adult rather than yearling males (Olpinski 1980, Jamieson 1982). There may be several reasons for this. First, because of inexperience and adult competition, yearling males may occupy sites that are not as safe as those of adults. Second, yearling courtship displays seem less perfected (Olpinski 1980), and yearlings may simply be less adept at attracting females. Third, male yearlings range widely and their locations are less predictable than those of adults. The female's selection of adult males in preference to yearlings in polygynous grouse species is the basic theoretical reason for the existence of nonbreeding yearling males (Wittenberger 1978).

Female choice of males in the steppe grouse, which advertise at communal display grounds, is especially contentious (Bradbury & Gibson 1983). Does she choose the genetically fittest male and thereby produce superior offspring (Trivers 1972), or does she mostly select a mating site contested between males (Wiley 1973)? Hartzler (Chap. 7) and Wiley watched sage grouse at the same lek and reached different conclusions. Wiley (1973b) concluded that females selected mating sites rather than individual males, and that males competed for these sites. Hartzler and Jenni (Chap. 7), however, provide convincing documentation that females do not go to mating spots per se, but rather select males that strut the most vigorously. In contrast, Kermott (1982) has concluded that female sharp-tailed grouse select mating spots. Hjorth (1970) diagrammed a sharp-tailed grouse lek watched by Brown (pers. comm.) where a dominant male was removed and three yearlings expanded their advertising stages to include his site. Females came to the former site and a yearling was successful in breeding. Again, however, others believe that the males themselves are chosen (Hamerstrom pers. comm., Emlen & Oring 1977, Sparling 1979). The 3–4 days or more that each female steppe grouse on average visits the lek suggests that females may be evaluating males (Wiley 1973b, Hamerstrom & Hamerstrom 1973, Robel & Ballard 1974, Hamerstrom 1980). Emlen and Oring (1977, Oring 1982) suggest that females patronize male clusters because it provides a forum for evaluating male quality, and this implies that male quality is an important determinant of female choice.

It is important to decide if the selection of males by females is really a means of altering the genetic constitution of the offspring (Williams 1975, Harpending 1979). If this is true, then additional problems are those of resolving the lek paradox question (Borgia 1979), the "sexy-son" controversy (Weatherhead & Robertson 1979, Wittenberger 1981, Taylor & Williams 1982, Kirkpatrick 1985), and run-away selection (Fisher 1958, Lande 1981, O'Donald 1983, Arnold 1983).

Most workers have documented that the more central males do most of the breeding (Scott 1942, Robel 1966, Wiley 1973); the Hamerstroms (1973) reported that 31% of 555 copulations were by exterior males. A problem is how to define peripheral and central males; on a small lek all males are peripheral and no one is completely bounded by other males. The mean lek size in Wisconsin over a 22-year period was 8.3 males ($n = 6,611$) (cf. Hamerstrom & Hamerstrom 1973). With leks of this size one could then expect a ratio of interior to exterior cocks of 1:7, assuming similar configurations as in Rippin and Boag (1974b), Sparling (1979), and Robel (1966). Thus, based on their frequency in the population, exterior cocks should have performed approximately 88% of the breeding if there was no female choice. In fact, however, the Hamerstroms reported that only 31% of the copulations were by exterior males. Thus the Hamerstroms' data also agree with data of other workers—i.e., that interior males breed more often than peripheral males.

Observations of females are consistent with the view that females want undisturbed breeding. Evans (1961) reported fewer attacks between sharp-tailed grouse males when females were present. This might explain the daily hen peaks reported in prairie chickens (Hamerstrom & Hamerstrom 1973). Hens arriving ahead of time could wait for more hens and less disturbance. Females spend more days on large leks, and large leks are generally less stable in social climate (Hamerstrom & Hamerstrom 1955). Sage grouse hens are much smaller than males (1:1.8 ratio) and harassment of hens often occurs. These hens move through the lek as a pack and this should reduce harassment from males (Chap. 7). Oring (1982) felt that birds on leks were safe from predators, but that leks were dangerous for females because of aggressive male behavior. He suggests that females avoid the lek centers at first, as well as other areas of overt aggressiveness, and that only after male relations are stable and aggressiveness subsides do the females move in to mate. This is consistent with Robel's (1972) finding; after the removal of three dominant, male prairie chickens he reported aggression increased among resident males and successful copulations declined from an average (6 years) of 34 per year to three.

Copulations are commonly interrupted by neighboring males (Evans 1961, Lumsden 1965, 1968, Hamerstrom & Hamerstrom 1973, Chap. 7). The Hamerstroms (1973) judged that based on behavior, 23% of 590 copulations by prairie chickens were unsuccessful. Mating was interrupted in 14% of 511 attempts by sage grouse (Chap. 7). Dominant cocks commonly knock subordinate males off females in coitus. By visiting the lek before the time when she is ready to copulate, a female can watch the activities of males and may learn where she will be least disturbed. By this hypothesis a female may benefit by using male dominance within his territory as a shield to reduce harassment.

Although females can be expected to choose undisturbed breeding situations—a phenotypic advantage of certain males or particular spots—we can also expect that, in an ultimate and proximate sense, females choose males on the basis of other phenotypic traits. Our hypothesis is that females should select those males at leks that are least likely to interfere with the maintenance of an inconspicuous nesting site. This is an extension of the least-costly-male hypothesis of Wrangham (1980), which attempts to explain the evolution of the lek mating system. Favored males should be those which move around less than other males, move out to meet incoming females less often than neighbors, and follow females to a lesser degree than other cocks. Peripheral males commonly follow females from leks; central males remain more in place (Oring pers. comm., Hartzler 1972, de Vos 1979, Gratson unpubl. data). Female black cocks prefer to breed when there are male clusters (de Vos 1979, 1983). In Texas, prairie chicken hens successfully bred at leks that had central males—10 copulations in 86 observations (12%)—but rarely bred at linear leks that had no central males—1 copulation in 76 sightings (1%) (Horkel & Silvy 1980). Males from linear leks commonly followed females away from leks (Horkel & Silvy 1980), and nesting success was low in that population (Chap. 15). Small, central territories may thus be used as a preliminary index of the tendency of males to "wait" for females rather than to seek or follow females into nesting habitats.

Hartzler and Jenni (Chap. 7) elegantly documented that female sage grouse select males that strut the most frequently. Their findings are consistent with our stationary-male or waiting-male hypothesis, because the mobility of strutting males is reduced (Hjorth 1970). Such dominant males assured of future matings (hens even line up in sage grouse) should not be interested in following females.

The stationary-male hypothesis we have briefly outlined here does not precisely predict how females choose, but which and why males are selected. The sampling strategies and cues females use may be many and varied, and include other females themselves (Gratson unpubl. data). In a system where males can gain no increased, relative fitness benefits from being dispersed (cf. Bradbury 1981), females should enforce the male dispersion pattern by exerting extreme choice. Perhaps the occasional copulation that occurs with peripheral lekking males reduces the tendency for these generally unsuccessful males to desert leks and seek females away from arenas in nesting cover. By initially spending more time with central males, females may force peripheral males to contest for sites toward the center of the lek (Rippin & Boag 1974b, Kermont 1982); the male dispersion is driven inward and the locations of leks are kept in place and prevented from expanding outward into nesting habitats, where males appear to impose costs on nesting females.

14.6 The strategy for improving chick survival

After the female finally succeeds in hatching her clutch, she must continue her investment; 50% of the chicks commonly die between the time of hatching and their independence from the hen in August and September (Fig. 15.1). Tactics to improve the survival of progeny should include: (1) frequenting areas where young chicks can optimally forage, and thus maximize growth during this critical stage in their life history; (2) avoiding predators by remaining inconspicuous; and (3) defending the brood from predators, if necessary.

14.6.1 The trade-off: Optimal foraging versus antipredator tactics

It is common for broods to move long distances in the first few hours and days of life (Fig. 14.14, Cebula 1966, Viers 1967, Silvy 1968, Schladweiler 1968, Barrett 1970, Schiller 1973, Haas 1974, Ramharter 1976, Maxson 1977, Sopuck 1979, Bakke 1980, Armleder 1980, Chap. 6). Long brood movements frequently take ptarmigan outside the territory defended by the male (Bergerud & Huxter 1969a, Erikstad 1978, 1985a, b, Steen & Unander 1985, Chap. 8).

These long initial movements suggest that many nests are not placed in optimal locations with respect to food and cover for the chicks. Nests are generally in dense growth and shaded canopies, because they are more successful where concealed. Young chicks, however, require plant communities with abundant insects, warm temperatures, and a plant structure that provides concealment but does not hinder movement; but females should not compromise nest security by locating nests near such communities. Thus, where there is not a good interspersion of dense (nest) cover and open (brood) cover, young broods, of necessity, must move.

Yearling forest grouse females commonly move farther from nest sites to

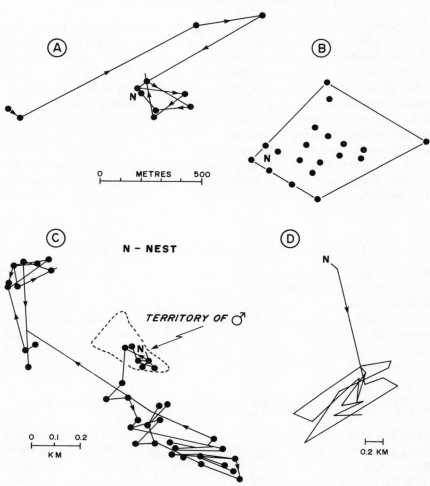

Fig. 14.14. (*A*) Prelaying movements of a yearling blue grouse hen suggest that she was searching for a nest site and narrowing her search area with time. (*B*) Prelaying range of an adult blue grouse hen indicates that she nested on the edge of her range. (*C*) Movements of a male and female willow ptarmigan with their brood. The birds left the territory defended by the male and made one long movement between two more localized ranges. (*D*) The long, initial movement of a yearling blue grouse hen with chicks after hatching suggests that the nest was not located near early brood habitat. (Adapted from Erikstad 1978, Sopuck 1979, Armleder 1980.)

brood ranges than do adults. This may also be true for sage grouse (Berry & Eng 1985). Yearling blue grouse females with broods traveled an average of 484 ± 333 m (*n* = 16) after 1 week, whereas four adults went 205 ± 81 m (Sopuck

1979, Armleder 1980). Some yearlings of ruffed and spruce grouse also make long movements (Herzog 1977a, Maxson 1977). These longer travels of yearlings may result in part from nest-site selection without consideration of where brood habitat is located, but probably another factor is the lack of knowledge about where brood cover is located once the nest has hatched. Further, yearling hens may have had to select inferior habitats to nest because of competition with adults in the spacing of nests. Sopuck (1979) showed seven yearling females nesting in second-growth forests; all would have had to take chicks long distances to locate more open habitat.

Young broods commonly move faster and farther than older broods (Bump et al. 1947, Hungerford 1951, Kupa 1966, Godfrey 1975). Godfrey (1975) and Schiller (1973) recognized an early-brood interval, the first 2 weeks of life, and a late-brood period, the remainder of the summer. The earlier time includes the critical days when chicks cannot thermoregulate and when many die. This is a period when chicks require a high-protein diet of insects, and warm, open habitats to forage in without constant brooding (Erikstad & Spidso 1982, Erikstad & Andersen 1983, Jorgensen & Blix 1985).

Brood ranges in the first 2 weeks are often larger than later ranges (Table 14.2). One hypothesis is that mobility is inverse to insect and forb abundance (Fig. 14.15). This has been documented for the Hungarian partridge (*Perdix perdix*) in England; broods move farther in areas with insecticides sprayed and less in those left unsprayed (Southwood & Gross 1969). Erikstad (1978, 1985a), working with willow ptarmigan in Norway, and Godfrey (1975) and Barrett (1970), using ruffed grouse, have also shown that movement of broods increases as insect abundance decreases. Movements may also be influenced by the dryness of the season (Fig. 14.16, Giesen 1977). In dry years, forb and insect distribution may be more patchy, resulting in longer movements and increased concentrations of broods (cf. Wallestad 1971).

An implication of this general hypothesis is that chick growth should vary between years, depending on the variability of insect abundance and warm weather, and that within years, broods that move the least should show faster growth than those which travel more in response to reduced insect abundance. Redfield (1978) found that blue grouse chicks had different growth rates in different years. Chicks that hatched late in the season when the weather was warmer and insects presumably common, had faster growth rates than early-hatched chicks (cf. Myrberget et al. 1977). Spruce grouse chicks also grew faster in a year of early phenology than in a late year (Quinn & Keppie 1981). Willow ptarmigan showed a negative correlation between growth and distance traveled in Norway (Erikstad, 1978, 1985a), and Mercer (1967) documented a similar sequence in Newfoundland. Growth of ptarmigan chicks was significantly slower in 1962 than in 3 other years, and this reduced growth was accompanied by increased movement (Fig. 15.35).

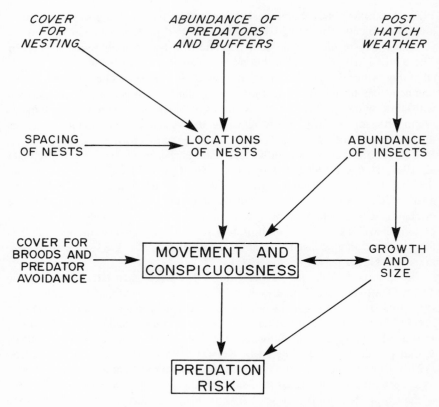

Fig. 14.15. Model of the hypothesized role of the environment in the movement and conspicuousness of broods, which influence their risk of predation.

An alternative explanation for continuous and long-distance movements by broods is that these movements represent behavioral adaptations to avoid encounters with predators that bring prey to a temporarily fixed place, such as a nest, and return to the last capture location to hunt again (Sonerud 1985). Goshawks, red-tailed hawks (*Buteo jamaciensis*), and gyrfalcons probably hunt in this manner. After encounters with humans, broods do move (e.g., Chap. 6), and chicks can be expected to be led away by the hen if she observes nearby raptors. As noted by Sonerud (1985), what is needed as a test of this hypothesis is a comparison of movements of broods provided with adequate insect supplies with those of broods with inadequate insect abundance, under the same predator conditions. If brood movements reduce the probability of detection by predators, broods with lots of food should move just as often and far as broods with less food.

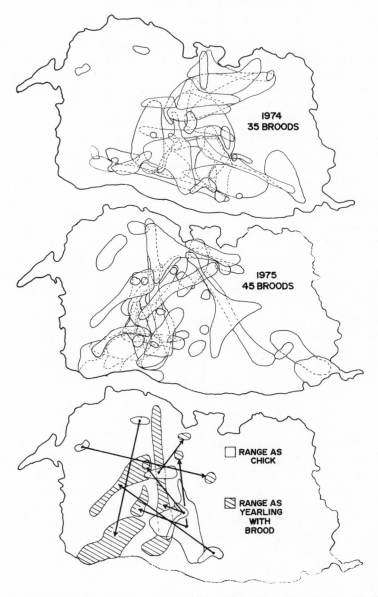

Fig. 14.16. Summer ranges of blue grouse hens with broods on Moresby Island, British Columbia (Chap. 2). In a wet year, 1974, broods were more centrally located in dry, upland habitats than in 1975, when the weather was drier. Brood ranges of yearling females with chicks did not correspond with ranges the yearlings had traveled the year before, when they were chicks.

14.6.2 Inconspicuousness of females and broods

Young chicks are especially vulnerable to predation before they can fly, and females should seek habitats with protective cover. But habitats used by broods are commonly more open than many nearby habitats. Small chicks can obviously find cover under much shorter vegetation than can mature females. The use of the open habitats, optimal for chicks but not for the larger female, thus results in a parent-offspring conflict (Trivers 1974). The conspicuous female must compromise her own safety so that her chicks can forage in warm, insect-rich habitats to maximize growth and hurry through the critical, first 2 weeks of life. Hens that lose their chicks generally seek denser cover than hens that still have broods (Haas 1974, Maxson 1978, Sopuck 1979). Ten of 11 radio-tagged, blue grouse females that lost their broods went to denser cover than did brood females (Sopuck 1979). Sopuck also found that 80% of 150 observations of broodless hens were in thickets, whereas only 24% of 133 observations of brood hens were in the same cover. Some unsuccessful, white-tailed ptarmigan and blue grouse females may actually leave the summer range and move to heavier cover if they lose their broods (Mussehl 1963, Giesen 1977, Sopuck 1979). The same pattern has been documented for ruffed (Maxson 1977) and spruce grouse (Ellison 1973, Haas 1974, Herzog 1977a). The increased conspicuousness of brood hens in chick habitat has its cost, these hens may often have a higher summer mortality rate than broodless hens (Christenson 1970, Maxson 1977, Table 15.7).

One tactic that females could use to remain more inconspicuous is to avoid other hens and broods. The ranges of broods commonly overlap (Fig. 14.16), but for forest grouse this overlap is spatial rather than temporal (Keppie 1977, Maxson 1978). Although broods may use the same ranges to forage, they may still avoid each other, using the same areas but at different times. Keppie (1977a) found only 8 of 428 sightings of broods within 50 m of each other. Females with broods should elect to show mutual avoidance of other broods since aggressive interactions between females would increase the conspicuousness of chicks.

An additional disadvantage of broods being in close proximity is that females risk the chance of mortality with distraction display for chicks that are not their own. On Brunette Island, Newfoundland, in 1962, when there were 20 broods per square kilometer (Mercer 1967), adults of up to three broods often responded simultaneously with distraction displays to distress calls from chicks that were not immediately nearby.

Keppie (1977a) showed that mixed broods occurred mostly when the maternal hen died; 10 of 11 chicks that joined a new hen lived till autumn, but such mixed broods may decrease the survival of the hens's own progeny, especially if they are younger than the adoptees. Since female distraction behavior is related to chick age and number (cf. Andersson et al. 1980), such displays may be inappropriate for the size and number of a mixed brood. Also, an increase in brood size and the unsynchronized stage of developing young should increase the conspicuousness of mixed broods. The escape tactics of maternal chicks of the adopting hen must also differ from the newcomers. This implies that mixed broods could decrease survival of the "adopting" hen's progeny, and should be avoided.

Many authors have noted that hens with chicks move to denser and taller cover as the chicks mature (e.g., Ammann 1957, Bergerud & Huxter 1969, Barrett 1970, Christenson 1970, Haas 1974). Ruffed grouse commonly seek dense, lowland, alder-conifer habitats (Fig. 14.17, Grange 1948, Eng 1959, Schladweiler 1965, Kupa 1966, Barrett 1970, Maxson 1974, Pietz & Tester 1982), where large owls infrequently visit (Nicholls & Warner 1972). After the critical, early chick stage is passed, the female no longer must compromise her safety to allow optimal foraging by her brood, and she should then seek denser cover. If predators are generally not a problem in the summer—as, for example, for spruce grouse at Gorge Creek, Alberta (Keppie 1979, Boag et al. 1979)—females could remain in relatively open habitats. These habitats may have a greater variety of foods than those with more protective cover. The priorities should be that optimal foraging for chicks takes preference over safety for the hen in the early brood period, and that safety takes preference over feeding in the late brood period. The trade-off can be reduced by using areas with sufficient vertical stems for cover and with reduced horizontal cover so that light reaches food species at ground level (Frandsen 1980). Patchiness in microhabitats provides the best of both worlds, safety and nutrition.

In all the grouse, females are smaller than males, with the possible exception of white-tailed ptarmigan (Johnsgard 1973, 1985). This dimorphism is accepted as being partly a result of intrasexual selection for increased size in males, but apart from this there could also be selection for reduced size in females. Small females would be less conspicuous if they visited effective cover when they had young broods. Effective cover is defined as cover that is sufficiently tall and dense to hide females bent over while feeding, but also short enough to permit the female clear visibility while standing (Mussehl 1963). Smaller females would have an advantage in survival compared with larger hens in short brood cover. The white-tailed ptarmigan female weighs approximately 320 g in July, and on high mountains these females use small rocks as cover (Weeden 1959b, Braun & Rogers 1971, Chap. 8). The rock ptarmigan is larger, at an average of 420 g, and frequents the short, dwarf-shrub communities (Weeden 1959b). Next in the continuum of both cover height and female height is the willow ptarmigan, at 450 g; she frequents the taller shrub communities (Weeden 1959b).

This continuum in larger body size also occurs in willow ptarmigan as one goes from north to south (Salomonsen 1972). Salomonsen argues that smaller birds in the northern environment would be favored because of the harsh environment, but Bergman's rule would suggest the converse. Also, ptarmigan in the far north commonly migrate and leave their harsh winter ranges. May (1975)

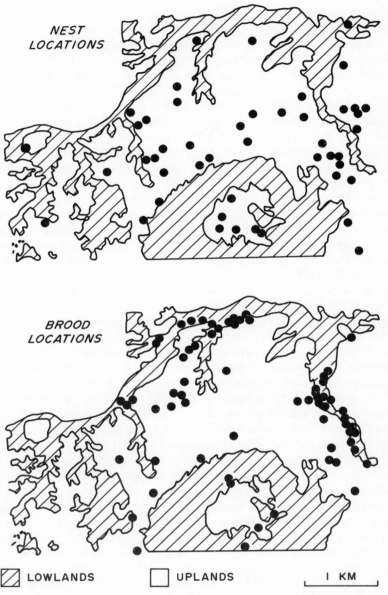

Fig. 14.17. Nests of ruffed grouse hens at Cloquet, Minnesota, were dispersed on upland sites, but brood locations were clumped in lowland situations, where there was probably more cover from predators (data from Kupa 1966). A similar pattern of dispersed early-brood locations (near nests) and clumped locations of older broods was described for blue grouse by Zwickel (1973).

documented that the small, 300+ g white-tailed ptarmigan is physiologically well adapted to its harsh mountainous environment. This size continuum both among and within species of ptarmigan may be the result of selection to match effective cover.

The spruce grouse is the smallest of the forest grouse and inhabits the most dense, coniferous cover, with the shortest shrub and herbaceous cover. Ruffed grouse are slightly larger, and herbaceous vegetation in the more open deciduous forests is taller. The blue grouse is the largest and frequents open canopies with tall ferns and herbs in the brood season (Bendell & Elliot 1967). The sage grouse is the largest of the steppe grouse, and sagebrush is commonly 0.5 to 1 m tall. The prairie grouse do not seem to conform to the effective-cover model. Prairie chickens are slightly larger than sharptails, but often frequent shorter cover. The lesser prairie chicken is smaller than the greater, but its cover is taller (Jones 1963). However, the original range of the prairie chicken may have included the more eastern mesic, tallgrass prairies and brushlands, and that of the sharp-tailed grouse the more western and shortgrass savannas and plains (Johnsgard 1985). Thus, they too could have evolved a morphology to help minimize the parent-offspring conflict; i.e., the chick's need for low, open cover and the female's need for effective cover.

A number of authors have reported the roosting behavior of broods. Before chicks can fly or thermoregulate, they must be brooded during the night. Broods presumably roost in the most secure habitats available. Older prairie chicken and sharp-tailed grouse broods may even roost in lowlands and wet areas, where cover is usually dense (Ramharter 1976, Chap. 6). At this stage the risks of predation if they were elsewhere may be greater than costs associated with cold and wet microenvironments.

The broods of some of the open-dwelling grouse abandon the tactic of inconspicuousness in August and join gang broods. Gang broods have been documented in sharp-tailed grouse (Ammann 1957, Sisson 1976, Brown pers. comm.), prairie chickens, sage grouse (Wallestad 1975b), and white-tailed ptarmigan (Choate 1963a, Giesen 1977, Chap. 8). The brood creche occurs at the same time that distraction behavior by hens is curtailed. These gang broods represent the first use of the flocking tactic as an antipredator strategy (see section 14.8.2. The increased vigilance permitted by this tactic leads one to expect that it should occur mostly in open-habitat grouse. Gang broods should also occur only after the young are capable of strong and prolonged flight.

14.6.3 Reducing interactions with predators

If a female with chicks encounters a predator, she might be expected to make a long movement to minimize the risk of another contact (see also section 14.6.2). Brood ranges may thus partly reflect the frequency and severity of such contacts with predators (Sonerud 1985, Table 14.2). A plot of brood sites often shows clusters of points separated by long distances (Barrett 1970, Schiller 1973, Erikstad 1978, Fig. 14.14). A sharp-tailed grouse brood moved 28 km in the fifth week after hatch, after it had previously used a radius of only 1.0 km (Schiller 1973). One spruce grouse female with older chicks ranged over 52 ha, whereas eleven other females ranged over a mean area of 16.6 $\pm$ 2.5 ha (Herzog 1977a). Svedarsky (Chap. 6) showed that prairie chicken broods remained in small areas for several days and then inexplicably shifted long distances. It seems improbable that foraging ranges should suddenly be abandoned if food was gradually diminishing. These large ranges and long-distance movements shown by some hens are probably tactics to avoid further encounters with a previously observed predator. Predators can be expected to return to sites where prey were located; to move seems a prudent strategy on the part of the hen (see also Sonerud 1985).

The large brood ranges of female steppe grouse may be partly in response to the higher density, diversity, and mobility of steppe predators (Fig. 15.8). Prairie grouse raise large broods and often lose fewer chicks than forest grouse, despite the high, inherent predator risk associated with steppe environments. Mobility, though costly in energy, may be a tactic to reduce predation risk.

14.6.4 Defense of young against predation

A female should be able to improve the survival prospects of her offspring by defending them against predators, but this entails some risk. Females should be prepared to risk more when the young are the most vulnerable, and when the brood is concentrated and all chicks are thus in danger (Andersson et al. 1980).

Most young grouse die in the first 2 weeks of life. This is the period of extreme vulnerability, as they can neither fly nor thermoregulate, and they are often together, being brooded. Female defense should be greater in this early stage. Apparently the only data available are for blue grouse. Distraction displays are most intense during the first 2 weeks of life, and are less intense when there are fewer chicks together (Kristensen 1973, Fig. 14.18). Kristensen also showed that brood defense is less intense when the chicks are very young, 1 to 4 days old; during these first few days they are still receiving nourishment from the yolk sac, and should not be as vulnerable to windchill when they are separated.

Intensity of defense by the hen should also vary in relation to danger to the young compared with danger to herself. Birds can probably distinguish among predator types (Simmons 1955, Curio 1975, Veen 1977). Killdeers (*Charadrius vociferus*) commonly fly at cattle and horses, who might trample the young but pose no danger to the hen. With more dangerous mammals, such as foxes, more impeded flights are shown (Simmons 1955). When willow ptarmigan, ruffed grouse, and blue grouse chicks are captured, and give distress calls, females commonly risk approaching humans to within 2 m; in these instances the danger to the young is extreme. If grouse could discriminate between naive and experienced

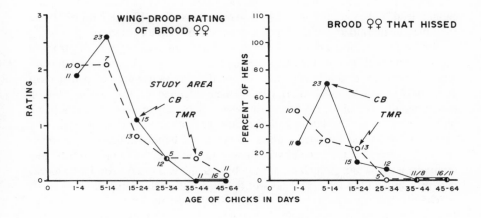

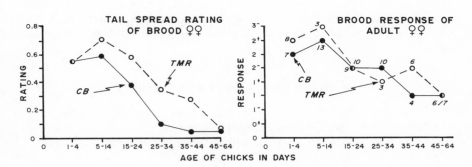

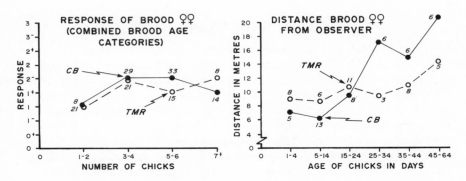

Fig. 14.18. Comparison of the intensity of distraction behavior among hens with chicks of different ages and among hens with different numbers of chicks. The two study areas are Comox Burn and Tsolum Main Road, Vancouver Island (Kristensen 1973).

predators, they could evaluate the risk and grade their responses. Grouse commonly "lead" if they are followed (Watson & Jenkins 1964, MacDonald 1970) and they may change their tactics depending on the predator's response.

Ruffed grouse, blue grouse, and willow ptarmigan hens often run in front of humans with their tails fanned and flicking back and forth. White-tailed ptarmigan hens do not fan their tails (Chap. 8), and the two prairie grouse species most commonly remain hidden and run without the tail fanned. Grouse species that fan their tails all have black markings on the rectrices; this makes the birds much more conspicuous. The tail of ruffed grouse is especially long (a ratio of wing to tail of 1:0.8) and includes a black, subterminal band. Ruffed grouse, especially, fly with their tails maximally fanned. In contrast, the steppe grouse have relatively narrow tails, which are mostly brown and white-mottled. These markings probably add to the crypticness of the bird, rather than emphasize the tail.

The black markings on the tails of some grouse likely act as deflectors (Fig. 14.19). There are common deflecting adaptations on the tails of several animal groups (Powell 1982, Caldwell 1982). An attacking predator is directed away from the body and to the less essential tail. Fanning and flicking of the black rectrices permit the female to increase the effectiveness of distraction, without increasing her own risk.

14.7 Brood disbandment and migration

There appear to be two distinct movements by grouse in the fall: (1) the dispersal of brood members and (2) the movement to cover on winter ranges. The first movement may involve an assessment of breeding opportunities by juveniles, whereas the second, involving both juveniles and adults, is clearly survival-oriented.

14.7.1 Brood disbandment

Members of ruffed grouse broods in Minnesota, sharp-tailed grouse broods in Wisconsin and Manitoba, and prairie chicken broods in Kansas initially disperse in September–October (Eng 1959, Godfrey & Marshall 1969, Caldwell 1976, Bowman & Robel 1977, Chap. 5). Juvenile males leave the brood before juvenile females in ruffed grouse, and this is also suggested for sharp-tailed grouse and prairie chickens (Chap. 5). Willow ptarmigan broods in Newfoundland and rock ptarmigan broods in Scotland also disband in September (Watson 1965, Mercer 1967); juvenile males search for territories and some advertise. No one has provided evidence that the aggressiveness of the adult hen is a factor in brood disbandment; nor is this suggested by laboratory work (Alway & Boag 1979). In fact, the hen commonly leaves the brood before the juveniles disband and disperse (Chap. 5). In natural populations where fall dispersal has been observed, juvenile males had time to prospect for advertising sites between the attainment of sexual

Fig. 14.19. Willow and rock ptarmigan have partly black tails, which may act to deflect the attack of predators to less-essential tail extremities. White-tailed ptarmigan live on high mountains, above most avian predators, and in areas often with low cloud cover, where the white tail aids them in remaining cryptic.

maturity and the arrival of winter. Further, juvenile males could remain cryptic (brown body on brown substrates) while prospecting.

Brood breakup and dispersal apparently does not occur in the fall in many other grouse populations. Failure to disband in the autumn in some species may result from late attainment of sexual maturity. Blue grouse juveniles do not reach full sexual maturity their first fall, and there is no brood disintegration; instead, in some areas they migrate to winter ranges with the adult hens (Lance 1967, Sopuck 1979), but in other locations females may leave the brood before migration (Hines 1986a). Apparently, once the period of rapid growth is over in July, it is advantageous for them to leave the open, logged, or burned habitats to return to the relatively safe, coniferous forests. Nor do sage grouse mature by autumn. Juveniles in broods join gang broods that later form the nucleus of winter flocks (Patterson 1952, Dalke et al. 1963, Wallestad 1975b). A second reason that some populations do not show brood disbandment is the simultaneous arrival of both snow and sexual maturity. The birds are brown against a white background, and cannot afford the risk of prospecting in open, unfamiliar habitats. This occurs in ptarmigan in northern or alpine environments (Giesen 1977, Chaps. 10, 11).

14.7.2. Fall migration

During the breeding season both males and females expose themselves to risk in order to frequent relatively open areas to advertise or to nest and rear chicks. As winter approaches, the tactics of survival take precedence over those of reproduction — birds must "beat" the winter in order to be alive the following spring to breed again and repeat the investment cycle.

A common explanation for fall migration of grouse is that birds move to places where their survival will be enhanced by a more plentiful food supply (e.g., Schorger 1944). An alternative explanation is that grouse migrate in order to find cover that will reduce predation risk (see also Chap. 10).

Two environmental changes appear to correspond with fall migration — leaf fall and snow cover. Gratson (Chap. 5) showed that sharp-tailed grouse begin to move to winter cover at snowfall. Mossop (Chap. 10) watched willow ptarmigan throughout the winter as their ranges shifted. As the snow cover increased, the birds became more restless, shifting downslope to taller, emergent willows only after they had lost most of their cover. Each time they departed, ample willow buds for food still remained; in fact, as snow depth increased, it allowed the birds to reach more abundant bud supplies on the upper branches. Nonetheless, they moved.

Eng (pers. comm.) reported that sage grouse migrate at the same time that snow appears, usually long before snow depth reduces the supply of available food. Some sage grouse populations are migratory and others more sedentary (Patterson 1952, Dalke et al. 1963), but all move to dense, tall sagebrush (Patterson 1952, Dalke et al. 1963, Eng & Schladweiler 1972, Beck 1977). These migratory and nonmigratory populations occur because of differences in the nearness of sagebrush of sufficient height to conceal birds as snow depth increases (Fig. 14.20). Populations that are not migratory have tall sagebrush nearby; those populations that migrate have sagebrush lower in height, or sagebrush inundated with snow and therefore ineffective as cover. Even the terminal branches of sagebrush emerging from deep snow cover should provide ample food. Food availability appears to be an insufficient stimulus to explain migratory movements in most grouse species.

White-tailed ptarmigan in Colorado migrate downslope and seek willows approximately 0.5 m in height (Braun & Schmidt 1971), and usually arrive with the

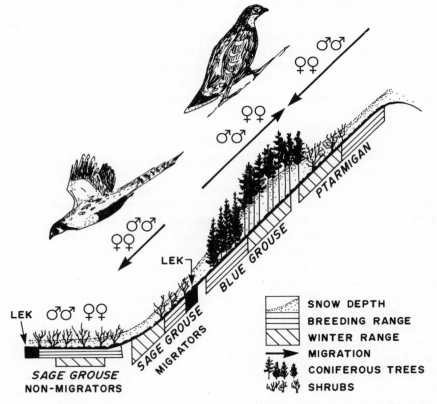

Fig. 14.20. Fall movements of grouse are generally to areas with denser "winter" cover. Birds in some populatons of blue grouse shift uphill when cover is reduced by snow on breeding ranges. Some sage grouse populations move downhill to find more cover. Ptarmigan generally move downhill to reach taller cover and brown backgrounds if they are still in pigmented plumage. In Iceland, ptarmigan may migrate uphill in the fall when they are in white plumage to find white backgrounds (Gardarsson 1971). In these fall and winter movements, males tend to remain closer to breeding ranges and use sparser cover than do females.

first major storm in September or early October (Braun et al. 1976). At this time birds are mostly in pigmented plumage. The first winter storms would not reduce their food supplies, especially on windswept, alpine slopes. These ptarmigan feed in the crepuscular period, appearing watchful and moving quickly across openings in search of denser, more centrally located vegetation. Mobility increases with reduced snow cover. At times, white-tailed ptarmigan even return to the breeding ranges in the winter if fair weather prevails, but only after they acquire their white, winter plumage. This movement would be away from more food in the valley, to less food in the alpine regions.

Even more elucidating are the movements of rock ptarmigan in Iceland. They move to alpine habitats with less plant biomass than the areas downslope that they leave, and find white backgrounds that match their white plumage, despite the lesser food supplies in the higher elevations (Chap. 9).

Blue grouse males on Vancouver Island migrate uphill as well, but in July, leaving open areas with a rich diversity of nutritious foods for a monotypic diet of needles in coniferous cover (King 1971, Sopuck 1979). Grouse that move long distances become partly segregated into male and female flocks. Invariably, males move to vegetation lower in cover value and in harsher climates, yet nearer their breeding ranges than females (Figs. 14.20, 14.21, 14.22, Chaps. 5, 10, Irving et al. 1967b). But even in these environments, with reduced food and cover in comparison to the locations of females, males maintain their fall weights as well as females (Fig. 16.10, 16.11).

The prairie chicken apparently migrated in the 1800s (e.g. Schorger 1944). Because it is the most granivorous grouse, it may have trouble finding seeds in deep snow and is thus the most likely candidate to demonstrate food-induced migrations. But the migrations of prairie chickens also took place at the same time cover characteristics changed, owing to leaf fall and snow, and before the time when food was in short supply. During these migrations, females moved farther than males, exactly what we see in the other grouse species.

In the past, sharp-tailed grouse have also made spectacular fall movements. In the autumns of 1892 and 1932 thousands moved out of the Hudson Bay lowlands in October and November (Snyder 1935). In both years, these populations were probably at cyclic highs (Keith 1963). No adequate explanation has been proposed for these emigrations (Snyder 1935, Hanson 1953, Keith 1963), but birds may have moved south to seek winter cover when large flocks first formed. Such enormous flocks would have been especially conspicuous in October and November after leaf fall, and when snow cover canceled their crypticness. The sex ratio of birds that reached the farthest south in the course of these migrations was 48 females to 17 males (from Snyder 1935). This segregation suggests a normal winter stimulus; males probably remained closer to the northern breeding grounds than females. Large areas of coniferous forest lie between the Hudson Bay lowlands and the birch and aspen forests north of Lake Superior.

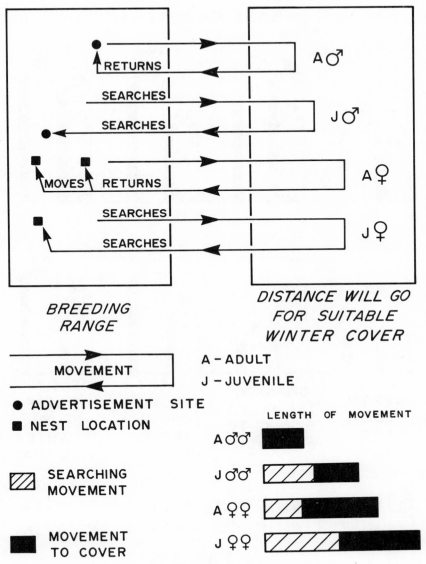

Fig. 14.21. Relative length of movements between breeding and nonbreeding seasons. Adult males move the least, followed by juvenile males; adult females and juvenile females move the farthest. These differences between sexes and ages can be explained by: (1) juveniles must travel farther than adults in finding a suitable breeding site, because adults show philopatry and juveniles are inexperienced, and (2) males are less prepared than females to travel long distances from breeding ranges; females seek cover that is optimal for survival, even if they must move far away.

SAGE GROUSE

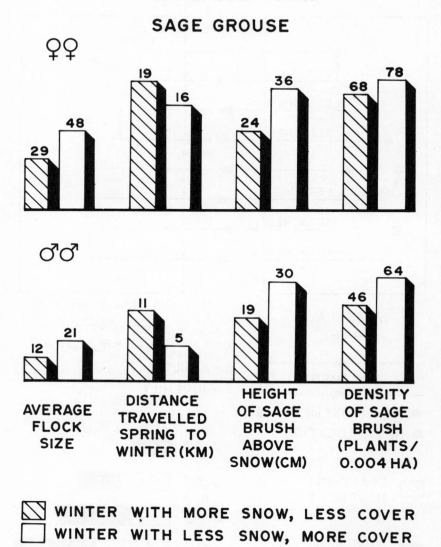

Fig. 14.22. Flock sizes, movements, and vegetation cover sought by female (*top*) and male (*bottom*) sage grouse in two winters of different snow and cover conditions. (Adapted from Beck 1975, 1977.)

Once the sharptails left the lowlands, they would have had to travel long distances before finding a suitable food and cover combination. Possibly this massive emigration was a winter shift to cover, and became a migration because birds found unsuitable habitat and were forced to continue their journey.

14.7.3. Movements between the breeding seasons

Investigators band adults and juveniles to learn of their movements and philopatry between seasons. Findings from these studies generally show a consistent pattern: adult males are the most sedentary; juvenile males and adult females move farther; and juvenile females travel the greatest distances between breeding seasons (Table 14.7, Fig. 14.21).

This consistency can be explained by the different tactics of adults and juveniles and of males versus females. A major component of this movement is a result of searching for advertising and nesting sites (Fig. 14.21). Because adults of both sexes generally show philopatry, their searching movements are shorter than those of juveniles. Adult males move shorter distances than adult females because males are returning to last year's advertising sites, whereas females, though likely returning as well, may shift farther. This will be especially true if the previous year's nest site was unsuccessful and another must be chosen. Some juvenile males may have located their sites the previous fall, but others are making a final decision in the spring and may therefore move farther than adult females. Juvenile females probably accumulate little nest-location information from the previous fall. They should delay their decision until they can assess spring cover and possibly predator activity, and they must also avoid adult females. This results in large movements. Included in the total distance traveled between seasons is the distance a bird moved to find winter cover. Females generally move farther than males. The combination of searching for breeding sites and for winter cover results in the four different distances of adults versus juveniles, and females compared with males. In effect, there is an *attraction* between males because some yearling males located themselves near proven advertising sites; and there is a *repulsion* between females, who most commonly avoid each other when nesting. These tendencies, coupled with the tactic in the winter of males staying near advertising sites because of intrasexual competition, and the female's strategy of searching for optimal winter cover and food to prepare for next year's nesting season, provide the four distinct movement modes.

14.8 Strategies for winter survival

The major problem for grouse in winter is to avoid predation. Many of the alternate prey of their predators have migrated south or live under snow. Forest and steppe grouse are conspicuous against their white background of snow. Deciduous leaves have fallen, shrubs are snowed in, and the ultimate predator of grouse—the goshawk—may range far and wide, from the prairie provinces of Canada south to Kansas.

Commonly, 40% to 50% of the grouse die between August and the next spring, when they are counted (Chap. 15). Some populations are relatively secure over winter; for example, spruce grouse in Alberta do well in coniferous cover, and white-tailed ptarmigan survive well in tall willows (Braun 1969, Keppie 1979). However, many other populations have less secure cover and/or more effective predators, and suffer high winter losses as a result; examples are ruffed grouse in Minnesota (Chap. 15), rock ptarmigan in Iceland (Chap. 9), and willow ptarmigan on Brunette Island, Newfoundland (Mercer 1967). The major tactic of grouse to escape detection by predators is to move to cover. There appears no exception to the general rule that birds are found in denser cover in winter than in the breeding season.

Even in winter, males are generally in more open cover than are females and they travel shorter distances from breeding ranges to find winter cover (Table 14.7). Male sage grouse in one population traveled only 5 km in a mild winter and used cover 30 cm tall, whereas females in this population traveled 16 km to cover 36 cm tall (Beck 1977, Fig. 14.22). In a winter of deep snow, both males and females traveled farther to find cover, 11 km for males and 19 km for females. Yet males used cover that averaged only 19 cm, whereas females remained in cover averaging 24 cm (Fig. 14.22). In the three ptarmigan species, the male stays closer to the breeding range and in shorter cover than the female (Weeden 1964, Braun 1969, Chap. 10). Robel et al. (1972) found more sharp-tailed grouse males in one study area (Kadoka), which contained mostly low grass cover, and more female sharp-tailed grouse at another study area along the Missouri River, where grass and shrubs were taller. King (1971) traveled the open subalpine region in search of blue grouse. Breeding males were on ranges used in both summer and winter, but females had left to seek denser cover. The differences in cover requirements between males and females is probably the least for spruce and ruffed grouse, both of which travel only short distances between breeding and winter ranges.

That males and females show different movements to winter cover, and that they often select cover of different heights and densities, should result in some segregation of the sexes in winter. Sexual segregation is most common in ptarmigan (Weeden 1964, Braun 1969, Chap. 10) and in some steppe grouse populations (Robel et al. 1972, Beck 1977). Spruce and ruffed grouse are the least segregated in winter, owing to restricted movement (cf. Doerr et al. 1974, Herzog 1977a).

14.8.1 Winter feeding tactics

Generally, grouse do not have winter food problems. Spruce and blue grouse may spend days, even weeks, in the same conifer (King 1971, Herzog 1977a). There they can both forage on needles and roost in the safety of a concealing fir or pine. The overlap of cover and food is also complete, for example, for sage grouse, which feed on sagebrush, ptarmigan, which use willows and birches, and red grouse, which both forage and hide in heather (*Calluna vulgaris*). Speaking of the winter foods of grouse Doerr et al. (1974, p. 614) said: "These species [one to two major foods] seem to have several common attributes; they are often abundant, easily available, can be fed on rapidly and efficiently [large leaves and buds], and are nutritious if consumed in large quantities." There may be constraints on which plants or plant parts may be taken, such as the level of antiherbivore resins produced by some shrub or tree species, certain ages, or parts (Bryant & Kuropat 1980). But in general, as Bryant and Kuropat (1980) have concluded about subarctic grouse (ruffed, spruce, and ptarmigan) and their foods, the browse species utilized by grouse are abundant in space and time, and grouse reside in and are adapted to, nutritionally and physiologically, these habitats.

The conspicuousness of dark-bodied grouse increases abruptly with leaf fall and snow cover. In summer and early fall their brown bodies are cryptic against a brown background—but in a matter of days, or after one heavy snowfall, they are in bold contrast to their physical environment. To minimize conspicuousness they must change feeding tactics abruptly; and if they must remain and be conspicuous, they seek heights from which they may watch for predators. Gratson (Chap. 5) reported that sharp-tailed grouse formed larger flocks after snowfall, became more mobile, and visited taller and more varied food sources (see also Marshall & Jensen 1937). In Europe, capercaillie and black grouse also feed less on the ground and more in trees just after snowfall (Koskimies 1957). Keppie (1977b) showed that a significant increase in feeding in trees by spruce grouse occurred only after the first snowfall (Fig. 14.23). Another example is ruffed grouse, which began to feed in aspen trees on 5 December 1968 at Rochester, Alberta—the same day as the first heavy snowfall. The next year, the first snow was 6 weeks earlier, on 22 October; and on 24 October the birds were again in trees budding on aspen (Doerr et al. 1974).

Grouse subject to heavy predation pressure limit their feeding to short bouts during crepuscular periods when fewer avian predators are about. Mossop (Chap. 10) documented how ptarmigan emerged from their snow burrows in the evening and fed vigorously, then returned to snow cover. The sequence was repeated in the morning just before there was enough light to see. Braun and Schmidt (1971) watched white-tailed ptarmigan feed from 1730 to 1900 hours. They normally engaged in intense feeding activity. No longer cautious, they would run or fly from one *Salix* bush to another. Their feeding appeared almost desperate and individual birds were observed "standing on their toes" or jumping off the ground to reach buds overhead. At such times they exhibited little fear or alarm. In contrast, in the middle of the day birds were mostly sedentary, and when they were active they moved slowly and cautiously, with their bodies positioned low to the ground. Braun and Schmidt (1971) called this "inconspicuous creeping."

The feeding schedule of ruffed grouse appears more complicated than that of ptarmigan. Ruffed grouse live in forests without clear views, and are faced with an effective nocturnal predator—the great horned owl, and an especially effective diurnal predator as well—the goshawk, an early riser. Ruffed grouse also feed

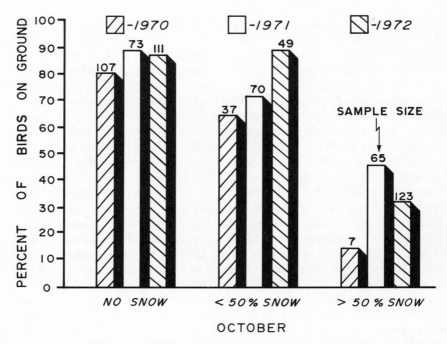

Fig. 14.23. Spruce grouse quickly shift from ground locations to tree cover when snow cover becomes complete and they are no longer cryptic against white backgrounds. (Adapted from Keppie 1977b.)

for short periods of from 15 to 30 minutes in early morning and late evening (Doerr et al. 1974, Chap. 4). A ruffed grouse probably needs less light intensity to relocate a large, vegetable food source than does a goshawk to pinpoint a mobile grouse in a new location, and it is within this brief margin of time that the grouse makes its move to feed.

Ruffed grouse feed in aspens later in the evening in winters with little snow cover for roosting (Chap. 4). This would allow them to leave with full crops, and the full crops would permit them to feed less the following morning when predator risk is high. It may also take the birds longer to fill their crops if they must remain more alert because of the lack of snow cover. Huempfner and Tester (Chap. 4) also noted that birds usually began to feed in the lower branches of the aspen, and that the rate of moving higher in the tree varied between years with different snow cover (Fig. 14.24).

Blue and spruce grouse generally do not have the winter predation problems of ruffed grouse. These two grouse live in dense conifer forests and eat needles. Their lower, annual mortality rates reflect this cover advantage; on average only 35% die over winter compared with 55% of the ruffed grouse (Chap. 15). Ellison (1971) reported that spruce grouse did not select spruce trees to feed in for either

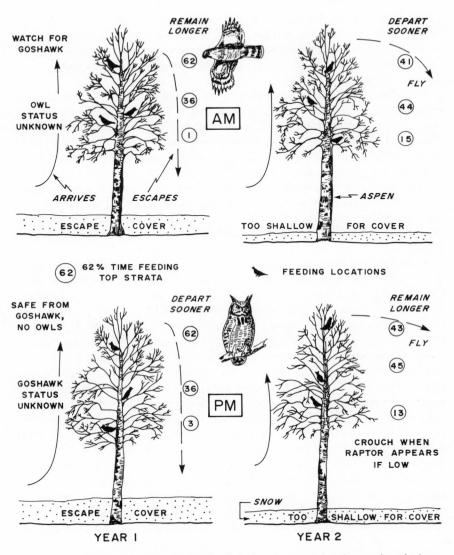

Fig. 14.24. Winter feeding behavior of ruffed grouse in aspens, based on one hypothesis of the findings presented in Chapter 4. In AM (morning) feeding bouts, birds remain higher in the tree in a winter with good snow (*year 1*) than in a winter without "escape" snow (*year 2*). In winters of good snow, birds in PM feeding bouts feed high in the tree, but depart sooner because snow-roosting helps them to conserve stored food and because they can feed in relative safety the next AM, owing to the nearness of escape snow. In a winter of little snow, they feed longer in the PM because it is a relatively safe period and they can leave with a full crop to reduce the length of feeding the next morning, when they will be more vulnerable to predators because of inadequate snow cover.

crown density or stand density. Birds are sometimes conspicuous on branches, but they can quickly move into the center of the tree where the tight whorls of branches provide concealment and obstruction when predators are near. Spruce grouse also commonly use the trunk of the trees for loafing and for roosting cover (Ellison 1971).

It is often argued that aspen, because of its nutritional qualities, is essential to ruffed grouse (Gullion 1970a,b,c, 1977a,b, 1982). Yet many ruffed grouse populations live outside the range of aspen. In southwest British Columbia there is no aspen, and ruffed grouse live in alders (*Alnus* spp.). In some winters in Minnesota, ruffed grouse feed prodigiously on aspen, in others they feed mostly on other species (Svoboda & Gullion 1972, Chap. 4). In the winter of 1968–69, ruffed grouse fed primarily on beaked hazel (*Corylus cornuta*), as aspen production was low; nonetheless, the grouse population increased in 1969. Also, production of aspen buds was the highest in eight years in 1964–65, yet the spring grouse population declined in 1965 (Gullion 1970a, 1981, Svoboda & Gullion 1972).

Ruffed grouse should use aspen when they can combine optimal foraging tactics with reduced predation risk. Birds can fill their crops quickly on aspen, since buds are larger, and then retreat to cover. This is perhaps its greatest advantage. Aspen grows in clones, and birds feeding on the periphery may be provided with more visibility than those feeding in a more uniform birch forest. Doerr et al. (1974) failed to show that the aspen stands selected by ruffed grouse had buds of higher nutritional quality than stands that were not utilized. Even the findings of Bryant and Kuropat (1980), which revealed a close association between the preferred foods of ruffed grouse and the lowered resin concentrations of those foods, have shown that selective pressures other than simply nutritional and energy demands are operating in the grouse-forage relationship. Aspen also provides sufficient height for birds to dive into snow below for escape (Fig. 14.24). Birds do not use aspen if the trees are lower than the surrounding canopy. Especially interesting is the finding that grouse stopped using aspen for 3 weeks after a sleet storm in Minnesota (Svoboda & Gullion 1972). Svoboda and Gullion felt that the grouse could walk on the snow crust, although against the white snow they would be quite conspicuous. The crust probably prevented them from using the snow as escape and roosting cover and the aspen was no longer as safe as being elsewhere. Huempfner and Tester (Fig. 4.1) showed earlier that use of aspen by ruffed grouse was much higher in the winter of 1971–72, a winter of good escape snow, than it was in two other winters when the snow cover was inadequate for escape. The exclusive use of aspen appears to depend on the presence of two conditions: goshawks and sufficient snow for escape and roosting cover. Aspen's primary benefits may be that it allows short feeding bouts and its structural characteristics permit its use as an antipredator tactic.

14.8.2 Winter flocking

Flocking by birds is generally explained as an adaptation to gain information on food distribution, or as a tactic to increase the speed at which predators may be detected. In the latter hypothesis, presumably the survival advantage of early warning outweighs the flocks' conspicuousness. Flock size or the proportion of flocked birds would thus vary with the need for vigilance; flocks should be larger or more birds should be in flocks in habitats where birds are more conspicuous and must react early to the approach of predators. If flocking is food-related, flock size should generally increase with the difficulty of finding food.

Flocking in grouse appears to represent a need for mutual vigilance rather than for finding patchy food supplies. Grouse feed in the winter on ubiquitous sagebrush, spruce, pine and fir needles, willow, birch, and aspen buds, all of which are abundant and can be found in large, extensive patches. Variability in flock size changes not with the availability of food but with the conspicuousness of the birds. Large flocks are characteristic of the steppe and tundra grouse which forage in open habitats where they would benefit from mutual vigilance. Open habitats allow birds to flush at long distances from predators and escape by flight. The forest grouse commonly form only small, temporary groups of two to four birds (Ellison 1972, Doerr et al. 1974). Hines (1986a) found 43% of the blue grouse in winter alone and 25% in duos ($n = 1,068$). Such small flocks would allow the birds to remain relatively inconspicuous, and to use the tactics of crouching and avoiding detection, rather than flight, which may be less effective as an escape tactic at shorter detection distances (cf. Chap. 4). Flock sizes of sharp-tailed grouse, which commonly feed in trees and shrubs in winter, decrease when birds can frequent cryptic backgrounds, or when deep snow permits the birds concealment in snow burrows (Chap. 5). Prairie chickens formed tighter packs as winter progressed and cover diminished (Hamerstrom & Hamerstrom 1949). Flocks are largest when birds are most conspicuous, after snowfall but before deep snow allows snow-burrowing. The flocks of sage grouse, which feed on the ground and use sagebrush for cover, are larger in winters with less snow, and correspondingly more cover and food, than in winters when snow is deep and cover is more restricted (Beck 1977, Fig. 14.22). The differences in flock sizes between open-land and forest grouse—cryptic and noncryptic grouse—are most consistent with the hypothesis that the flocking habit and flock size represents a trade-off between the benefit of mutual detection and the cost of increased conspicuousness.

Koskimies (1957) stated that the first line of defense in black grouse was to be cryptic, to crouch and to escape detection, and that flight to escape was the second line of defense. This may not apply to sharp-tailed grouse and prairie chicken on top of the snow, because they usually cannot avoid detection in large flocks and may flush while predators are far off (Brown 1966a). Because they are not totally synchronous in feeding, some birds are usually alert while the others feed. Prairie grouse rely on a long lead-time to reach cover; the predator should know it has been detected and that pursuit is usually unprofitable (Baker & Parker 1979).

The crouch-or-fly decision for all grouse should involve an assessment of: (1) the seriousness of the predator threat, (2) the escape options, and (3) the predictability of detection (Fig. 14.25). Grouse are able to distinguish among predators; for example, prairie grouse commonly crouch at leks when marsh hawks (*Circus cyaneus*) appear, and flush "hard" at the approach of goshawks and peregrine falcons (*Falco peregrinus*) (Berger et al. 1963, Sparling & Svedarsky 1978). Several possible costs must be weighed against the benefits of flushing; these may include increased conspicuousness and flight energetics, among others.

The crouch-or-fly decision may also be influenced by intrinsic differences in approachability; blue grouse and ruffed grouse, for example, may be polymorphic in their approachability (Chaps. 1, 2, 3). Grouse at cyclic highs may be more reluctant to flush than when the populations are low and increasing (Keith 1963, Chap. 4).

The means of escape should vary with the availability of escape habitat. Koskimies (1957) distinguished between a "cover-taking response," in which birds fly low and for short distances if they are cryptic against the background and cover is nearby, and an "escape by flight," in which birds fly long distances at high elevations. If ruffed grouse can plunge into the snow, they should take the first option. Mossop (pers. comm.) has watched rock ptarmigan attempt to fly above approaching raptors. He has also observed willow ptarmigan flush at the approach of a helicopter; the birds flew low and downhill and headed for taller vegetation, where the female took cover first. In Iceland, rock ptarmigan used a fence in the local village to avoid gyrfalcons (Chap. 9). Willow ptarmigan generally fly low and duck into the most available cover. The ptarmigan's black rectrices may provide a final strategy, which can result in a strike at the tail and some missing rectrices—but the bird often escapes (Fig. 14.19).

The escape options of grouse may be restricted if they face a *variety* of predators. In Newfoundland, willow ptarmigan flushed at farther distances in foggy weather, when they were relatively safe from raptors. The crouch-or-fly decision under these conditions could thus be directed solely toward the approaching ground disturbance. To assist in the capture of blue grouse females on Moresby Island, British Columbia, it often helped to imitate the call of a red-tailed hawk. When the females heard the call they would crouch and freeze, allowing us a closer approach so that we could "noose" them. Mossop's observations of ptarmigan in snow burrows successfully bursting from their roosts to avoid a fox, only to be captured by a gyrfalcon (which was probably watching the fox), illustrate the problems that arise when a normally effective tactic is used against odd combinations of predators. Ptarmigan at Chilkat Pass would sometimes not flush from

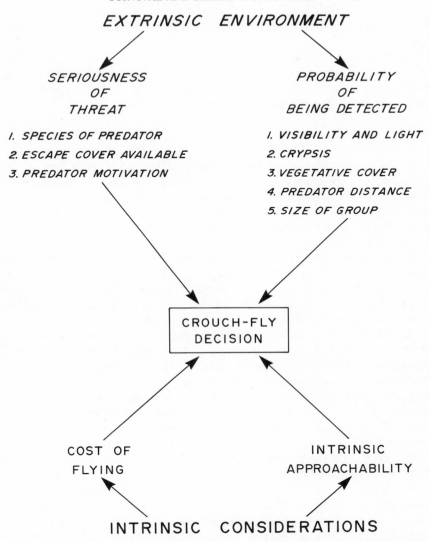

Fig. 14.25. Grouse should consider the seriousness of the predator threat and the probability of being detected in comparing the benefits and costs of the option of crouching and the option of flying when predators are detected. There are also intrinsic differences among individual grouse in the tendency to flush Chaps. 1, 2, 3).

willow cover because of possible gyrfalcon predation, but this permitted a golden eagle to land and walk into the willow and snatch a grouse. Is there any longtime grouse biologist who has not seen a goshawk mysteriously appear when he or she had captured or flushed a grouse (e.g., Gratson 1981)? Grouse must compromise

escape tactics when faced with a number of predators with varying hunting reper-
toires.

Flocking may not only increase vigilance, but it may also spread the risk
among flock members and help to confuse predators as well. In Iceland, large
flocks of ptarmigan may fly in close formation and wheel together, possibly hin-
dering the stoop of gyrfalcons (cf. Chap. 9).

14.8.3 Winter roosting tactics

Grouse spend the long, winter nights roosting. If they are detected, they may be
in trouble with nocturnal predators. Many daylight hours are also spent in non-
feeding activities, at which time inconspicuous behavior should be a high priority
and should not be compromised by moving about. Roosting places should be
selected in areas not searched by predators and where there are good opportunities for escape if detected.

Grouse commonly burrow under snow cover in order to roost. One explanation for snow-burrowing is that it provides a warmer microclimate, so that heat
energy may be conserved (Gullion 1970a, Hoglund 1980), although Grange
(1948) believed it served an antipredator function. Although the snow certainly
conserves heat, perhaps a burrow's greater benefit is as cover to avoid predators.
By insulating the bird, snow cover makes it possible for a grouse to stay in the
burrow for many hours, slowly digesting the food gathered during brief feeding
bouts and stored in the crop. Huempfner et al. (pers. comm.) found that ruffed
grouse that used snow burrows were able to restrict feedings to only two daily
periods, during crepuscular hours. Otherwise they remained under cover and
avoided goshawks. When they were unable to snow roost, they fed at least three
times daily, and the third bout occurred in the middle of the day when goshawks
were hunting.

Bump et al. (1947) provided anecdotal evidence that predators, specifically humans and foxes, could capture ruffed grouse in snow burrows. But Huempfner
(pers. comm.) examined 1,100 snow burrows of ruffed grouse and could not find
a single burrow that showed signs of a successful predator attack. Mossop followed a partly tame fox at Chilkat Pass as it hunted; the fox never succeeded in
capturing a ptarmigan in a burrow. Invariably, as the fox became too close to a
burrow, first one and then all the ptarmigan would burst forth and escape.

Ruffed grouse apparently do not need to snow-burrow to survive cold weather.
Our evidence for this is that the mortality rate of ruffed grouse was not correlated
with the suitability of snow for roosting in an 8-year study in Alberta, or for a
13-year period in Minnesota (Gullion & Marshall 1968, Little 1978, Rusch et al.
1984). The average overwinter mortality rate of ruffed grouse males during two
winters in Minnesota, during which there was little snow for roosting (1958–59
and 1960–61; Fig. 14.26) was 55% ($n = 95$) (Gullion & Marshall 1968). In con-

trast, the mortality rate estimated from six other winters in which there was adequate snow for roosting was 53% ($n = 483$) (Gullion & Marshall 1968). Ruffed grouse actually showed a weight gain in spring 1961, after a winter without snow (Fig. 14.26). Above-average mortality of ruffed grouse occurred in Minnesota in three winters — 1963–64, 1972–73, and 1973–74 (Fig. 14.26). In these three winters, the numbers of days of snow at least 20 cm in depth (adequate for burrowing) were only 40, 61, and 67 days, respectively, whereas the mean for a 13-year period was 78 days. These 3 years were also those in which goshawks came south to Minnesota (Mueller et al. 1977). Grouse, conspicuous against their white backgrounds, were forced to feed between the relatively safe, crepuscular periods. These birds did not die from physiological or nutritional stress — spring weights were not low (Fig. 14.26). Rather, they died because they foraged in the daytime, at a time when goshawks were abundant, and when snow was frequently not deep enough to permit escape dives.

If snow-burrowing is an antipredator strategy, the blue and spruce grouse should snow-burrow less frequently than other grouse, because they can stay in the cover of conifers. Ruffed grouse should also seek dense conifer cover for roosting when snow is not available. Some blue grouse at Mt. Washington, British Columbia, occasionally spend several days in conifer forests without snow-roosting (King 1971); however, some do burrow. The alpine forest at Mt. Washington is open, and all locations may not provide cover. Furthermore, some grouse may have to move to snow as an escape tactic. Apparently, spruce grouse in New Brunswick, Alberta, and Montana, and on the Kenai Peninsula, Alaska, usually do not snow-roost (Stoneberg 1967, Ellison 1971, Hedberg 1980). The winter range in Alberta and Montana, in particular, is comprised of dense forest stands (Stoneberg 1967, Boag et al. 1979). On the Kenai Peninsula, the snow is often crusted, preventing snow-burrowing (Ellison 1971). Spruce grouse snow-burrow in Michigan, where they feed in more-open stands of jack pine (*Pinus banksiana*) (Robinson 1980), and where the sparsely branched and scattered trees may not protect them at night from horned owls. Ruffed grouse usually roost in dense conifers near available food supplies (Grange 1948, Barrett 1970, Doerr et al. 1974). At Cedar Creek, Minnesota, ruffed grouse roosted at the base of cedars (*Thuja occidentalis*) when snow was not available, and were occasionally captured by horned owls (Huempfner pers. comm.). Thus there are a number of examples of grouse roosting successfully in conifers in cold regions.

Grouse often use snow burrows or snow depressions in relatively warm weather, and in the daytime. Rock ptarmigan have used snow for cover even in the summer. The birds cover their bodies with snow and leave their heads exposed. This has been reported for rock ptarmigan (Watson 1972), willow ptarmigan (Mossop pers. comm., Chap. 10), ruffed grouse (Bump et al. 1947), sage grouse (Patterson 1952), sharp-tailed grouse (Chap. 5), and prairie chickens (Hamerstrom et al. 1957). These burrows or depressions are not needed for heat

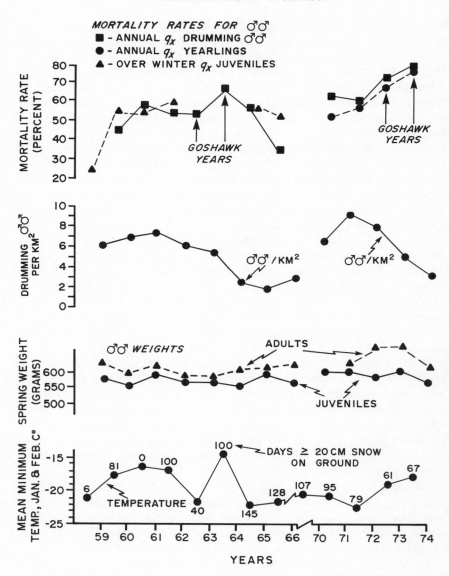

Fig. 14.26. Annual mortality rates of ruffed grouse males in relation to densities, spring weights, temperatures, and days suitable for snow-roosting. (Grouse data from Gullion & Marshall 1968, Little 1978; weather statistics from Cloquet and Pine River, Minnesota; goshawk data from Hofslund 1973, Mueller et al. 1977.)

conservation; rather, the birds have camouflaged their brown bodies and can now watch for predators.

Snow burrows should be located where predators are seldom present. Rock ptarmigan burrow on steep slopes next to rocks (Watson 1972); sharp-tailed grouse prefer to roost in marshes, where there may be fewer alternative prey for fox (Chap. 5). Other antipredator behaviors also indicate that snow is used for cover. Sharp-tailed grouse often tunnel far from the snow opening, making it difficult for a fox to know where to pounce (Chap. 5). Burrows are also spaced apart, and once one bird flushes the others can also flush away from the intruder (Chap. 5, 10).

Snow-roosting may at times allow birds to remain close to food supplies, thereby reducing mobility and conspicuousness. Ruffed grouse stay predominantly in deciduous forests where they can both snow-roost (Grange 1948) and feed at nearby aspen (Svoboda & Gullion 1972, Chap. 4). The snow provides cover when not foraging and also escape cover while feeding in aspen.

That some populations do not use suitable snow for roosting, even in cold weather, is not consistent with the thermoinsulation hypothesis. Cold—the hypothesized cause—is present, but the expected effect—snow-roosting—is not. Birds may roost in trees instead. Cold is not, therefore, a sufficient cause for snow-roosting.

14.9 Polymorphic spacing strategy

In an ideal world, a bird would select a habitat type for nesting and advertising on the basis of its inherent fitness prospects (Levins 1968). However, the ideal-free world would not consider competition. Fitness should decline within habitats as density increases (Fig. 14.27). One can visualize two options: (1) A bird can settle in the intrinsically best habitat; but this habitat will also be selected by others, thus detracting from its utility. (2) A bird can settle in lower-quality habitats, where there will be fewer good sites but also fewer competitors. The trade-off is that the quality of the best habitat is reduced by competition for nesting and advertising sites, and the increased conspicuousness of the birds to predators. In the second option birds will be farther apart, less conspicuous, and may face fewer predators. The evolutionary advantage of spacing is never without qualification—dispersion and aggregation confer conflicting advantages and dis-advantages (Waser & Wiley 1979).

Grouse do have density options. Females space themselves relative to nesting sites (Figs. 13.7, 14.12); the hen's territory is spatiotemporal (Wilson 1975), and her defense space travels with her. Male forest grouse defend advertising sites and, as with females, there are no distinct boundaries with adjacent birds; rather, there are areas of little use and no clear ownership (Fig. 14.7) (Zwickel & Bendell 1972, Archibald 1975, Herzog & Boag 1978). Even in the vigorously defended

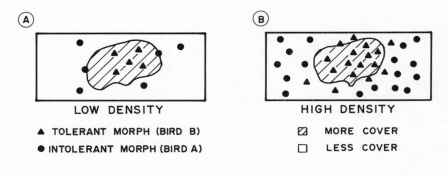

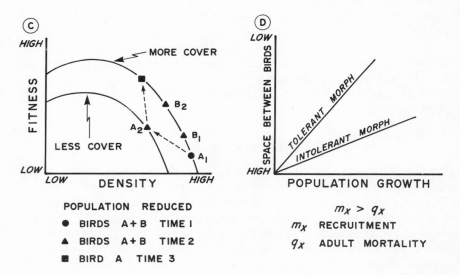

Fig. 14.27. Two behavior morphs are density tolerant and density intolerant. (*A*) When a population is low, the density tolerant will be clumped in the best cover. (*B*) When the population increases, the habitat will be more uniformly occupied. (*C*) *Bird A*, reared in good cover, is intrinsically more density intolerant than its brood mate *B*. *Bird A* prospects for a breeding location in a lower density-less cover situation (A_1 to A_2). The fitness of *B* improved (B_1 to B_2) with the departure of *A*. If the density is reduced in the best cover by a removal experiment before *A* is committed to a breeding site, the bird may shift back (*time 3*) to the better cover to improve fitness. (*D*) The space between both morphs decreases as the population increases (Fig. 2.17).

territories of ptarmigan, the size of the male's territory is correlated with the number of male competitors (Fig. 15.24, Bergerud et al. 1985). Thus, new birds can squeeze in. In steppe grouse, males can join the perimeter of established leks or move elsewhere. It is the bird's option to select the site for maximum fitness. Avoidance of high-density situations is an alternative to competition.

Genetically influenced and determined, polymorphic strategies in spacing behavior could occur in heterogeneous environments when the resources are distributed, coarse grain, and the birds settle in patches (Levins 1968, Gadgil 1971, Gillespie 1974, Hedrick et al. 1976, Wiens 1976, Austad 1984). Polymorphic spacing behavior has been shown for fish, mice, toads, frogs, and others (Williams 1966a, French et al. 1968, Krebs et al. 1976, Wells 1977, Davies & Halliday 1979). Alternative reproductive behaviors and evolutionarily stable strategies (ESS) are currently very active areas of research in other animal groups (see *American Zoologist* 24, p. 307).

Grouse settle in patches, and patch sizes and quality appear hierarchical. When prairie chicken populations declined in Wisconsin, the reduction was most apparent in marginal habitats (Hamerstrom et al. 1957). When the willow ptarmigan population in Newfoundland reached a cyclic high, densities were comparatively homogeneous; the second-best hunting barrens, Portugal Cove, had numbers comparable to the prime habitat at St. Shotts (Bergerud 1970a). But at the cyclic low, the Portugal Cove population declined more than that at St. Shotts. Ruffed grouse populations in optimal habitat in Ontario showed little population change through a provincewide cycle (Theberge & Gauthier 1982), and ruffed grouse densities at Watch Lake, British Columbia, were more stable in a small study area than in a wide area (Chap. 3, Fig. 3.3). Another example is blue grouse, which were patchily distributed on Moresby Island, British Columbia, in 1971 when there were only 26 males, and more uniformly distributed in 1976 when there were 42 males that selected advertising sites (Chap. 2).

A number of workers have removed territorial birds in optimum habitats (Jenkins et al. 1964, Bendell et al. 1972, Zwickel 1972, Hannon 1978, 1983). Generally, birds from other areas arrived to repopulate the high-quality habitats (Fig. 14.27). Although we would not predict such replacements in cyclic populations starting to increase (Chap. 15), these replacement birds verify that birds are dispersed in patches and suggest that they can improve their fitness by exercising particular density options. We can recognize at least two morphs: (1) a high-density, tolerant morph, which is adapted to squeeze into habitats with abundant resources (more nest and advertisement sites per area) and adapted to living in close proximity with others and (2) a low-density, intolerant morph, more inclined to seek low-density situations where resources are more dispersed. These morphs may be analogous to Chitty's (1967) two types: π selected and α selected animals (review in Krebs 1978).

Our knowledge of phenotypic polymorphism in spacing strategies is most advanced in forest grouse. All three forest grouse—ruffed, spruce, and blue—live in habitats liable to forest succession. Blue grouse colonize newly logged, coniferous forest sites (Redfield et al. 1970) or following fire successions (Martinka 1972, Bendell 1974). Spruce grouse are frequent in early successional stages of lodgepole and jack pine forests (Szuba & Bendell 1982). The boreal forest occupied by spruce grouse is a fire-driven ecosystem (Kelsall et al. 1977). Advertising, ruffed grouse males find young aspen stands safe as soon as the canopy closes (DeStefano & Rusch 1982). Aspen is another species of early successional stages and is adapted to regenerate following forest fires (cf. Doerr et al. 1971). The temporal favorableness of these seres for grouse lasts longer than the birds' generation time. A genetically based, polymorphic spacing system would allow birds to persist in older successional stages, and at the same time permit their progeny to pioneer the newly created, unoccupied habitats (Gadgil 1971). This system would be the result of individual fitness strategies.

The pioneering work on polymorphism in forest grouse was Mossop's study of the behavior of birds at three locations—Copper Canyon (CC), Comox Burn (CB), Middle Quinsam (MQ)—on Vancouver Island (Chap. 1). He showed that birds in a population at high densities showed behavior that reduced their conspicuousness to predators. Birds had long flushing distances, were nonaggressive, and were seldom seen on the ground. A population at low density (MQ) was comprised of birds that were more mobile, aggressive, and more conspicuous in spacing behavior. Comox Burn birds were intermediate.

Bergerud captured birds from these three stocks and released them on three islands: Moresby Island received birds from all three stocks (CC, CB, MQ); Portland Island received founders from CC: Stuart received birds from MQ (see also Chap. 2). To review briefly the conclusions of this experiment: the founders retained their distinct behaviors throughout their lifetimes in these new and very different habitats on the islands. Also, progeny raised on Stuart acted like their (originally) MQ parents. The progeny on Portland behaved like the parent stock from CC for half the birds, but the other half was much more conspicuous and aggressive, like MQ stock. The conspicuous MQ and the inconspicuous CC types of progeny both occurred in the population on Moresby, as well as an intermediate type. These behavioral types of progeny occurred in ratios that suggested a heritable basis. The more constant behavior of MQ progeny versus CC progeny suggests that CC stock had more underlying genetic variations than did MQ. These high- and low-density morphs have different dispersal patterns.

Males and females of the low-density phenotype were mobile on Moresby and sought low-density habitats on the island's edge. Birds of the high-density phenotype settled near each other and had small advertising and preincubation ranges. Both types of birds were present in the closed system on Portland Island. But in the open populations on the mainland, where Bergerud had originally captured the birds, he could not find both types near each other. At Copper Canyon, where the founders of Portland Island were captured, he found only the high-density type. We believe that the low-density type in this open system had dispersed away from the high-density sites occupied by their parents, similar to what occurred on Moresby Island, with mixed stock. On Vancouver Island Bergerud (pers. files) found a high-density population at the top of a mountain near Cowichan. These birds were closely spaced, flushed at long distances, and could not easily be captured. Surrounding these birds, but downhill, were birds spaced farther apart and in denser vegetation cover. In contrast to the hilltop birds these could be approached closely and would come to arena tests and fight their mirror images. Bergerud also found at Mt. Washington, Vancouver Island, widely spaced birds that would fight their mirror images, this time on the subalpine habitat (pers. files). Hannon (1978), working at Comox Burn immediately beneath Mt. Washington, found blue grouse more closely spaced and less aggressive than the widely dispersed birds on Mt. Washington. Hand-reared progeny from low-density, blue grouse populations fought their mirror images more, and were more mobile pacers than chicks raised from parents who lived in higher-density situations (Chap. 2, Cooper 1977). Hines (1986b) recently radio-tracked blue grouse and classified birds as dispersers and nondispersers. Both types had similar reproductive success and mortality rates. There is ample evidence of suites of tactics grouped within alternative reproductive behaviors (ARBs *sensu* Austad 1984), which permit blue grouse to select either high- or low-density situations.

The genetics at one locus (Ng) of colonizing blue grouse have been documented in two populations (Redfield 1974, Zwickel et al. 1977). At Alberni, Vancouver Island, Redfield (1974) found an excess of homozygous, yearling blue grouse settling in vacant, newly logged areas. At Comox, Vancouver Island, Zwickel et al. (1977) removed birds from second-growth forests 9 years after logging. At Comox, the frequency of Redfield's (1974) colonizing genotype was similar for the removed birds and the colonizing replacements. Although densities were essentially zero at both Alberni and Comox after removal, homozygotes could adapt to the reduced cover and extensive space at Alberni, whereas heterozygotes should have sought in the more optimal and advanced plant cover at Comox. These results are consistent with the spacing hypothesis (Fig. 2.26) outlined earlier to explain the existence of blue grouse types on the Gulf Islands. Together these studies suggest that: (1) density-tolerant birds most often occur in resource-rich habitats; (2) more density-tolerant birds are heterozygous; (3) density-intolerant, dispersal types seek lower densities in more resource-limited habitats; and (4) more density-intolerant birds are homozygous.

Spruce grouse also appear to show behavioral polymorphism. Yearling males and females exhibit a wide or a restricted nest (females) and advertising site (males) searching pattern (Herzog 1977a). Keppie (1981) documented sedentary, wide-ranging, and intermediate types of juvenile birds dispersing from the same broods. Herzog and Keppie (1980) and Schroeder (1985) recognized that a complex ingress-egress (sorting) occurred in both fall and spring; some birds left as others came into the study area. Juveniles in one area dispersed in the fall even though Keppie (1979) had removed all the adults. The complex movements of spruce grouse (Fig. 14.28) can be explained by five processes: (1) their study area was of optimal habitat, where density-tolerant types should breed; (2) in the fall, progeny of both density-tolerant and density-intolerant birds sought winter cover nearest to their breeding ranges; (3) birds in spring dispersed either into the study area or left the study area, according to whether they were density-tolerant or intolerant types; (4) there was positive assortment of these two morphs, as argued for blue grouse (Fig. 2.26); and (5) the density-tolerant morph produced both density-tolerant and density-intolerant phenotypes. Keppie (pers. comm.) has confirmed that his study area was of more nearly optimal habitat than the surrounding land. His study also suggests that the extensive shuffle in fall and spring, which has been documented for forest grouse, may be exaggerated when we select small, high-density areas to study populations in open systems.

Ruffed grouse have a similar pattern of fall dispersal. Some birds leave and others arrive (Rusch & Keith 1971b). These movements cannot be explained by social explusion; rather, birds must be seeking their own best-fitted environment. Behavioral studies of ruffed grouse have shown that most gray-colored males flush at longer distances than red-colored ones (Chap. 3). In that study, the same red-phase birds fought trespassers (mirror images) in their advertising ranges and at their drumming logs more vigorously than did gray-phase birds. Also, red-phase females were more conspicuous than gray females in distraction displays (Fig. 3.13; see also Haas 1974 for spruce grouse). In Minnesota, red-phase birds have a shorter life expectancy than gray-phase birds (Gullion & Marshall 1968, Little 1978), possibly because of their conspicuous behavior (Chap. 3). In the Minnesota studies the red phase increased in frequency as numbers increased (Gullion & Marshall 1968, Little 1978). This was also true for two periods of increase in 15 years at Watch Lake, British Columbia (Chap. 3). Differences in spacing behavior thus seems to vary according to phenotype (color), and these differences are more striking between years than between places within years (cf. Gullion 1981).

Whereas the spacing patterns of phenotypes in the forest grouse may be best-adapted to different stages of forest succession, climate may be the dominant extrinsic variable that affects spacing in steppe grouse. In the prairies and savannas, drought cycles affect the abundance of herbaceous nesting cover. An abnormally wet or dry year that varies 25% above or below the mean can be expected, on average, every 2.5 years in the shortgrass prairie, every 3 years in the mixed-grass prairie, and every 4 years in the tallgrass prairie (Wiens 1974). This variable template means that steppe grouse should be flexible in searching behavior. In some years they will have to search large areas to find suitable nesting patches; at other times nest cover will be abundant. Some females should be prepared to nest near each other when the environment is patchy, and to be widely spaced when conditions permit. Density-tolerant and density-intolerant types may exist in the steppe grouse. Gratson (Chap. 5) has recognized a bimodalism in move-

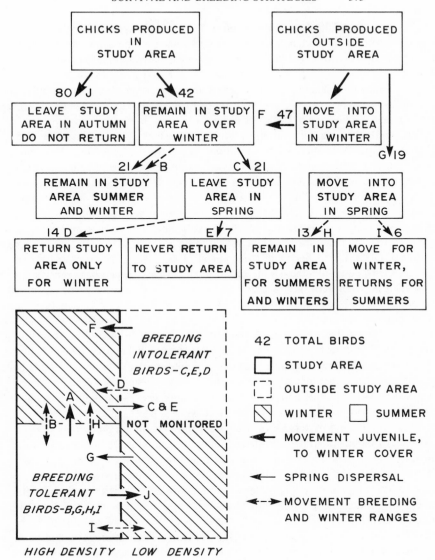

Fig. 14.28. Fall and spring movements of juvenile spruce grouse documented by Herzog and Keppie (1980). This complex movement pattern can be explained by assuming that most of the breeding birds in the study area were density tolerant (suggested because the study area had a high density—Keppie pers. comm.) and that these birds produced both density-tolerant and density-intolerant progeny. These movements are explained by: (1) both morphs seeking the nearest winter cover (fall movement) and (2) each morph showing positive assortment the next spring (spring movement), when they space themselves to establish nesting and future advertising sites.

ment patterns in male sharp-tailed grouse. One would expect alternative mating tactics in colonizing tendencies. When populations are increasing, the best tactic might be for yearlings to establish new leks near new, female nesting ranges. When the population is decreasing, it would be a better tactic to contest lek positions at established display grounds. The grouse cannot predict if the population is increasing or decreasing, and both types may be maintained where different phenotypes are favored at different times.

The tundra grouse have the most constant physical environment of the three grouse groups. Plant succession is minimal on the arctic-alpine floor. Vegetation is not buffeted by wet and dry growing seasons as it is on the prairie. The major environmental variable that changes is the number of birds, because nesting success is usually high (Chap. 15). Many ptarmigan populations show regular changes in number-cycles. The aggressive behavior of rock ptarmigan varies between increasing and decreasing phases in cyclic abundance (Watson 1965). Aggressive spacing behavior has been shown to be at least partly innate (Theberge & Bendell 1980), and heritable (Moss et al. 1982, 1984, 1985) in ptarmigan. Mercer (1967) documented a suite of parameters that changed between years in an insular population of willow ptarmigan as it declined, and Bergerud has noted that birds were more conspicuous and vulnerable to hunting at high densities than when populations declined and were low (Bergerud 1972). Henderson's (1977) work has shown that more colonizing red grouse were homozygous than birds living in higher densities. These marked differences in behavioral tactics in ptarmigan at high and low densities, together with high probability of a heritable basis, suggest the occurrence of a genetic polymorphic system in which one morph is fittest at low densities and another at high densities, as predicted in Chitty's (1967) polymorphic behavior hypothesis (Chap. 12).

There is a gambit of behavioral tactics for tolerant-intolerant density morphs. Each set of tactics (a strategy) will be ineffective unless there is positive assortment of phenotypes. Dispersal is the assortment mechanism. Phenotypes seek a density habitat that contains "like-minded" birds. The density-tolerant tactic of spacing near other advertising males in habitat with good vegetation cover would be counterproductive if a neighbor were more aggressive or more mobile, and monopolized females. Density-tolerant females are sedentary and docile, to remain inconspicuous while nesting in high numbers. Their strategy would be ineffective if an aggressive, more intolerant female were to settle in their midst. Mutual avoidance of different phenotypes by sorting into preferred density habitats would result in optimal spacing for individuals and maintain divergence of aggressiveness in the population.

The temporal and spatial sequence of sorting of these behavioral types may vary among populations and species with different life expectancies. The behavior of the long-lived blue grouse at Copper Canyon varied little from 1970 to 1980, yet densities were much less in the latter years. Conversely, there were major temporal changes in aggressive behavior in a short-lived, ruffed grouse population as densities changed (Chap. 3). For the long-lived species, these behavioral polymorphisms seem more striking between areas than between years. In the shorter-lived species, changes between years appear more striking (Jenkins et al. 1963, Watson 1965, 1967, Mercer 1967, Bergerud 1970a, Watson & Miller 1971). The aggressive phenotype of blue grouse is found in situations where densities were low, whereas the aggressive phenotypes of ptarmigan and ruffed grouse appear more frequently at high densities and when populations decline. But, blue grouse are noncyclic, whereas ruffed grouse and ptarmigan populations in northern areas show 10-year cycles of abundance (Chap. 15, Figs. 15.30, 15.32). A major distinction between cyclic and noncyclic species may be the spatial-temporal pace of sorting morphs moderated by longevity. In noncyclic populations, phenotypes orient themselves in space, whereas polymorphisms in cyclic populations occurs temporally.

There has been a discussion of whether density and demography are causal in behavior, or if behavior is causal in demography (e.g., Chitty 1967, Charlesworth & Giesel 1972, Gaines 1978). Like many earnest debates, the truth may lie between the poles. Aggressive and spacing behavior have a heritable basis in grouse (Moss et al. 1982, 1984, 1985) independent of density, but these polymorphic suites of tactics preadapt birds to maximize fitness in different density environments (Fig. 2.27). "Two fundamental antithetical sets of behavior are always present between individuals, repulsed behaviour to maximize resources and thus separate from others, and attraction behaviour to maximize current resource availability and thus congregate where resources are most abundant" (Taylor & Taylor, 1977, p. 418). These conflicting, fundamental forces provide the template of the behavioral, polymorphic sorting system in grouse.

14.10 Summary

This chapter reviews the strategies and tactics grouse have adopted to maximize their fitness, first by enhancing their survival and second by maximizing breeding opportunities. The male's primary concern, besides survival, is advertising for and breeding with females. The female is less concerned about breeding, which is easily accomplished. Her most important decision is where to nest to minimize predation of her clutch. A second important decision for her is where to take the chicks so that they can rapidly grow and yet escape detection by predators.

Males have adopted several tactics to successfully advertise for females; they show fidelity to sites they have selected, and in many populations they display in the fall, months before breeding, to assure ownership of these locations. Males also select safe sites near nesting females and commonly display in the crepuscular periods to avoid diurnal predators. Yearling males are capable of breeding but generally are not chosen by females. Thus, yearling males devote their time to prospecting for future advertising sites that are safe and will attract females in later years.

Females prospect early for suitable nesting sites. Factors that may influence a female's decisions are: extent of nesting cover, local abundance of predators, and locations of other females and males that may "blow her cover" by overt display directed at her. Females avoid other females to reduce the chances for density-dependent nest predation to occur and to minimize conspicuous, aggressive interactions, which may also attract predators. Females of all the grouse, except some prairie chickens and sharp-tailed grouse in pure grasslands, nest adjacent to logs, trees, or rocks, or under shrubs to avoid being ambushed on the nest, which permits them to "sit-tight," concealing their eggs. Laying and incubating hens show a variety of behaviors on and near the nest that minimize nest conspicuousness. Females of some species often abandon nests and renest, and the factors influencing these decisions are discussed in this chapter.

The phenotypic cues and ultimate factors that females use to select males are still contentious. We believe that choice is made on the basis of factors that will assure the female a safe, successful coitus and will minimize the conspicuousness of herself and her nest site. We suggest that females of the steppe species generally select those males on leks that are less likely than other males to approach and follow females off the lek and into nesting habitats. This reduces the conspicuousness of nests in habitats with many nest predators. Forest grouse females may select males displaying at intermediate distances from their nest sites. A male that is too close may bring unwanted attention to the nest site. If a female moves to a male far away, she increases her conspicuousness. Ptarmigan hens select males with large territories that contain ample space, to maximize distances to other nests, and high-quality cover to hide nests.

The brood-rearing strategy of hens includes moving from the nest site to find optimal foraging habitats for young chicks. Later, when the chicks can thermoregulate, hens take their broods to denser cover, decreasing their conspicuousness to predators. The intensity of distraction displays by brooding hens is proportional to the potential loss in fitness from chick mortality and wanes after the risk to chicks is reduced at 2–3 weeks of age.

Following the breeding season, grouse are concerned primarily with survival. Migrating in the fall to denser and taller cover, flocking, and snow-roosting are all viewed as tactics that reduce predation-risk rather than tactics to cope with weather or food factors. In winter, males will compromise their safety more than females to remain nearer to breeding areas and thus enhance breeding opportunities the following spring.

This chapter closes with a discussion of two alternative suites of breeding tactics that grouse may have evolved in a cover-space trade-off. This polymorphic spacing system involves a density-tolerant morph and a density-intolerant morph. Density-tolerant birds select habitats of high intrinsic cover value for breeding and are prepared to compromise space in a high-density context for this ideal cover. These birds have adopted behavioral tactics that promote inconspicuousness and close-living, at the expense of social interactions to enhance space. Density-intolerant birds, in the face of competition, elect to compromise cover value to select sites with more space to avoid predators. This morph is more aggressive and conspicuous than the density-tolerant birds, and more adept at prospecting widely to find satisfactory sites for nesting and advertising. It is hypothesized that these two traits of attraction and repulsion are present in all grouse groups. The variation in the frequency of these phenotypes will be primarily in space for noncyclic populations, and positive assortment will occur through dispersal; for cyclic populations the frequency of the morphs will vary with time.

15

Population Ecology of North American Grouse

A. T. Bergerud

15.1 Introduction

The first synthesis of the demography of North American grouse was thirty years ago when J. J. Hickey (1955) reviewed the then current literature. His review emphasized census methodology, the age and sex structure of populations, and the question of fluctuations and cycles in the numbers of grouse. Johnsgard (1973) also reviewed the current literature, but emphasized life-history characteristics of species. In the past ten years, wildlife biologists have been actively counting grouse, determining the sex and age composition of the living and the dead, calculating mortality rates, and searching for nests. Radiotelemetry has allowed biologists at last to find nests, to evaluate the use of space, and to investigate and document the factors that cause death. Unfortunately, many of these data on grouse are unpublished—in government reports or in doctoral and master's theses. I used these sources because not to have done so would have excluded many important findings and prohibited a current synthesis. This review chapter of the population ecology of North American grouse is my interpretation of the literature and does not, therefore, necessarily represent the views of the authors of this book nor those from whose works I have collected the statistics.

The annual change in the number of grouse can be considered to begin when yearlings and adults arrive on the breeding range in year 1. The first potential influence that could reduce the intrinsic rate-of-increase (r_m) is the percentage of hens that nest. Next, there is variability in the size of clutches and in hatching success. After hatching, some chicks die. Further, some adult birds die during the summer. Indexes to production in year 1 include the mean size of broods in autumn, and the ratio of juveniles per adult in the harvest. These indexes of production are not valid measures of recruitment, because juveniles die over winter at greater rates than adults (Hickey 1955), but the fall juveniles:adult ratio (as a breeding success index) remains the common yardstick, in the literature, of the abundance of the new generation. The juveniles, yearlings, and adults then face the winter season, and more losses ensue. Dispersal should not be considered, a priori, a variable in demography; birds that have left probably remain alive, and the impact of the loss of such birds on the dynamics of a population says much about the adequacy of the size of the study area. After winter we have a new breeding population in the spring of year 2. Recruitment and mortality have failed to balance and the size of the breeding population has changed. What drives these changes and what prevents the population from continuing to increase is the subject of this chapter.

15.2 Percentage of hens nesting

Darwin (1871, p. 417) was one of the first to suggest that all females do not nest. He asked "How is it there are birds enough to replace immediately a lost mate of either sex?" His interpretation was based on the removal of territorial birds and the observation that replacements appeared.

A major theory of population regulation of grouse is, simply put, that females prevent other females from breeding. This notion has been advanced to explain changes in numbers of willow ptarmigan (*Lagopus lagopus*) (Watson & Moss 1972, Hannon 1982, 1983), blue grouse (*Dendragapus obscurus*) (Zwickel 1972, Hannon & Zwickel 1979), and spruce grouse (*Dendragapus canadensis*) (Boag et al. 1979). The main evidence for this theory is that females arrive to replace birds that are removed, as Darwin noted (Watson & Jenkins 1968, Bendell et al. 1972, Zwickel 1972, Zwickel 1980, Hannon 1983). These experimental results provide convincing evidence that territorial behavior spaces breeding birds, as argued by Lack (1966). They do not demonstrate that some females are prevented from breeding by social interaction. Birds may simply be relocating in habitats with reduced densities, resulting from removal, to improve their fitness prospects (Fig. 14.27); this sequence has been shown for great tits (*Parus major*) (Krebs 1971).

Two removal experiments conducted in closed systems (no ingress or egress) with blue grouse males and willow ptarmigan males and females failed to find surplus nonbreeding birds (Chap. 2, Blom & Myrberget 1978). Myrberget and Blom provided evidence that ptarmigan pairs in fact shifted from where they would have nested to the vacancies created. The replacement females observed in the removal experiments of Zwickel (1980) and Hannon (1982, 1983) appeared relatively early in the season, when some hens were still searching for sites. After the hens had begun to nest, little replacement occurred (Zwickel 1980, Hannon 1982, 1983). The failure of hens to appear later is consistent with the idea that they are nesting elsewhere. No studies have documented large numbers of nonbreeding females during the peak of incubation. It seems unlikely that nonbreeding females could be available just before incubation and then disappear 2 to 3 weeks later.

The most convincing method to detect nonbreeding females is to radio-track females throughout the preincubation period. For the test to be valid, these females must be captured before they visit males. Forest grouse have been monitored extensively by telemetry, and the results suggest that nearly all adult females breed and nest and that most yearlings attempt to do so. All 18 adult, blue grouse females that were radio-tracked on Vancouver Island nested, and of 46 yearling hens that were followed, 38 nested, 5 more were believed to have nested, 1 was killed too early to decide, and 2 (4%) definitely did not nest (Hannon 1978, Sopuck 1979). The results of Herzog's (1977a) study of spruce grouse in Alberta are less clear; Herzog and Boag (1978, p. 867) said, "We have no direct evidence to indicate all females do not breed," but later Boag et al. (1979) said that only 60–70% of 47 females nested. Herzog (pers. comm.) said that of the 11 questionable yearlings, some indeed had nested, but that others, based on evidence from their movement patterns, probably had not. In Minnesota, Haas (1974) radio-tracked 17 female spruce grouse and Maxson (1974) tracked 13 yearling ruffed grouse (*Bonasa umbellus*), and both concluded that all had nested.

Evidence from studies of the steppe species indicates that nearly all female sharp-tailed grouse (*Tympanuchus phasianellus*) and prairie chickens (*Tympanuchus cupido*) nest (Table 15.1). In the longer-lived sage grouse (*Centrocercus urophasianus*), some yearling females probably do not breed (Stanton 1958, Eng 1963).

I can find no evidence of nonbreeding females in rock (*Lagopus mutus*) or willow ptarmigan (Table 15.1). Conceivably there could be a shortage of males in these monogamous species, owing to predation by gyrfalcons (*Falco rusticolus*) on displaying males. When this occurred in Iceland, however, some females simply mated and nested with the same males (Gardarsson 1971). In Svalbard, one cock was seen to mate with four different hens (Unander & Steen 1985). Choate (1963a), working with white-tailed ptarmigan (*Lagopus leucurus*), observed females moving into his area late in the nesting season and called these females "nonbreeders"; again these may have been unsuccessful females that had tried to breed elsewhere. Other workers who have studied white-tailed ptarmigan have reported that all females breed (Table 15.1).

Conceivably, it might benefit a yearling of a species with a long life expectancy to delay breeding until 2 years of age. The greatest mortality of hens occurs during nesting and the brood season; if a female waited for better nesting conditions as an adult, she might live longer and thus contribute more offspring than commencing with a yearling breeding option. Blue grouse are one of the longest-lived grouse species, and F. Zwickel has provided enough statistics on yearling and adults to test the delayed-option strategy. If 100 yearlings delayed breeding until 2 years of age, they would still contribute fewer young throughout the lifetime of the cohort than 100 yearlings that first bred at 1 year of age—800 compared with about 875 young (calculations based on Zwickel 1975, Zwickel et al. 1977, 1983). This would occur even if the first-year survival rate of nonbreeding yearlings that delayed breeding was 80% and only 69% for yearlings that nested.

Theoretically, all females should breed in their first year. Their life span is too short to delay breeding, and the experience they accumulate as yearlings should benefit their later attempts. The demographic data indicate that, indeed, nearly all adult females nest, but also that at times there are some nonbreeding yearlings in the long-lived species: blue grouse, spruce grouse, sage grouse, and white-tailed ptarmigan. Even if some females do not breed, this does not necessarily suggest that they are prevented from doing so by other females, nor that such non-breeding would be a mechanism that regulates numbers.

15.3 Clutch size in grouse

Lack (1947, 1954) proposed that the clutch size of each species of bird has been set by natural selection at that which provided the maximum number of surviving young. For the nidifugous species, Lack (1968) hypothesized that selection favored the clutch size that provided eggs of high quality and hence, survival of precocial young; also clutch size, proximately, should be affected by the hen's physical condition as influenced by her diet. An alternative ultimate hypothesis is that species have evolved their characteristic clutch sizes to minimize losses from predation (Skutch 1949). Large clutches require more trips to the nest by a female and thus extend and increase the vulnerability of the nest to predators. Also, large broods would be more conspicuous and female defense behavior could entail higher risk; thus, the increased vulnerability does not end after the eggs have hatched. Although this hypothesis has been discounted by some (Klomp 1970), it remains an alternative to the food hypothesis for nidifugous species (Cody 1966, Johnsgard 1973, Safriel 1975, Perrins 1977, see also Slagsvold 1985).

A valid hypothesis of clutch size in grouse must explain: (1) the wide variation in the mean number of eggs laid among species, ranging from five to six eggs in some of the spruce grouse and white-tailed ptarmigan populations to 12 to 13 eggs in prairie grouse, and (2) the extreme variation between populations within species. For example, the mean clutch size of spruce grouse shows wide variation (Rand 1947); in Alaska the mean clutch is 7.5 eggs (Ellison 1974), but in Minnesota it is only 4.7 (Haas 1974). Rock ptarmigan in Scotland have a clutch of 6.6 eggs (Watson 1965), but in Iceland the average is 11 eggs (Gardarsson 1971).

15.3.1 Maternal condition and clutch size

If clutch size both ultimately and proximately is principally determined by maternal nutrition, it should vary among places, years, and individuals in relation to the physical condition and spring foods of females. However, there was no correlation between the weights of prairie chicken females in Minnesota in the spring and their clutch sizes (Table 14.4). Ruffed grouse females in Minnesota laid an average of 11.9 $\pm$ 0.39 ($\pm$ SE) eggs ($n = 11$) in 1971 and 10.5 $\pm$ 0.58 eggs ($n = 10$) in 1972, but females weighed significantly more in 1972 than in 1971 (Maxson 1974). Myrberget (Fig. 11.7) found no correlation between the weights of willow ptarmigan hens on Tranøy Island, Norway, and their clutch sizes for 11 years (1965–76), but in 1977, 1978, and 1980, the clutch was two eggs larger than the mean of the previous 11 years, and this increase was accompanied by a major increase in female weight.

Table 15.1. Comments in the literature on the proportion

"Greater than 90% of the females nest."

Tundra grouse

Willow ptarmigan: "Probably all hens attempted to nest once" (Bergerud 1970a, p. 305). "So surplus birds apparently did not exist at that season" (Pedersen et al. 1983, p. 267).

Rock ptarmigan: "No non-breeding females were observed" (Gardarsson 1971, p. 97). "Specimens collected . . . failed to uncover evidence that only female(s) did not breed (Weeden 1965, p. 340). "Polygamy . . . ensured that almost all hens bred every year (Unander & Steen 1985, p. 204).

White-tailed ptarmigan; "There were no unmated females on the study area" (May 1975, p. 197). "The evidence obtained indicated that all females attempted to nest" (Braun & Rogers 1971, p. 39). "Field observations indicated that all females nested" (Giesen 1977).

Forest grouse

Ruffed grouse: no references found.

Blue grouse: "Practically all hens on the summer range . . . were breeding birds." (140 of 143 had broods or brood patches – Zwickel & Bendell 1967:829), "96 percent, 66/69 of adults hens . . . were breeding." (Bendell & Elliot 1967:53), 4 of 43 yearlings may not have nested and 2 of 88 adults (1974–74) may not have nested. On Moresby Island 84 of 86 tagged adults nested, as did 27 of 34 yearlings (pers. files).

Spruce grouse: More than 90 percent of the hens nested (Ellison 1972). "We found brood patches on all females examined in late May and June with one exception." (Robinson 1980:60); 174 of 186 spruce grouse hens nested (Keppie 1975b).

Steppe grouse

Sage grouse: 97 percent (379/390) of the females had ovulated (Stanton 1958, Dalke et al.

Generally, the mean size of clutches for a particular species increases with latitude. In prairie grouse, for example, the correlation between clutch size and latitude is $r = 0.573$, using 29 studies. Females in many of the northern populations of grouse begin laying eggs before or coincident with new plant growth. Presumably, these populations would have little variation in clutch size if variability resulted from changes in the spring condition of females following spring "green-up." Contrary to this hypothesis, clutch size varied one to two eggs among years in willow ptarmigan populations in Newfoundland (Bergerud 1970a) and rock ptarmigan in Alaska (Weeden & Theberge 1972, pers. comm.). Prairie chickens lay three to four fewer eggs in Texas and Missouri than in Minnesota (Lehmann 1941, Arthaud 1968, Svedarsky 1979). Egg-laying in Minnesota is coincident with the start of the growing season (Table 14.4), but the southern

---

of females that nest (excluding radiotelemetry studies)

===

1963) (this does not necessarily mean all nested); "All field observations indicated that the entire female population conducted at least one nesting attempt." (Patterson 1952:103); 242 of 256 adults ovulated (Braun 1979).

Sharp-tailed grouse and prairie chicken: no references except Robel and Ballard (1974), who believed some female prairie chicken might not get bred.

"Less than 90% of the females nest."

Tundra grouse

Rock ptarmigan: "Some non-breeding was suspected but this was not certain." (Watson 1965, p. 159).

Forest grouse

Ruffed grouse: "Non-nesting varied from 0 to over 25 percent of all females . . . in different years" (Bump et al. 1947, p. 359).

Spruce grouse: "We estimate only 60–70 percent (yearling females) bred" (based on brood patches, $n = 47$ and radio-tracked females—Boag et al. 1979). But Herzog (1977a, p. 42) said of the 4 "nonbreeding" radio-tracked hens: "Movements were localized and nests may have been destroyed before discovery."

Blue grouse: Substantial number of sub-adults (nonbreeders?) of mixed sex were found during the breeding season (Boag 1966). "76 percent (29/38) of yearling hens were breeding" (Bendell & Elliot 1967, p. 53). 44% of yearling females were classified as nonbreeders (Hannon and Zwickel 1979).

Steppe grouse

Sage grouse: "5 of 20 (sub-adults) failed to ovulate (Stanton 1958:64); 119 of 139 yearlings ovulated (Braun 1979).

populations have several weeks of new, spring growth before egg-laying. They should, according to predictions of the nutrition hypothesis, have larger clutches than the more northern races; this is the converse of what occurs.

We have provided evidence that nesting commences with the disappearance of snow (Fig. 14.10); under these conditions annual variations in nesting schedules should nevertheless start from a common-food baseline. The food hypothesis predicts that females should delay nesting in late springs until they can accumulate sufficient nutrient and energy reserves; contrary to the hypothesis, hens begin laying in the north before new and nutritious foods are available, even though chicks from late initial nests and renests appear to have good survival (Bergerud 1970a, Parker 1981).

Females that nest early generally lay more eggs in their initial attempt than do females initiating nests later in the same year (Jenkins et al. 1963, Bergerud 1970a, Svedarsky 1979). This applies to willow ptarmigan, in which yearlings and adults have similar clutch sizes. Presumably, females that start nesting later in a given year assimilate more higher-quality foods than do early hens. If these late hens were in poor physical condition initially, one might still expect that their improved physical condition owing to their delay would compensate, and clutch sizes would be similar — but this does not occur. Further, in the aviary, late-starting red grouse have smaller clutches even though food quality and availability are held constant (Moss et al. 1981).

The food hypothesis is neither a necessary nor a sufficient explanation of the variability in clutch size. It provides no explanation for differences in clutch size between populations of the same species in which birds are eating similar foods and initiating nests at approximately the same time. All the populations in which grouse have long life spans (i.e., annual survival rate > 60%) show clutches of fewer than seven eggs (section 15.3.3), yet plant phenology and food show no consistent pattern among populations. The largest North American grouse, the sage grouse, and the smallest, the white-tailed ptarmigan, have a similar clutch size; but the egg expressed as a percentage of the total weight of the sage grouse is 3.4% and of the white-tailed ptarmigan is 6.4% (Johnsgard 1973). The food hypothesis has been related only to maximizing fitness in the current breeding season, and ignores that grouse should evolve life-history traits to optimize lifetime production (Williams 1966b, Charnov & Krebs 1974).

15.3.2 Clutch size determined by chick survival

Safriel (1975) proposed that for birds with precocial young, clutch size was dependent on the optimal brood size that could be defended by the parents as modified by the density of food. Parents would have more difficulty defending chicks while searching for a dispersed food supply. The survival of grouse chicks in broods, however, is largely independent of clutch size; commonly 40–50% of the chicks die before autumn (Fig. 15.1), regardless of whether the hens laid large or small clutches. Also, the frequency distribution of brood sizes in the autumn is essentially normal for most grouse unless cyclic polymorphism is involved (Bergerud 1970a). This suggests that survival of chicks from different clutch sizes is approximately equal. Willow ptarmigan chicks have mortality rates similar to the other grouse even though both parents provide protection. Also, the mean sur-

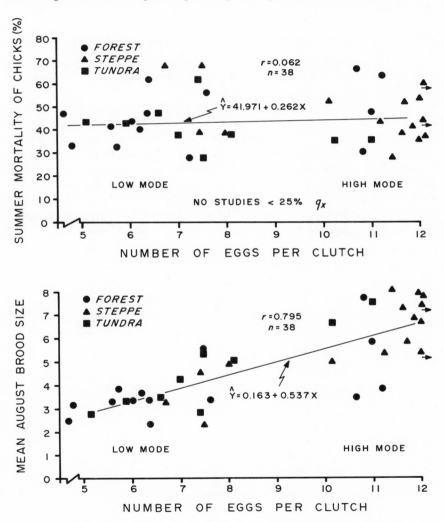

Fig. 15.1. *Top*: Summer mortality of chicks is not correlated with clutch size. *Bottom*: Hence, brood size increases linearly with clutch size (data from 38 studies). References for this and other figures with many data points are found beneath tables (see especially Table 15.2).

vival rates of chicks do not increase with latitude, even though ground predators are less abundant in the north. Safriel's (1975) hypothesis is not supported in the tetraonids. He makes the interesting point that if the young themselves take protective action, parents could successfully raise more young. He offers this as an explanation for the larger clutches of gallinaceous birds compared with those of shorebirds.

15.3.3 Clutch size determined by life span and predation risk of eggs

The mean clutch size of the various grouse increases as the annual mortality rate of adults increases, or stated conversely, clutch size declines as survival improves (Fig. 15.2). This correlation between fecundity and longevity is most precise in the arctic, where man has not upset natural predator systems, altered nesting habitats, or harvested grouse populations to the same degree as in southern latitudes. In my view the more independently evolved variable in this correlation is the mortality rate; mortality is not explained as the density-dependent result of a maximized reproductive rate as argued by Lack (1966). Nor do these parameters simply covary fortuitously or covary in response to a common, environmental resource antecedent as argued by Ricklefs (1977). Species evolve a clutch size that optimizes the trade-off between the benefits of high reproduction and the cost of reproductive risk. By prorating its reproductive effort over its

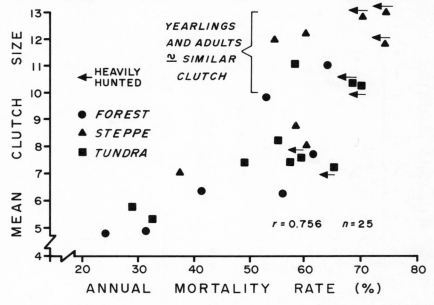

Fig. 15.2. Mean clutch size of grouse in 25 populations regressed against annual mortality rate. Natural mortality rates of birds in heavily hunted populations (indicated by *arrows* along data points) are lower than those shown.

greater life span, a long-lived individual can afford to invest less in annual reproduction than can a short-lived individual (Williams 1966b, Murphy 1968, Gadgil & Bossert 1970). Experimental confirmation of this trade-off is the recent work of Rose et al. (1984), who showed a reduction in ovary weights of young-adult fruit flies (*Drosophila*) in populations exhibiting postponed senescence.

The greater independence of mortality than reproduction is explained by the fact that each grouse species inhabits a fairly specific biotype; sage grouse live in the distinct sagebrush biome; ruffed grouse have taken a niche in deciduous forests; and spruce and blue grouse have evolved adaptations that permit their exploitation of coniferous forests. These distinct habitats provide different escape-cover characteristics, and are coinhabited by different arrays of coevolved predators. This distinct predator-cover complex, coupled with the specific antipredator tactics of each grouse species, has shaped the mortality rates of populations and species. Risk associated with reproductive activity may contribute to mortality, but the predator-cover dyad will be the major determinant of annual mortality rates and is mostly independent of fecundity and density (section 15.6).

My model for the clutch size of tetraonids distinguishes between the factors that influence clutch size differences among species and among populations within species. The differences in clutch size among *species* are hypothesized to be caused by different reproductive optimization schedules that result from the

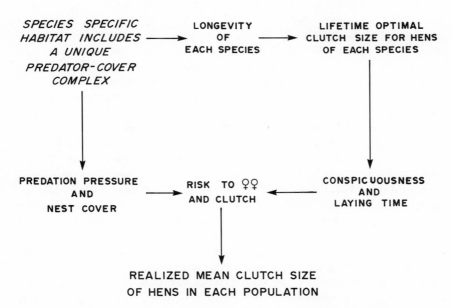

Fig. 15.3. Environmental factors that determine clutch size. The realized clutch size for birds in each population may be less than the optimal for each species, based on longevity, in order to reduce conspicuousness and predation loss.

unique longevity of individuals of each species. Life span is the result of the species-specific habitat (Fig. 15.3). This habitat includes a characteristic type of escape cover and is coinhabited by specific coevolved predators. I have termed this the predator-cover complex. The fine-tuning of *populations within species* results from different levels of egg predation, and possibly predation of females. Hens in populations faced with heavy predation risk individuals could reduce their clutch so that the length or the egg laying period is shortened, thereby reducing the number of trips to the nest and thus the conspicuousness of the clutch (Johnsgard 1973).

The clutch sizes of grouse can be segregated into high and low modes (Fig. 15.4). The low mode, from 5 to 8 eggs, is characteristic of grouse with annual survival rates greater than 50%, and the high mode, from 9 to 13 eggs, is characteristic of grouse with survival rates equal to or less than 45% per year. Within these two reproductive strategies, yearling hens lay significantly fewer eggs than adults only in the low-clutch group, and the difference between yearlings and adults is greatest where nest predation is low within this group (Fig. 15.5).

These differences in clutch size between yearlings and adults are consistent with the optimization hypothesis that females of species with long life spans invest less in the initial clutch because of increased risk resulting from lack of experience and a longer life span over which they can maximize their effort. Yearlings in the high-survival group are, for the most part, less successful in nesting than adults (Keppie 1975a,b, Herzog 1977a, Zwickel et al. 1977, Petersen 1980, Smyth & Boag 1984). If nest predation is high in the long-lived group, the nests of both adults and yearlings will be at high risk, and adults may have clutches closer in size to those of yearlings. In general, the clutch-size data fit the hypothesis that long-lived grouse can afford to invest less in each attempt and to commit more resources to maintenance and later reproductive efforts than can birds expected to live only a short while.

The validity of this hypothesis requires a significant loss of eggs during egg-laying (see Myrberget 1985, Boag et al. 1984). Admittedly, there are few relevant data; most nests are found only after incubation has begun. Two of 22 radio-monitored, ruffed grouse hens lost their incomplete clutches during the laying period (Maxson 1974). Four of 37 sage grouse hens lost their clutches while still laying (Petersen 1980), and Svedarsky (1979) reported 5 of 36 prairie chicken hens that lost incomplete clutches. For bobwhite quail (*Colinus virginianus*), Klimstra and Roseberry (1975) found a 6% predation rate per day for the first 3 eggs laid; 3% per day for the remainder of egg-laying; and a rate of 2% per day during incubation ($n = 863$). Most eggs were lost to foxes (*Vulpes vulpes*). Mortality of waterfowl nests in North Dakota was generally highest during the early laying period, moderately high for later eggs, and lowest during incubation, according to Klett and Johnson (1982). They speculated that the presence of hens at nests reduced predation.

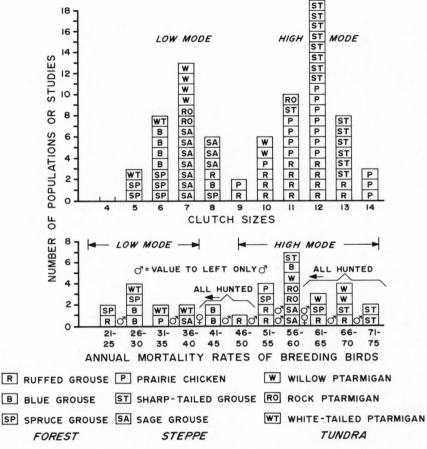

Fig. 15.4. There are two distinct modes of clutch sizes – a low clutch mode of five to eight eggs in populations in which birds have an annual mortality rate of 21%–41%, and a high clutch mode of ten to 14 eggs, corresponding to annual mortality rates of from 51% to 75%. Natural mortality rates of heavily hunted populatons would be less than the reported mortality rates. (Many references to clutch size in literature cited in Table 15.2.

Another consideration is that eggs are easy to steal when hens are laying and generally absent from the nest. An incubating female probably defends her clutch against several important predators including squirrels (*Spermophilus* spp.), snakes, and corvids (*Corvus* spp.). Predators may also search more for undeveloped eggs, which may be more nutritious than eggs with developing embryos (Sargeant pers. comm.). The evidence is substantial that females should improve their nesting success by reducing the period of egg-laying and the resulting vulnerability of unattended eggs.

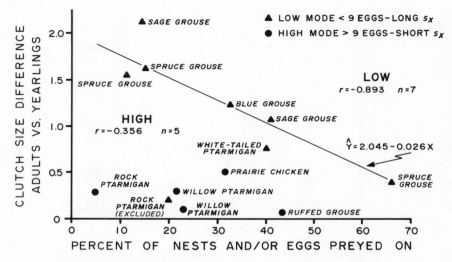

Fig. 15.5. The difference in mean clutch size between yearlings and adults is greatest in populations with the low clutch mode, and the difference is greatest in habitats where relatively few nests are destroyed by predators. (For references see Table 15.2.)

The principal evidence for the hypothesis that clutch size is primarily determined between populations by the risk of predation is that most grouse have smaller clutch sizes in those populations exposed to heavy nest predation (Fig. 15.6). A similar sequence has been reported for the passerine birds (Ricklefs 1969). In earlier papers, Ricklefs (1969, 1970) attributed the difference in clutch size to predation pressure, but later he supported a resource-oriented explanation (Ricklefs 1977).

A typical finding is that the commonest clutches are smaller than the clutch size that yields the most chicks per hen (Klomp 1970, Hussell 1972), contrary to the Lack hypothesis. In red grouse, hens that lay clutches of 10 to 11 eggs rear more young than females with clutches of the most common size, 7 to 8 eggs (Jenkins et al. 1963, Moss et al. 1981). The red grouse moors are managed to reduce nest predators, but if predators were common, the field clutch mode of 7 to 8 eggs might be more productive than the larger clutches because of its improved chance of escape from predators. The most productive clutch size in grouse should be evaluated based on survival of eggs, rather than on the survival of chicks from successful nests.

The clutch size of grouse decreases with increased longevity of adults and with reduced nesting success (Figs. 15.2, 15.6). I found no examples of a population in which birds have a long life expectancy ($q_x < 0.50$) and also have a mean clutch size of greater than 7 eggs, regardless of nesting success. But populations in which birds have short life expectancies ($q_x > 0.50$) have large clutches (> 9 eggs) if nesting success is low, but may have either large clutches (> 9 eggs)

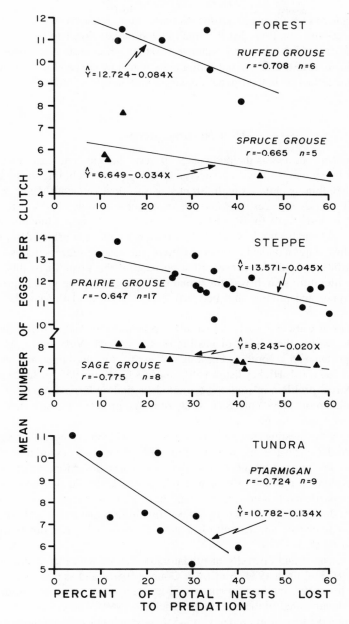

Fig. 15.6. The mean number of eggs per clutch is low in populations where hens can expect a high probability of nest predation, and is greater where hens can expect a low rate of nest predation. (For references see Table 15.2.)

or small clutches ($<$ 9 eggs) if nesting success is high. High survival is a sufficient but not necessary condition for the small-clutch mode. This suggests that long-lived birds cannot further reduce clutch size to make their nests more inconspicuous if predation risk is high, but individuals with low survival may be able to afford some reduction in their generally larger clutches, to mitigate risk if nesting success is relatively low.

15.4 Nesting success

I define nesting success as the percentage of nests that hatch at least one young. There are many biases in nesting-success investigations, including those that result from combining clutches in different stages of development (Miller & Johnson 1978). Biases also result from unrepresentative samples because the most conspicuous nests were found; attraction of predators to nests; human-induced desertion; and small sample sizes. In this review I could not arbitrarily exclude many studies. Any statistical comparison involving nesting success that is statistically significant should be conservative because of the great variability in the data. The literature search was for broad differences between grouse groups — forest, steppe, and tundra — and between species and populations within these groups.

All the grouse are extremely vulnerable to predation because of their relatively large clutches and their habit of nesting on the ground. Very early, M. Nice (1942) reported a 55% combined nesting success for the phasianiae and tetraoninae ($n = 5,597$). J. J. Hickey listed a 58% success figure in 1955 for seven grouse studies. A real problem in studying tetraonids is finding large samples of nests. Only the mammoth New York State study of ruffed grouse had a sample of nests in excess of 1,000 (Bump et al. 1947).

In this review, nesting success was 58% ($n = 5,422$) the same as that reported in 1955. Predation on average accounted for 79% of the unsuccessful nests (Table 15.2). The second most frequent cause of loss was nest desertion, which is especially prevalent in the sage grouse and prairie chickens. Furthermore, prairie chickens in particular lost nests to flooding, fires, and agricultural practices (Lehman 1941, Bowen 1971, Svedarsky 1979). In addition, desertion and predation losses are correlated. Species with low nesting success desert more frequently (Tables 14.6, 15.2).

The abundance and diversity of predators decreases with increasing latitude (Fleming 1973, Wilson 1974, McCoy & Connor 1980), and as the abundance of predators increases, the nesting success of hens decreases (Fig. 15.7); this has also been documented in the passerines (Ricklefs 1969). Hens south of latitude 40°N averaged a loss from predators of 45%, whereas hens nesting north of latitude 46°N had an average loss from predation of only 26%.

Grouse in the southernmost regions face extreme predation problems. Hardy

Table 15.2. Nesting success and predation of grouse nests based on total nests for each species and unweighed means from different studies (excludes studies without normal predators)

Grouse groups and species	Sample size		Nesting success (%) successful total		Predation rate (%) preyed on total	
	Nests	Studies	Nests	Studies	Nests	Studies
Forest grouse						
Ruffed grouse	1,783	13	62	61 ± 5.4	33 (86)[a]	30 ± 4.7
Spruce grouse	148	5	55	62 ± 11.3	39 (87)	33 ± 12.5
Blue grouse	260	4	53	53 ± 3.8	36 (76)	34 ± 6.4
Totals and means	2,191	22	60	60 ± 4.0	34 (84)	32 ± 4.0
Steppe grouse						
Sharp-tailed grouse	540	16	54	54 ± 4.4	37 (73)	36 ± 4.2
Prairie chicken	934	22	49	48 ± 3.1	39 (77)	38 ± 3.1
Sage grouse	699	12	35	38 ± 4.0	50 (76)	47 ± 6.3
Totals and means	2,173	50	46	48 ± 2.5	42 (76)	40 ± 2.6
Tundra grouse						
White-tailed ptarmigan	70	2	60	65 ± 5.0	39 (93)	35 ± 5.0
Rock ptarmigan	213	2	70	73 ± 3.5	20 (68)	22 ± 1.5
Willow ptarmigan	775	6	71	72 ± 4.5	21 (75)	22 ± 3.9
Totals and means	1,058	10	70	72 ± 3.3	22 (76)	24 ± 3.3
Totals and means	5,422	82	57	59	36 (79)	31

[a] Percentage of unsuccessful nests destroyed by predators.

Sources for nesting success and for many clutch sizes: Ruffed grouse – Fisher 1939, Bump et al. 1947, Grange 1948, Hardy 1950, Fallis & Hope 1950, Tanner 1948, Banasiak 1951, Kupa 1966, Neave 1967, Barrett 1970, Cringan 1970, Maxson 1974, Rusch et al. 1984. *Spruce grouse* – Ellison 1974, Haas 1974, Herzog & Keppie 1978, Robinson 1980, Redmond et al. 1982, Keppie 1982. *Blue grouse* – Mossop 1971, Zwickel 1975, Zwickel & Carveth 1978, Sopuck 1979, Hoffman 1979. *Sharp-tailed grouse* – Gross 1930, Hamerstrom 1939, Grange 1948, Hart et al. 1950, Blus & Walker 1966, Bernhoft 1969, Christenson 1970, Artmann 1970, Pepper 1972, Schiller 1973, Rice & Carter 1975, 1976, 1977, Sisson 1976, Kohn 1976, Ramharter 1976, Caldwell 1976. *Prairie chicken* – Gross 1930, Hamerstrom 1939, Lehmann 1941, Schwartz 1945, Ammann 1957, Copelin 1963, Yeatter 1963, Silvy 1968, Arthaud 1968, Watt 1969, Bowen 1971, Horak 1974, Rice & Carter 1975, 1976, Sisson 1976, Drobney & Sparrowe 1977, Horkel 1979, Horkel et al. 1978, Riley 1978, Sell 1979, Svedarsky 1979, Vance & Westemeier 1979. *Sage grouse* – Dargan and Keller 1940, Keller et al. 1941, Batterson & Morse 1948, Patterson 1952, Nelson 1955, Gill 1965, Carr 1967, Klebenow 1969, May 1970, Wallestad & Pyrah 1974, Petersen 1980. *White-tailed ptarmigan* – Choate 1963a, Giesen et al. 1980. *Rock ptarmigan* – Watson 1965, Weeden & Theberge 1972. *Willow ptarmigan* – Hagen 1935, Kristofferson 1937, Bergerud 1970, Watson & O'Hare 1979, Hannon 1982, Hannon & Smith 1984, Myrberget Chap. 11).

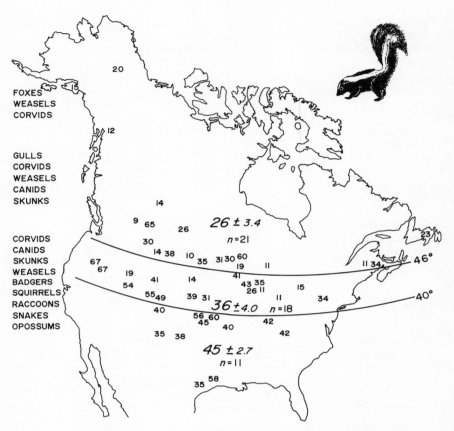

Fig. 15.7. The percentage of nests destroyed by predators decreases with a decrease in number of predator species and in populations farther north.

(1950) found that only 3 of 12 (25%) ruffed grouse nests hatched in Kentucky. Snakes were a serious predator. The southernmost grouse, the Attwater's prairie chicken, hatched only 17 of 54 (31%) nests (Horkel et al. 1978). In that study, the loss of hens was as serious a problem as the destruction of nests. Nine of 59 radio-tracked hens were lost during egg-laying; 22 additional hens were killed during incubation. The sex ratio of Attwater's prairie chicken is one of the most unbalanced in the grouse literature–approximately two males per one female (Horkel & Silvy 1980). The southern distribution of grouse appears limited by predation of nests and of females.

Grouse in the middle latitudes fare better (Fig. 15.7), but both sage grouse and prairie chickens have generally low nesting success, approximately 35% and 49%, respectively (Table 15.2); in addition, prairie chicken hens are commonly killed on the nest (Table 14.6). Desertion and renesting of adults are tactics both species use to reduce predation loss (Fig. 14.13).

The ptarmigans enjoy significantly higher nesting success than do either the forest or steppe grouse. One reason is that they face fewer kinds of predators of nests (Fig. 15.8), and these predators are at lower densities. In addition, ptarmigan are monogamous, and the males help distract predators from the nests (Chap. 13).

Little information exists on the total density of predators in the three habitat types—steppe, forest, and tundra. The available evidence, discussed in Chapter 13, indicates that the steppe has the most predators. The comparative sequence is:

Nest predation: steppe > forest > tundra
Number of predator species: steppe > forest > tundra
Density of predators: steppe > forest > tundra

In addition to abundance of predators, there are other reasons for the low nesting success in the steppe. The extent of grass and sagebrush communities has been reduced by agriculture—this concentrates nesting females and thus reduces the size of areas that predators need to search for prey.

Furthermore, nesting cover has been reduced by grazing and herbicides. We have also aided the predator's access to nesting habitats by providing perching posts, travel lanes, and culverts to be used as dens. Further we have increased the abundance of alternate prey with domestic animals and by roadkills. Man has upset the predator-prey adaptive race more in the steppe than in the other two habitat zones.

15.4.1. Frequency of renesting

The renesting decision of female grouse should be based on the benefits and costs of the increased parental investment in laying a second clutch (Fig. 14.13). Early grouse biologists doubted the importance of renesting (Hamerstrom 1939, Bump et al. 1947, Ammann 1957). Even as late as the 1970s, Johnsgard (1973), in a review of the literature, reported little renesting in the tetraonids.

Now we can measure accurately the frequency of renesting, based on radiotelemetry. Renesting can also be judged by the distribution of copulations for lek species and by hatching distributions. Using these distributions is valid because females revisit males at leks between first and second nestings to secure viable sperm (Lake 1975, Parker 1981a) and because hatching frequencies in the absence of predation are essentially normally distributed (Fig. 15.9, Hannon 1982). Skewed hatching distributions can result from renesting.

I have calculated the renesting frequency for seven species using the presence of late-hatched broods or second peaks in the frequency of matings (Table 15.3).

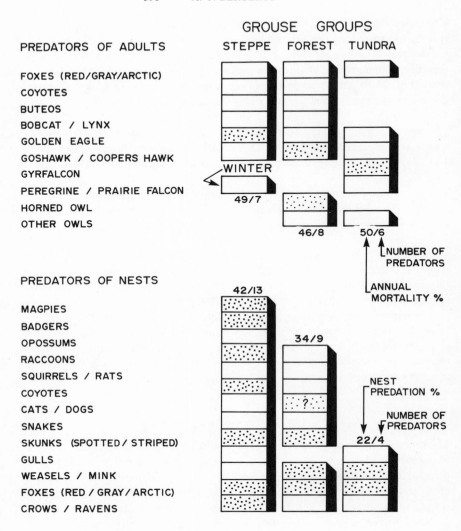

GROUSE GROUPS

PREDATORS OF ADULTS

STEPPE   FOREST   TUNDRA

FOXES (RED/GRAY/ARCTIC)
COYOTES
BUTEOS
BOBCAT / LYNX
GOLDEN EAGLE
GOSHAWK / COOPERS HAWK
GYRFALCON
PEREGRINE / PRAIRIE FALCON
HORNED OWL
OTHER OWLS

WINTER

49/7   46/8   50/6

NUMBER OF PREDATORS

ANNUAL MORTALITY %

PREDATORS OF NESTS

42/13   34/9

MAGPIES
BADGERS
OPOSSUMS
RACCOONS
SQUIRRELS / RATS
COYOTES
CATS / DOGS
SNAKES
SKUNKS (SPOTTED / STRIPED)
GULLS
WEASELS / MINK
FOXES (RED / GRAY / ARCTIC)
CROWS / RAVENS

?

NEST PREDATION %

NUMBER OF PREDATORS

22/4

CAUSES MAJOR MORTALITY

Fig. 15.8. *Top*: For the three grouse groups, the diversity of predators that kill adults is similar, as are mean mortality rates. *Bottom*: The greatest diversity of nest predators is in steppe habitats and the least diversity is in the tundra. Nesting success in steppe < in forest < in tundra.

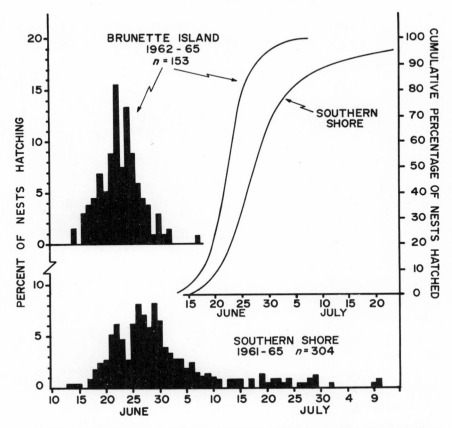

Fig. 15.9. The hatching curve of nests of willow ptarmigan on Brunette Island, Newfound-land, was normally distributed because there was no predation of nests by mammals and little renesting. On the southern shore, Newfoundland, hatching distribution was skewed to the right — to the later dates — because most females renested after their first nests were destroyed by foxes and weasels (Mercer 1967, Bergerud 1970a).

An assumption of this method is that nesting success in first and second attempts is the same. This assumption may not be valid for some species, especially those nesting in the steppe, where cover improves with the growing seasons.

Forest grouse appear to renest less frequently than steppe species (Table 15.3). These grouse face effective predators in forests with little herbaceous growth — they also have small preincubation ranges, with less space than the lek species to move nest locations (Table 14.2).

Radiotelemetry data are not yet available for tundra grouse. Parker (1981b) found that 14 of 56 (25%) willow ptarmigan hens renested when their eggs were removed during *incubation*. Tundra grouse probably have a high inclination to renest — but it has escaped notice since hens are usually successful with their first nests. Also, corvids and weasels (*Mustella* spp.) commonly steal the eggs of ptarmigan one at a time; such a gradual, nontraumatic loss may go undetected by the hen.

Grouse of the steppe show a high propensity to renest (Table 15.3). Nesting

Table 15.3. Estimations of renesting based on radio-tracking females that lost their nests and the sighting of late-hatched young or late matings

Grouse groups and species	% of females that renested		References
	From telemetry	Based on sightings	
Tundra grouse			
Willow ptarmigan		88 (55/249)[a,b]	Bergerud 1970a
Rock ptarmigan		13 (8/201)	Weeden 1965, pers. comm.
White tailed ptarmigan		30 (18/138)	Choate 1963a
Forest grouse			
Ruffed grouse	22 (9)[c]	26 (149/1473)	Maxson 1974, Barrett 1970, Bump et al. 1947
Spruce grouse	10 (10)	20 (3/18)	Ellison 1974, Haas 1974, Keppie 1975b
Blue grouse	26 (31)		Sopuck & Zwickel 1983
Steppe grouse			
Sharp-tailed grouse	86 (14)		Schiller 1973, Christenson 1970
Prairie chicken	83 (6)	72 (609/1655)	Svedarsky 1979, Hamerstrom & Hamerstrom 1973
		59 (32/89)	Robel & Ballard 1974
Sage grouse		43 (≈52/343)	Hartzler 1974
	41 (17)		Petersen 1980

[a] Sample size: 55 females with late-hatched chicks, and 249 females with chicks hatched at normal time. Calculations based on 0.75 nesting success: (a) $249 \times 1.00 = 0.75x$ = 332 females started 1st nests; (b) $332 - 249 = 83$ females failed 1st nests; (c) $55 \times 1.00 = 0.75x$ = 73 females failed 1st nest and started 2nd nests; (d) $73/83 = 88\%$ of the females that failed first nests started 2nd nests.

[b] A check of method is: If 100 hens in Newfoundland hatched first nests at 0.75 (Bergerud 1970a), and 25 unsuccessful hens renested at 0.88 and also had a renesting success of 0.75, females seen with broods in August should be 91.5% (75 hens + 16.5 hens ($25 \times 0.88 \times 0.75$) = 16.5; 91% of the hens seen 1955–65 had chicks ($n = 841$, Bergerud 1970a, p. 308).

[c] 9 hens radio-tracked

success was higher in second attempts than first attempts for sharp-tailed grouse in Minnesota and North Dakota (Christenson 1970, Schiller 1973). Robel (1970) argued that early-nesting prairie chickens had a higher success than later-nesting prairie chickens in Kansas. If drought conditions existed, it is conceivable that residual growth could be denser than new growth. But in years with normal rainfall, nesting success should improve as new cover appears. Schiller (1973) provides convincing arguments of how increased growth can help disperse and conceal renesting attempts.

In general, yearlings renest less often than adults. This has been documented for blue grouse (Sopuck 1979), spruce grouse (McCourt 1969), and sage grouse (Wallestad 1975b). The initial nesting success of radio-tagged, yearling sage grouse in Colorado was 34% (5 of 16) compared with 33% for adults (4 of 12) (cf. Petersen 1980), but the success of both age classes, based on the molt sequency in the harvest for 5 years, was 32% for yearlings and 58% for adults (Braun 1979). This sequence suggests greater renesting in adults.

Yearling hens are generally less successful in concealing their nests (Sopuck 1979, Redmond et al. 1982) and generally have reduced nesting success in forest and steppe populations, which are faced with effective nest predators (Table 15.4). It might benefit the inclusive fitness of yearlings of long-lived populations that lay small clutches to forgo renesting. As adults the next season, they would face less intraspecific constraint in the selection of nest sites. Also they could lay at the optimum time. Yearlings, at least in the blue and spruce grouse, lay their eggs about one week later than do adults (Keppie 1975b, Hannon et al. 1982, Smyth & Boag 1984). As nesting becomes progressively more difficult it could be expected that yearlings would fare less well than experienced adults (Fig. 15.10).

15.4.2 Annual variations in nesting success

All the grouse show variation between years in nesting success. These differences may reflect annual differences in weather as in white-tailed ptarmigan (Braun & Rogers 1971); changes in age structure of nesting females, as in sage grouse (Eng, pers. comm.); and variation between years in predator searching and nesting cover (Chap. 14).

The percentage of yearling females in a population changes from year to year based on prior survival. In a year with few yearlings, nesting success may be higher than in a year when there are many inexperienced yearlings (Eng. pers. comm.). This can be an important density-dependent, dampening mechanism; i.e., the difference between adult and yearling nesting success in Table 15.4 is correlated with the nesting success figures in Table 15.2 ($r = -0.837$, $n = 8$). The variables in this correlation are not strictly independent, but the correlation is still instructive. If sage grouse have a good nesting season in one year, there is more than an even chance that they will be less successful the next. The more

600 A. T. BERGERUD

Table 15.4. Nesting success compared between adults and yearlings based on nests, broods seen, or molt sequence

Grouse groups and species	Sample size	% females successful			References
		Adults	Yearlings	Difference	
Forest grouse					
Ruffed grouse	24 nests	71	61	− 10	Maxson 1974, Barrett 1970
Blue grouse	682 females	81	71	− 10	Redfield 1972
Blue grouse	647 females	73	67	− 6	Hoffman 1979
Blue grouse	911 females	76	53	− 23	Zwickel et al. 1977
Blue grouse	56 nests	38	58	+ 20	Sopuck 1979
Spruce grouse	257 females	41	30	− 11	Keppie 1975b, McCourt 1969
Spruce grouse	48 females	82	44	− 38	Robinson 1980
Spruce grouse	36 nests	48	7	− 41	Redmond et al. 1982
Mean		64	49	− 15	
Steppe grouse					
Sharp-tailed grouse	(no studies)				
Prairie chicken	20 nests	61	43	− 18	Svedarsky 1979
Sage grouse	22 nests	77	44	− 33	Wallestad & Pyrah 1974
Sage grouse	35 nests	41	39	− 3	Petersen 1980
Sage grouse	large wing sample	77	61	− 16	Wallestad & Watts 1972
Sage grouse	large wing sample	58	36	− 22	Braun 1979
Mean		63	44	− 19	
Tundra grouse					
White-tailed ptarmigan	209 females	78	49	− 29	Braun & Rogers 1971
White-tailed ptarmigan	49 nests	58	61	+ 3	Giesen pers. comm.
Rock ptarmigan	57 nests	82	76	− 6	Weeden & Theberge, pers. comm.
Rock ptarmigan	315 females	77	60	− 17	Weeden pers. comm.
Willow ptarmigan	50 nests	83	94	+ 11	Myrberget 1970c
Willow ptarmigan	49 nests	85	74	− 11	Hannon & Smith 1984
Mean		77	69	− 8	

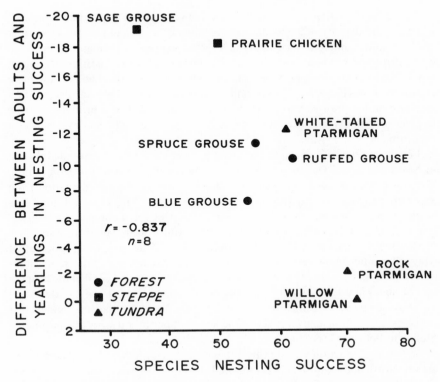

Fig. 15.10. The reduction in nesting success of yearlings from that of adults is greater in species that have lower nesting success. The X and Y axes are not strictly independent. (For references to differences between adult and yearlings see Table 15.4, and for species nesting success see Table 15.2.)

problems a species encounters in nesting, the more yearlings will lag behind experienced adults in being successful, and the more prior production will dampen population changes.

Nesting success should vary between years with the number of predators searching for nests. The New York State inquiry on ruffed grouse documented that nest predation increased when mice populations were low, and predators— mostly foxes—were probably more inclined to hunt for clutches. Weasels are the major predator of nests in many rock ptarmigan populations, and weasel predation was more severe in some years than others, probably in response to a shortage of mice (Weeden & Theberge 1972). Willow ptarmigan in Norway had high losses of eggs in 1963, 1967, and 1979—these losses followed years with high populations of rodents and probably involved more predator searching and reduced nest cover from rodent eat-outs (Chap. 11). A similar sequence has been documented in black grouse (*Tetrao tetrix*) (Angelstam 1983). Prey switch-over can add significant variation in nesting success between years.

Herbaceous nesting cover should vary between years, depending on spring weather, and thereby influence the concealment of nests and rates of predation. This variability should be most important for the steppe species that rely on herbaceous plant cover to hide nests. The prairie grouse commence nesting in residual cover from the previous growing season. While they are incubating, new plant growth becomes increasingly important as the dead material falls and decays. Soil moisture on the prairies varies between years and should be a primary variable in plant growth (Williams & Robertson 1965) because it affects cover and nest concealment.

I evaluated the role of rainfall in breeding success for the sharp-tailed grouse in North and South Dakota and Minnesota by calculating a soil-mixture index. The soil-moisture index was based on summing the monthly precipitation from September in year 1 until July in year 3 (23 months). The 23-month total was needed to account for both residual cover and new cover. I compared this moisture scale to an index of the percentage of successfully nesting hens from statistics of sharp-tailed grouse in North and South Dakota. This index was calculated: [(juveniles/adult in harvest) $\times$ 2 $\div$ mean brood size in late summer]. Assumptions of this index were (1) that all hens attempted to nest and (2) that the proportion of males and females in the population was equal. Next I compared the soil moisture to juveniles/adult ratios in Minnesota. Last, the moisture index was tested by correlation analysis against the late-summer brood sizes of sharp-tailed grouse in both the Dakotas.

Sharptail production was significantly correlated with the soil-moisture index in both North and South Dakota (Fig. 15.11), but not in Minnesota (not shown). The importance of moisture in the variability of plant growth increases as one moves down the rainfall gradient going from east to west (Wiens 1974). Grasslands in Minnesota are less influenced by variations in moisture than those in the central and western Dakotas.

The moisture index was correlated with both the successful nesting hens and chicks/brood statistics for sharptails in the Dakotas (Fig. 15.11). My interpretation is that annual vagaries in plant cover affect predator/grouse interaction both at the nest (nesting success) and with the brood, but that the annual changes in nesting success contribute considerably more to the variabililty in total chick production than does variation in the survival of chicks in broods.

Additional evidence that annual moisture-cover changes affect nesting success in prairie grouse is that there is a higher proportion of adult males in years of low production (Fig. 15.12). This correlation was also satisfactory if I used juveniles per adult male rather than the juveniles/adult figures; the latter would be biased by female deaths. Prairie chicken females in disturbed habitats commonly get killed on the nest (Table 14.6) and this type of ambush could be more frequent when cover was short and sparse or patchy during dry cycles.

An extensive literature substantiates the view that soil moisture affects nesting

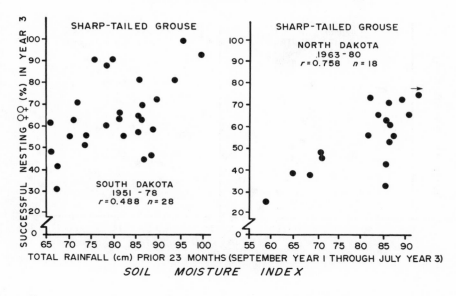

SOIL   MOISTURE   INDEX

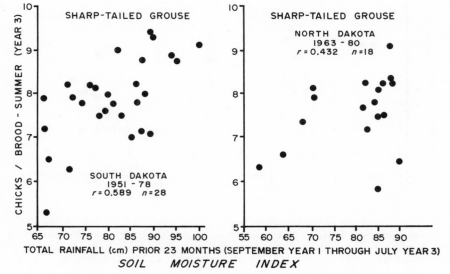

SOIL   MOISTURE   INDEX

Fig. 15.11. Breeding success of sharp-tailed grouse is correlated with soil moisture, which influences plant growth and hence also residual cover. Vegetative cover influences both nesting success and survival of chicks in broods in South and North Dakota. The correlation for juveniles/adult statistics and the moisture index were for South Dakota, $r = 0.608$, $n = 30$ (1949 to 1978), and for North Dakota, $r = 0.553$, $n = 32$ (1949 to 1980).

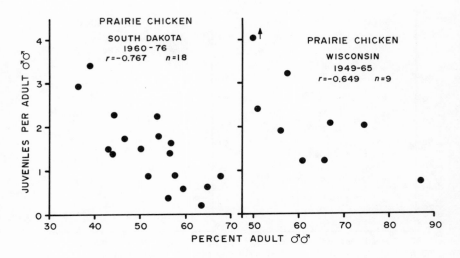

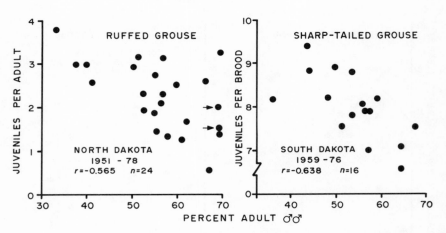

Fig. 15.12. Four grouse populations that showed significant declines in breeding success with an increase in percentage of adult males in the harvest. Summer predation of hens probably occurs in these populatoins and results in unbalanced fall and winter sex ratios of adults. (Grouse data from Hamerstrom & Hamerstrom 1973, Hillman & Jackson 1973, Linde et al. 1978, Schulz 1981.)

cover and the dynamics of grouse. Hamerstrom (1936) and Errington (1935, 1937a) recognized 50 years ago that drought cycles would reduce vegetation cover and increase predation losses of pheasants. Janson (1951) and Wallestad (1975a) mention declining populations of prairie chickens and sage grouse during dry cycles. Breeding success for sage grouse increased in wet years (Carr 1967,

Blake 1970). Several workers have commented on the concentration of nests or broods in dry seasons or following overgrazing. Pheasants in South Dakota showed low productivity in warm, dry springs (Martinson & Grondahl 1966). Wagner (1957) emphasized the low production of pheasants and deaths of hens in dry, warm springs, but felt these losses were caused by physiological stress. However, more recent studies show that females do get killed when nesting cover is sparse. The loss of eggs from dummy pheasant nests to crows in South Dakota was highest early in the season before new growth appears (Grondahl 1956, Mitchell 1957). Mallard (*Anas platyrhynchos*) females are commonly killed on the nest by foxes (Johnson & Sargeant 1977), and the production of dabbling ducks, as in sharptailed grouse, is related to soil moisture (Boyd 1981). A major annual variable in sharp-tailed grouse production, and probably in prairie chickens and sage grouse as well, is the abundance of nesting cover as it is influenced by soil-moisture conditions in regions of low rainfall.

15.4.3 Nesting success and densities

The proportion of young in grouse populations in the fall generally declines as spring numbers increase (Fig. 15.13). This principle of inversity (Errington 1945) is, I believe, commonly a result of density-dependent nest predation. Relevant data to directly evaluate the hypothesis are meager in the grouse literature, but evidence is extensive for other ground-nesting birds that do not defend their nests. Nesting success declined as the spacing of nests diminished in dabbling ducks (cf. Weller 1979, Livezey 1981, Cowardin et al. 1985) and in phasianids (Wagner et al. 1965, Gates 1971, Potts 1980), as well as in shorebirds and passerines (Horn 1968, Krebs 1971, Andersson & Wikund 1978, Page et al. 1983). Tinbergen et al. (1967) conducted the first experiments that demonstrated that dispersion of nests can affect survival from predation. Lack (1968) felt that predation was the driving force in the dispersion of breeding birds in habitats vulnerable to predators. Taylor (1976) has modeled the advantages of the prey's spacing out to avoid predators that search randomly.

Changes in clutch size do not sufficiently explain inversity. Spruce and ruffed grouse populations show inverse rates of gain with density (inversity) (Fig. 15.13), but clutch size is relatively constant (Bump et al. 1947, Keppie 1975b). Lack (1954) and Hickey (1955) felt that changes in adult mortality did not explain inversity.

Invariably, those grouse populations that had production indexes negatively correlated with density were populations that had nest losses greater than 55%. Ptarmigan populations seldom show inversity and they commonly have nest losses less than 40% (Table 15.2).

The percentage of ruffed grouse and spruce grouse hens with broods (% successful nests) decreased significantly with increased spring numbers (Fig. 15.13,

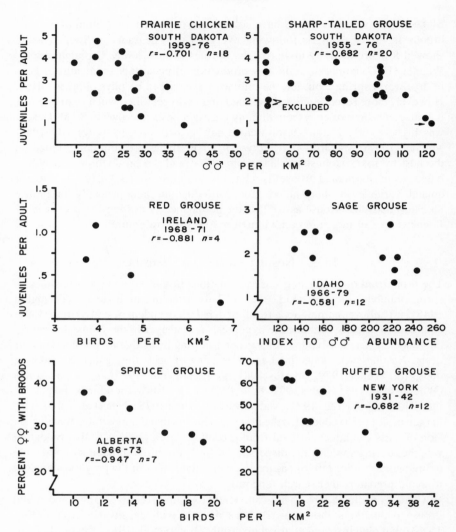

Fig. 15.13. Six grouse populations that demonstrated a decline in breeding success as spring densities increased – i.e., inversity. (Data from Bump et al. 1947, Hillman & Jackson 1973, Linde et al. 1978, Boag et al. 1979, Watson & O'Hare 1979, Autenrieth 1981.) The correlation no longer held for spruce grouse when observations were extended to 1981 (Smyth & Boag 1984). In later years, red squirrels (*Tamiasciurus hudsonicus*), which probably do not hunt in a density-dependent manner, were important predators (Boag et al. 1983).

Bump et al. 1947, Boag et al. 1979). But the percentage of female blue grouse with young was lowest when birds first colonized newly logged habitats on Vancouver Island, and increased with density, contrary to inversity principles

(Zwickel & Bendell 1967, Redfield 1972, Zwickel et al. 1977). This contrary trend is consistent with the density-dependent predator hypothesis; because these habitats were newly logged when first colonized, nest cover increased coincident with population growth and increased density.

The annual nesting success of prairie grouse also declined in three populations as spring numbers increased (Fig. 15.14). The decline was more rapid at high than low densities for the two sharptail populations. For sharptails, the mean proportion of successful nesting hens was 55 $\pm$ 4% (n = 18) in North Dakota and 66 $\pm$ 3% (n = 28) in South Dakota; for prairie chickens in South Dakota, the mean proportion was 64 $\pm$ 6% (n = 19). All three populations generally increased after a year of above-average success and declined when hens were less successful (Fig. 15.14).

Another generalization was that populations that showed inversity had large nest losses from canids. Examples are spruce grouse at Gorge Creek, Alberta, with 30% nesting success and coyotes (*Canis latrans*) the suspected predator (Keppie & Herzog 1978), and ruffed grouse in New York, with 62% success and red fox the major predator. Bump et al. (1947, p. 314) said, "There is some evidence that when high breeding density exists certain animals, particularly the fox, often happen on enough nests to associate the flushing of the bird with the possibility of dining on omelet."

If predators of nests—particularly canids—cause inversity, then areas without effective foxes and coyotes should not show inversity. The red grouse populations are intensively managed in Scotland and fox populations are reduced. The red grouse population shows little inversity relative to summer gains and density (Jenkins et al. 1963, 1967). In Ireland, however, where nesting success is approximately 20% lower and foxes are more common, the summer gains of red grouse were inverse to density (r = -0.989, n = 4; from Watson & O'Hare 1979). In summer, the ruffed grouse population at Connecticut Hill, New York, demonstrated a nesting success that was negatively correlated with breeding numbers (Fig. 15.13), but when foxes and other predators were removed during a 4-year study this summer rate-of-gain was not correlated with density (r = -0.146, n = 4; from Bump et al. 1947, p. 349). The number of juvenile blue grouse in the harvest was inverse to adults in Washington—where foxes are a potential predator–but on Vancouver Island, where foxes are rare, inversity has not been documented in blue grouse (Zwickel & Bendell 1967, Redfield 1973, Zwickel et al. 1977).

The forest grouse can benefit the most, in terms of nesting success, by dispersing under canopies with nest backstops. In steppe habitats, overhead cover is paramount for these species and may compromise spacing between nests in patchy cover, thereby facilitating searching images in predators and leading to reduced nesting success. Inversity should be more apparent in steppe species when populations are high in dry years, when hens are forced to nest closer together.

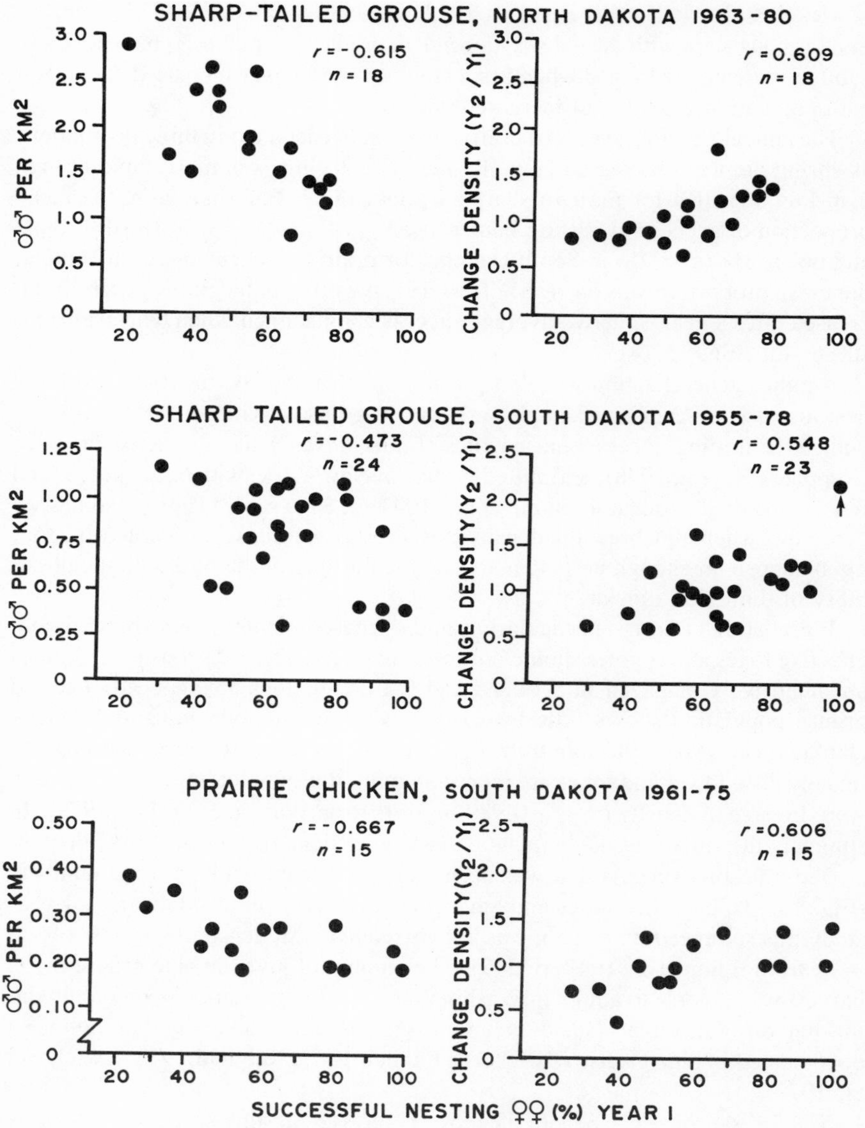

Fig. 15.14. *Left*: In three prairie grouse populations, the proportion of successful nesting females was correlated with density (% successful hens calculated by: [(juveniles/adult × 2) ÷ mean brood size]). *Right*: The proportion of successful females was also correlated with changes in population size. (Data from Hillman & Jackson 1973, Kobriger 1975, 1981, Linde et al. 1978.)

The percentage of yearlings in a populations will affect overall nesting success since yearlings are less successful than adults. As populations increase in density, there will be a greater proportion of yearlings and their productivity will contribute to an inverse relationship between breeding numbers and summer rate-of-gain. This influence is greatest in the steppe grouse where the success rates of yearlings and adults are most disparate (Table 15.4).

In summary, two explanations for inversity in grouse are: (1) nesting success decreases with increasing spring density because the nests are closer together and attract more predator attention and (2) nesting success declines when the proportion of the population comprised of yearlings increases. The first explanation of reduced space between nests seems a dominant factor in forest grouse and the second explanation based on naive yearlings is more appropriate for steppe grouse. However, annual changes in nesting success correlated with density are the common explanations of inversity in both grouse groups.

15.5 Mortality of chicks

Chicks in their first summer die at high rates and the survivors represent production. When the survivors are expressed at the autumn proportion of juveniles to adults (J:A) the parameter is termed *breeding success* (Jenkins et al. 1963) or the *production ratio* (Bump et al. 1947). To understand breeding success, the mortality of chicks must be quantified and the mortality factors determined. I estimated chick mortality by comparing the mean number of eggs per completed clutch with the mean number of chicks in broods at about 2 months of age. This index ignores the fact that some eggs in successful nests do not hatch and that some females successfully hatch their eggs but lose all the chicks. Infertility of eggs is quite constant among species, and represents approximately 8% of all eggs (Johnsgard 1973). Failure to quantify the loss of entire broods means chick mortality is underrepresented by this method.

15.5.1 Mortality rates

The mean mortality rate of chicks between hatch and autumn for the nine species is 44% (28 studies) (see Fig. 15.1). There is no significant difference among the three groups of grouse: forest grouse incur 46.6% ± 3.7% mortality; steppe grouse 40.5% ± 1.9%; and tundra grouse 40.3% ± 3.3% mortality.

The only major differences I have found in mortality of chicks among species within the groups were in spruce grouse (37% ± 2.7%) compared with blue and ruffed grouse (56% ± 6.8%). Within the steppe grouse, prairie chickens appear to have higher mortality rates than either sharp-tailed or sage grouse. The only prairie chicken mortality estimate *less* than 40% was from Michigan (0.27), based on small samples of clutches and broods (Ammann 1957). In comparison, only 2 of 10 studies of sharp-tailed and sage grouse showed chick losses *greater* than 40%.

15.5.2 Mortality factors

The common causes of death of chicks mentioned in the literature are: (1) chilling from weather, (2) predation, and (3) starvation. There is no consensus on the importance of these extrinsic factors. An acceptable explanation must account for the high early loss of chicks that universally occurs before 3 weeks of age (see Fig. 1.3), during the period chicks cannot thermoregulate. Some examples are blue grouse hens, which lost 40% of their charges within 2 weeks of hatching (Zwickel & Bendell 1967); spruce grouse hens had about a 40% loss of chicks when counted at about 40 days posthatch (Keppie 1975b). White-tailed ptarmigan broods were reduced 20%–44% by 2 weeks of age (Choate 1963a, Braun & Rogers 1971).

One problem in determining the causes of death is that few dead chicks are found. In the 13-year, intensive study of ruffed grouse in New York, biologists found only 83 chicks of approximately 4,300 (2%) that died (data from Bump et al. 1947). A second problem in determining the cause of mortality is that many of the decimating agents are interrelated. Cold weather may cause chilling (Myhre et al. 1975), but it may also prevent chicks from feeding while they are brooded (e.g., Boggs et al. 1977, Erikstad & Spidsø 1982), or it can affect plant growth for food or escape requisites and the availability of insects. Thus for all three grouse groups, the evidence directly linking weather and substantial losses is tenuous, especially when we consider that females should be able to brood chicks and insulate them from the extrinsic environment.

Cold spring weather is a common explanation for early mortality before chicks can thermoregulate, especially for ptarmigan (Slagsvold 1975, Marcstrom & Hoglund 1981, Choate 1963a). Dead ptarmigan chicks were found after inclement weather in Alaska and Iceland (Weeden 1965, Gardarsson 1971). But other workers have found no correlation between weather and mortality (Myrberget 1972, Bergerud 1970a, Watson 1965, Weeden & Theberge 1972, Jenkins et al. 1963, and Braun & Rogers 1971). Theberge & West (1973) discounted weather as a factor in mortality for rock ptarmigan young, noting that young chicks need to feed only 6 minutes per hour and can thus be brooded by their mothers at least 90% of the time. Complicating the argument for ptarmigan is that female fidelity in brooding and distraction behavior may vary between hens and cohorts, possibly with chick behavior, independently of weather vicissitudes (Jenkins et al. 1963, Mercer 1967). Also confounding this is evidence that the intrinsic viability of ptarmigan chicks may vary between years (Jenkins et al. 1963, Theberge & Bendell 1980, Bergerud 1970a, Watson & Moss 1980). A further problem is that cool weather could make insects more sluggish and easier to capture, therein compensating for the greater need for brooding (P. Hudson pers. comm.)

The role of unfavorable weather in causing deaths in forest grouse is also argued. Zwickel (1967) felt that cold, wet weather was not a factor in the deaths of young, blue grouse chicks. Storms were thought to result in the loss of some ruffed grouse chicks, but predators and other "undetermined causes" were considered more important (Bump et al. 1947). Survival of ruffed grouse and spruce grouse chicks was higher in warm springs than in cold ones (Larsen & Lahey 1958, Ritcey & Edwards 1963, Dorney & Kabat 1960, Robinson 1980, Fig. 3.8).

The steppe grouse actually showed improved survival of chicks in wet springs, which is especially damaging to the hypothesis that weather causes chick mortality in all cases (Fig. 15.11). Again, heavy rain may cause direct losses (Svedarsky 1979).

Predators certainly take large numbers of chicks; mortality that occurs beyond the thermoregulating interval can possibly be ascribed to predation, but ground predators would be most serious before chicks can fly and thermoregulate. Small chicks are commonly together and thus this period of vulnerability to predators coincides with the known and universal heavy loss of chicks prior to 3 weeks of age.

Chicks are killed mostly by raptors and foxes. Bump et al. (1947, p. 335) listed 46 of 64 ruffed grouse chicks taken by raptors and 16 of 64 taken by foxes. A crow (*Corvus brachyrhynchos*) and weasel each took one chick. A fox disturbed a prairie chicken hen that was brooding her chicks, and the brood hen was lost. The chicks then died from chilling (Svedarsky 1979). Dorney and Kabat (1960) reported larger broods of ruffed grouse in areas of Wisconsin where foxes are less common. On Vancouver Island, where foxes are rare, few blue grouse chicks disappeared after 2 weeks of age (Zwickel & Bendell 1967).

Juveniles/adult ratios were correlated with the adult sex ratio in several studies (Fig. 15.12, Dorney & Kabat 1960). The unbalanced sex ratios probably result from the loss of females to predation. The correlation between fewer females and fewer chicks could be explained by the predation of females, resulting in the death of both the hen and the entire clutch. Predators may kill nesting or brood hens, and the eggs or brood will die from exposure; when predation is heavy, females and chicks may be killed independently. These correlations between sex ratios and breeding success suggest that predation can be a sufficient cause of changing survival of chicks.

If predation was a serious factor, one might predict that brood mortality would increase with clutch size. Large broods would be more conspicuous and more difficult to defend. But the mortality of chicks was not correlated with clutch size (Fig. 15.1). A large sample of brood sizes for sharp-tailed grouse in North Dakota was normally distributed (Kobriger 1981). Chicks from larger-than-average clutches survived as well as chicks from smaller clutches. A female can expect to raise one additional chick if she can afford the cost of two additional eggs (Fig. 15.1).

Some studies have been conducted in areas where predators have been reduced; others have been conducted on islands where there were few predators.

In all cases a considerable percentage of chicks disappeared between hatching and the fall (Fig. 15.15). Further, I regressed summer mortality of chicks against nest predation (%) for 34 studies and found no correlation ($r = 0.268$); there was also no correlation between chick mortality and increasing latitude and reduced predator diversity ($r = 0.184$, $n = 34$). Predation of chicks is a sufficient but not necessary explanation of the high, constant mortality of chicks in the first 3 weeks of life.

Many authors must feel that grouse chicks starve — students commonly measure the abundance of arthropods. Bump et al. (1947) felt that invertebrates for chicks were superabundant at about $75/m^2$. Barrett (1970) was more concerned about a shortage of insects for ruffed grouse even though he measured 210 invertebrates/m^2 in habitats where young broods traveled. If females seek to nest as early as inconspicuousness permits (Chap. 14), it does not necessarily follow that chicks would hatch coincident with a flush of chick food (cf. Elliot 1979).

But the vagaries in insect foods may be a major influence on chick survival. The growth rate of chicks has been shown to vary between years for willow ptarmigan (Mercer 1967, Myrberget et al. 1977, Erikstad 1985), blue grouse (Redfield 1978), and spruce grouse (Quinn & Keppie 1981). These differences in growth rates appear to relate more to posthatch weather than to prehatch factors, i.e., female nutrition (Myrberget et al. 1977, Redfield 1978, Quinn & Keppie 1981). Temperature can be expected to influence insect abundance as well as the competition of thermoregulatory processes for metabolizing energy (Ricklefs 1972). When insects were scarce for ruffed grouse and ptarmigan, the broods moved farther (Barrett 1970, Erikstad 1978), and brood survival decreased with increased mobility, in both ptarmigan and blue grouse (Armleder 1980, Erikstad 1978). Wet, cool springs may provide more cover and insects for the steppe grouse; warm, dry springs may do likewise for forest grouse living in more shaded, mesic communities.

I found in my blue grouse study (Chap. 2) that chicks survived less well on Portland Island, where there was thick undergrowth, than on Moresby Island, where logging had occurred. Blue grouse populations generally declined as canopies closed in (Redfield et al. 1970), and brood sizes were generally lower at Middle Quinsam than at Comox Burn, when Middle Quinsam was at a late stage of succession (see section 15.7.5). Armleder (1980) documented fewer insects in blue grouse habitats as forest canopies increased.

The detailed laboratory studies of Jørgensen and Blix (1985) of ptarmigan chicks explain much of the weather-food paradox in chick survival. They showed that chicks had the same browsing time whether the temperature was 2°C or 12°C, and this browsing time exceeded the lower critical minimum of 6 min/hr (Theberge & West 1973). Chicks always tried to fill their crops, and thus they were unable to compensate for increased energy expenditure and a reduced food quality in a spring with late phenology and reduced insect abundance. Jørgensen

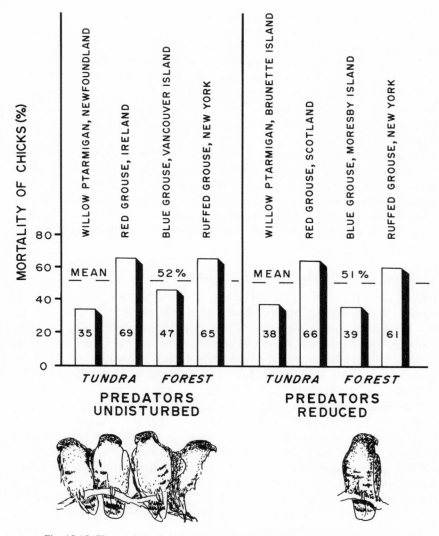

Fig. 15.15. The survival of chicks in four populations where predators were reduced was similar to that in four closely related populations where predators were left undisturbed (Bump et al. 1947, Jenkins et al. 1963, Mercer 1967, Bergerud 1970a, Zwickel et al. 1977, Watson & O'Hare 1979, Chap. 2).

and Blix concluded that the availability of high-quality food was critical for growth and survival, and low ambient temperatures, if they did not affect food quality and intake, were of little consequence.

The reduction of insect populations has occurred following chemical spraying programs. The English workers (Southwood & Cross 1969, Potts 1980) saw a clear connection between production in Hungarian partridge and DDT. Early survival was reduced in ruffed grouse broods in areas in New Brunswick that were sprayed for spruce budworm, compared to unsprayed areas in control blocks (Neave & Wright 1969).

Grouse should have evolved physiological and life-history schedules to hurry through critical life-history stages (Williams 1966a). The need for a high-protein diet for thermoregulation and rapid growth is not liable to compromise (Wise 1982). Variations in weather, maternal behavior, and intrinsic viability may all influence survival, but the abundance of insect supplies or other high-quality food in good cover may be the necessary pacemaker to successfully pass through the critical, first 2 weeks of life.

15.5.3 Density-dependence of mortality

If chick mortality was density-dependent, it would help to buffer population changes. Another possibility for density-dependent mortality is that yearlings may be less successful mothers. In high populations there would be more yearlings, who might raise fewer chicks per female; however, the difference in brood size noted between yearlings and adults appears explicable on the basis of differences in clutch size, rather than different brood survival (Zwickel et al. 1977, Keppie 1975b).

One explanation for density-dependent mortality of chicks relates to the spacing of nests. At least in spruce and blue grouse, females space their nests; at high numbers more females may be in more marginal habitats (Sopuck 1979) and may need to take their broods farther to find suitable insect and cover habitats. Yearling blue grouse females travel farther initially with their broods than do adults (Sopuck 1979, Armleder 1980). Increased movement might stress the chicks, or it might result in contact with more predators (Fig. 14.15). Blue grouse had increased mortality with increased movement and large home ranges (Armleder 1980). This explanation for a relationship between density and chick survival would seem most applicable to forest grouse, and least to steppe grouse, which may nest near each other and often take their chicks long distances (Schiller 1973, Svedarsky 1979).

Chick mortality is not correlated with breeding densities in rock ptarmigan ($r = -0.224$, $n = 11$; Weeden & Theberge 1972); willow ptarmigan ($r = 0.105$, $n = 9$; Bergerud 1970a) or ruffed grouse ($r = 0.452$, $n = 13$; Bump et al. 1947, pp. 527, 539). Also, there is no correlation between size of the brood and density in white-tailed ptarmigan ($r = -0.406$, $n = 18$; Braun & Rogers 1971); spruce grouse ($r = -0.380$, $n = 14$; Smyth & Boag 1984); or prairie chickens ($r = 0.009$, $n = 18$; Sisson 1976, Robertson 1979). Nor is there a correlation for sharp-tailed grouse in Nebraska ($r = 0.209$, $n = 18$; Sisson 1976, Robertson 1979, Mitchell & Vodehnal 1982); North Dakota ($r = 0.275$, $n = 18$; Kobriger 1975, and government reports); or South Dakota ($r = 0.411$, $n = 24$; Hillman & Jackson 1973, Rice & Carter 1976, Linde et al. 1978). These data provide little evidence for density-dependent mortality of chicks.

15.6 Mortality of juveniles and adults

This discussion to this point has centered on parameters that affect breeding success: (1) percentage of hens nesting, (2) clutch size, (3) nesting success, and (4) survival of chicks in their first summer. All contribute to the abundance of the new generation and recruitment (m_x). These additions are balanced in stable populations by the deaths of juveniles—birds from 4 to 10 months of age—and of adults. This section focuses on mortality rates of juvenile and adult birds (q_x). I emphasize mortality rather than survival rates (s_x), because the factors that cause death are more tractable than those which contribute to the absence of death and continued survival.

15.6.1 Mortality factors

Grouse die from many causes, but predation accounts for 85% of reported mortalities (Table 15.5). The importance of predation has been further documented in numerous telemetry investigations. There may be biases—a bird that is weak from disease or starvation may be more susceptible to predation, or a bird with a radio harness may not be the equal of a bird without. Still, many workers have argued that results from radio tracking are representative—at least after initial losses—and one can always compare mortality rates between tagged and untagged birds to evaluate these assertions. Accidents are the second most common cause of mortality. These fatalities are usually the direct intrusion of humans into the birds' environment with power lines, fences, highways, and other constructions. No cause of death was determined for a large class of dead birds. The birds may have died from disease—generally such birds are not emaciated. Documented cases of starvation are exceedingly rare. Apparently red grouse die from both disease and starvation—females have even been found dead on the nest (Jenkins et al. 1963, 1967), but these red grouse populations live in extremely dense populations where the natural predators have been reduced. These results cannot be extrapolated to more natural populatons with normal assortments and densities of predators.

Table 15.5. Causes of mortality of North American grouse
(excluding hunting and accidents from research)

Grouse groups and species	Sample size of birds	% of mortality				
		Raptor predation	Mammal predation	Unknown predation	Accidents	Other
Tundra grouse						
Willow ptarmigan	50	mostly gyrfalcon	a few by foxes	—	—	—
Rock ptarmigan	278	96% gryfalcon and foxes	—	—	4	—
Rock ptarmigan	9	100	—	—	—	—
White-tailed ptarmigan	44	59	20	—	9	11
Forest grouse						
Ruffed grouse	642	70	24	—	3	3
Ruffed grouse	186	72	12	8	8	—
Ruffed grouse	72	79	10	1	4	3
Ruffed grouse	107	73	25	—	2	—
Ruffed grouse	13	77	23	—	—	—
Ruffed grouse	26	54	12	—	35	—
Spruce grouse	19	95	5	—	—	—
Spruce grouse	18	39	44	—	6	—
Blue grouse	77	57	4	35	—	4
Steppe grouse						
Sharp-tailed grouse	28	4	50	46	—	—
Prairie chicken	10	30	70	—	—	—
Prairie chicken	20	16	43	40	—	5
Sage grouse	10	10	30	40	20	—
Approximate means	1,591	58	27	—	10	5

Sources: *Willow ptarmigan* — Mossop Chap. 10; *Rock ptarmigan (278)* — Weeden 1965; *Rock ptarmigan (9)* — Gardasson 1971; *White-tailed ptarmigan* — Braun and Rogers 1971; *Ruffed grouse (642)* — Bump et al. 1947; *Ruffed grouse (186)* — Eng & Gullion 1962; *Ruffed grouse (72)* — Huempfner pers. comm.; *Ruffed grouse (107)* — Rusch & Keith 1971b; *Ruffed grouse (13)* — Maxson 1974; *Ruffed grouse (26)* — Hager 1954; *Spruce grouse (19)* — Ellison 1971, 1974; *Spruce grouse (18)* — Robinson 1980; *Blue grouse* — Hines 1986a; *Sharp-tailed grouse* — Hart et al. 1950; *Prairie chicken (10)* — Svedarski 1979; *Prairie chicken (20)* — Schwartz 1945; *Sage grouse* — Nelson 1955.

15.6.2 Mortality rates

I calculated the mortality rate of juvenile birds 4 to 10 months of age in populations based on: (1) band returns, (2) counts of juveniles in the fall versus yearlings in the spring, and (3) by combining adult mortality and the fall breeding success (J/A) needed to stabilize numbers. The formula was [1.00 − (annual adult mortality/juvenile per adult needed to stabilize breeding numbers)]. To illustrate method 2, the rock ptarmigan at Eagle Creek had an average of 395 juveniles/year from August 1960 to 1970 and 136 yearlings the subsequent springs. $J_{q_x} = (395 - 136)/395 = 0.66$. Based on method 3, the juvenile mortality rate was 0.69; the number of August young/adult needed to maintain breeding numbers was 1.87, and the adult annual mortality rate was 0.58: $[1.00 - (0.58/1.87)]$. All three mortality methods are based on the assumption that birds still alive the next spring will return and be identified. This assumption is probably violated in some studies of open populations.

The mortality rate of adults was calculated (1) from yearlings/adult ratios that result in stable populations (Hickey 1955), (2) based on band recoveries (life-table analysis), or (3) comparing the number of adults and yearlings in year 1 with number of adults in year 2. None of the methods permit a distinction between natural and hunting deaths. The adult mortality calculations are more robust than the juvenile rates since yearlings and adults that have bred once can be expected to return in later years if still alive (Chap. 14).

The mortality rates for juvenile birds over winter averaged 50%–70% (Table 15.6) and were generally about 15% greater than adult mortality rates. Juvenile birds are naive when broods disband and should be more conspicuous than adults in seeking winter cover, joining winter flocks, and finding their first breeding locations. Also juveniles may be more vulnerable than adults to fall hunting. This is especially relevant to ruffed grouse (Dorney 1963, Rusch & Keith 1971b).

The most unusual mortality rate for juveniles was a low 13 percent winter loss of spruce grouse at Gorge Creek, Alberta (Table 15.6). This mortality rate was based both on banded birds (the survival of 123 of 141 juveniles in three winters (Keppie 1979) and on the stabilizing recruitment method. By the latter method, adult mortality equaled 32.5 (Boag et al. 1979) and stabilizing recruitment for the years 1966–73 was 0.37; hence $[1.00 - (0.325/0.37)]$ the juvenile mortality was 0.12. Conversely, this population had one of the highest known losses of nests for forest grouse, 45 of 64 nests (70%) (Redmond et al. 1982). The population was able to persist in the face of this high nest loss because of the high survival of juveniles and adults.

Mortality rates for adult grouse ranged from about 25% to over 75% (Fig. 15.4). Unlike with egg losses there was no significant difference in the mean mortality rates of grouse between steppe, forest, and tundra groups, and all the grouse face similar assortments of predators (Fig. 15.8). Hunted populations had higher losses than unhunted populations (Fig. 15.4) suggesting that hunting was additive (see section 16.3).

15.6.3 Bimodalism of mortality rates

The mortality rates of grouse fall into two distinct modes: a low mortality mode of less than 45% and a high mode of greater than 45% (Fig. 15.4, Table 15.6).

Table 15.6. Comparison of clutch size and mortality rates for grouse

Grouse group and species	Clutch size	Mortality rates				Total q_x of new ♀♀ to = loss of ♀♀
		Nest	Chick	Juvenile	Adult ♀♀	
Tundra grouse:						
White-tailed ptarmigan (Colo.)	5.9	0.43	0.42	0.60	0.41	0.86[a]
White-tailed ptarmigan (Mont.)	5.2	0.30	0.44	0.58	0.44	0.83
Rock ptarmigan (Iceland)	11.0	0.08	0.35	0.81	0.46	0.92
Rock ptarmigan (Alaska)	7.5	0.31	0.47	0.69	0.56	0.85
Willow ptarmigan (Nfld.)	10.2	0.25	0.35	0.79	0.50	0.90
Willow ptarmigan (B.C.)	7.3	0.12	0.33	–	0.54	0.85
Forest Grouse:						
Ruffed grouse (Minn.)	10.9	0.39	0.67	0.55	0.66	0.89
Ruffed grouse (Alta.)	11.0	0.23	0.47	–	0.64	0.88
Spruce grouse (Alta.)	4.8	0.71	0.33	0.13	0.34	0.86
Spruce grouse (Mich.)	5.7	0.22	0.32	0.71	0.55	0.81
Spruce grouse (Alaska)	7.6	0.19	0.28	0.77	0.57	0.85
Blue grouse (B.C.)	6.4	0.45	0.47	0.50	0.31	0.90
Steppe Grouse:						
Prairie chicken (Wisc.)	12.0	0.50	–	–	0.56	0.91
Sharp-tailed grouse (Mich.)	12.1	0.30	0.36	–	0.70	0.88
Sharp-tailed grouse (N.B.)	12.8	0.46	0.39	0.63	0.63	0.90
Sage grouse (Colo.)	7.0	0.59	0.29	–	0.37	0.89
Means	8.6	0.35	0.38	0.62	0.51	0.88
Coefficient of Variation	32%	49%	27%	31%	22%	4%

[a] 100 females lay 580 eggs of which 290 are females; 41 adult females die. Total mortality of new females to equal annual loss of adult females $(290–41)/290 = 0.86$.

Sources: *Tundra grouse*—Choate 1963a,b, Braun 1969, Bergerud 1970a, Braun & Rogers 1971, Gardarsson 1971, Weeden & Theberge 1972, Giesen et al. 1980, Hannon 1982, Mossop pers. comm. *Forest grouse*—Kupa 1966, Gullion & Marshall 1968, Gullion 1970, Ellison 1974, Zwickel 1975, Zwickel et al. 1977, Keppie 1979, Boag et al. 1979, Robinson 1980, Zwickel et al. 1983, Rusch et al. 1984. *Steppe grouse*—Hamerstrom 1939, Ammann 1957, Hamerstrom & Hamerstrom 1973, Kohn 1976, Braun 1979, Kobriger 1981, Petersen 1980.

These mortality rates are for populations rather than for species. There are ruffed grouse, spruce grouse, and blue grouse populations with mortality rates below 45%, and other populations with mortality rates above 45%. Sage grouse females in Colorado die at a rate $\leq 40\%$, but in Montana, where the clutch size is larger mortality rates are 60% (Wallestad 1975b, Braun 1979). The two white-tailed ptarmigan populations that have been studied in Colorado and Montana both fall into the low mortality mode (Choate 1963a, Braun & Rogers 1971), but white-

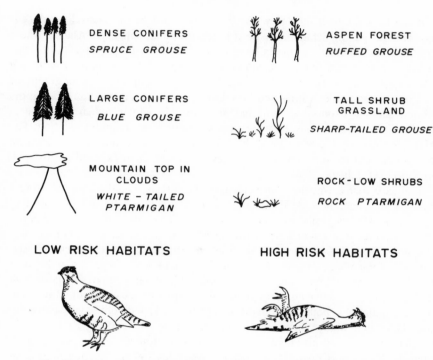

DENSE CONIFERS
SPRUCE GROUSE

ASPEN FOREST
RUFFED GROUSE

LARGE CONIFERS
BLUE GROUSE

TALL SHRUB
GRASSLAND
SHARP-TAILED GROUSE

MOUNTAIN TOP IN
CLOUDS
*WHITE - TAILED
PTARMIGAN*

ROCK-LOW SHRUBS
ROCK PTARMIGAN

LOW RISK HABITATS

HIGH RISK HABITATS

Fig. 15.16. Comparison of the escape features of three low-risk habitats and three high-risk habitats.

tailed ptarmigan farther north, in British Columbia and Alaska, occupy ranges with gyrfalcons and can be expected to have higher mortality rates. Young white-tailed ptarmigan broods in northern British Columbia averaged seven chicks; hence, clutches would have to be eight or nine, and mortality may be greater than 45% (Fig. 15.2).

The low and high mortality modes can be explained by differences in the predation of adults. The low-mortality populations live either where there are few raptors or in habitats where they are relatively safe from these predators (Fig. 15.16). High-mortality populations face more raptors and/or live in less secure habitats.

Spruce grouse populations may be in either the high or low mortality mode. Spruce grouse in southwestern Alberta face high predation of nests—70%—but have low mortality rates of adults—less than 33% (Boag et al. 1979, Redmond et al. 1982). Spruce grouse on the Kenai Peninsula, Alaska, lose few nests but the mean longevity of adult birds is short: 276 days versus 1,022 days for Alberta birds (calculated from Ellison 1974, Herzog 1978, Boag et al. 1979). Both populations lose few chicks in the summer—28% and 33%, respectively (Table 15.6).

Females have a higher mortality rate than males in Alberta, where losses occur mostly in the summer, but males die at faster rates than females in Alaska, where mortality occurs mostly in the fall and winter (Ellison 1974, Keppie 1979). The grouse in Alberta live in a closed canopy of dense pine (*Pinus contorta*) averaging 3,936 stems per ha (Boag et al. 1979). The weakest link in the demography of Alberta grouse is the nesting and brooding seasons, when they must be on the ground and are exposed to mammal predators. In winter, when they live in conifers in the thick forests, they are almost invulnerable to raptor predation. The Alaska grouse, on the other hand, have few mammals to contest with when on the ground, but the more-open forest canopies leave them exposed to goshawk predation (cf. Ellison 1974).

I suggest that it was the dense stems of the forests inhabited by the Alberta grouse rather than the lack of predators that accounted for the superior survival rates of the Alberta grouse over the Alaska birds. Two other spruce grouse populations also have low mortality—birds in Montana (Stoneberg 1967) and Minnesota (Anderson 1973, Haas 1974). Both populations inhabited dense forests. Females in the Minnesota population quickly sought dense forest when they lost their broods. Additional evidence that secure environments can make up for high predation pressure is that adjacent to the Alberta spruce grouse are ruffed and blue grouse populations, both living in more open habitats, and both having mortality rates 17%–24% higher than those of spruce grouse (Boag 1966, 1976b).

Adult white-tailed ptarmigan in Colorado and Montana have low mortality rates of 29%–33% (Choate 1963a, Braun 1969, May 1975). All other ptarmigan populations studied have died at annual rates of approximately 50% or more (Watson 1965, Bergerud 1970a, Gardarsson 1971, Weeden & Theberge 1972, Myrberget 1975b, 1976b). The mortality rates of white-tailed ptarmigan can be explained on the basis of low predation from raptors. First, they are hunted mostly by prairie falcons (*Falco mexicanus*) and golden eagles (*Aquila chrysaetos*), the very effective predators—gyrfalcons and peregrine falcons (*Falco peregrinus*) are absent from these southern habitats. Second, white-tailed ptarmigan frequent rock fields of approximately their body size (Schmidt 1969, May 1975). Their strategy is to squat and crouch adjacent to or beneath such rocks. These ptarmigan are inconspicuous and difficult to detect in such situations. Third, the birds are distributed in widely scattered, small patches on high mountains. This dispersal requires raptors to distribute themselves coarse-grained relative to the patches of birds—they must spend time traveling between patches and cannot afford to be as specialized for ptarmigan as are gyrfalcons in more continuous distributions in the arctic. Finally, whitetails live high in the mountains in heavy cloud cover, which hinders raptors. Sometimes they are safe from raptors for days on end. It is this unique, safe mountain habitat exploited by the white-tails that has provided them with their low, annual mortality rate.

Rock, white-tailed, and willow ptarmigan are found in the same mountain ranges in northern British Columbia (Weeden 1959b), where gyrfalcons hunt them. Even here, white-tailed ptarmigan are less vulnerable to raptors. The gyrfalcons at Chilkat Pass, British Columbia, commonly hunt from perches of approximately 1,200 m in elevation (Mossop pers. comm.). These rock ledges are below the elevation used by whitetails and at the same elevations as the rock ptarmigan (Fig. 15.17). Both species are therefore relatively safe from attack from above.

Blue grouse on Vancouver Island are another of the long-lived populations. Goshawks and eagles are the common raptors—blue grouse are likely too large for Cooper's hawks. Blue grouse, like spruce grouse, live in conifers in winter. Birds are able to sit high in dense foliage and eat needles without exposure. As noted in Chapter 14, birds are often close to the main stem and surrounded by branches. The birds do not have to go to the ground to snow roost. In contrast, ruffed grouse visit leafless aspen trees early and late in the day to feed when light is least favorable for raptors, and depend on snow-roosting for cover overnight (Fig. 4.7). In some years there is inadequate snow for roosting, and mortality rates increase. The needle/conifer habitat is responsible for the low mortality rates of some blue and spruce grouse populations compared to ruffed grouse.

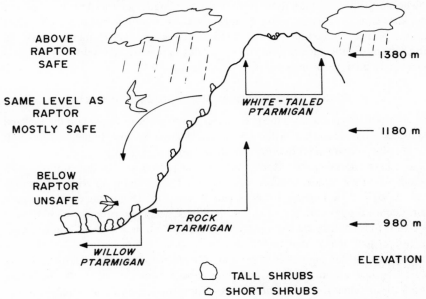

Fig. 15.17. Gyrfalcons at Chilkat Pass, British Columbia, commonly hunt from perches at about 1,200-m altitude. Perches are below the habitats frequented by white-tailed ptarmigan and at the same elevation as terrain inhabited by rock ptarmigan. White-tailed and rock ptarmigan are relatively safe because gyrfalcons search below them on the valley bottom for willow ptarmigan. Mountain outline and ptarmigan distribution from Weeden (1959a).

One ruffed grouse population living along the shores of Puget Sound in Washington shows a low mortality rate. Brewer (1980) provides an annual mortality rate of approximately 23% for 31 banded, ruffed grouse males. In this example, the forest did not provide cover, since it was relatively open and logged (Salo 1978), having perhaps only 500 stems per ha, which is well within the hunting tolerance of goshawks (Reynolds et al. 1982). However, the area lies outside the breeding range of goshawks (Cramp et al. 1980). Thus the low mortality rate results from the lack of predators, and not from effective cover.

This predator/cover hypothesis predicts that the survival rates of individuals will be improved if the effective raptor populations are substantially reduced. In Scotland, two raptors of red grouse — goshawks and peregrine falcons — no longer hunt red grouse, and red fox populations have also been lowered on many intensely managed moors. Red grouse lay clutches of approximately 7 eggs (Jenkins et al. 1963) and their predicted natural mortality rate should be about 45% (Fig. 15.2). Consistent with this reduction in predation, the mortality rate of the lightly hunted, Kerlock population (1962–65) was only 39%, calculated from Jenkins et al. (1967). The predation/cover hypothesis also predicts that the grouse in North America living south of the goshawk distribution should have lower mortality rates than those farther north. Male lesser and Attwater's prairie chickens can be expected to have mortality rates less than that reported for the greater prairie chicken in Wisconsin (53%, Hamerstrom & Hamerstrom 1973). The return of Attwater's prairie chicken males to their former leks in Texas was 65%; only 35% were missing (n = 20; Jurries 1981).

15.6.4 Mortality rates and reproductive risk

An alternative hypothesis to the predator/cover hypothesis to explain the low and high mortality modes is that these differences arise because females with small clutches have lower reproductive risks than females with large clutches. Females have a high mortality rate during the nesting period and in the summer with broods when they frequent short, open cover. The mortality of chicks in broods is about 40%–50% independently of clutch size (Fig. 15.1); therefore, a female that hatches 6 eggs can expect to lose 3 chicks, whereas a female with 12 will lose 6. If these chicks die from predation, the risk to a hen with 12 chicks might be greater than that to one with a smaller brood.

One index of female risk is to compare the observed number of females dying in nesting and brood activities, with the expected number of deaths based on prorating the annual survival of the population (both males and females) to the total number of days that females have been monitored nesting and raising chicks. The reproductive-risk index is the observed deaths of hens divided by the expected deaths.

All six polygynous grouse species have been radio-monitored during the summer reproductive season, and the deaths of females are known. The sample is undoubtedly biased by the radio-tracking technique, but this bias should allow a comparison of reproductive risk between the low and high clutch modes. Females of the high clutch mode—prairie chicken, ruffed grouse, and sharp-tailed grouse —were monitored in Minnesota, and all suffered significantly greater mortality during the reproductive period than that expected, based on the annual survival statistics (Table 15.7). In contrast, three populations with small clutches—spruce grouse in Alberta, blue grouse on Vancouver Island, and sage grouse in Colorado—had approximately the same number of deaths per time unit as would be expected based on the annual survival rate (Table 15.7). The correlation between reproductive risk and clutch size is $r = 0.943$ $(n = 6)$.

Is this clutch-mortality correlation one of cause and effect, or are clutch and mortality parameters correlated because they are both causal with a third factor? I have called this third factor the predator-cover complex (Fig. 15.3). The three populations within the high clutch mode live in the steppe or in deciduous forests and have high mortality rates (Table 15.6). Blue and spruce grouse, with the low clutch mode, live in conifer forests and have a low mortality rate. Sage grouse females with small clutches also live in open habitats and have low mortality rates, but the mortality rate of the male sage grouse is similar to that of the species with large clutches (Braun 1979). Sexual dimorphism in sage grouse may deflect predators from less conspicuous females to males.

The cause-effect dilemma between clutch size and survival may be evaluated

Table 15.7. Number of radio-tracked females observed to die from predation during the breeding season compared with the number expected to die prorating the annual mortality rate to the time period radio-tracked.

Clutch mode and species	Clutch size	Days radio tracked[a]	Different females[b]	♀♀ that died Obs.	♀♀ that died Exp.[c]	Risk (O/E)
High mode						
Prairie chicken	13.5	1,192	21	11[d]	2.5	4.4
Sharp-tailed grouse	12.5	1,018	15	8	2.3	3.5
Ruffed grouse	11.0	2,420	17	12	5.0	2.4
Low mode						
Spruce grouse	4.7	1,718	29	2	2.0	1.0
Blue grouse	6.4	4,661	49	6	4.6	1.3
Sage grouse	7.0	2,361	42	2	2.8	0.7

[a] Major references for radio tracking: Schiller 1973, Haas 1974, Maxson 1974, Herzog 1977a, 1979, Sopuck 1979, Svedarsky 1979, Petersen 1980.

[b] Some radio-tracked females excluded from sample in most studies for a variety of reasons.

[c] Expected calculated (total days tracked/ [-0.4343/log. s_x] [365]).

[d] Figures are conservative because many terminations of radio-tracked females were probably caused by predation but were not considered dead unless radio or carcass was found.

by looking at the mortality rates of males, which in these populations do not assist females in their reproductive effort. If mortality rates of males are vastly different than those of females, female reproductive risk could be the causal factor in the differences in the low and high modes; but if male mortality parallels that of females, the predator-cover complex, which they both share, can be hypothesized to be the causal factor.

The annual mortality rates for the low clutch populations are: (1) spruce grouse in Alberta, males 28% versus females 37% (Keppie 1975b, Boag et al. 1979); (2) blue grouse on Moresby Island, males 32% versus females 26%; at Middle Quinsan, Vancouver Island, males 31% versus females 33%; at Comox Burn, Vancouver Island, males 25% versus females 29% (Chap. 2, Boag et al. 1979, Robinson 1980, Zwickel et al. 1983); and (3) sage grouse in Colorado, males 57% and females 37% (Braun 1979). For the high clutch mode the mortality rates for prairie chickens in Wisconsin are males 53% versus females 56% (Hamerstrom & Hamerstrom 1973). There are no mortality figures for ruffed grouse females; males commonly have annual mortality rates of approximately 50% ± 5% (Table 3.2, Dorney & Kabat 1960, Gullion & Marshall 1968, Rusch et al. 1984). The adult sex ratio in ruffed grouse is generally 55% males and 45% females (Table 15.8), or a mortality rate for females of approximately 56%. There are no natural mortality rates for unhunted, sharp-tailed grouse populations. The proportion of adult males to females in the harvest is commonly 55:45 (Table 15.8). Male and female sharp-tailed grouse banded in South Dakota had similar mortality rates (Robel et al. 1972).

The difference in the mortality rates of males between the low and high clutch modes is about 20% (35% versus 55%), but within populations, there is little difference in mortality between males and females. Only in the sage grouse is the difference between male and female mortality rates (20%) similar to the difference between the low and high mortality rates of females (20%). This lack of difference in mortality between males and females supports the view that the greater mortality rate of grouse with large clutches compared to those with smaller clutches is not cause and effect. The greater mortality of birds with larger clutches likely results from the less secure, predator-cover complex of their habitat.

15.6.5 Differential mortality of males and females

Parental investment differs between males and females. Males advertise for females and invest little in care of the young, but females nest and defend their young, and direct their movement. Hence, the two sexes have different mortality regimes and there is no theoretical reason for equal proportions of male and female adults in a population (cf. Angelstam 1984). On Moresby Island, British Columbia, the male:female ratio in 1975 of the blue grouse raised on the island

Table 15.8. Proportion of males in harvested collections and birds trapped in the winter (sample size in parenthesis)

Grouse groups and species (place)	% males Juveniles	Adults	References
Tundra grouse			
Willow ptarmigan (Nfld.)	51 (1633)	55 (917)	Bergerud 1970a
Willow ptarmigan (Fin.)	51 (482)	62 (595)	Pulliainen 1975
Rock ptarmigan (Ice.)	48 (14943)	47 (5009)	Gardarsson 1971
White-tailed ptarmigan (Col.)	45 (66)	65 (233)	Braun & Rogers 1971
Unweighed means	49	57	
Forest grouse			
Blue grouse (B.C.)	46 (2502)	–	Zwickel et al. 1975
Blue grouse (Wash.)	47 (302)	47+ (303)	Zwickel & Brigham 1970
Spruce grouse (Ont.)	49 (766)	55 (423)	Lumsden & Weeden 1963
Ruffed grouse (Mass.)	51 (680)	57 (600)	Hager 1954
Ruffed grouse (Ohio)	51 (12971)	55 (5365)	Dorney 1963
	49 (2972)	59 (2562)	Davis & Stoll 1973
Ruffed grouse (N.D.)	53 (2496)	55 (1265)	Schulz 1981
Ruffed grouse (B.C.)	51 (1753)	60 (813)	Chap. 3
Ruffed grouse (Alb.)	53 (1000)	59 (264)	Rusch & Keith 1971[b]
Ruffed grouse (Alb.)	51 (341)	53 (793)	Hilton & Wishart 1981
Unweighed means	50	56	
Steppe grouse			
Sharp-tailed grouse (Alb.)	50 (2623)	47 (1781)	Hilton & Wishart 1981
Sharp-tailed grouse (N.D.)	49 (28777)	51 (16693)	Kobriger 1981
Sharp-tailed grouse (S.D.)	54 (5324)	52 (2263)	Robel et al. 1972
Sharp-tailed grouse (Mich.)	56 (2018)	60 (889)	Ammann 1957
Prairie chicken (Kan.)	55 (306)	55 (298)	Baker 1953
Prairie chicken (Wis.)	62 (950)	63 (740)	Hamerstrom & Hamerstrom 1973
Prairie chicken (Okl.)	53 (491)	47 (532)	Lee 1950
Sage grouse (Wyo.)	46 (2693)	30 (1964)	Patterson 1952
Sage grouse (Ida.)	47 (67103)	34 (43028)	Autenrieth 1981
Sage grouse (Wyo.)[a]	41 (6451)	25 (4358)	Game Dept.
Sage grouse (Colo.)[a]	47 (5775)	34 (4588)	Braun 1979, Braun & Hoffman 1979
Unweighed means[b]	51	54	

[a] Adults include yearlings in which sex was known: Wyoming yearlings 28% male and adults 20% male, Colorado yearlings 40% male and adults 28% male.
[b] Excludes sage grouse.

was 43:57 ($n = 76$), when the entire population was classified. In this insular situation, nearly all females successfully raised young (Chap. 2) because of the absence of ground predators, and females had a low mortality of 26%. Males, on the other hand, showed normal mortality rates of 32% (Fig. 2.6) – red-tailed hawks (*Buteo jamaicensis*) and occasional goshawks apparently took some males when they advertised and occasionally both males and females in the winter. Unbalanced sex ratios can provide insights into the mortality agents at work.

In general, males predominate in the harvests of white-tailed and willow ptarmigan, sharp-tailed grouse, prairie chickens, and ruffed grouse (Lee 1950, Baker 1953, Ammann 1957, Dorney & Kabat 1960, Bergerud 1970a, Table 15.8). Males predominate also in large samples of winter-trapped, adult sharp-tailed grouse (Robel et al. 1972) and prairie chickens (Hamerstrom & Hamerstrom 1973). But females are more common in sage grouse, as shown both by band returns and observation of birds in the winter (Dalke et al. 1963, Beck 1977, Braun 1979, Table 15.8). There is no consistent male or female predominance in either spruce or blue grouse (Lumsden & Weeden 1963, Zwickel & Bendell 1967, Zwickel 1972, Ellison 1974, Zwickel & Brigham 1975, Zwickel et al. 1975, Keppie 1979).

The adult sex ratio does not necessarily only reflect differences in the mortality rates of males and females resulting from their different investment strategies. The adult sex ratio could also be modified by the sex ratio of the new recruits.

In 10-year-cyclic populations of ptarmigan there is some evidence of fewer juvenile females than males during high populations and/or during declines. Gardarsson (1971) reported the sex ratio of rock ptarmigan chicks 4–25 days old as 56% male. There was a male:female ratio of 62:38 in 93 willow ptarmigan chicks collected in Newfoundland (Bergerud 1970a). The proportion of male rock ptarmigan yearlings at Eagle Creek, Alaska, decreased as breeding success improved; the correlation of percent male yearlings and breeding success the prior season was $r = -0.574$, $P < 0.10$, $n = 9$ (Weeden pers. comm.). The proportion of males in the breeding population in Scottish rock ptarmigan also decreased as breeding success the prior year improved, $r = -0.718$, $P < 0.01$, $n = 18$ (data from Watson 1965). These combined findings suggest that cyclic ptarmigan populations may have a higher proportion of male than female chicks when there is high summer mortality of young – female chicks may be intrinsically weaker than males (Bergerud 1970a).

Several forest grouse populations show little deviation from unity in the proportion of juvenile males and females (Table 15.8), nor were the adult male:female proportions significantly correlated with the percentages of juvenile males ($r = 0.554$, $n = 9$, Table 15.8). Thus, here, adult departures from unity will need an explanation apart from the influence of the survival of juveniles.

For the prairie grouse there are more juvenile males than females in the harvest in most states (Table 15.8). Samples secured from winter trappings are also skewed to males. Males could be more vulnerable than females if they prospected for advertising sites at leks coincident with hunting and traveled widely between leks in small groups. However, the bias would not explain the predominance of males in the winter trapping. The correlation between the percent juvenile males and adult males was $r = 0.852$, $n = 7$. The possibility remains that male chicks in prairie grouse may be more viable than females, as postulated for ptarmigan.

The sex ratio of both adults and juveniles in sage grouse is weighted to females (Table 15.8). This disparity is also present in yearlings. These differential mortalities of male juveniles and yearlings represent a significant portion of the unbalanced sex ratio seen in adults, but the large-bodied, adult males can also be expected to die at greater rates than females (see Braun 1979). In dimorphic sage grouse, male chicks may suffer a higher mortality than female chicks, owing to differential growth and energy requirements, a sequence noted for dimorphic Capercaillie (*Tetrao urogallus*) in Europe (Wegge 1980, Moss & Oswald 1985).

The sexual imbalances present in grouse are in part a result of different predation mortality. In general, nest predators decrease in abundance and diversity from south to north (Fig. 15.7), whereas effective raptors increase. The most effective grouse raptors are the gyrfalcon and goshawk, and are found in the north; the golden eagle covers the entire North American grouse range except the high arctic and the east. Ground predators of females should be most serious in the south, especially in the steppe, and predators of adults, especially of conspicuous, displaying males, should be least in the steppe and most in the tundra if the natural predators are still present. All three grouse groups fit these predictions and show an increase in the proportion of females with increasing latitude (decline in ground predators) and a decrease with increased nest predation and declining nesting success (Fig. 15.18).

The predation hypothesis also explains the variability of the sex ratio between populations of the same species, for example, for spruce grouse (Table 15.9). Male spruce grouse are more common in Alberta than in Alaska; in Alberta, nest predation is high (Keppie 1980) and 29% of the females disappear in summer, versus 11% in winter (Keppie 1979). Males in Alberta are relatively safe from goshawks because of the high density of lodgepole (*Pinus contorta*) stems. In Michigan predation of males and females is more balanced (Table 15.9). The Yellow Dog plains of Robinson's Michigan study area are on the south edge of the goshawk range—grouse use the more open and less secure, Jack pine coverts (Robinson 1969), but also nesting success is high. The sex ratio is predicted to be nearly balanced. In Alaska nearly all the hens rear chicks—nest predation and predation pressure of females are minimal. But males are commonly taken by goshawks (Ellison 1974). The adult sex ratio there favors females (Table 15.9).

The north-south cline in nest-adult predation can be documented further with ptarmigan (Table 15.9). Ptarmigan in Colorado have few raptors that take adults, and mortality is low, but nest predation is the highest recorded for ptarmigan

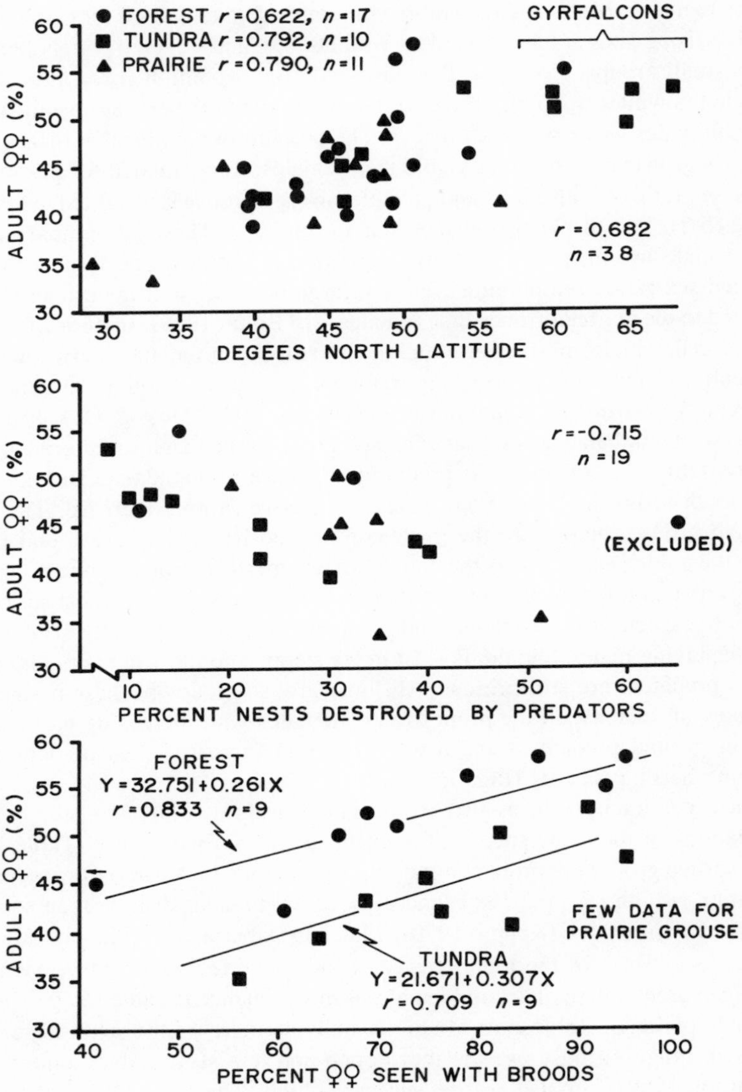

Fig. 15.18. Differential mortality of females is associated with predation during the nesting and brood-rearing seasons. *Top*: The proportion of females in populations increases with latitude because there are fewer mammalian predators of nests farther north. In the Arctic, gyrfalcons take more male ptarmigan, further increasing the proportion of females. *Middle*: There are fewer females in populations in which many nests are destroyed by predators. *Bottom*: There are more females in populations in which a high proportion of hens are seen with broods in July and August.

Table 15.9. Comparison of population parameters between grouse populations subject to different intensities of nest and adult predation[a]

Population parameters	Many nest predators but few predators of adults	Predation of nests and adults is similar	Few nest predators but many predators of adults
Forest grouse	Spruce grouse, Alberta	Spruce grouse, Michigan	Spruce grouse, Alaska
Clutch size	4.8 (64)	5.7 (9)	7.6 (26)
Nesting success	30% (64)	78% (9)	81% (26)
Females with young	29% (171)	72% (117)	93% (214)
Mortality adult females	0.33	0.55	0.57
Mortality adult males	0.22	0.50	0.68
Adult sex ratio (:)	55:45	54:46	45:55
Tundra grouse	White-tailed ptarmigan, Colorado	Rock ptarmigan, Michigan	Rock ptarmigan, Iceland
Clutch size	5.9 (60)	7.5 (198)	11.0 (301)
Nesting success	57% (60)	69% (198)	92%[b]
Mortality adult females	0.41	0.56	0.46
Mortality adult males	0.27	0.63	0.65
Adult sex ratio	64:36	49:51	47:53

[a] Boag et al. 1979, Keppie 1979, Redmond et al. 1982, Robinson 1980, Ellison 1974, Braun 1969, May 1975, Weeden & Theberge 1972, pers. comm., Gardarsson 1971.
[b] Based on eggs rather than nests.

(Giesen et al. 1980). Females in Colorado have a higher mortality rate than males (Braun 1969). Ptarmigan in Alaska face considerable predation by weasels (Weeden 1965), which are probably more interested in eggs than killing females. Some gyrfalcons are present and displaying males should be selected. Adult males have a higher mortality (63% versus 56%) at Eagle Creek, Alaska, and are less common than adult females in the spring (49% males, $n = 857$). Ptarmigan in Iceland nested on an island without mammalian predators but where gyrfalcons selectively hunted males (Chap. 9). Thus, the population included more females than males. (Table 15.9). In Svalbard, there are no gyrfalcons, and the chief predator is the Arctic fox (*Alopex lagopus*) that searches for nests and chicks. The sex ratio there favors males 56% ($n = 151$), since males do not defend nests or broods (Unander & Steen 1985).

15.6.6 Mortality and density

If the mortality rate of juveniles and adults is density-dependent, this would dampen population change. Lack (1954, 1966) felt that the regulating factor in birds was density-dependent starvation during the winter. I evaluated this hypothesis when possible, by comparing the annual mortality rates of banded birds with spring numbers. However, there were very few data. My second technique was to regress fall numbers against spring numbers the next season. If these plots were linear, they indicated density-independence relationships in overwinter mortality. A curvilinear plot in which spring numbers declined more rapidly as a proportion of fall numbers as the population increased would signify that overwinter mortality was density-dependent.

Forest grouse show little annual variation in mortality with density. The mortality rate of banded, adult blue grouse was relatively constant at Middle Quinsam from 1959 to 1976, as the population declined, and at Comox Burn, both when the population first colonized this area from 1962–65, and when numbers increased 1969–77 (Zwickel et al. 1983). The mortality of females at Middle Quinsam increased when the population declined. Forest succession may have played a part in this. The spruce grouse population at Gorge Creek shows a linear plot between fall and spring numbers, not suggestive of density-dependence. The correlation between spring numbers and annual mortality was $r = 0.154$ ($n = 5$) (Boag et al. 1979). The spruce grouse of the Yellow Dog plains in Michigan showed a correlation of $r = 0.644$ ($n = 4$) between spring numbers and annual mortality (Robinson 1980). Ruffed grouse populations in New York, Minnesota, and Alberta showed significant linear relationships between spring numbers and previous fall numbers; winter mortality was density-independent for the most part (Figs. 15.19, 15.20).

Of special interest is the mortality of advertising, ruffed grouse males in relation to density. These displaying males are commonly killed by goshawks near their display sites in the spring (Eng & Gullion 1962), but they are seldom killed on the actual display stage (Meslow 1966, Gullion & Marshall 1968, Rusch & Keith 1971a). I think there is competition for these safe sites and that males at high densities may opt to be silent as a survival tactic rather than advertise at a dangerous site (Fig. 15.21, see also Lewis & Zwickel 1982). The regression of mortality on total number of males in the Cloquet population of Minnesota was similar to the regression of mortality of advertising males, suggesting that silence tactics did reduce density-dependent mortality (Fig. 15.21). The mortality of advertising males was positively correlated with density in Minnesota ($r = 0.549$, $n = 20$; Fig. 15.21), but in Alberta the mortality of advertising males *decreased* coincident with increasing density ($r = -0.724$, $n = 8$; Rusch et al. 1984). The mortality rate in Minnesota changed in nonrandom runs as the population cycled (Fig. 15.21). I do not believe that these contrasting mortality correlations are causal based on numbers per se, but that they reflect changes in density-dependent selection for aggressiveness during cycles and increased vulnerability in the years of high numbers—because of both behavior and the switch-over of predators from preferred snowshoe hares (*Lepus americanus*) to grouse (Chap. 3).

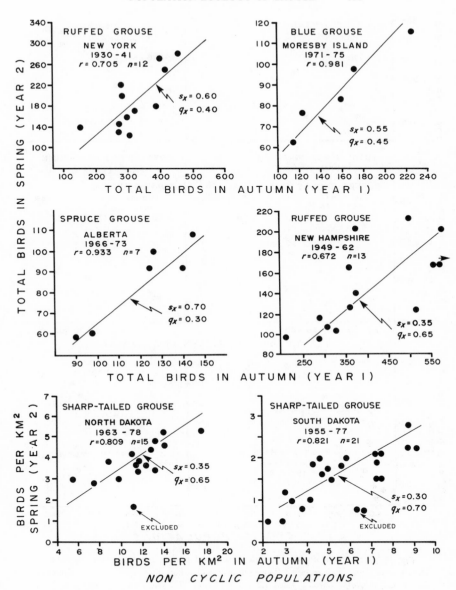

Fig. 15.19. Six noncyclic populations show a linear plot between numbers in the fall and numbers the next spring, indicating a relatively constant winter mortality and a lack of density-dependence in winter mortality rates (q_x). (Data from Bump et al. 1947, Allison 1963, Kobriger 1975, 1981, Linde et al. 1978, Boag et al. 1979, Chap. 2).

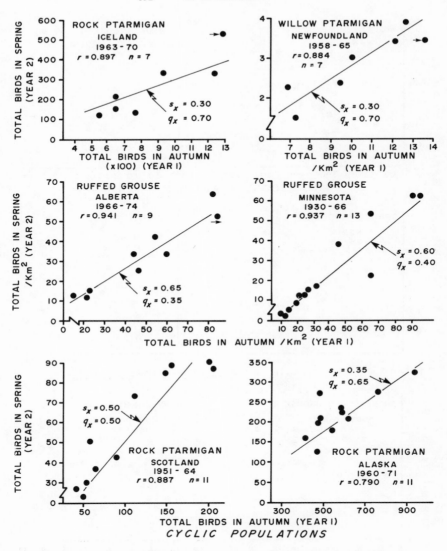

Fig. 15.20. Six cyclic populatons show a linear plot between numbers in the fall and numbers the next spring, indicating a relatively nonvariable winter mortality and a lack of density-dependence in winter mortality rates. (Data from King 1937, Watson 1965, Bergerud 1970a, Gardarsson 1971, Weeden & Theberge 1972, Rusch et al. 1984, pers. comm.)

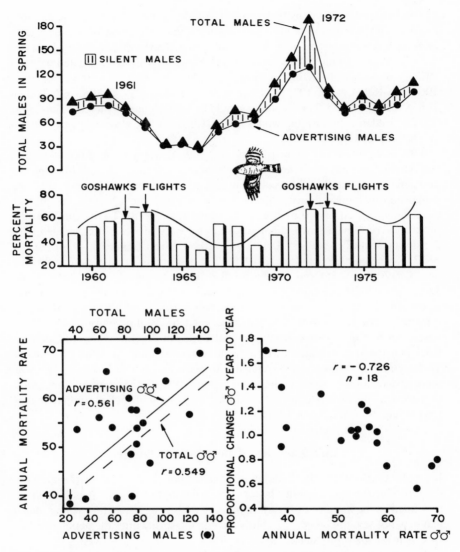

Fig. 15.21. *Top*: Total number of males in spring at the Cloquet ruffed grouse study area in Minnesota, 1959 to 1978. The proportion of silent males increased when the population was high. There were annual runs in mortality rates and high mortality occurred in years when goshawks came south. *Bottom left*: Mortality rates are correlated with the number of males advertising. The correlation does not improve when regressed against total males, which includes silent males. *Bottom right*: Changes in the number of males in spring between years are correlated with annual mortality rates. (All data adapted from Gullion 1981.)

Data to evaluate the density dependence of mortality in steppe grouse are few. There are no long-term studies of banded birds, and workers seldom use a study-area approach to count birds in the fall and spring. The mortality of female sharp-tailed grouse in South Dakota and males in Montana was not correlated with the number of males displaying in the spring (South Dakota, $r = 0.423$, $n = 4$, 1964–67; Robel et al. 1972) (Montana, $r = 0.449$, $n = 4$, 1963–67; Brown 1966b, 1967, 1968b). These species should be able to counter increased suscepti-bility to predation by forming winter flocks (Chap. 14; see also review by Pulliam & Millikan 1982).

Of special interest is the possibility of density-dependent mortality of greater prairie chicken hens while nesting. These hens are frequently ambushed on the nest, and there is reduced breeding success at high numbers (Fig. 15.14). The proportion of female prairie chickens in the South Dakota harvest declined as numbers increased ($r = 0.579$, $n = 16$; Linde et al. 1978). To the contrary, the proportion of female sharp-tailed grouse in the harvest was not correlated with density in South Dakota, $r = 0.129$, $n = 20$; or North Dakota, $r = -0.275$, $n = 17$ (Kobriger 1981, Linde et al. 1978). The nest ambush rate of prairie chicken hens is 9% ($n = 185$) and for sharp-tailed females only 4% ($n = 206$) (Table 14.6). This difference may partially account for the differences in the density-dependent mortality of hens between the two prairie grouse species. Mortality rates in tundra grouse were not density-dependent. Willow ptarmigan in New-foundland had relatively constant, annual losses in 7 years (Bergerud 1970a). Rock ptarmigan in Alaska showed a cyclic pattern in adult mortality (Weeden & Theberge 1972) that was not correlated with density ($r = 0.432$, $n = 9$). Nor was there a correlation between adult mortality and density for Myrberget's long study of ptarmigan in Norway (Chap. 11), nor a 7-year study of rock ptarmigan in Ice-land (Chap. 9, Gardarsson 1971).

15.7 Theories of population change

Populations are constantly changing in size, and population ecologists search for the reproductive and mortality factors that drive these changes. Population size is defined as the *number* of breeding birds in the spring, including young males that may not actually breed, i.e., birds alive in the spring after the population has spaced itself for reproductive activity.

Five common, density-dependent hypotheses explain changes in numbers (Fig. 15.22). (H_1) The *threshold-of-security* hypothesis specifies that winter cover is inadequate to shelter fall populations; numbers above a threshold are vul-nerable to predation or dispersal, and spring populations are more constant than fall populations. (H_2) The *winter bottleneck* hypothesis specifies that the avail-ability of winter food is variable and commonly in short supply. Birds starve and the magnitude of the loss varies with winter severity, and possibly with numbers.

HYPOTHESES   **TEST IMPLICATIONS**

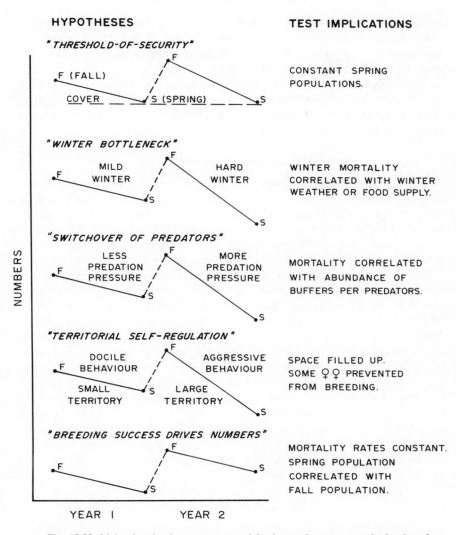

"THRESHOLD-OF-SECURITY"

CONSTANT SPRING
POPULATIONS.

"WINTER BOTTLENECK"

WINTER MORTALITY
CORRELATED WITH WINTER
WEATHER OR FOOD SUPPLY.

"SWITCHOVER OF PREDATORS"

MORTALITY CORRELATED
WITH ABUNDANCE OF
BUFFERS PER PREDATORS.

"TERRITORIAL SELF-REGULATION"

SPACE FILLED UP.
SOME ♀♀ PREVENTED
FROM BREEDING.

"BREEDING SUCCESS DRIVES NUMBERS"

MORTALITY RATES CONSTANT.
SPRING POPULATION
CORRELATED WITH
FALL POPULATION.

Fig. 15.22. Major theories that attempt to explain changes between years in the size of a population of breeding birds.

(H₃) The *predator switch-over* hypothesis states that mortality rates are lower and populations increase when predators are rare or buffers (alternative prey) common; when buffers decline, predators switch over, winter mortality increases, and populations decline. (H₄) The fourth hypothesis I will call the *territorial self-regulation* hypothesis, which proposes that breeding space is in short supply. Birds establish territories in the fall or spring, and those unable to successfully compete for space are surplus and doomed to die. (H_5) The fifth hypothesis states that *breeding success drives spring numbers*. Unlike the first four hypotheses, a test implication of this hypothesis is a relatively constant, winter mortality rate (Fig. 15.22). The first four hypotheses predict variable winter-mortality rates dependent upon the requisites postulated in short supply: H_1 – cover; H_2 – food; H_3 – buffers; H_4 – space. Population changes in H_5 are mostly explained by changes in nesting success and chick survival between years, dependent on variations in cover, predators, and weather.

15.7.1 Threshold-of-security

The threshold-of-security hypothesis dates to Errington's (1945) study of bobwhite quail at Prairie du Sac, Wisconsin, 1929–44. He noted that spring populations were generally constant and hypothesized that habitats had well-fixed capacities to protect animals; individuals in excess of this capacity were not safe from predators and died or disappeared (for ruffed grouse, cf. Errington 1937b). Romesburg (1981) felt that the hypothesis was nearly impossible to test.

One test implication of this hypothesis is that spring populations should be relatively constant in size compared with variable fall numbers. This implication does not hold for grouse because spring numbers parallel fall numbers (Figs. 15.19, 15.20) and often can change tenfold between years (Keith 1963, Schulz 1981, see Fig. 15.30).

I believe that the constancy in numbers that Errington saw was a function of the size of the window he used to view the population. If one picks a small study area of optimal habitat, numbers are often relatively constant (cf. Theberge & Gauthier 1982). Birds will always be attracted, regardless of total numbers, as they space themselves to maximize fitness (Fig. 14.27). Self-contained populations do fluctuate between years (Mercer 1967). When large, regional areas are censused, fluctuations are evident (see Fig. 15.30). Radiotelemetry has shown that dispersal for breeding occurs in all grouse and is the means of spacing. This spacing dampens fluctuations in small, optimal study areas.

15.7.2 Winter bottleneck

David Lack (1954) argued in favor of the view that birds face a density-dependent shortage of winter food. Many students then took to the field to test the hypothesis, but even the best examples that Lack marshaled in his final evaluation (Lack 1966) are unconvincing (cf. Chitty 1967). It is really difficult to envisage blue or spruce grouse living in a sea of green conifer needles faced with a food problem. Blue grouse apparently gain weight in winter (Redfield 1973b), and spruce grouse show a minimal decline over winter (Ellison & Weeden 1979, Robinson 1980). Also, both species have constant, winter mortality rates (Boag et al. 1979, Zwickel et al. 1983, Hines 1986). They have no food problem. The sage grouse also gains weight in winter (Beck & Braun 1978), and it lives in a sea of sagebrush leaves. If snow accumulates, the sage grouse has the ability to make long movements. Nor do the ptarmigan face winter food problems. Gardarsson (Fig. 9.9) and Mossop (Fig. 10.4) have documented ample food remaining when high populations of rock and willow ptarmigan declined. Willow ptarmigan generally maintain or gain weight in winter (Figs. 10.26, 16.11), as do white-tailed ptarmigan (Fig. 16.11).

If birds generally face winter shortages of food, they should feed for long periods, and feeding bouts might be correlated with the severity of the shortages. But the winter feeding budget for grouse appears to represent less than 5% of a 24-hour period.

Further evidence against this hypothesis is that biologists do not find starved birds in winter. Lack argued that dead birds would be hard to locate, but even with radiotelemetry workers have not found birds that died of food problems. Biologists are in the field in winter: Mossop found no obviously starved willow ptarmigan in winter, and birds on his study areas gained weight (Chap. 10); the Hamerstroms winter-trapped prairie chickens for some 20 years and they have never found starved birds (pers. comm.). The dead ptarmigan I have found died mostly in the spring at the very moment foods were becoming more abundant (cf. Weeden 1965, Mercer 1967). Ruffed grouse and prairie chickens are discussed in more detail in Chapter 16.

15.7.3 Switch-over of predators

The predator switch-over model dates back at least to Lack's (1954) treatise on the natural regulation of numbers (see also Hagen 1952). He suggested that when snowshoe hares crashed, northern predators would cause a severe impact on alternate prey such as grouse. Later, based on the advice of J. J. Hickey and L. B. Keith, he rejected the hypothesis. Keith (1963) showed that hares peaked in numbers before grouse in nine declines; hares and grouse declined together in five examples; and declines of grouse preceded those of hares eleven times. Later Keith (1974) revitalized the hypothesis, suggesting that grouse could be driven down by switch-over even though the local hare population was still high. Hare populations were not in perfect synchrony and predators might, through numerical responses, concentrate where hares and grouse were still common. Rusch et al. (1978) found support for this hypothesis for a ruffed grouse decline in Manitoba, where predators took more ruffed grouse when hares disappeared.

Keith and Rusch, and their students, at Rochester, Alberta, counted hares, ruffed grouse, sharp-tailed grouse, coyotes, lynx (*Lynx canadensis*), red-tailed hawks, horned owls, goshawks, and mice for one 10-year cycle, 1966–75 (Fig. 15.23). Hares peaked in 1971, whereas the local, ruffed grouse population reached a peak in 1968 and a provincewide peak of ruffed grouse occurred in 1970

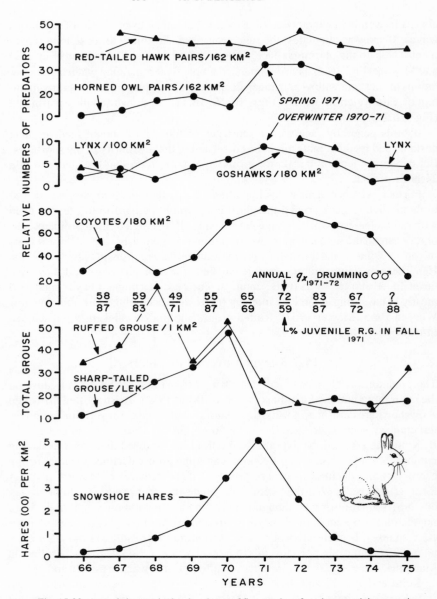

Fig. 15.23. Annual changes in the abundance of five species of predators and three species of prey during one 10-year cycle of snowshoe hares at Rochester, Alberta. Also shown are mortality rates of advertising males and percent young birds in harvests of ruffed grouse. (Data from Keith et al. 1977, Adamcik et al. 1978, Rusch et al. 1984.)

(Rusch et al. 1984). In this study grouse were already beginning to decline before predators were numerous and while hares were still increasing (Fig. 15.23). Also, the survival of young grouse was highest when hares were low; predators should not have been switching from hares to grouse nests and chicks.

The mortality rates of advertising male ruffed grouse at Rochester, Alberta, were not highly correlated with predator abundance (goshawk: $r = 0.101$, $n = 8$; owls: $r = 0.752$, $n = 8$; coyotes: $r = 0.480$, $n = 8$; lynx, $r = 0.573$, $n = 5$). Increased predators may have boosted mortality rates. But the population declined from 1968 to 1969, even though adult survival was the highest in eight years (Fig. 15.23). The population also declined 1970–71 and 1971–72, when breeding success was the lowest in 8 years. It increased when the ratio of percent juveniles to percent adult mortality was greater than 1.4 (e.g., 1969–70, 87/55 = 1.6), and the population declined 1970 to 1973 when the ratio was less than 1.1. Breeding success was certainly involved in the dynamics of this ruffed grouse population (see Fig. 15.26), and it was not highly correlated with the abundance of the important predators (goshawk: $r = -0.514$, $n = 9$; horned owls: $r = -0.370$, $n = 9$; coyotes: $r = -0.415$, $n = 9$). Predator switch-over cannot explain the decline in this ruffed grouse population.

I think that the predator switch-over model is useful for forecasting prolonged declines, but should be restricted to changes in goshawk predation following changes in hare abundance (Chap. 3). Goshawks are the ultimate predators of grouse (Eng & Gullion 1962). These birds are mobile, and their flights south occur at 10-year intervals coincident with hare declines (Mueller et al. 1977). Ruffed grouse mortality rates increased in all 4 years that goshawks came south in large numbers in northern Minnesota (Fig. 15.21). Goshawk predation appears responsible for major declines in red-phase males at Watch Lake, British Columbia. (Chap. 3). There are large declines of ruffed grouse in Manitoba at 10-year intervals. Ransom (1965) reported the near disappearance of ruffed grouse between November and January 1962–63. A count of drumming males in Rusch's Manitoba study area was 100 birds in 1971 and only three in 1972 (Rusch et al. 1978). The birds simply vanished in both crashes. I believe goshawk predation is the major factor responsible for these fall and winter crashes that occur after hares have declined.

The impact of goshawk predation on ruffed grouse, in addition to a functional response to hare declines, should be influenced by the availability of snow for roosting and plunges (Fig. 14.26), and the flushing behavior of grouse (Chap. 3). Grouse should flush at short distances and take greater risks when the birds are at cyclic highs or declining. At such times goshawks may be moving widely, searching for prey other than hares. It appears that greater variation exists in the annual mortality rate for ruffed grouse than for other grouse species (Figs. 15.21,

15.23, Gullion & Marshall 1968, Little 1978). This variability may relate to the mix of three factors: (1) abundance of goshawks and buffers, (2) cyclic flushing behavior of grouse, and (3) annual differences in the suitability of snow for cover.

Predator switching from hares to grouse is not necessary to explain grouse declines or the 10-year cycle of grouse. Grouse populations such as ptarmigan in Iceland show major 10-year cycles (Gudmundsson 1960), although they do not live in ecosystems that contain cyclic hare populations.

15.7.4 Territorial self-regulation

A controversy that has lingered since the 1950s is whether territorial behavior actually limits breeding numbers or if it acts primarily as a dispersal mechanism and means of assessing density (Lack 1954, 1966, Wynne-Edwards 1962, Fretwell & Lucas 1969, Watson & Moss 1970, Davies 1978, Patterson 1981, Wittenberger 1981a). The most-quoted and best-documented examples used to support the territorial-limitation hypothesis is the 30-year, ongoing study of red grouse in Scotland (Jenkins et al. 1963, Moss et al. 1984, Watson & Moss 1985). Modifications of their hypothesis have also been applied to blue and spruce grouse (Zwickel 1972, 1980, Boag et al. 1979) and willow ptarmigan (Hannon 1983).

In the 1972 red grouse model of population regulation, the quality of spring and summer food affects egg quality and breeding success, as well as the intrinsic spacing behavior of males and females contesting for territories in the fall and early winter. Territory size in turn determines stocking and population density (Watson & Moss 1972, 1980). Birds that do not secure territories are surplus and face a short life expectancy. This model implies that populations are always at a socially induced carrying capacity based on behavior as it determines territory size, and surpluses are available every autumn.

In the spacing model, food quality affects not only spacing behavior but also the viability of young. Thus, spacing behavior and breeding success covary together; i.e., following a winter and spring that results in good nutrition, birds will be less aggressive and have smaller territories; coincident with this, they will have improved breeding success. The covariance of both breeding success and spacing behavior makes it extremely difficult to distinguish between the influence of breeding success versus that of territorial size on the subsequent population size. Spacing behavior could drive breeding numbers as Watson & Moss propose, or breeding success could be *causal* to changes in breeding numbers. With the latter hypothesis, spacing behavior and territory size would be the *effects* of competition between different numbers of competitors, and territory size would be dependent on prior breeding success and would not drive breeding numbers. The two hypotheses can be diagramed as follows:

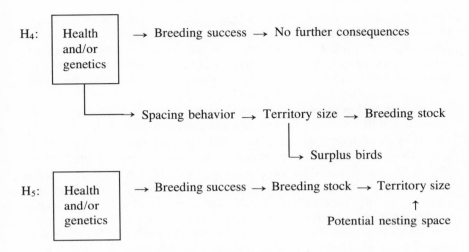

H₄:

Health and/or genetics → Breeding success → No further consequences

→ Spacing behavior → Territory size → Breeding stock

↳ Surplus birds

H₅:

Health and/or genetics → Breeding success → Breeding stock → Territory size

↑

Potential nesting space

Watson and Moss (1972, 1980) rejected the second hypothesis (H_5), arguing that spacing behavior and territorial size were independent of breeding success.

Most recently the Scottish workers have rejected the nutritional aspect of their model as well as Chitty's hypothesis that genetic changes are the major cause of population cycles (Moss et al. 1984). However, they still believe that spacing behavior (territorial competition) limits numbers (Watson & Moss 1985) and now suggest that emigration is a key variable in declines (Moss et al. 1984, Watson et al. 1984b).

The major research findings that lead to the spacing model in red grouse include: (1) a staircase decline in breeding numbers coincident with territorial behavior; (2) the presence of large numbers of birds—floaters—during the winter, which do not have territories; and (3) the discovery of large numbers of dead floaters in marginal habitats. Finally, when birds were removed from the territories, they were replaced by the floater birds (Jenkins et al. 1963, 1967, Watson & Jenkins 1968, Watson 1985).

But the replacement of territorial birds by other birds does not constitute evidence of territorial limitations in an open system. The red grouse populations were open systems. For example, the number of red grouse on the Low study area in Scotland *increased* after the breeding season in November-December 1957 and again in October-December 1959. The Kerlock population increased in October 1965. The High area population increased in October 1960. The Glen Muick study had an estimated 124 birds in August 1958, even though 147 birds were shot, 106 were present in the spring of 1959. The Corndavon population was estimated at 307 in August 1957; 265 were shot, but 89 birds were present in 1958. Clearly there was considerable movement between moors in Scotland. Documentation of small dispersal distances of tagged birds, especially when tagged on heavily hunted and productive moors (Jenkins et al. 1967) does not constitute evidence that the populations were self-contained; ingress could easily exceed egress. Replacement of the vacated territories can be explained by birds shifting to optimal breeding densities (Fig. 14.27), and does not mean that these birds would not have bred elsewhere (Brown 1964, Watson & Moss 1970).

The mechanics of population change of spring numbers in the red grouse, territorial model (H_4) is density-dependent winter mortality. Fall territorial behavior is postulated to determine territory size, and the nonterritorial birds expelled die before the next spring. Predation was the major cause of death in the Kerloch, High and Low study areas (Jenkins et al. 1963, 1964, 1967). But winter predation of red grouse was not strongly density-dependent, contrary to the model (Fig 15.24A). Actually, the dead birds that the Scottish workers located from October to May represented a relatively constant proportion of the posthunting population; for the Low area, the known winter losses were: 1957–58, 39% (233/537); 1958–59, 27% (172/633); 1959–60, 22% (66/302); 1960–61, 25% (115/468). A constant proportion of birds died over winter, yet the breeding population (1957–61) for the Low area changed from a high of 371 birds in 1957 to a low of 157 birds in 1960 (C.V. = 34%, $n = 5$). These changes in breeding numbers were not correlated with total dead birds found between fall and spring (Fig. 15.24B). Winter mortality in the study was mostly density-independent and noncompensatory, contrary to the test implication of the territorial-limitation model (Fig. 15.22).

The question of whether some red grouse females were prevented from breeding should be addressed, since males can be polygynous, and for grouse in general, females are the sex in short supply. The red grouse population declined at Glen Esk between November and May 1957–58; between September and February 1958–59; and between September and October 1960–61 (Jenkins et al. 1963). Because the sex ratio remained relatively constant, females as well as males must have left or died. The loss of males can be explained by territorial expulsion on territories in the fall, but males would not expel females. Thus, the females themselves must force other females to leave (Hannon 1983). The literature suggests that female red grouse are not strongly territorial until well into the winter (Jenkins et al. 1963), yet large numbers of females left as early as September (1961) and October (1958). Females departed in 1958 even after an estimated 43% of the population had been harvested.

An alternative hypothesis to explain this dispersal is that many birds left simply to improve their survival and later breeding prospects, which has been documented in spruce (Keppie 1979, see Fig. 14.28) and ruffed grouse (Eng 1959), and were not "forced" out. The detailed counts of red grouse at Kerloch, Scotland (Jenkins et al. 1967), generally show declines in numbers in October–November and increases in February–March. These observations are con-

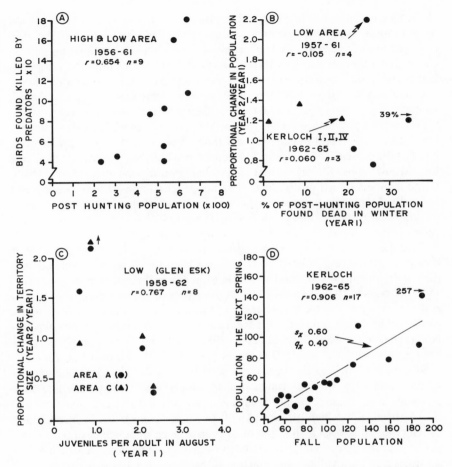

Fig. 15.24. Population statistics from early red grouse studies (Jenkins et al. 1963, 1964, 1967) to evaluate the hypothesis of population limitation through territorial self-regulation (spacing). (*A*) Winter losses from predation were largely density-independent, 1956–61. (*B*) Changes in the size of the breeding population from year to year were not correlated with proportions of the posthunting population found dead. (*C*) Proportional changes in territory size from year to year correlated with prior breeding population; (*D*) The spring population at Kerloch (unhunted) changed as a constant proportion of the prior year's fall population.

sistent with a two-direction dispersal schedule, as reported for blue, spruce, and ruffed grouse (Rusch & Keith 1971b, Herzog & Keppie 1980), and proposed in the polymorphic model in Fig. 2.26. Female red grouse floaters were seen throughout the winter but few were seen in May (Jenkins et al. 1963). Is it reasonable to believe that females suddenly died in May? A more realistic possibility is that with breeding finally upon them, females no longer could delay choosing a nesting site while hoping for a vacancy in a preferred habitat, but had to settle for a second-best location. Because some red grouse moors have been managed to provide vigorous heather growth they should be optimal for nesting cover. The difference between the best and the "other" may be more discontinuous in these red grouse areas than in unmanaged grouse habitats where a more gradual continuum exists. Hence hens at high density may delay their decision to the last moment, and ingress-egress could be considerable and confounding.

The principal evidence for the territorial hypothesis should be that nonbreeding females are present in late May and June when productive hens are incubating. But the presence of a large proportion of such hens has not been documented for red grouse or, for that matter, any other grouse population (Table 15.1). Large numbers of red grouse hens have never been radio-tracked to document conclusively that many do not nest because of social behavior. A major radio-tracking study, such as that conducted by Hines (1986) with blue grouse, would certainly help clarify the demography of red grouse.

Changes in territory size in red grouse are correlated with changes in prior breeding success (Fig. 15.24C) and have not been shown to be correlated with the quality or quantity of food available to males in the fall (Henderson 1977, Miller & Watson 1978, Lance 1978b). A more parsimonious explanation than H_4 is that territory size is the consequence of breeding success and is inverse to the number of birds that compete for space, as documented for other ptarmigan populations (Pedersen 1984, Bergerud et al. 1985) (i.e., H_5). Spring numbers in red grouse are correlated with fall numbers (Fig. 15.24D, see also Watson et al. 1984b), as predicted by the breeding-success hypothesis. There are examples of vacant advertising sites for ruffed grouse, blue grouse, and willow and rock ptarmigan—populations are not always at a "socially induced carrying capacity" (Gardarsson 1971, Chap. 9, Little 1978, Lewis & Zwickel 1982). Bendell and Elliott (1967, p. 78) said, "It follows that even in dense populations of 0.44 males per acre, more males could have joined the breeding population." A growing consensus is that the evolutionary function of territory in birds is to space an individual away from others, as Lack (1966) argued (Davies 1978). Gardarsson (1971, Chap. 9) rejected territorial spacing as a means of control in rock ptarmigan, as did Myrberget and Mossop for willow ptarmigan (Chaps. 10, 11). The birds studied by Gardarsson and Myrberget left their study areas on islands in the fall. Heavy winter mortality occurred in winter flocks in the absence of territorial behavior. Nearly all the ptarmigan that returned in the spring in both areas were able to secure breeding space.

Watson (1985) believes that the extremely high densities of red grouse in Scotland are a valuable vehicle to address the question of inherent mechanisms of population limitation. It is my opinion that since these populations are so intensively managed and unnatural, they are not an adequate laboratory to address questions of natural population control and adaptive behavioral strategies. The chapters in this book have emphasized the role of predation as a prime mover in the evolution of reproductive tactics to enhance survival. The ground predators in Scotland are controlled and reduced in numbers, and nesting success is unusually high for a noninsular population. Further, the nesting habitat is managed by cultural practices and is discontinuous. Birds without territories must frequent habitats that are less safe (Jenkins et al. 1963), and these birds may be weak from atypical nutritional and disease problems (Jenkins et al. 1963, 1967, Hudson et al. 1985). Thus, it is not surprising that these "waiting birds," of reduced social status, may suffer increased mortality, and this compensatory mortality has been considered the means of population regulation (Watson & Moss 1979). Nonbreeding birds in other, more natural grouse populations may actually improve their longevity by avoiding the risks of advertising and nesting by seeking protective cover (Maxson 1977, Little 1978, Sopuck 1979, Lewis & Zwickel 1982). Again, dense populations restricted to discontinuous and limited habitats should display ingress-egress tendencies atypical of birds with a wider, more continuous range of habitat options. But the red grouse studies do provide insight into the ultimate limits of increase, where numbers are maintained above the natural controls of the extrinsic environments. These studies also provide an experimental laboratory where we can make comparisons with natural populations; but it may be unwise to extrapolate findings from these managed systems to more natural situations (Lack 1965, 1966).

15.7.5 Breeding success drives numbers

The earliest grouse biologists believed that breeding success drove numbers. Ralph King pioneered ruffed grouse studies in Minnesota in the 1930s and said (1937, p. 524), "The first essential, of course, is an October population in excess of the desired April population. It must be in excess in order to allow for winter losses." The granddad of all studies, the mammoth, New York ruffed grouse study of 1932–42, resulted in the following conclusion: "The factors of increase include primarily the various components of the reproductive potential for the species" (Bump et al. 1947, p. 512).

My primary technique to evaluate whether breeding success is paramount to changes in breeding numbers was to regress population change between years (total birds, or density, in year 2 divided by total birds, or density, in year 1) against the breeding success in year 1 (young birds per adult in August, or young per brood in August). A second method of evaluation was to calculate the coefficient of variation of breeding success versus mortality statistics. The test implication of the breeding-success hypothesis (Fig. 15.22) is that adult mortality is relatively constant compared to variation in breeding success.

Variations in population size in the steppe grouse are generally conceded to result from changes in prior production. The standard management techniques for these three grouse species include the counts of summer broods and the determi-

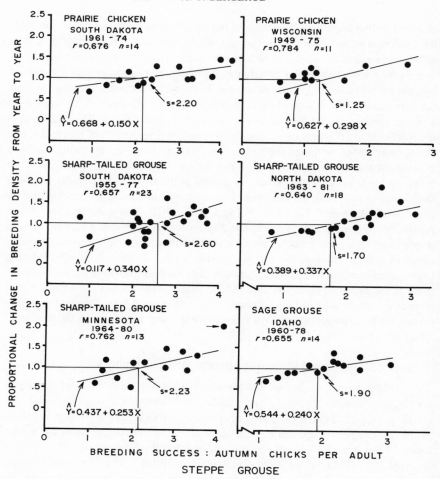

Fig. 15.25. The proportional change in density between adjacent years is correlated with breeding success the previous year in six populations of steppe grouse; *s* equals the mean number of juveniles per adults in the autumn required to balance average overwinter losses of juveniles and adults and maintain mean population size. (Data from Hillman & Jackson 1973, Kobriger 1975, 1981, Berg 1977, Linde et al. 1978, Autenrieth 1981; some years unavailable or excluded for various objective reasons.)

nation of breeding success by assessing age ratios of harvested birds. Changes in breeding numbers are correlated with prior production in prairie chickens in Kansas (data from Horak 1971), Wisconsin, and South Dakota (Fig. 15.25). Annual changes in the density of sharp-tailed grouse males on leks are correlated with production in Montana (Brown 1966b, 1967, 1968b), Saskatchewan, Minnesota, South Dakota, and North Dakota (Fig. 15.25). Similarly, the abundance of strutting, male sage grouse in Idaho reflected prior production. The correlation between sage grouse production and subsequent numbers was not significant for statistics from North Dakota or Colorado (Rogers 1964, Braun 1979, Hoffman 1979, government reports). However, the census technique of counting males on leks can be misleading (Beck & Braun 1980). The number of males attending a particular lek shows great variation between days (Hartzler 1972, Jenni & Hartzler 1978, Emmons & Braun 1984), and young males do not arrive until late in the season. Yearling:adult ratios are positively correlated with prior chick production in sage grouse (Dalke et al. 1963), indicating that production does drive numbers and that census methodology is inadequate to determine spring numbers.

In general, steppe grouse show large annual variation in juvenile:adult ratios, but mortality rates are relatively constant. The variation in production results primarily from changes in nesting success, because the coefficient of variation (C.V.) in brood size is less than that in juvenile:adult ratios. For example, the C.V. for annual brood size of sharp-tailed grouse during 18 years in North Dakota was 11%, whereas for juvenile:adult ratios it was 38% ($n = 32$). In South Dakota, the C.V. in brood size of prairie grouse for 28 years was 12%, the C.V. in the number of juveniles per adult is much greater (prairie chickens: 44%, $n = 18$; sharp-tailed grouse: 32%, $n = 31$) (Hillman & Jackson 1973, Kobriger 1975, 1981, Linde et al. 1978). The mean C.V. in annual mortality rates for steppe grouse in two studies was 11% (Brown 1966b, 1967; Robel et al. 1972), whereas the mean C.V. in the juvenile:adult ratios was an average of 46% for 11 studies. In the steppe environment, productivity varies much more than does mortality and is the major force in population change.

The annual fluctuation in breeding numbers of forest grouse is also correlated with prior breeding success. Ruffed grouse populations changed in relation to variations in breeding success in New York, Alberta, Wisconsin, New Hampshire, and British Columbia (Fig. 15.26). Spruce grouse numbers changed in response to the percentage of juveniles in the autumn for populations in Alberta and Michigan (Fig. 15.26). Like the steppe grouse, there is greater variation in breeding success (C.V. = 31%, $n = 8$ studies) than in annual mortality (C.V. = 19%, $n = 7$ studies).

A major problem in evaluating the factors responsible for changes in forest grouse numbers is that many workers rely on counts of advertising males to detect population changes. But there is a large component of silent males in most populations, and this component varies between years and is positively correlated with densities (Gullion 1981, Rusch et al. 1984). Most silent males are yearlings and are overlooked in census techniques such as drumming counts (ruffed grouse) and hooting tallies (blue grouse).

Populations that showed changes correlated with production were only those in which researchers included census techniques that accounted for silent males,

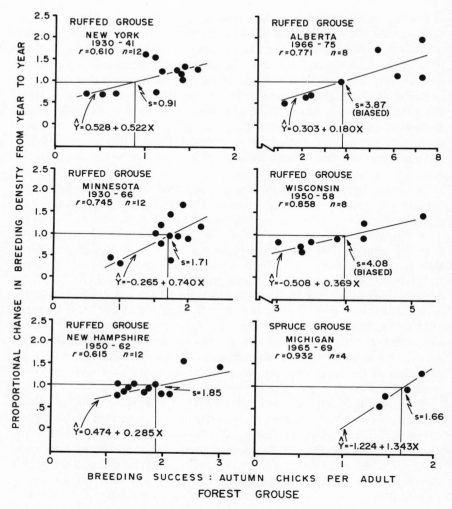

Fig. 15.26. The proportional change in density between adjacent years is correlated with breeding success the previous year for six populations of forest grouse; the *s* values (see legend for Fig. 15.25) for ruffed grouse in Alberta and Wisconsin are biased by the increased vulnerability of juvenile birds to hunting. (Data from King 1937, Bump et al. 1947, Dorney & Kabat 1960, Allison 1963, Gullion 1970c, Robinson 1980, Rusch et al. 1984; some years unavailable.)

such as the complete counts of spruce grouse in Michigan (Robinson 1980) and the King strip census in Minnesota.

Authorities disagree whether breeding success determines breeding numbers of blue grouse. Fred Zwickel, from his studies of blue grouse on Vancouver Island, has argued that there are more than enough juveniles alive in the fall to replace annual adult losses, and breeding success does not determine breeding numbers (Zwickel & Bendell 1967, Zwickel, 1982, Zwickel et al. 1983). However, Redfield (1972) also studied blue grouse on Vancouver Island and felt that changes in breeding success did alter spring numbers. His data show a correlation between production and the abundance of yearlings the next year (Fig. 15.27, middle). Fowle (1944), who pioneered blue grouse studies on Vancouver Island, also felt that when losses among chicks were high it could result in stabilized or declining populations. I found that in the closed, blue grouse system on Moresby Island that when the number of chicks per hen in August was greater than 1.3, the population increased the following spring (Fig. 2.10).

The most intensively studied population of blue grouse on Vancouver Island is that at Comox Burn (Zwickel & Bendell 1967, Lance 1967, 1970, Mossop 1971, Zwickel 1972, Zwickel et al. 1977, Zwickel 1980). This population has clearly responded to annual changes in production; there is a significant correlation between chick production and yearling females the next year ($r = 0.796$, 1969–76; Fig. 15.27) and between the number of chicks per hen and yearling females again the next spring ($r = 0.728$, 1967–74; data from Mossop 1971, Zwickel et al. 1977, 1983). Also, overwinter survival of juveniles was not density dependent in 8 years, and thus could not be the means of population regulation (data from Lewis 1979, Zwickel 1983, Zwickel et al. 1983). The survival of adults at Comox Burn has been relatively constant from 1969 to 1978, and cannot explain annual changes in numbers (Zwickel et al. 1983).

If productivity drives numbers of blue grouse on Vancouver Island, breeding success should differ significantly between decreasing and increasing populations. The mean number of chicks per brood in August for the Vancouver Island populations that were increasing was 3.8 ± 0.14 ($n = 14$), whereas for stable or declining populations it was 2.9 ± 0.13 ($n = 29$; $t = 5.265$, $P < 0.01$; data from Zwickel & Bendell 1967, Mossop 1971, Redfield 1972, Zwickel et al. 1977, Bendell pers. comm.).

The Comox Burn (CB) population increased from 1968 to 1972, at the same time the population at Middle Quinsam (MQ) decreased. During these years, the Comox Burn birds had 61%–80% of the females with broods and a mean brood size of approximately 3.8 chicks per brood female; birds in the decreasing population at MQ shared a nesting success of 53% and an annual brood size of about 2.5 (Fig. 15.28). Brood hens are more easily sighted than nonbrood hens and need to be corrected at a 1.9:1 ratio (Mossop 1971). Mortality rates of yearlings and adults were similar for both populations, approximately 42% of the adults and yearlings died each year at MQ from 1970 to 1976, and about 40% of the adults and yearlings from 1969 to 1977 disappeared at CB (Fig. 15.28) (Zwickel

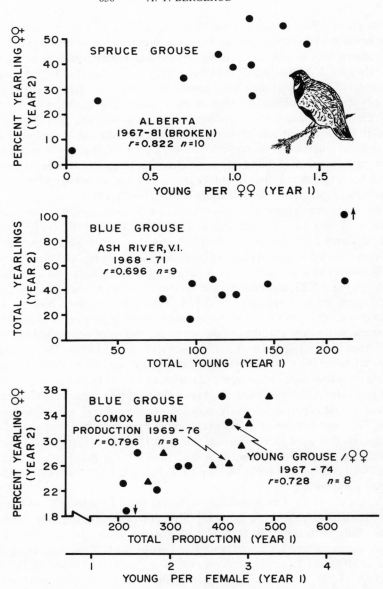

Fig. 15.27. The percent yearlings or total yearlings is correlated with prior breeding success in three forest grouse populatons in which clutch sizes are small and mortality rates are low. (Data from Mossop 1971, Redfield 1972, Zwickel et al. 1977, 1983, Smyth & Boag 1984.)

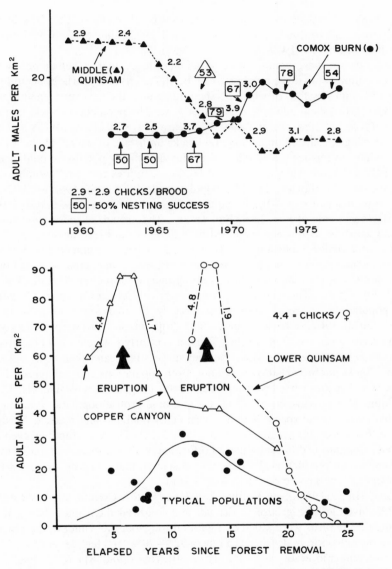

Fig. 15.28. *Top*: Population changes of blue grouse at Comox Burn and Middle Quinsam, Vancouver Island, British Columbia, in relation to nesting success and chicks per brood statistics (averaged by 2-year intervals). *Bottom*: The eruption of two blue grouse populations when breeding success was very high and the more typical blue grouse populations that increase following colonization of newly logged areas and that finally decline as the forest canopy closes in. (Data from Redfield et al. 1970, Mossop 1971, Zwickel et al. 1977, 1983, Frandsen 1980, Bendell pers. comm., and British Columbia game-check data.)

et al. 1983). Overwinter survival of juveniles was calculated at about 50% in both areas for 1959 to 1964 (Zwickel & Bendell 1972), but only 40% for older juveniles at Comox, 1969–76 (Zwickel 1983).

We can use these demographic parameters to evaluate whether production alone is sufficient to drive numbers. At CB, 100 adults and yearlings should provide 138 chicks by fall, of which 55 should live until the next spring and replace the 40 yearlings and adults that died that year. The population should increase from 100 to 115 birds, or at a rate-of-increase of $r = 0.14$. At MQ, 100 adults and yearlings produced on average 66 chicks until fall, of which 33 should live over winter to replace the 42 older birds that die; this population should change from 100 to 91 individuals, or $r = -0.09$. These figures compare favorably with the real-world estimates. The MQ population declined from 1968 to 1972 at a rate-of-increase of $r = -0.10$, and the CB population increased between 1968 and 1972 at a rate of $r = 0.13$ (Fig. 15.28). The growth of these populations, 35 km apart, is adequately explained by differences in breeding success.

Two population explosions of blue grouse have been documented on Vancouver Island that provide insight into the cause of population fluctuations. At Lower Quinsam (LQ), the number of birds rapidly increased to over 90 males/km^2 by 1951 (Fig. 15.28). The second eruption occurred at Copper Canyon (CC), where the population increased from approximately 58 males/km^2 in 1964 to 86 males/km^2 in 1967. In both instances these eruptions were accompanied by very high breeding success (Fig. 15.28). Thus, it is clearly possible for a blue grouse population to double in 3 years if nesting success is greater than 80% and four or five chicks per brood survive until fall. Both populations plunged quickly from these high densities when breeding success returned to more typical levels. These eruptions also provide further evidence that blue grouse populations cannot be limited by territorial space. Within 3 years they doubled, and reached densities four to five times greater than normal (Fig. 15.28). The two eruptions even occurred in habitats in different stages of reforestation. The common ingredient was unusually high production. Evidence is substantial that breeding success drives numbers of blue grouse on Vancouver Island.

Last, Hines (1986a), on Hardwicke Island, British Columbia, placed radios on 293 juvenile blue grouse in the fall and followed them until they died or recruited. The birds were killed by raptors throughout the winter in the absence of spacing behavior; males died at a rate of 72%–79%, and females at 65%–72%. This overwinter mortality was 74% (1979–80), 76% (1980–81), 67% (1981–82), and 73% (1982–83) (C.V. = only 6%), and was independent of population size. Five of 28 yearling females did not nest, but they were *not* prevented from holding space in the breeding habitat—a test condition of the territorial limitation model (Watson & Moss 1970). The number of recruits in year 2 was linearly correlated with prior production in year 1; for females $r = 0.97$, and for males r

= 0.92 (n = 4 years). Hence variation for breeding success was the mechanism of population change between spring numbers.

The spring abundance of tundra grouse also changes in relation to variations in the breeding success the previous year (Fig. 15.29, Chaps. 10, 11, May 1975, Pedersen et al. 1983, Pedersen 1984). But unlike the steppe and forest grouse, in ptarmigan the coefficient of variation for the annual mortality statistics is approximately equal to the C.V. of juvenile:adult ratios—31% (n = 3 studies) and 39% (n = 5 studies), respectively. Weeden and Theberge (1972) also concluded that vagaries in rock ptarmigan numbers in Alaska were influenced both by changes in production and by mortality.

Red grouse populations also respond principally to changes in breeding success (Bergerud et al. 1985). There is a significant correlation between breeding success and the proportional changes in numbers of red grouse in the Glen Esk, Low and High populations (r = 0.883, n = 7; from Jenkins et al. 1963), and for three lightly hunted areas (Kerloch, Forvie, and Locknagar, r = 0.681, n = 26) (Fig. 15.29). But the statistics from two other red grouse populations, on two "rich" Scottish moors—Glen Muick and Corndavon—failed to show positive correlations between breeding success and subsequent densities (Jenkins et al. 1967). It was based on these two exceptions that Jenkins and Watson rejected the hypothesis that production drives numbers of red grouse. Both populations were highly productive and at high densities, and both sustained harvest losses of approximately 45% from 1958 to 1965 (Jenkins et al. 1967). These harvests were sufficiently high to negate the role of production in altering subsequent breeding numbers. The mean estimate of breeding success in August was 144 young per 100 adults (1958-71). In a fall population of 244 birds, 110 would have been harvested and an additional 50 would have died from other causes between fall and spring. I estimated this 50-bird loss (38%) from the overwinter mortality of birds in an isolated red grouse population at Forvie, 1957-65, excluding 1958-59 (from Table 2 in Jenkins et al. 1967). In addition, in an earlier study of red grouse, Jenkins et al. (1963) reported posthunting loss before spring of greater than 25%, based on dead birds found at their Low study area and the disappearance of banded birds from December to March. This 25%-plus loss would be conservative because some birds would not be found. If we subtract the 110 birds killed during the hunting season plus the 50 that died from natural causes from a fall population of 244, there would be insufficient birds to maintain 100 breeding birds. To evaluate this in another manner, assume that these red grouse suffer a 65% annual mortality (Jenkins et al. 1967). Then a population of 244 with a survival rate of 35% would have only 85 remaining at the end of the year—again, this is inadequate to maintain numbers. Production could not drive numbers in these two rich moors, because there was an excess of hunting mortality.

However, these populations did maintain their numbers from 1957 to 1971

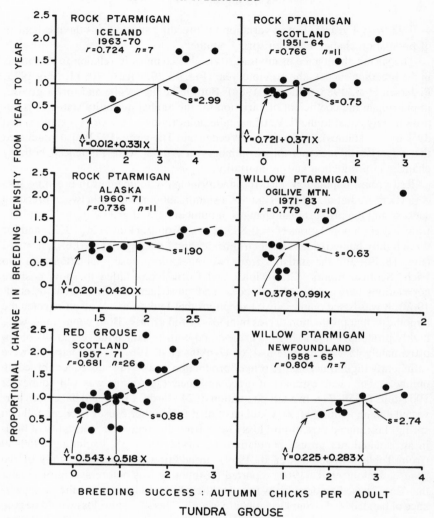

Fig. 15.29 The proportional changes in density between adjacent years are correlated with breeding success the previous year for six populations of tundra grouse. (Data from Jenkins et al. 1963, 1967, Watson 1965, Bergerud 1970a, Gardarsson 1971, Weeden & Theberge 1972, pers. comm., May 1975.)

(Jenkins et al. 1967, Moss et al. 1975). Additional birds must have come from less productive moors where hunting losses were lower. For example, the Locknagar population maintained a breeding-success estimate of 1.05 juveniles:adult (1961–71) and had a low hunting loss (Jenkins et al. 1967). If these birds sustained a 38% overwinter loss (205 − 78 = 127), there would still be sufficient stock to maintain their own numbers (using an index of 100) and yet have sufficient colonizers (127 − 100 = 27) that could improve their fitness by shifting to the more productive Glen Muick or Corndavon moors.

The Scottish, red grouse biologists have done interesting fertilizer experiments (Miller et al. 1970) that provide evidence that breeding success determines numbers in red grouse. They fertilized heather in May 1965. Birds invaded the improved heather cover in 1966, but the density of birds did not increase in that year, as expected if nutrition influences spacing behavior (Watson & Moss 1972). Instead, the population increased in size the second year after fertilization (1967), when the increased production of young from 1966, which resulted from the improved nutrition in 1966, first took territories. The experimental population also remained higher than the control population in the third year (1968) after fertilization, when the heather no longer showed the improved growth or nutritional quality brought about by the fertilizer. This further increase is consistent with the hypothesis that, again, it was the high breeding success the previous year that determined the density of birds the next season. Watson and O'Hare (1979) noted that in 19 populations of red grouse in Ireland with low brood survival, 14 decreased the next year, but in 5 areas where brood survival was high, 4 increased the following year. Production appears to drive numbers in red grouse in Ireland as well as in Scotland.

Another example in which hunting probably negates a direct link between production and subsequent changes in numbers is the several small populations of white-tailed ptarmigan in Colorado studied by Braun and Rogers (1971). These populations were harvested at rates ranging from 14% to 63%. These hunted populations seem to have maintained their numbers, but again there is extensive movement between these small populations and ingress from less hunted populations likely explains stability. Heavily hunted populations do not provide a fair test of the breeding-success hypothesis.

Recently, Watson and Moss (1985) appear to have rejected their original model (Watson & Moss 1972, 1980) in which breeding success has no further consequence for the subsequent size of spring numbers, and the dynamics of the system, in their view, was determined by compensatory winter mortality (Watson & Moss 1979). They state (Watson & Moss 1985, p. 283): "Changes in spring numbers from one spring to the next could be predicted from the observed chick production ratio each year." This is clearly the breeding-success hypothesis proposed (Bergerud 1970a). But in the same paper, Watson and Moss also say that the density of grouse at Glen Esk and Kerloch is limited by territorial behavior; do they equate density with total numbers? Since territorial behavior occurs after breeding success is determined, and territory size and breeding success are negatively correlated (Bergerud et al. 1985), territorial behavior must be an effect of earlier events, and breeding success lies closer to the core of population regulation.

The observation that there are more than enough chicks in the fall to replace adult losses is not evidence that production does not drive numbers. These chicks are not surplus. Each population has a unique and relatively constant, overwinter mortality regime dictated by the particular cover characteristics and predators in a given region. In some years, high production of chicks would provide more than enough recruits to compensate for the typical, density-independent adult losses, and the population the next spring would increase. Yet in another season, reduced production or survival of chicks in their first summer will fail to provide sufficient recruits to replace the largely constant loss of yearlings and adults, and next year's population will be lower. Clearly, if production did not provide recruitment that on average balances adult losses, the population would become extinct.

In all, I have examined 37 sets of data from substantial studies of grouse. Thirty studies show significant or nearly significant correlations between changes in breeding success and population changes the next year. The exceptions include the white-tailed ptarmigan and red grouse populations that are heavily hunted, and some sage and ruffed grouse populations that probably are inaccurately censused. One blue grouse population in Alberta showed satisfactory breeding success, but numbers continued to decline from 1955 to 1964; high adult mortality was the suspected cause (Boag 1966). My conclusion is that change in breeding success is a sufficient variable to drive numbers. This does not mean that it is a necessary factor. Clearly, if mortality rates do change between years, this can affect breeding numbers, as was true for ruffed grouse in Minnesota (Fig. 15.21). But variations in mortality rates of the majority of grouse populations are only about half those found in breeding success. A generalization from this review is that breeding success is the dominant demographic parameter that alters spring breeding numbers. Similar conclusions have been reached for Hungarian partridge (*Perdix perdix*) (Potts 1980), black grouse (Anglestam 1983), and pheasants (Linder et al. 1960).

15.8 The 10-year cycle in grouse

Since the 1930s, grouse biologists have been intrigued by and have inquired into the underlying causes for the recurring periods of scarcity and abundance of northern grouse. The 10-year cycle in grouse is well recognized (Keith 1963). Leopold (1933, p. 50) spoke of cycles as "periodical associations of more or less fixed length and amplitude." Davis (1957) felt that cycles could be distinguished on the basis that abundance changed in a nonrandom sequence, wherein one could predict the future growth of a population. This discussion is limited to the long, nonrandom fluctuations in abundance of 9- to 11-year intervals. Myrberget (1984 and Chap. 11) has provided a comprehensive explanation for the shorter 3- to 4-year cycles (phase-forgetting, quasi-cycles; Niebet & Gurney 1982) in willow ptarmigan, based on cycles in mice, plant cover, and the predator switch-over phenomenon. This switch-over model as an explanation for the 3- to 4-year cycle has also been documented for black grouse (Angelstam 1983, Angelstam et al. 1984).

The 10-year cycle is most pronounced in northern ruffed grouse (Keith 1963) and arctic ptarmigan populations. Willow and rock ptarmigan in North America, Iceland, Greenland, and Scotland all show 10-year cycles (Salomonsen 1939, Braestrup 1941, Gudmundsson 1960, Watson 1965, Bergerud 1970a, Weeden & Theberge 1972). The cycle has become less pronounced or has disappeared in populations of ruffed grouse in New York, New Brunswick, and Maine, where earlier naturalists once recorded the periodic rises and falls in numbers (cf. Bump et al. 1947, Palmer 1949, Keith 1963). The prairie chicken population in Wisconsin also showed 10-year cycles in abundance from about 1850 to 1940 (Schorger 1944, Grange 1948), and then the pattern was broken (Hamerstrom & Hamerstrom 1973). At present, the cycle of ruffed grouse appears to be damping out in the Cloquet study area in northern Minnesota, where ruffed grouse research began and where field biologists have been using the King census in the spring since 1932 (King 1937, Gullion 1981).

Two other generalizations are that cyclic populations are found in large, continuous blocks of habitat (Leopold 1931) and in northern latitudes (Keith 1963). These continuous habitats include aspen parkland, coniferous forests, and arctic tundra. The boundary between the northern, cyclic populations and more southern, noncyclic populations stretches from Alberta to Minnesota, following the southern edge of the aspen parkland (Fig. 15.30). Prairie grouse in the farmlands and grasslands south of the aspen parklands are not cyclic, but sharp-tailed and ruffed grouse in the parkland show regular changes in abundance. One can distinguish further differences in the continuity of habitats used by cyclic ruffed grouse in northern Minnesota and Wisconsin, and those of noncyclic ruffed grouse in the southern portions of these states. The cyclic populations live in more homogeneous, conifer-aspen forests on glacial moraines, whereas the random, fluctuating populations reside in small blocks of relic habitats interspersed with farmland. This forest-farm interface is plainly evident on county forest maps of Wisconsin (see also Curtis 1959), and crosses the state at about 45°N. latitude, just north of the Hamerstroms' prairie chicken study area at Buena Vista Marsh, Wisconsin (Fig. 15.30, see also Curtis 1959).

15.8.1 Frequency- and density-dependent selection

In 1970 I proposed that the mechanics of change for 10-year, cyclic populations resulted from regular changes in breeding success (Bergerud 1970a). In this model, breeding success varied in response to density-dependent selection among genotypes that produced chicks of different intrinsic viability, as predicted by Chitty's (1967) hypothesis of density-dependent selection between behavioral morphs. My argument then was that variations in amplitude, periodicity, and syn-

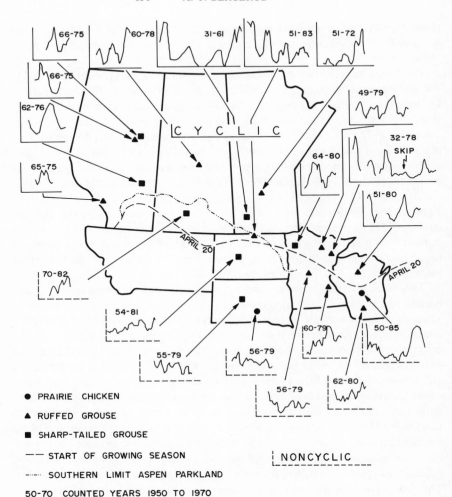

● PRAIRIE CHICKEN

▲ RUFFED GROUSE

■ SHARP-TAILED GROUSE

— — START OF GROWING SEASON

–·–·· SOUTHERN LIMIT ASPEN PARKLAND

50-70 COUNTED YEARS 1950 TO 1970

NONCYCLIC

Fig. 15.30. Comparison of the regular, cyclic fluctuations of grouse populations in the aspen parkland and boreal forest and the irregular fluctuations of populations south of the aspen parkland. All graphs are based on counts of birds in the spring except those from Manitoba and Saskatchewan, which are based on harvest statistics and thus influenced by breeding success. The increasing amplitude in the graphs using the latter four indexes reflects increasing hunting pressure rather than increasing natural amplitude. The cycles are damping out in ruffed grouse in the Turtle Mountains, North Dakota, and in the Cloquet area in Minnesota. (Data from Gullion 1970c, 1981, Hamerstrom & Hamerstrom 1973, Hillman & Jackson 1973, Kobriger 1975, 1981, Boag 1976b, Rusch 1976, Berg 1977, 1979, Keith et al. 1977, Linde et al. 1978, Anonymous 1980, Thompson & Moulton 1981, Schulz 1983, Rusch et al. 1984, pers. comm., R. K. Anderson pers. comm., S. R. Barber pers. comm., Alberta Game Dept. records.)

chronization in cycles could be explained by superimposing the vagaries of posthatch weather on these smooth alterations in chick viability. Ricker (1954) had suggested that cycles of different amplitude could result from the interaction of smooth reproduction curves and a sequence of random factors.

The polymorphic, density-dependent selection hypothesis is consistent with theoretical research into density-dependent selection (Charlesworth 1971, Roughgarden 1971, Giesel 1974, Slatkin 1979). Anderson and Arnold (1983, p. 649) stated that "when resources are limited, the genotypes in a Mendelian population will be forced into competition as the population grows in size. If the selective values of the genotypes respond differentially to population size, then density selection will occur. Experimental studies with a variety of organisms have shown that such density-regulated selection does in fact occur" (see review in Prout 1980).

Breeding-success statistics are available for five cyclic grouse populations (Fig. 15.31). Breeding success was highest when these populations increased their numbers and less when the populations were declining. In all cases, breeding success was correlated with subsequent population changes (Figs. 15.20, 15.29). There are no reported examples of cyclic grouse populations that do not display rather smooth annual changes in breeding success (Figs. 15.31, 15.32, 15.33). These relatively nonrandom changes in breeding success are probably a necessary condition to generate the 10-year cycle in grouse.

The smooth variation in chick survival in cyclic populations is not directly related to density. Chick survival generally declines before peak populations and remains low for several years after numbers fall. However, this delayed, density-dependent impact can be traced back to the competition faced by parent birds in breeding. Chick survival improves when at low densities there is no longer competition for requisites and the parents that compete at high densities have died. These results are consistent with the theory of density-dependent, polymorphic selection in which birds with less genetic variation (homozygotes) are more successful in competing for nest sites and/or mates at high densities, but in so doing provide less-viable young and the seeds of decline (see MacArthur 1968, Bergerud 1970a). In red grouse, chick survival was higher in heterozygous broods than in homozygous broods (Henderson 1977).

In Newfoundland, ptarmigan showed differences in calling frequency, vulnerability to hunting (Fig. 15.34), dispersal distances, renesting frequency, autumn weights, and male fidelity to broods, among cohorts (Bergerud 1970a). The ptarmigan on Brunette Island varied in many parameters between cohorts as the population declined from a high in 1962 (Fig. 15.35). Rock ptarmigan in Scotland called more when their numbers were declining (Watson 1965). Captive-breeding studies have now shown that calling frequency is at least partly inherited in red grouse (Moss et al. 1982b).

Reduced nesting success is also suggested in ptarmigan when numbers are high

660   A. T. BERGERUD

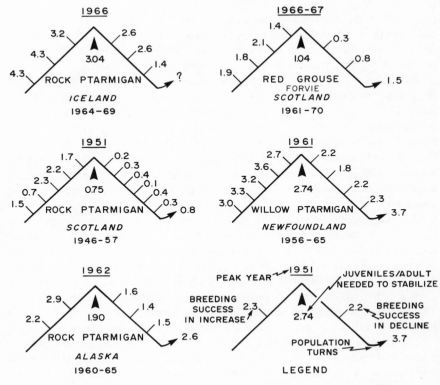

Fig. 15.31. Juveniles per adult statistics for five cyclic populations (legend, bottom right). Breeding success was greater than the number of juveniles per adult needed to maintain numbers (*s*) in years before the peak. Just before the peak year (highest breeding population), breeding success declined in six of seven population peaks recorded. After the peak, breeding success was inadequate to maintain numbers (i.e., < *s*). Breeding numbers again began to increase in four of the populations when breeding success was greater than *s*. (Data from Watson 1965, Jenkins et al. 1967, Bergerud 1970a, Gardarsson 1971, Weeden & Theberge 1972, Moss et al. 1975.)

or declining (Jenkins et al. 1963, Watson 1965, Bergerud 1970a). Experimental evidence shows differences in intrinsic viability and behavior of hand-reared chicks between cohorts in red grouse (Jenkins et al. 1965, Moss et al. 1981, Moss et al. 1984), willow ptarmigan (Bergerud 1970a), and rock ptarmigan (Theberge & Bendell 1980). In general, the survival of chicks in aviaries parallels that of those in the wild. Clutch size may also change between cohorts, as there are significant correlations between densities and clutch size in cyclic, Alaskan rock ptarmigan ($r = -0.568$, $n = 9$), cyclic ruffed grouse in Alberta ($r = -0.538$, $n = 8$), willow ptarmigan in Newfoundland ($r = 0.600$, $n = 9$), and rock ptarmigan in Iceland ($r = -0.816$, $n = 8$) (Bergerud 1970a, Gardarsson 1971, Weeden

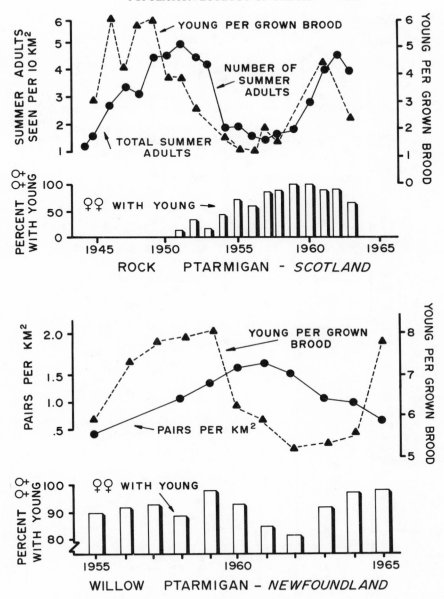

Fig. 15.32. Nesting success (estimated by the proportion of females with broods) and chick survival in relation to density for cyclic rock (*top*) and willow (*bottom*) ptarmigan populatons. Breeding success changed in smooth patterns, was highest just before peak spring densities, and began to increase again just before the population started to increase. (Data from Watson 1965, Bergerud 1970a.)

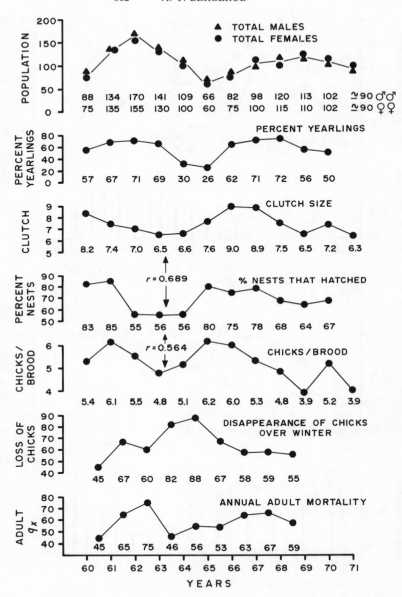

Fig. 15.33. Demography of the cyclic rock ptarmigan population at Eagle Creek, Alaska (39km²), 1960 to 1971. (Data from McGowan 1972, Weeden & Theberge 1972, pers. comm.)

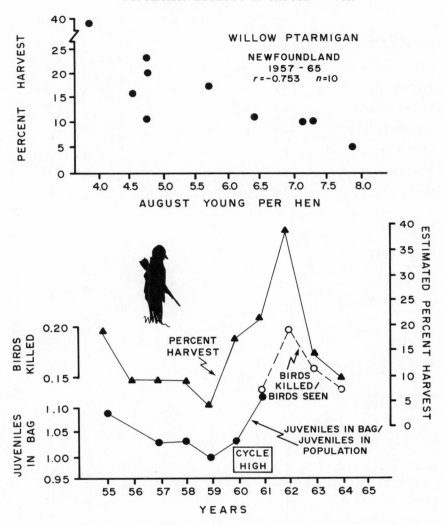

Fig. 15.34. Vulnerability of willow ptarmigan to hunting in Newfoundland showed a cyclic pattern. Birds were most susceptible to hunting after the peak, in 1962, when they were probably the most aggressive. Vulnerability was also correlated with chick viability. (Data from Bergerud 1970a, 1972.)

& Theberge 1972, Rusch et al. 1984; see Fig. 15.33). These correlations can be explained better by differences in the fecundity of genotypes than from density-related or nutritional-physiological stress.

The breeding success model builds on the foundation that all grouse populations, whether cyclic or noncyclic, are polymorphic in spacing behavior. I

	1962	1963	1964	1965	62	63	64	65
DEMOGRAPHY								
TOTAL POPULATION	392	63	81	41				
CLUTCH SIZE	6.3	8.0	8.8	10.0				
CHICKS / BROOD	3.9	4.6	5.3	6.2				
% PAIRS WITH YOUNG	70.0	86.4	97.3	95.0				
q_x CLUTCH–AUGUST	62	48	45	41				
% JUVENILE MALES	53	62	78	71				
% ADULT MALES	65	56	52	50				
BEHAVIOR								
CALLS / COCK								
APRIL	—	10.1	9.1	8.0				
OCTOBER	—	6.9	5.1	4.0				
LENGTH OF HATCH (DAYS)	25	19	17	16				
% ADULTS GOOD DEFENSE	—	5	19	50				
RATIO ADULTS CAUGHT TO ADULTS IN POP.	11.9	4.7	2.9	1.9				
MEAN MOVEMENT OF BROODS (M)	398	267	257	213				
PHYSICAL INDEX								
WING GROWTH PER DAY (MM)	2.49	3.13	3.59	3.59				
WEIGHT JUVENILES	534	556	620	608				
WEIGHT ADULTS	576	607	635	632				

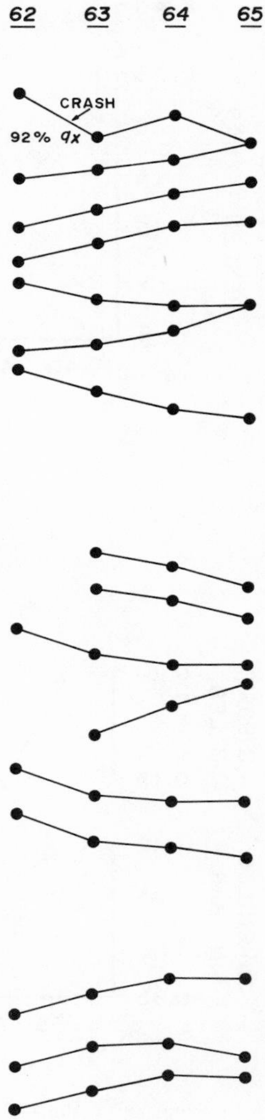

Fig. 15.35. In the cyclic population of willow ptarmigan on Brunette Island, Newfoundland, birds showed a high correlation among demographic, behavioral, and morphological parameters as their numbers declined from 1962 to 1965, suggesting a smooth change in intrinsic quality (Data from Mercer 1967.)

hypothesize that there are two suites of tactics, density-tolerant and density-intolerant phenotypes (section 14.9). The relative success of these tactics varies in space and time as populations fluctuate. Space and dispersal are the more important mediators for noncyclic populations, whereas time is the dominant pacer in cyclic populations. The evidence is extensive for these two suites of tactics (Chaps. 1,2,3).

15.8.2 The single locus, density-dependent model

The genetic background underlying the density-tolerant, intolerant phenotypes is not known. In red grouse, aggressive behavior and dominance had an additive heritability component of 0.6 between fathers and sons (Moss et al. 1982b). The aggressive behavior of blue grouse males on Stuart Island showed no detectable change in 7 years between fathers and sons (Table 2.7), whereas the docile phenotype introduced to nearby Portland Island produced both aggressive and docile progeny in the first generation (Fig. 2.21). In our genetic model of the 10-year cycle (Chap. 12), we equated aggressiveness with homozygosity (aa) and docility (density-tolerance) with heterozygosity (Aa) based on the behavioral outcomes of the island introductions. Thus, the cyclic fluctuations were generated on the basis of a single locus with Mendelian segregations and complete penetrance. The cycle was driven by genetic changes in the viability of chicks and competition for space between three genotypes.

Our model in Chapter 12 had several components of realism. Actual brood sizes observed in Newfoundland (Bergerud 1970a) were used in the simulation (high chick survival was attributed to heterosis). The amplitude of the cycles varied in response to stochastic changes in chick survival from spring weather (Bergerud 1970a). At approximately 100-year intervals, cycles were skipped, consistent with the real world. The cycle damped out in grouse populations with low mortality rates, again in tune with actual observations. But was the model too simple?

Many researchers feel that complex behavior is best explained by polygenic inheritance—the additive action of many loci (Cade 1984). Possibly the correlations of so many morphological and behavioral parameters in cyclic grouse (see Fig. 15.35) might result from major chromosome differences in inversions or karyotypes. The aggressiveness of house mice varied between 2n = 26 and 2n = 24 karyotypes (Capanna et al. 1984). At this time we know practically nothing about the genetic basis of behavior in birds. Single-locus segregations are a common finding for polymorphisms in morphology for vertebrates (Chap. 3). The substitution of alleles at a single locus can cause changes in rate of wing vibrations in *Drosophila* (Schicher 1973) and female receptivity in mosquitoes (*Aedes atropalpus*) (Gwadz 1970). Regardless of the genetic foundation of the density-tolerant, density-intolerant behavior suites, the genetic mechanism would need to be discontinuous in segregations in random mating systems to explain the rapid changes between adjacent cohorts.

Another criticism of the single-locus model in Chapter 12 is that the switching mechanism between increase and decrease phases was density-dependent competition for limited space and nonbreeding of the docile genotype. However, the evidence is that nearly all hens in each of the 9 grouse species generally nest regardless of densities (Table 15.1). Females of the lek species do not appear to have mutually exclusive nesting ranges that could provide a means of density-dependent restraint in nesting.

15.8.3 The female choice, density-dependent model

The cycle model might be made more robust by dropping the simplistic restriction of single-locus genetics and the space limitation. Instead, assume that adaptive gene combinations are maintained by linkage disequilibrium or pleiotropy for each of 2 (or 3) density phenotypes. The cycle is still driven by changes in chick survival owing to genetic influences, but the switching mechanism is not mediated by space but by hens pairing nonrandomly at high and low densities, preferring males of a similar phenotype. For ptarmigan in Newfoundland, I noted positive pair assortment within cohorts in 1962 and 1963 when the population was generally aggressive and displayed bimodalism in chick survival (Fig. 15.36, Bergerud 1970a). Pairing was more random in 1964 and 1965 as the population declined and the bimodalism in the viability of chicks became less clear (Fig. 15.36).

I have provided a diagram (Fig. 15.37) of how a female-choice paradigm could operate based on data from the cyclic, Scottish rock ptarmigan population studied by Adam Watson (see Fig. 15.32). In 1950–51 the Scottish population was high and the best habitat continuously occupied by males (Watson 1965). Under these conditions females should select males with large territories and avoid those with small territories (Chap. 10, Miller & Watson 1978, Hannon 1983). Pairing monogamously with males with the largest territories would ensure maximum spacing of nests, which would minimize nest predation within the constraints of the relatively close spacing (Fig. 15.37). Males with large territories would be aggressive (Watson 1964, Watson & Miller 1971). Likewise, aggressive females would have the pick of territory sizes by excluding docile females (Hannon 1982). Hence, the social competitions of male vs. male and female vs. female would lead to positive assortment of the density-intolerant phenotype. These aggressive pairs in the best habitats would produce less-viable young (Jenkins et al. 1963, Mercer 1967, Bergerud 1970a, Theberge & Bendell 1980). Docile pairs in secondary habitats might also fare poorly (Bergerud & Mercer 1972). The Scottish population declined after 1952 when the birds were generally aggressive and breeding success was low (< 0.5 chicks per adult, Fig. 15.32). The correlation between spacing behavior (1952, 1954–56, 1960–62; aggressive acts/100 min) and breeding success was $r = -0.833$, $n = 7$, $P < 0.05$) (data from Watson 1965). Not only did the population decline, but the sex ratio of adults shifted heavily to males. The correlation between aggressiveness and the proportion of males the next year was ($r = 0.878$, $n = 7$, $P < 0.01$); the correlation between breeding success and the proportion of males the next year in 18 years was highly significant ($r = -0.718$) (from Watson 1965).

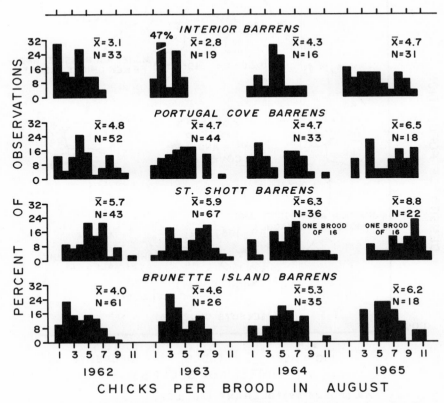

Fig. 15.36. The August brood sizes of willow ptarmigan in Newfoundland were often significantly bimodal in local populations in the years after a cyclic peak in 1960–61. (Data from Bergerud 1970a.)

A generalization is that males increase in cyclic ptarmigan populations as numbers decrease (Watson 1965, Bergerud 1970a, Fig. 15.33). In Newfoundland and Iceland more young, female chicks died than males (Bergerud 1970a, Gardarsson 1971). The significance of these deaths imbalance is that they provide changes in the frequency of the phenotypes because the viability of aggressive chicks is less than that of docile chicks (Bergerud 1970a, Theberge & Bendell 1980, Moss et al. 1984). Also, aggressive parents may provide less care (Jenkins et al. 1963, Bergerud 1970a).

By 1954–56 the Scottish population had declined by one-third; under these circumstances females could be less particular in the selection of various-sized territories—hence pairs should be a more random assortment between phenotypes. However, there would be lag effects because each new cohort pairs at densities different from that faced by the parents (Bergerud 1970a). The age structure would become progressively older because of reduced cohort contributions. In

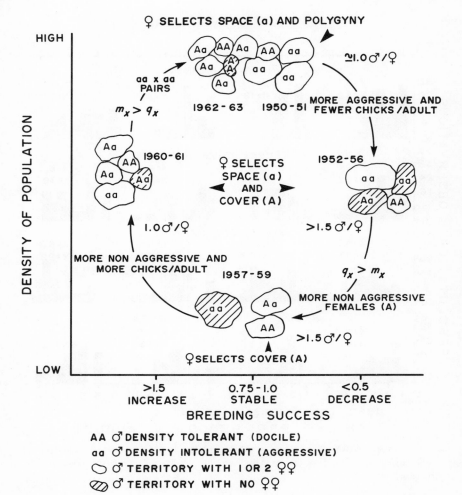

HIGH

♀ SELECTS SPACE (a) AND POLYGYNY

aa x aa
PAIRS

$m_x > q_x$

1962-63   1950-51

≃1.0♂/♀

MORE AGGRESSIVE AND
FEWER CHICKS/ADULT

1960-61   ♀ SELECTS
SPACE (a)
AND
COVER (A)

1952-56

1.0♂/♀

>1.5♂/♀

MORE NON AGGRESSIVE AND
MORE CHICKS/ADULT

1957-59

$q_x > m_x$

MORE NON AGGRESSIVE
FEMALES (A)

>1.5♂/♀

♀ SELECTS COVER (A)

DENSITY OF POPULATION

LOW

>1.5
INCREASE

0.75-1.0
STABLE

<0.5
DECREASE

BREEDING SUCCESS

AA ♂ DENSITY TOLERANT (DOCILE)
aa ♂ DENSITY INTOLERANT (AGGRESSIVE)
⬭ ♂ TERRITORY WITH 1 OR 2 ♀♀
⬭ ♂ TERRITORY WITH NO ♀♀

Fig. 15.37. The density-selection model of female choice to explain the 10-year cycle.
Data are adapted from Watson (1965). In 1950–51 the population was high; females should
have chosen aggressive males (*aa*) with large territories to increase their space away from
other nesting females. An increase in the frequency of the *a* allele should have resulted in
reduced viability and survival of chicks, especially (*aa*) females, and in a decline in the population. At midcycle, in 1952–56, females could choose either aggressive males or docile males
that defended good nesting cover. With no change in *a/A* frequency, chick survival would
have remained low and the population would have continued to decrease. In 1957–59, when
the population was small and territories were hardly touching, females would choose males
that defended good nesting cover (*A*). With an increase in frequency of *A*, chick viability improved and breeding success was greater than needed for stability (*s*). In 1960–61, as density
increased, females could choose either (a) or (*A*) males, and breeding success remained
greater than *s*. At high densities, 1962–63, females again chose aggressive males (*aa*), setting
into place another decline. Females may choose to be polygamous and select males with relatively large territories when densities are high, and territories are small overall.

1974, declining populations of willow ptarmigan at Chilkat Pass had the following age structure: $\geq$ 4 years—15%; 3 years—27%; 2 years—23%; and yearlings—35% (Mossop pers. comm.; $n = 26$ banded males and females on territory). This array is significantly different from that which would result considering only a constant, annual adult mortality of about 50% (Chap. 10).

At the bottom of the cycle in Scotland in 1957–59 the population had declined by two-thirds. By then, females, which I believe were predominantly nonaggressive, had a maximum choice of males since males outnumbered them 3 to 2 (Fig. 15.37). The territories of males should have been generally large and uniform in size (see Figs. 9.6, 10.19), hence females could have chosen males that incorporated the best nesting cover into their defended space. On Moresby Island it was the docile blue grouse males (CC stock) that defended the smallest advertising ranges (Bergerud & Hemus 1975), but in the best cover (Fig. 2.4). If this sequence held for rock ptarmigan, there should have again been positive assortment in pairing, but unlike the nonrandom pairing at the "high," at the "low," nonaggressive hens would have selected nonaggressive (density-tolerant) males. These mating combinations would produce more-viable progeny. After 1958, chick survival improved for the Scottish birds and breeding success exceeded 0.75 young per adult, which was the stabilizing breeding-success figure for that population (Fig. 15.29). The increase phase had been triggered. By 1962–63 the population in Scotland was again dense (Watson 1965), favoring pairing by aggressives, setting in place another decline and cycle.

The hypothesis of female choice to explain switching in growth phases of the cycle (Fig. 15.37) requires that there be changes in delayed density-dependence in spacing behavior that can be traced to a genetic basis. Moss et al. (1984) have now documented a regular change in aggressive behavior in cock red grouse during one complete 8-year cycle that had a heritable basis of $h^2 = 0.6$ (Moss et al. 1982b). They state, "The results confirm that genetic changes in aggression take place during a population fluctuation" (Moss & Watson 1985, p. 275). Further, by selectively pairing ptarmigan, these workers developed high and low aggressive lines in a captive population ($H_r = 0.9$, Moss et al. 1985). They report (p. 258): "The results are consistent with simple quantitative genetic inheritance of the ability to dominate others, with equal contributions from each sex." This simple inheritance system is facilitated if birds mate assortatively, and Gjestal (1977) has documented this for captive ptarmigan.

The Scottish workers rejected the genetic-aggression explanation for cycles of red grouse because the proportion of subordinate birds increased before the population started to decline, and the most submissive birds occurred just after the peak in numbers (Moss et al. 1984, Watson & Moss 1985). They reasoned that these sequences suggest changes in behavior as a result of, rather than as the cause of, population change. But the female-choice explanation (Fig. 15.37) predicts delayed sequences. When numbers are high and territories contiguous, assortative pairing of aggressive birds should result in their progeny being more homozygous for aggressiveness, and these birds will contest for breeding space in later years (Bergerud 1970a). In Newfoundland, ptarmigan were most approachable and aggressive just after the peak in numbers (Fig. 15.34, Mercer 1967, Bergerud 1970a), as were ruffed grouse at Watch Lake (Fig. 3.16).

In Scotland the peak in inherited docility in red grouse occurred in 1973 after the high in numbers in 1972 (Moss & Watson 1985). This sequence is the converse of that in Newfoundland (Fig. 15.34) and Watch Lake (Fig. 3.16), and of the Chitty hypothesis (Moss & Watson 1985). However, in Scotland there was extensive emigration when numbers were high; the birds that left should have been the density-intolerant phenotype (Fig. 2.4). The remaining birds and their progeny would then have been less aggressive. The Scottish results may have resulted because a closed system was not studied.

A robust female-choice explanation for the 10-year cycle in grouse should account for the cycles not only in monogamous ptarmigan, but also in polygynous ruffed grouse and sharp-tailed grouse (Fig. 15.30). A major difference in the two mating systems is that with polygyny some males breed several females and males do not defend nesting space or cover that females could choose. Females for these species must generally choose between the males that continue to advertise after male vs. male competition. The most complete data available for polygynous grouse is the ruffed grouse study presented in Chapter 3.

Red-phase, ruffed grouse males at Watch Lake, British Columbia, were more aggressive than gray birds, and their frequency in the advertising population increased with density (Fig. 15.38). The frequency of red hens also increased as numbers expanded (Fig. 15.38), and these hens were more aggressive than gray hens (Fig. 3.13) and raised fewer chicks per successful female (Table 3.5). Positive assortment should have occurred in mating for ruffed grouse, on the basis of frequency alone. If birds of the color-behavior phenotype sorted themselves in space as did blue grouse on Moresby Island and Vancouver Island, there would have been positive assortment. The ruffed grouse in Area 1 at Watch Lake were generally more aggressive than those in Area 2 (Figs. 3.10, 3.11, 3.15). Positive pairing assortment between color morphs has been recorded in snow geese (*Anserr caerulescens*) (Cooke & Cooch 1968) and the Arctic skua (*Catharacta skua*) (O'Donald 1977). For both species there were differences in behavior between morphs. If we combine assortive matings in grouse, plus genetic linkage combinations involving color-behavior and possibly chick survival, we have the necessary basis for density-dependent selection resulting in cycles. A confounding factor at Watch Lake was the appearance of goshawks in 1972–73 and 1980–81. These raptors probably killed many more red cocks than gray males. This predation should have altered the underlying genetic frequencies in one season and could have affected the switching of the cycle from declining to increasing. Still that population experienced negative recruitment 1971–74 and 1979–82, before

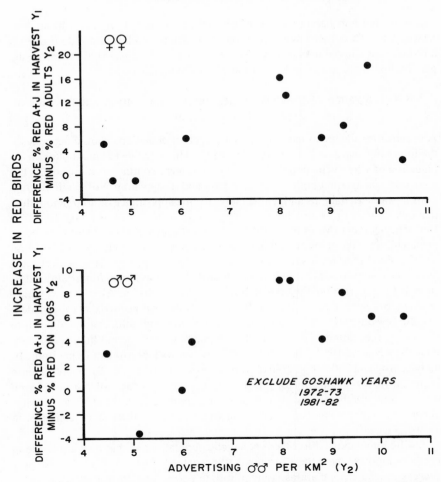

Fig. 15.38. *Top*: Proportion of red grouse hens in the ruffed grouse population at Watch Lake, British Columbia (Chap. 3), increased when densities increased. *Bottom*: Proportion of red cocks advertising at Watch Lake also increased as numbers increased.

and after the goshawk flights. Further there was positive recruitment in both 1974 and 1975 when the frequency of the color phases did not change (Table 3.1). An underlying, intrinsic cyclic mechanism is still suggested.

Females of the steppe grouse, like sharptails, generally mate with more centrally located males at leks, but they also choose which leks they will visit (Fig. 14.9). As populations increase, new, small leks of yearlings appear. Males at these leks may be more density-intolerant and aggressive. Such males could improve their breeding success in increasing populations as density intolerant females expand into habitats that are less densely occupied, and visit these new, nearby leks. This is strictly speculation; there are no studies to decide if there is a positive assortment in pairing for steppe grouse, and we have only the first suggestion that there are even behavioral phenotypes (Chap. 5).

15.8.4 Relevance of the density-dependent model to characteristics of cyclic populations

A satisfactory theory to explain 10-year, cyclic fluctuations should account for the following characteristics of tetraonids. (1) The hypothesis should offer an explanation of why cyclic populations are in northern, continuous biomes. (2) The theory should account both for the damping and disappearance of cyclic fluctuations in southern habitats and, conversely, for the appearance of nonrandom fluctuations such as those that have recently occurred in red grouse populations at Kerloch, Scotland (Moss et al. 1984). (3) A valid model should also provide an explanation for the skips that often occur in a series of cycles (Leopold 1931, Fig. 15.30). Furthermore, a satisfactory account should specify (4) why cyclic behavior is absent in populations in which birds have low, annual mortality rates, such as blue grouse on Vancouver Island, spruce grouse in Alberta, and white-tailed ptarmigan in Colorado. In addition, a hypothesis is needed that (5) can identify the reasons why one population is cyclic, and one immediately adjacent to it is noncyclic. Some of the red grouse populations in Scotland fluctuate irregularly (MacKenzie 1952, Hudson et al. 1985), yet rock ptarmigan living immediately nearby and 200 m higher in elevations are cyclic (Fig. 15.32). Ruffed grouse in the Turtle Mountains of North Dakota are cyclic but sharp-tailed grouse living only a few kilometers away fluctuate in a noncyclic fashion. The density-dependent selection model is sufficient to account for these characteristics in grouse.

Cyclic populations differ from noncyclic populations in that they are found in northern biomes where there are few nest predators (Figs. 15.7, 15.30). Nesting success in cyclic populations is invariably in excess of 60% (cf. Watson 1965, Kupa 1966, Bergerud 1970a, Gardarsson 1971, Weeden & Theberge 1972, Rusch et al. 1984). This high nesting success, coupled with typical brood attrition and overwinter loss, provides sufficient recruits for cyclic populations to increase (Table 15.10) so that ultimately density-dependent competition will occur. Females in noncyclic populations generally have a nesting success of less than 60%. This high loss, coupled with chicks lost in summer and overwinter mortality of juveniles and adults, does not provide sufficient recruitment for continuous population growth (Table 15.10). A necessary but not sufficient condition for cyclic populations is high nesting success.

Originally, Maine, New York, and New Brunswick were covered with contiguous forests. Nest predation would have been lower than now, and nesting suc-

Table 15.10. Life equation of a hypothesized, typical, cyclic grouse population compared with that of a noncyclic population

---

Cyclic population

Population parameters: 50 breeding males and 50 breeding females; mean clutch size that hatches = 9 eggs (reduced to account for infertility, etc.); 0.70 nesting success (Table 15.2); 0.55 survival of chicks in broods; 0.45 survival of juveniles overwinter; annual mortality of adults 0.50 (Table 15.6).

Population change year 1 to year 2:

Recruitment (m_x): 50 females × 9 eggs × 0.70 nesting success × 0.55 brood s_x × 0.45 overwinter s_x = 78 yearlings.

Mortality (q_x): 100 adults (year 1) × 0.50 s_x = 50 adults

50 adults + 78 yearlings = 128 birds (year 2) (m_x > q_x): *Population increases*

Noncyclic population

Population parameters: 55 breeding males and 45 breeding females (Table 15.8); mean clutch size that hatches = 9 eggs (reduced to account for infertility, etc.); 0.50 nesting success (Table 15.2); 0.55 survival of chicks in broods; 0.45 survival of juveniles overwinter (Gullion & Marshal 1968); annual mortality of adults 0.50 (Table 15.6).

Population change year 1 to year 2:

Recruitment (m_x): 45 females × 9 eggs × 0.50 nesting success × 0.55 summer survival of young × 0.45 overwinter s_x = 50 yearlings.

Mortality (q_x): 100 adults (year 1) × 0.50 s_x = 50 adults.

50 adults + 50 yearlings = 100 birds (year 2) (m_x = q_x): *Population stable*

---

cess of ruffed grouse in these areas would have been comparable to the still-high nesting success of cyclic ruffed grouse in Alberta, about 76% (Rusch et al. 1984). When settlers arrived, small farms appeared; domestic animals accompanied the homesteaders, and habitat diversity increased. The common nest predators found in settled landscapes—red foxes, skunks (*Mephitis mephitis*), raccoons (*Procyon lotor*), and corvids—all should have increased.

The cycle has disappeared in New York (Bump et al. 1947, Keith 1963), where from 1930 to 1942 the nesting success of ruffed grouse was 61% (Bump et al. 1947). This is borderline nesting success for a cyclic population. Noncyclic ruffed grouse in Massachusetts had a 50% success rate (Banasiak 1951), and in New Brunswick, where the cycle has also disappeared, on average only 47% of the hens were successful from 1965 to 1966 (Neave 1965).

Nest predation not only reduces potential recruitment, it also brings extrinsic "noise" to what was a more intrinsic, self-contained system. Mice and insect populations fluctuate and foxes, skunks, and weasels increase and switch from buffer species to grouse (Bump et al. 1947; Chap. 11). Random weather effects influence plant cover, hence, the rate of nest predation (Fig. 15.11). Populations cannot show smooth changes in breeding success when predation of nests is high and variable.

The cycle of ruffed grouse in northern Minnesota is becoming less pronounced. There was no clear peak for an expected high in 1960–61 at Cloquet (Fig. 15.30). Predation of eggs had been 24% from 1933 to 1934 ($n = 477$), but increased to 32% by 1959–66 ($n = 169$) (Kupa 1966). Overall success at Cloquet was 69% (Kupa 1969, Gullion 1970c), whereas in central Minnesota a marginally cyclic population (Fig. 15.30) showed nesting success of approximately 59% (Maxson 1974). Nest predation should increase in the years ahead because the aspen forests of northern Minnesota are becoming fragmented, and the cycle will disappear.

In the Turtle Mountains of North Dakota the amplitude of the 10-year cycle of ruffed grouse has moderated in the past 30 years (Fig. 15.39). The forest in the United States portion of the mountains is rapidly being converted to farmland (Schulz 1983). Foxes are replacing coyotes as the dominant canid (A. Sargeant pers. comm.). Foxes are a much more effective nest predator of grouse than are coyotes because of the much higher density of foxes—a home range of 13 km^2 versus 62 km^2, respectively, in North Dakota (Scott 1982). The percentage of females in the population has declined in each of the peaks of the last three cycles (Fig. 15.39), possibly owing to increased predation. This cycle is probably being damped because predators can destabilize nesting success ($< 60\%$) at progressively lower population peaks.

When predation increases, populations can generate positive growth only at lower densities than formerly (Fig. 15.39). Only at low densities can individuals be spaced in cover of good quality and remain inconspicuous in the face of more species and numbers of effective predators. Also, when densities are reduced, competition among individuals for advertising and nest sites will be less intense—space buffers social interaction and competition among genotypes, thereby damping cyclic fluctuations.

The prairie chicken population in Wisconsin once showed 10-year cycles of abundance. Peaks were about 1857, 1867, 1878, 1887, 1897 (Schorger 1944), 1909, 1915, 1923 (Leopold 1931), and 1933 (Grange 1948, Anonymous 1976). Minor peaks may have occurred in about 1940 and 1950 (Hamerstrom & Hamerstrom 1973), but the cycle was damping out, and the major peaks in the 1960s and 1970s never occurred (Fig. 15.30). In the mid-1800s this chicken population had rapidly increased following clearing of the land (Leopold 1931, Schorger 1944). The creation of habitat was a necessary but not a sufficient condition for

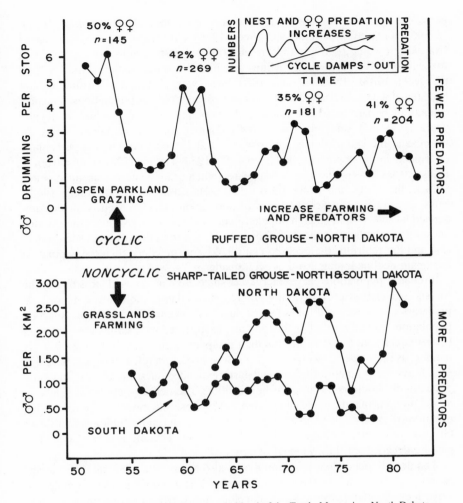

Fig. 15.39. Ruffed grouse in the aspen parkland of the Turtle Mountains, North Dakota, are cyclic, whereas sharp-tailed grouse in the grasslands farther south are noncyclic. The grasslands have sufficient kinds and numbers of predators to reduce nesting success so that density-dependent selection seldom occurs. However,the cycle of ruffed grouse is damping out. With each successive peak, there were fewer females, consistent with the hypothesis of increased rates of predation and the disappearance of the cycle in the future. (Data from Hillman & Jackson 1973, Kobriger 1975, 1981, Linde et al. 1978, Schulz 1981.)

population expansion; to increase, a population must also have positive recruitment. When new habitats are created quickly, grouse can spread out and avoid nest concentrations, and thus reduce nest losses. But possibly more important, in this example there was a lag in predation pressure following settlement. Red foxes did not enter southwestern Wisconsin until about 1895 (Leopold 1931). Skunks increased after settlement (Scott 1956) and trapped raccoons increased from an estimated 6,000 in 1930 to 200,000 by 1975 (Anonymous 1976). Red foxes increased throughout the Midwest to high levels during the period 1931–45 (Sargeant 1983). By 1940 and 1950 birds were losing the nesting habitat (Westemeier 1971b) needed to counter *increasing* predator populations. The percentage of female prairie chickens in the population during the low, noncyclic years (1949–65) was 36% ($n = 890$) (Hamerstrom & Hamerstrom 1973), whereas at the end of the cycling phase, 10 to 15 years earlier, the percentage of females in the population had been 47% (1934–41, $n = 528$; Hamerstrom & Hamerstrom 1949). The cycle disappeared when nesting success dropped below 60% in the 1930s and 1940s (Gross 1930, Hamerstrom 1939, Grange 1948). Missing were the consecutive years of population increase needed for density-dependent selection. The high population in 1982 (Fig. 16.18) raises the exciting question of whether this increase forecasts the return of density-dependent selection and the return of the cycle to central Wisconsin. Since then the population has again declined, suggesting a cyclic pattern.

Predator populations have increased since humans caused erosion of the forests and altered prey diversity. Increased predators include the major nest predators of grouse—red foxes (Sargeant 1984), skunks, and corvids. Raccoon populations moved north. Other predators disappeared with settlement—the wolf (*Canis lupus*), lynx, and so on—but their disappearance meant little in grouse dynamics, as these species were not serious nest predators (cf. Johnson & Sargeant 1977). As the predators of field and farm expanded, nesting success in cyclic populations should have dropped below 60%. The density-dependent selection model predicts that the cycles will disappear in these situations. In the future, the question of cycles will be even more contentious and more biologists will ask: Grouse cycles: are they real (Gullion 1973)? They become less real with each passing decade, but they were of our past.

The density-dependent selection model also offers an explanation for the appearance of cycles where formerly none existed. Harvest statistics for red grouse at Kerloch, Scotland, showed irregular fluctuations from 1921 to approximately 1937 (Jenkins & Watson 1970). Population counts starting in 1962 showed non-random fluctuation; there were four runs of increase and decrease in population growth in the 14 years from 1963 to 1977 (Watson et al. 1973, Watson & Moss 1980). Because of the reduction of predators in Scotland, red grouse enjoy nesting success in excess of 75% (Jenkins et al. 1963, 1967), and thus the potential to cycle is present, although there has been extreme variability in the survival of chicks in summer. The research in Scotland documented that the quality of heather affects the hens' nutrition and the viability of chicks at birth—the Siivonen hypothesis (Moss et al. 1975). Disease of chicks may also be a problem (Hudson et al. 1985). The quality of heather, in turn, is affected by random variation in weather, which would add phenotypic "noise" to population growth.

However, from 1969 to 1971 there was a progression of good breeding seasons (Watson & Moss 1980, Moss et al. 1984) that allowed the population to build up. This high density could then have resulted in competition between density-tolerant and density-intolerant phenotypes, providing the template for cycles. This competition did occur; cocks at Kerloch were less aggressive when the population was increasing than when it was declining (Moss et al. 1984). Also, egg size, chick viability, and chick growth rates were higher when the population was expanding than when it was high and declining. These behavioral and physical parameters have a heritable component (Moss et al. 1982b, 1984), yet the red grouse workers reject a genetic explanation for their findings because results from wild eggs and subsequent progeny did not agree with those from the common lines of birds bred and reared in captivity. However, the genotypic recombinations from aviary crosses would not replicate field crosses because female choice of mates or their territorial requisites would not be duplicated in the aviary.

Rock ptarmigan in Scotland live only a few hundred meters higher in elevation than some neighboring, noncyclic red grouse. These rock ptarmigan in Scotland also have the high nesting success needed for true cycles, 76% (Watson 1965). In addition, these birds initiate nesting at the same time that spring green-up occurs (Watson 1965). Thus, compared with red grouse, there should be reduced variability in maternal nutrition and chick viability in rock ptarmigan. Our genetic simulation of the population dynamics of this rock ptarmignan population studied by Watson (1965), gave a cycle slightly longer than 10 years, in close agreement with the actual cycle periodicity (Chap. 12, Fig. 15.32).

The potential phenotypic variability between years for laying hens of changing nutrition is generally absent for northern cyclic grouse. For example, the sharp-tailed grouse in Saskatchewan and Manitoba generally hatch their eggs in the second or third week of June. Females are thus laying eggs in the last week of April. The growing season generally begins about 20 April along the cyclic/noncyclic interface through North Dakota and Minnesota (Fig. 15.30). Grouse north of this line have a reduced potential for nutrition to affect intrinsic chick viability. For grouse south of the line this potential is present, but the sequence has not yet been documented in North American grouse.

A more important environmental perturbation between cyclic sharp-tailed grouse in Alberta, Manitoba, and Minnesota, and noncyclic sharp-tailed grouse in North Dakota is nest predation. The Dakota birds live in grasslands where herbaceous nesting cover varies between years depending on rainfall. These birds face an array of prairie and farm predators. In contrast, cyclic sharp-tailed grouse in Manitoba live in the aspen parklands where the moisture regime is more constant and nesting cover more diversified. In addition, these latter populations are hunted by fewer kinds of predators, which exist at lower densities. One of the main predators in the aspen parklands is the coyote, which exists in much lower densities than does the fox in the grasslands to the south.

The potential for smooth changes in breeding success resulting from density-dependent selection is now absent in the prairie grouse of the grasslands. How-ever, prairie grouse could have cycled in the brief period between the disappear-ance of the buffalo and the wolves, and the increased arrival of the new contingent of field and farm predators on the coattails of settlement. During this period nest cover should have improved and only few predators were about (Chap. 16).

The density-dependent selection hypothesis provides an explanation for skips that occasionally occur in cyclic populations. Our simulation of competition among genotypes with different fitnesses has failed to demonstrate cycles at ap-proximately hundred-year intervals (Fig. 12.3). Skips in cycles will occur when-ever breeding populations remain low, so that genotypic sorting would not occur.

A prediction of the Chitty hypothesis relevant to this discussion is that popula-tion declines can be prevented if competition is reduced by removal experiments (Krebs 1978a). A series of random, inclement springs or disasters could reduce chick survival so that populations failed to increase as predicted using past trends. The Newfoundland willow ptarmigan skipped a cyclic peak in about 1930; there were large forest fires in 1927 and 1929 (Bergerud 1971), and these fires could have killed young birds, destroyed nests, and removed nesting cover. The willow ptarmigan at Chilkat Pass failed to decline in number in 1980–81 (Hannon 1982, pers. observ.), whereas other populations in the Yukon crashed in 1981 (Mossop pers. comm.). The Chilkat population was extremely heavily harvested, and we could not find "waiting" birds in 1980–81, as Mossop had in 1972 (Figs. 10.20, 10.22). This harvest could have delayed selection for density-intolerant birds, the forerunners of decline.

Many grouse populations do not cycle—even some in which birds begin nest-ing before new plant growth appears. Hens in nearly all noncyclic populations have nesting success that on average is less than 60%. For example, white-tailed ptarmigan have a 57% nesting success (Giesen et al. 1980); blue grouse on Van-couver Island, a 55% success rate (Zwickel 1975, Zwickel & Carveth 1978); and spruce grouse in Alberta hatched only 19 of 66 nests, or 29% (Keppie & Herzog 1978, Keppie 1982).

More important, we could not generate cycles in our simulation when popula-tions had low, annual mortality rates less than 40–50%. Birds in these populations that show low mortality rates also have smaller clutches and raise smaller broods (Figs. 15.1, 15.4). The low turnover of adults thus reduces the potential for large variations in brood size and prohibits a rapid, cyclic, polymorphic response be-tween adjacent cohorts. However, these populations had the potential to erupt in our simulation (Chap. 12) if they encountered a run of good breeding seasons. Such eruptions have indeed occurred in blue grouse (Fig. 15.28).

Adjacent cyclic populations are often synchronized (Keith 1963), but popula-tions become more out-of-step when one compares populations that are ge-ographically well-spaced (Bergerud 1970a). The interaction of smooth reproduc-tive curves of chicks with different viability and vulnerability to random extrinsic weather can partly explain both this synchronization and the absence of it (Leslie 1959, Chitty 1960). The susceptibility of chicks to mortality caused by weather would vary among genotypes. Adjacent populations face the same weather systems and would thus become more uniform in genetic character. Predation by raptors that range widely between populations might also improve the synchronization of adjacent populations if this predation resulted in differential culling of genotypes. In one cycle of ruffed grouse at Watch Lake, British Columbia, red-phase birds represented one-third of the population, but in the second peak, they represented only one-fourth (Fig. 3.4). However, in both instances, after the winter crash in which goshawks killed proportionally more red-phase than gray-phase birds, the percentage of reds was similar, 2–4% (Figs 3.4, 3.16).

In summary, the density-dependent selection hypothesis to explain the 10-year cycle in grouse is based on the belief that all populations are polymorphic in density preference, with some individuals more adapted to living in high densities (density-tolerant) and others to living in low densities (density-intolerant) (Chap. 14). Given that the extrinsic environment is relatively benign, recruitment can generally exceed mortality for several consecutive years. As the population builds, the relative advantages of the density-intolerant birds increase because of the competition among males for advertising sites and because of female choice of successful, aggressive males. In effect, all females breed annually but many males do not; thus fitness paces genotypic variability between genotypes. Aggressive, density-intolerant genotypes that are favored with intense competition are postulated to be more homozygous (Fig. 2.26), produce less-viable young (Bergerud 1970a), and contribute less to population growth than heterozygotes. These young die for a variety of reasons, but the summed result is that recruitment becomes insufficient to replace the more-or-less constant, natural mortality of adults, and the population then declines. The 10-year periodicity results from the relatively constant mortality rates of cyclic grouse (50%–60%); hence, a two-generation turnover period with its inherent lag effects. Extrinsically induced weather and predator mortality have different impacts on the genotype percentages in populations, thereby reducing genetic variability and adding some generation synchronization to nearby populations exposed to similar extrinsic regimes.

15.9 Limitation of breeding numbers

No simple hypothesis of population regulation can be expected to explain the great diversity of numerical responses observed in grouse, but a reasonable, comprehensive body of theory can be fashioned from a few general principles. Any model must include those population parameters that have clearly been documented in the literature to influence breeding numbers.

A viable population is maintained only if production to autumn equals overwinter losses (Table 15.6). A population cannot sustain both a high loss of eggs and young and a high mortality rate of adults. The first generalization is that there is a south-north continuum for these parameters; loss of nests is greatest in the south, where there is more predation of nests. Adult mortality is probably higher in the north, where there are more effective raptors; however, there are few studies of adult mortality in the south to verify this. The southern distribution of grouse is probably limited by nest predation, and the northern distribution limited by protective cover to avoid predators.

A second generalization is that grouse die primarily from predation. There is no substantial evidence that grouse of North America, other than young chicks, starve or succumb to disease in normal populations. The vulnerability of grouse to predation changes seasonally. They are most susceptible when they must compromise their inconspicuousness to advertise and to nest and rear chicks. It should be expected that the mortality rates of males and females will be different, because they differ in their investment in offspring.

A third principle is that individuals of each species are preadapted to a specific predator-escape cover complex, i.e., their species-specific habitat. Willow ptarmigan are found in the tall-shrub zones of the tundra. Gyrfalcons also occupy this zone and ptarmigan depend on willow shrubs for cover to escape this raptor (Chap. 10). Each habitat has its own array of coevolved predators and vegetation with unique morphological characteristics used by grouse to escape these predators. Birds of each grouse species, indeed of each *population*, will be subject to a unique mortality rate that is extrinsically determined by resident predators and cover.

Annual mortality rates are more constant than breeding success rates. But mortality can be expected to vary if predator abundance changes, or if the searching pattern of predators varies with changing, alternate-prey abundance. Mortality rates may vary among years if the inconspicuousness of the grouse is altered. Grouse behavior will add another dimension—density-intolerant birds have a suite of behaviors that improves their fitness in some intraspecific competitive situations, but at the same time may increase their vulnerability to predation.

If mortality rates change among years, they must alter breeding numbers. But mortality rates are only about half as variable as changes in breeding success. Mortality is induced by predator populations in which individual grouse have evolved their own adaptations to maximize fitness. This coevolution lends stability to the mortality rates of grouse. Breeding success, in contrast to mortality rates, varies more in response to the extrinsic environment, outside biological adaptation, and without lag effects or buffers.

I can find little evidence of density-dependence in the mortality rates of adult grouse. A relatively constant proportion of the population dies between breeding seasons. There were exceptions—the death of prairie chicken hens in summer increased with numbers as did the mortality of advertising, male ruffed grouse. A major predator like the goshawk generally hunts ruffed grouse, regardless of population size, but the goshawk may change its range in response to encounter rates.

It is the breeding-success side of the population equation that most influences changes in breeding numbers of grouse. Nearly all hens nest; clutch size varies among species and populations, but it shows little variation between years that is correlated with population change. Nesting success varies markedly in relation to: (1) changes in nesting cover, (2) predator pressure, (3) age structure (experience of the hen), and (4) female behavior. Nesting success of grouse is the most variable parameter in the dynamics of their populations, and through its influence on breeding success, contributes more to changes in population size between years that any other parameter.

The survival of chicks also has a fairly large coefficient of variation (Table 15.6). As in other bird species, very young grouse are the weakest link in the life-history of a cohort; chicks die from many causes before they can thermoregulate. Apparently no populations do not lose at least 25% of the chicks that hatch (Fig. 15.1). The major variables that likely alter chick survival are spring temperature, insect abundance, intrinsic viability, predation, concealing cover, and maternal condition. Also, the parental solicitousness may change between cohorts in cyclic species and affect chick survival.

We can recognize at least five extrinsic patterns and one intrinsic pattern to breeding success. (1) Chick survival can be influenced by the viability of young at hatch, which in turn is affected by maternal nutrition or parasitism mediated through weather and food in the prelaying period. Red grouse are an example (Fig. 15.40). (2) Breeding success can be influenced by nesting cover, which is influenced by rainfall. Sharp-tailed grouse in South Dakota are an example. (3) Breeding success can vary with stages of plant succession, as for blue grouse on Vancouver Island. When birds first colonize a newly logged area, nesting success and breeding survival are low (Zwickel & Bendell 1967). When after a period of years the forest grows too dense and homogeneous relative to the food for chicks, recruitment declines. (4) Breeding success can vary in relation to cycles in mouse populations and cover and predators switching to nesting grouse. The willow ptarmigan in Norway is an excellent example. (5) Breeding success can vary with June temperatures that affect insect abundance and the need to thermoregulate; the ruffed grouse at Watch Lake (Chap. 3) is an example. (6) The one intrinsic pattern is that breeding success can vary with density-dependent selection between genotypes. Rock ptarmigan in Scotland may be an example. These annual changes in productivity are the driving forces of population changes (Fig. 15.41).

The density of grouse, in turn, is a function of the species-specific habitat (space) prorated to the total number of birds alive (Fig. 15.41). It is an effect of last year's population demography; however, the density of birds is the arena in which density-tolerant and density-intolerant morphs compete for forthcoming

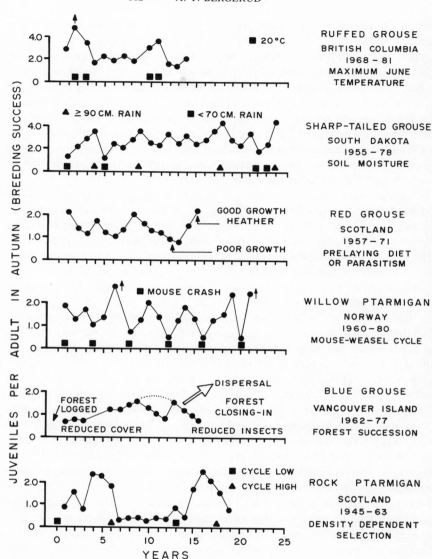

Fig. 15.40. Summary of six scenarios that can affect breeding success and drive numbers:
(1) the scenario of June temperature from Chap. 3; (2) soil moisture based on Fig. 15.11; (3)
maternal food or parasitism based on Moss et al. 1975 or Hudson et al. 1985; (4) predator
switch-over from Chap. 11; (5) forest succession based on Zwickel & Bendell (1967), Redfield (1970), Zwickel et al. (1977, 1983), and Frandsen (1980); (6) the 10-year cycle scenario
based on Fig. 15.32—data from Watson (1965).

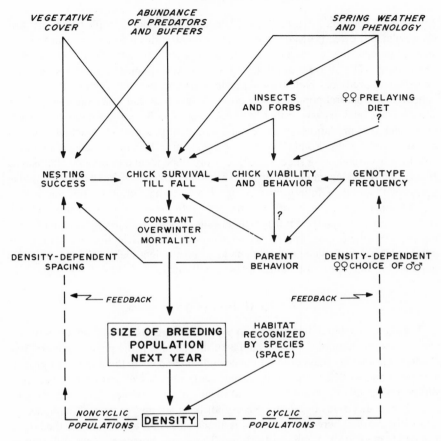

Fig. 15.41. Summary model of population limitation in grouse.

fitness. For noncyclic populations with high nesting losses, the sorting takes place primarily by dispersal of these morphs to seek those densities that suit their evolved suite of breeding characteristics and will result in maximum fitness (Chap. 2). For the cyclic populations living in more homogeneous and stable environments, with fewer extrinsic restraints to breeding success, dispersal is less important. For these birds, density-dependent competition for advertising and nesting sites is more intense.

The ultimate question—the lead sentence in the introductory lecture on population ecology—What prevents the unlimited increase of a population; why don't natural populations continue to increase as does man?—can be partly answered with respect to grouse. Many populations fluctuate free of density-dependent restraint; they may increase when food is favorable for chicks or again decrease when nesting cover is reduced in dry cycles. These populations fluctuate in response to a shortage of time, as explained in the random-walk theory of Andrewartha and Birch (1954). To study these populations is to never secure an answer to the question of the ultimate check of population growth. But there are a few insights. The ultimate limit of natural, *noncyclic* populations coexisting with undisturbed predators is density-dependent nesting success. If the environment is benign and natural populations continue to increase, the first requisite in short supply is adequate space so that hens can nest at sufficient distances from each other such that predation is reduced and sufficient progeny are hatched to equal natural, adult losses. Potts (1980) and Angelstam (1983) have reached a similar conclusion — that nesting success is the density-dependent damping mechanism in Hungarian partridge and black grouse. The inverse relationship between population growth and density in grouse comes down, in the end, to nesting success as it is influenced by space, cover, and predators. In those cases where there are insufficient predators in the environment to cause negative, density-dependent nesting success — the *cyclic* populations — density-dependent selection between genotypes at high densities can result in chicks of insufficient viability to maintain the population, and again population growth is limited.

15.10 Summary

The number of breeding grouse in a population constantly changes between years. Documentation of the mechanics of this change is the primary aim of this chapter. Parameters that could influence annual changes in the number of grouse are: percentage of hens that nest, variations in clutch size and nesting success, survival of chicks in summer, survival of juveniles in winter, and variations in annual mortality rates of adults. Nearly all hens attempt to nest. Clutch size is relatively constant between years and is also insufficient to account for the large, annual changes in the number of grouse. There are, however, large differences in clutch size between populations of the same species. The characteristic clutch size of each population is hypothesized to have arisen from selection with respect to lifetime fitness as influenced by the characteristic longevity of individuals in specific populations. Clutch size may have been further modified in some populations from that predicted by the expected longevity of an individual female because of directional selection from nest predators against females that lay large clutches. Nesting success of grouse is generally low; as a group only about 58% of the nests hatch. Predation accounts for an average of 79% of nest failures. Mortality of chicks is also high; on average 44% of chicks die before fall. But chick mortality is not correlated with clutch size and occurs regardless of the presence or absence of predators. Abundant insect food appears to be a necessary precondition for high survival of chicks. Mortality rates of juveniles and adults show large differences among populations, ranging from 18% to 81%. The differences can be attributed to the unique, predator-cover complex in which each population lives. Birds in some populations are quite secure from predators. In populations that show this low mortality mode ($<$ 45% annual q_x), selection favors females that lay small clutches. In noncyclic populations with a preponderance of males, mortality of females is high during the nesting period. The greater proportion of males in cyclic ptarmigan populations is possibly explained by the increased mortality of female chicks during population declines. The model of the 10-year cycle proposed by Bergerud (1970a) is further refined by the hypothesis that the switching mechanism between density-tolerant and density-intolerant phenotypes and population increases and declines is mediated by female choice of aggressive males with large territories when the density of birds is high, and by choice of docile males that control high-quality nesting cover when populations are low and birds are spaced far apart. The major conclusion of this chapter is that variations in breeding success drive population changes between years; overwinter mortality is relatively constant. The ultimate damping mechanism to the growth of noncyclic populations is postulated to be density-dependent nest predation; that to the growth of cyclic populations, density-dependent changes in mate choice between genotypes that provide chicks with differing intrinsic viabilities.

16

Increasing the Numbers of Grouse

A. T. Bergerud

16.1 Introduction

A tendency of management biologists is to proceed on the basis that if there is more habitat, it follows that there will be more grouse. It is true that habitat is the template for population growth, but it is only a necessary, and not a sufficient, precondition. Mortality rates are generally fixed by the predator-cover complex in which grouse live. For a population to increase, breeding success must be greater than that needed to stabilize numbers. The strategy of management should be to improve reproductive success.

The format of this chapter generally follows the topic outline discussed by Aldo Leopold in *Game Management* (1933). He proposed five major management schemes: control of hunting, control of predators, control of food and water, control of cover, and control of disease. Disease and water are not major limiting factors of grouse in North America (but see Potts et al. 1984 for red grouse [*Lagopus lagopus scoticus*] in England), and are not included. In lieu of those factors I have added control of space, which represents manipulation of the interaction of birds with their predator-cover complex, to enhance survival and breeding opportunities. Before addressing these limiting factors, however, I will discuss the determinants of density.

16.2 Mechanisms of density

16.2.1 Nesting success and density

In general we count males to obtain an index of density, but males space themselves to be near females (Bradbury 1981, Chap. 14). Thus, it is of paramount interest that the locations of females are the basic spacing unit. Females, in turn, space their nests to remain inconspicuous (Chap. 14.). They reduce their contact with males and other females to minimize the risk of predation. The major determinant of density in grouse is, I believe, the space needed for successful nesting so that m_x (recruitment) = q_x (mortality).

Evidence now indicates that the prelaying ranges of female blue (*Dendragapus obscurus*), spruce (*Dendragapus canadensis*), and possibly ruffed grouse (*Bonasa umbellus*) are generally mutually exclusive (Rusch & Keith 1971a, Zwickel 1972, Herzog & Boag 1978, Bergerud & Butler 1985). The prelaying ranges of females of the three ptarmigan species (*Lagopus* spp.) are also mutually exclusive (see Chap. 13). Anglestam (1983) reported that the ranges of female black grouse (*Tetrao tetrix*), a lek species, also were mutually exclusive, but this has not been shown in the literature for females of the three North American lek species. However, M. Gratson (pers. comm.) indicates that the nests of sharp-tailed grouse (*Tympanuchus phasianellus*) are mostly spaced. Also, a recent increase in prairie chickens (*Tympanuchus cupido*) in Minnesota has been accompanied by an increase in the number of leks and not in the number of displaying males per lek (Fig. 16.1). This association suggests that spacing occurs in prairie chickens. The prelaying ranges of the lek species are large (Fig. 16.2), and, because such large ranges could not be easily defended without a serious trade-off in energy and loss of inconspicuousness, the spacing mechanism that probably occurs is mutual avoidance rather than mutual exclusion.

Females of each grouse group (forest, tundra, and steppe) travel in prelaying ranges of different sizes (Bradbury 1981), and these ranges are larger where nest predation is serious (Fig. 16.2). My interpretation is that females faced with more predation pressure search larger prelaying ranges before investing in a specific nest site (Chap. 14).

The difference in the size of prelaying ranges, coupled with the fact that males space themselves to maximize contact with females, suggests that males of lek species will always be at lower densities than forest grouse males, when the entire habitat is considered. Also, the larger the prelaying ranges of the females, the greater the number of males that will be clustered at advertisement sites (Bradbury 1981). Similarly, tundra grouse should, and do, generally occur at higher densities than forest grouse because prelaying ranges of ptarmigan are smaller than those of forest grouse (Fig. 16.2). The low densities reported for ptarmigan in the high Arctic (Weeden 1963) resulted from the inclusion of large blocks of unsuitable habitat in the tabulations rather than from actual, low densities.

A more meaningful index to density would be to measure the mean distances between displaying males, or, if there were data, between nesting females. Lance (1970) gave the distance between five blue grouse nests at Comox Burn, British Columbia, as 274 ± 101 m. The distance between four adjacent, willow ptarmigan (*Lagopus lagopus*) nests at Chilkat Pass, British Columbia, was 120 ± 26 m (Fig. 13.5). The mean size of the prelaying ranges for five adult, blue grouse

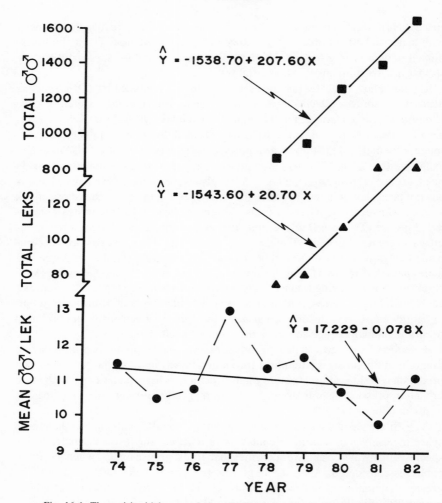

Fig. 16.1. The prairie chicken population in Minnesota recently increased. This increase was accompanied by an increase in the number of leks and not by an increase in the number of males per lek. (Data from Svedarsky pers. comm.)

hens at Comox Burn was 6.3 ± 3.19 ha (Hannon 1978), and for 18 willow ptarmigan hens at Chilkat Pass, approximately 2.7 ha (Hannon 1982). Using either measurement (distances between nests or sizes of prelaying ranges), ptarmigan were spaced 2.3 times closer together than were blue grouse hens.

How does this compare with male densities? The mean density of advertising, blue grouse males at Comox Burn from 1960 to 1967 was approximately 17 males/km^2 (Zwickel et al. 1983), whereas willow ptarmigan males at Chilkat Pass from 1958 to 1976 occurred at an average density of 36 males/km^2 (Fig.

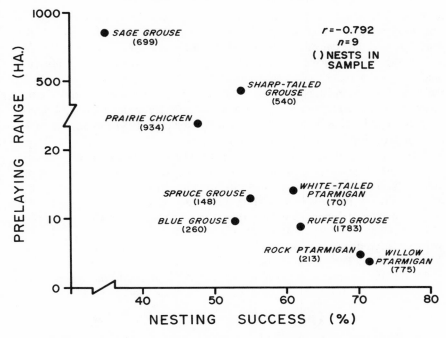

Fig. 16.2. Sizes of prelaying ranges of females are larger where there is more nest predation. Nesting statistics from Table 15.2; prelaying ranges from Table 14.2.

10.2). Thus, the ratio of blue grouse density to that of ptarmigan is similar to the ratio obtained from nest spacing and prelaying ranges. The hypothesis that the size of prelaying ranges generally determines density predicts that the density of populations faced with few nest predators will be higher than that of populations coping with many predators and high losses. In the former populations, females can nest closer together—reduce their space—and still have sufficient nesting success such that $m_x = q_x$. The fairly distinct, prelaying ranges of each grouse species may reflect an evolutionary stable strategy (ESS) (*sensu* Maynard-Smith & Price 1973). Selection may have favored females that invested the appropriate search effort in their specific predator-cover complex, which maximized their lifetime breeding success.

An alternative hypothesis to explain densities is that the spacing of grouse in a specific habitat is determined by food supplies (Jenkins et al. 1967). Red-grouse biologists noted early in their work that territories were smaller and densities of grouse were greater when heather (*Calluna vulgaris*) was abundant (Miller et al. 1966). But heather serves as both the primary nest cover and food for red grouse. Watson (1964, 1970) and Watson and Moss (1970) proposed that the quantity of heather would influence the visibility of males, hence their interactions, and that the quality of heather as food would further mediate the intrinsic aggressiveness of males, and hence territory size. However, they have been unable to document that food resources working through the behavior of males determine fall territory size and thus densities (Lance 1978b, Miller & Watson 1978).

An alternative explanation is that the correlation between heather abundance and red grouse densities is a function of the cover value of heather for nesting hens. Males can afford to advertise and defend smaller territories and still attract hens when their territories include heather of high quality for nesting. Territory sizes are smaller after fertilization (review Watson et al. 1984) because of the improved growth of nesting cover for females.

Densities of ptarmigan are positively correlated with nesting success (Fig. 16.3). Three populations that showed extremely high numbers lived on islands relatively free of mammal predators: Brunette Island, Newfoundland (Fig. 15.35); Tranøy Island, Norway (Fig. 11.1); and Hrisey Island, Iceland (Fig. 9.1). The other high-density populations are red grouse in Scotland, where predators are controlled, and willow ptarmigan at Chilkat Pass, British Columbia, where nest predation is relatively light (Weeden 1959b, Hannon 1982, Hannon & Smith 1984). The ptarmigan hens in six populations nested farther apart and had a reduced nesting success (Fig. 16.3); had the males in these populations

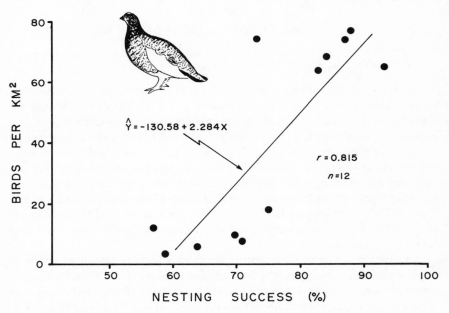

Fig. 16.3. Spring density of ptarmigan is higher for populations in which there is little nest predation. (Data from Choate 1963a, Jenkins et al. 1963, 1967, Watson 1965, Bergerud 1970a, Braun & Rogers 1971, Gardarsson 1971, Myrberget Chap. 11, Weeden & Theberge 1972, Watson & O'Hare 1979, Giesen et al. 1980, Hannon 1982.)

defended much smaller territories, they would have reduced their fitness by not attracting females or by an increased loss of nests. By avoiding males with small territories (Fig. 10.19), females may set the lower limit of territory size.

Forest grouse also space their nests, and densities should increase when nests can be spaced close together. The highest mean density reported for ruffed grouse occurred at Rochester, Alberta — 32 males and females/km^2 in the spring. Nesting success there was 76% (Rusch et al. 1984). A lower density of ruffed grouse occurred in Kentucky — 6 males/km^2, and nesting success was low, approximately 25% (Hardy 1950).

It has been argued that the abundance of aspen (*Populus tremuloides*) is the essential factor determining the density of ruffed grouse (Gullion 1977a, 1977b, 1982), but the demographic aspects of why densities could be higher in aspen forests than in other forest types have not been specified. The annual mortality rates of ruffed grouse are similar for several populations, from Wisconsin to Alberta (Dorney & Kabat 1960, Gullion & Marshall 1968, Boag 1976b, Rusch et al. 1984). All these populations live in aspen forests. But the ruffed grouse population with the lowest reported mortality rate lives in the Pacific Northwest, in an alder-maple (*Alnus* spp., *Acer* spp.) forest (Brewer 1980). The correlation presented by Gullion between aspen and ruffed grouse density may be in fact a nesting success-density relationship, since nesting improves with latitude (Fig. 15.7).

16.2.2 The concept of a stabilizing density

An older argument in the literature is whether a population's mean density averaged over many years represents a biological balance (Nicholson 1933) or is merely a statistical average of random, varying fluctuations (Andrewartha & Birch 1954). If nesting success mediates density, the mean density of a population represents the average density that just provides sufficient recruitment to equal mortality—i.e., the stabilizing density that provides stabilizing breeding successes (Fig. 16.4).

Prairie chicken and sharp-tailed grouse (*Tympanuchus phasianellus*) in South Dakota provide statistics showing fluctuations around different mean densities (Fig. 16.4). The populations are partly sympatric and the areas are censused by similar methods. These populations are probably affected by randomly varying soil moisture that influences plant cover, hence nesting success (see Fig. 15.11). They show similar juvenile:adult ratios in the autumn, but the stabilizing recruitment (prairie chicken, $s = 2.20$; sharp-tailed grouse, $s = 2.60$) occurs at a much lower density for prairie chickens than for sharp-tailed grouse (Figs. 15.25, 16.4). Prairie chickens nest mostly in grasslands in open landscapes; sharp-tailed grouse nest mostly in heterogeneous, grass-shrub cover (Chap. 5), as well as enjoy slightly less predation pressure on nests (Table 15.2). It is possible that chickens compromise plant cover more often than sharp-tailed grouse and use

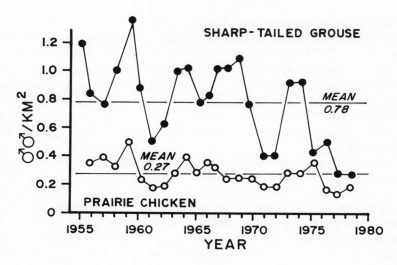

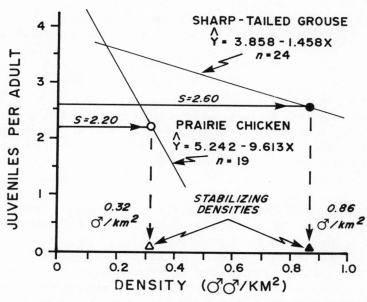

Fig. 16.4. Sharp-tailed grouse maintained a mean breeding density higher than that of prairie chickens in South Dakota (*top*). The stabilizing breeding success (*s*) is similar for both sharp-tailed grouse and prairie chickens, but the decline in breeding success with increased density is much more pronounced for prairie chickens than for sharp-tailed grouse, resulting in a lower stabilizing density for prairie chickens (*bottom*) (see Figs. 15.13, 15.14; data from Linde et al. 1978).

space more often as a nesting tactic. Their lower stabilizing density supports this hypothesis.

Pheasants (*Phasianus colchicus*) in South Dakota occupy much of the prairie grouse range, nest in similar cover, and face similar predators. Wagner et al. (1965) discussed in depth their observation that the mean density of pheasants was greater in South Dakota than in Wisconsin or Indiana. They recognized that these differences in mean densities resulted from compensatory intraspecific competition, but they did not specify the mechanism. Their hypothesis that females died more in warm, dry springs from physiological stress had no density-dependent connotation. However, such mortality could be explained by the lack of nesting cover in dry cycles and increased predation. Later, Gates and Hale (1974) documented spacing of nesting pheasants, and Dumke and Pils (1973) and Gates and Hale (1975) showed that nest predation and summer predation of hens were density-dependent.

The highest density of pheasants reported in the literature was on Pelee Island (Stokes 1954). Pheasants there had a consistently high rate of increase, irrespective of densities (Wagner et al. 1965), and nesting success was higher than elsewhere in the pheasant range (Gates & Hale 1975). With few predators, females could nest near each other and still be successful.

The combined findings of these pheasant investigations are consistent with the hypothesis that stabilizing densities have biological reality in that they provide on average stabilizing breeding success. There should be a unique stabilizing density for each predator-cover complex.

The density of grouse is driven primarily by nesting success, as it contributes to breeding success; density, in turn, feeds back through inversity to influence nesting success (Fig. 16.5). But these relationships are not a closed circuit. If adult mortality is density-dependent it would moderate nesting numbers and nesting success. Except for the mortality both of nesting, prairie chicken hens and of advertising, ruffed grouse males, I have found little evidence of such density-dependent mortality. Grouse have adopted breeding strategies to minimize such mortality. The major short-circuit in the nesting success-density interaction is brought about by changes in nesting success in response to random changes in the extrinsic environment. Nesting cover and the abundance of buffers and predators change between years, independent of grouse density, and thereby importantly moderate the role of density in influencing nesting success (Fig. 16.5).

In Figure 16.6 I have attempted to diagram how breeding success influences mean breeding densities. Consider again prairie chickens and sharp-tailed grouse in South Dakota. Both populations have high nesting success when densities are low (Fig. 15.13, 15.14). The reproductive success of females in the sharp-tailed grouse population declined at an increasing rate as numbers increased. The rate of successful, nesting female prairie chickens also declined as numbers rose, but the decline was more rapid and less curvilinear (Fig. 15.13). Consider that the

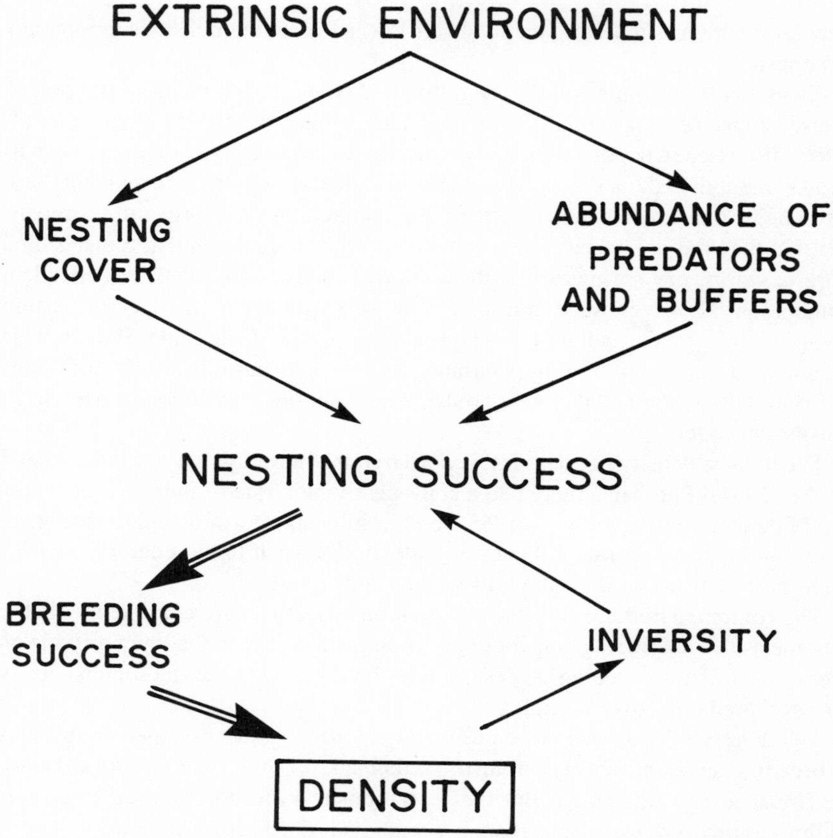

EXTRINSIC ENVIRONMENT

NESTING COVER

ABUNDANCE OF PREDATORS AND BUFFERS

NESTING SUCCESS

BREEDING SUCCESS

INVERSITY

DENSITY

Fig. 16.5. Nesting success is the principal parameter that drives density, but density feeds-back and influences nesting success. Nesting success is modified from year to year by extrinsic factors (cover, predators, and buffer species) that further change the influence of density (competition for nesting sites) on nesting success.

two m_x lines in Figure 16.6 (top) represent the prairie chicken (I) and sharp-tailed grouse (II) populations—the prairie chicken requiring a more favorable mixture of cover and space than sharp-tailed grouse at similar densities for similar recruitment. Adults in both populations probably have similar natural mortality rates. The stabilizing densities of these two populations should result when recruitment (m_x) and mortality (q_x) equal each other. Prairie chickens will stabilize at a lower density than will sharptails. The favorableness of the nesting habitat will override other factors in determining the mean breeding densities of these populations.

The variation in the number of grouse seeking space each spring *within* a population will be a major factor in nesting success and will ultimately influence the density next year (Fig. 16.6, bottom). This is a space-cover trade-off. As numbers

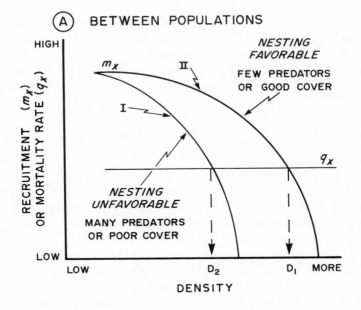

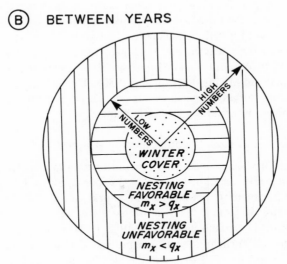

Fig. 16.6. *Top, A:* Difference in the stabilizing density of two populations depends on how cover and predation affect the balance between recruitment and mortality; recruitment varies more between populations than does adult mortality. *Bottom, B:* The difference in nesting success between years that drives density in a population (Fig. 16.5) is greatly influenced by differences between favorable and unfavorable nesting cover in the spacing of birds in spring; this success in turn depends on prior recruitment and the toal numbers competing for the space.

increase, the best cover for avoiding predators is compromised; some birds (density-intolerant morphs) will seek habitats that have more marginal cover, but that are less populated and thus will have more space per bird. Space will partly compensate for cover in fitness. Still, breeding success will be reduced in such marginal habitat, thereby dampening population fluctuations and annual variations in density.

16.3 Control of hunting

The history of hunting has passed through several stages. There was a time in pioneer days when there was no thought of conservation; hunters killed what they desired. However, even as early as 1708, New York State had a closed season on ruffed grouse in the summer to protect young and females (Schorger 1945). The attitude of game preservation increased and was discussed in some detail by Leopold (1933), who realized himself that populations could be overhunted. He remarked, "The virtual disappearance of both quail hunting and bird dogs from some shot-out quail states is a case in point" (Leopold 1933, p. 211). However, wildlife biologists argued that surpluses of game birds were available for harvest. For example, Bump et al. (1947, p. 370) concluded that "the general effect of man's hunting on grouse as currently practiced is not detrimental," in referring to 17% of the preseason ruffed grouse population that was harvested. In the mid 1940s a cyclic low in ruffed grouse approached in the Midwest; Minnesota and Wisconsin closed their season, but Michigan "hung tough." When the season opened in 1948 in Wisconsin and Minnesota, these states appeared to have no more grouse than did Michigan (Ammann 1950). The hypothesis was supported that cycles were natural ecological events not caused by hunting, and the belief was in place that you could not stockpile game.

16.3.1 Compensation principle

The compensation principle was ushered in during the 1950s. Allen (1954, p.131) said, "If we fail to take a hunting harvest, Nature does it for us. It is quite possible, and usual, for the hunter to get in ahead of natural mortality factors and convert the annual surplus of game to his own use merely by taking it before something else happens to it." DeStefano and Rusch, (1982, p. 31) recently said, in questioning the compensatory principle, that "generations of students digested the principle and many biologists came to accept the idea that most game animals present in summer and fall would succumb to late fall and overwinter mortality and that fall hunting would mainly harvest surplus animals."

The primary evidence that biologists use to argue that compensatory natural mortality occurs is that hunted populations are commonly the same as unhunted populations when spring counts are taken (Palmer 1956); however, this by itself is not evidence that natural mortality is compensatory. We could expect birds to fill voids created by hunting when they seek advertising and nesting sites in the spring. By moving to habitats of lower densities, birds should be able to improve their fitness, as predicted by one hypothesis of the Fretwell-Lucas habitat model (see Fig. 14.27). Hunters commonly seek grouse in "optimum" habitats, in which sometime after harvest, yearling birds should prospect and settle in their attempt to optimize the space-cover trade-off. Despite this, examples of populations that are being reduced by hunting pressure are now filtering into the literature. In these cases, the size of the buffer (unhunted) zones appears inadequate to provide sufficient recruitment to give the resemblance of compensatory natural mortality (cf. Gullion 1982, Kubisiak 1982).

16.3.2 Is hunting mortality additive to overwinter mortality?

One irrefutable test of the question of whether hunting is additive is to compare the annual mortality rates of banded adults between areas with different exploitation levels. For the test to be valid, birds on these areas should have taken part in breeding activities, and thus could be expected to show philopatry.

Fred Zwickel banded blue grouse at Comox Burn, on Vancouver Island, British Columbia, from 1962 to 1965 and again from 1969 to 1977 (Zwickel & Bendell 1967, Zwickel et al. 1983). During the first period hunting was light, but hunting pressure increased in the later period (Zwickel 1982). Of particular interest is that mortality rates of banded females were significantly greater during the second period (Fig. 16.7). Zwickel (1982, p. 1,060) said, "This selective removal of females has apparently increased the mortality rate of females." Fortunately, this study had a built-in control: most blue grouse males migrate before the hunting season. Mortality rates of males did not significantly increase between the periods 1962–65 and 1969–77. This indicates that hunting was the principal cause of the changes in mortality of blue grouse between the two periods. Are there other examples?

Clait Braun banded white-tailed ptarmigan (*Lagopus leucurus*) in the high mountains of Colorado from 1966 to 1969 (Braun 1969, Braun & Rogers 1971). Birds in two populations, Crown Point and Mt. Evans, were hunted each fall, whereas ptarmigan in Rocky Mountain National Park were not hunted. The life-table data Braun (1969) presented indicate that birds in the two hunted populations had mortality rates approximately double those of birds in the unhunted populations (Fig. 16.7). In this example, hunting appears completely additive. At Mt. Evans 51% of the population was harvested. If we assume that the remaining 49% alive at the end of the season died at the natural mortality rate (46% for females at Rocky Mountain National Park), then 49% × 46% = 23%; and 23% plus 51% harvested equals 74%, compared to the observed total mortality of 76% (Fig. 16.7). Braun (1969, p.86) felt that hunting increased the annual mortality rate by 15% at Crown Point and by approximately 27% at Mt. Evans. He remarked that

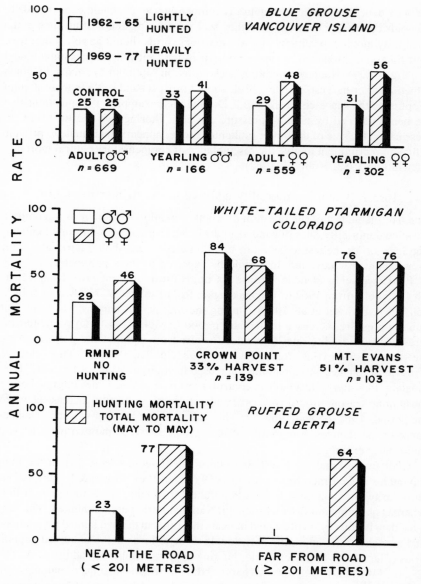

Fig. 16.7. Mortality rate of banded yearlings plus adults in populations that were subjected to different intensities of hunting pressure. (Data from Braun 1969, Fischer & Keith 1974, Zwickel et al. 1983.)

"perhaps hunting mortality was not entirely replacive and was partially additive." These populations in Colorado were maintained by immigration from surrounding areas (Braun & Rogers 1971).

Hunting of banded ruffed grouse at Rochester, Alberta, was also additive (Fig. 16.7). The harvest of banded birds within 201 m of roads was 23%, and the total annual mortality was 77% (Fischer & Keith 1974). Birds harvested at distances greater than 201 m from roads had only a 1% mortality rate caused by hunting, and their total annual mortality was 64%. Again we can look at unshot birds to confirm the estimates. After the hunting season 77% of the birds should still be alive near the road, and they should have a natural mortality rate of 63%; 0.77 × 0.63 = 0.485, thus a 48.5% natural mortality rate plus the 23% hunting mortality rate equals 71.5% total mortality. This is reasonably close to the observed mortality of 77%. Fischer and Keith (1974, p. 593) concluded that "fall hunting increased total annual mortality of males less than 201 meters from roads, and was therefore in part additive."

Frederick and Fran Hamerstrom banded prairie chickens in central Wisconsin from 1949 to 1965 (Hamerstrom & Hamerstrom 1973). The hunting season was closed during these years except in 1951. The two cohorts exposed to this hunting harvest had mortality rates higher than later cohorts that were not hunted (Fig. 16.8). The Hamerstroms concluded (p. 36), "It would seem that the hunting season increased mortality by about 25%."

Gordon Gullion has been banding ruffed grouse males for the past 30 years in central Minnesota, 1956–1985. Terry Little (1978) also banded males in central Minnesota at Crow Wing County, 1970–74. The hunting pressures for three study areas in Minnesota lined up as follows: Mille Lacs > Crow Wing > Cloquet. Cloquet is a refuge, but birds are harvested when they move outside (Gullion & Marshall 1968). Grouse at both Crow Wing and Mille Lacs had significantly greater mortality rates than Cloquet (Fig. 16.8). The mortality figures from Cloquet are similar to the losses reported for other ruffed grouse populations living in lightly hunted areas in North America, i.e., 50–60% (Dorney & Kabat 1960, Davies 1973, Boag 1976). Gullion (1982, p.21) concluded for the Mille Lacs region: "This population depression appears to be the result of excessive hunter harvest each fall. Evidently too many potential breeders are being removed by hunting." It is important to note that Mille Lacs is being intensively managed, whereas the surrounding areas have lower densities, thus reducing the potential of ingress by birds to fill vacancies created by hunting (see also Kubisiak 1982).

David Jenkins and Adam Watson began studies of red grouse in 1956 and the work continues under the direction of Watson and Robert Moss. In an early paper they reported a mortality rate of 71% for banded adults that were hunted on their study areas (Jenkins et al. 1963). The overall mortality rate of 828 banded adults on hunted moors in Scotland was 67% (Jenkins et al. 1963). It was concluded that

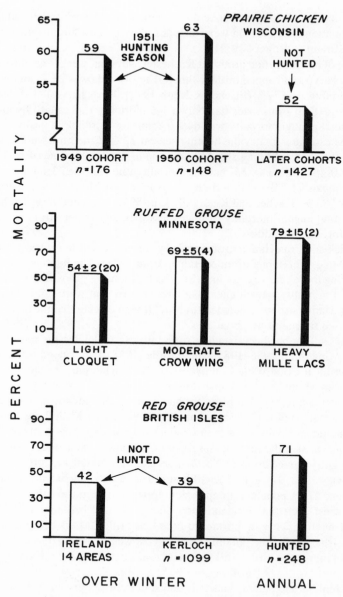

Fig. 16.8. Mortality rates of banded yearlings plus adults in populations that were subjected to different intensities of hunting pressure. The red grouse in Ireland and Kerloch were not banded. (Data from Jenkins et al. 1963, 1967, Hamerstrom & Hamerstrom 1973, Little 1978, Watson & O'Hare 1979, Gullion 1981, 1982.)

natural mortality was compensatory, "shooting exploited part of the surplus, and natural mortality mostly eliminated other birds that could not obtain or hold territories" (p. 375).

Two largely unhunted populations of red grouse are reported in the literature; one is at Kerloch, Scotland, and the other in Ireland. The overwinter mortality figures for these populations, computed by comparing fall populations with spring numbers (no banded birds available), were 39% for Kerloch (1962–65) and 42% for Ireland (1969–71) (Fig. 16.8 data from Jenkins et al. 1967, Watson & O'Hare 1979). The Kerloch birds also had an overwinter loss of approximately 41% in the years 1966–71 (data from Moss et al. 1975). Red grouse have a high survival rate over the summer, hence losses between fall and spring should approximate losses for the entire year. A comparison of the overwinter mortality rate of approximately 41% for the two unhunted populations with the annual mortality rate of 67–71% for the heavily hunted populations suggests that, contrary to the view of Moss et al. (1982a), hunting is additive in red grouse.

A second index that can be used to decide if hunting is additive is to compare the rate of population change over winter across an array of densities. If hunting is additive, spring numbers should be linearly correlated with fall numbers. As fall numbers increase, there would be no increase in compensatory, overwinter natural loss. If natural overwinter mortality is compensatory, the rate of overwinter loss should increase with increased numbers, and the plot of spring numbers on fall numbers should be curvilinear.

Spring numbers were regressed on the previous fall numbers for 12 populations (Figs. 15.19, 15.20). Ten populations show a linear plot. Neither the sharp-tailed grouse population in South Dakota nor the rock ptarmigan (*Lagopus mutus*) population in Scotland showed a completely linear relationship. In the case of rock ptarmigan, the curvilinear relation resulted from 2 years with maximum fall numbers.

A third index I used to evaluate whether hunting was additive to overwinter mortality was to compare the natural mortality of birds that were heavily hunted with the expected natural mortality based on clutch size (Fig. 15.1). Three populations that received considerable harvests and for which small clutch sizes are the rule are those of red grouse in Scotland, blue grouse on Comox Burn, Vancouver Island, and spruce grouse in Alaska (Jenkins et al. 1963, 1967, Ellison 1974, Zwickel 1977). A regression of mortality rates on clutch sizes for the seven populations with the lowest clutch sizes in Fig. 15.2 (all lightly hunted) is $Y = -6.76 + 7.112X$. Substituting the representative clutch size for red grouse (mean of 7.2 eggs), the expected natural mortality is 45%; for blue grouse (6.4 eggs) it is 39% and for spruce grouse (7.6 eggs) it is 47%. However, the annual mortality rates reported for these hunted populations are 71% red grouse, 50% female blue grouse, and 61% spruce grouse (Jenkins et al. 1963, Zwickel et al. 1983, Ellison 1974). The observed natural and hunting mortality rates of birds in these populations are 26%, 11%, and 14%, greater, respectively, than the predicted values based on clutch size. Hunting mortality is additive in all three populations, and red grouse show the largest additive component.

16.3.3 Compensatory aspects of hunting

Although hunting is clearly additive to overwinter mortality, it is probably not additive to the mortality that occurs in the breeding season. If densities are reduced by hunting, the density-dependent effect of competition for optimum sites will be reduced when birds space themselves in the spring to advertise and search for nesting sites. We know that birds enjoy a higher breeding success when densities are low (Fig. 15.14).

I propose the generalization that hunting mortality will be additive to natural mortality whenever the natural mortality occurs at the time birds are not spaced, such as in winter when they seek safe feeding sites in conifers, as do spruce and blue grouse; or travel in winter flocks, as do the tundra and steppe grouse. The hypothesis of *why* natural overwinter mortality is additive to hunting losses is that natural mortality is caused mainly by predators (Table 15.5). The major predators of grouse—the great horned owl (*Bubo virginianus*), the red fox (*Vulpes vulpes*), the goshawk (*Accipiter gentilis*) and the gyrfalcon (*Falco rusticolus*)—all have winter territories (Errington et al. 1940, Sargeant 1972, Pils & Martin 1978, Petersen 1979, Newton 1979). The spacing of these predators prevents marked numerical responses to grouse abundance. The number of raptors observed overwinter increased as the posthunting, red grouse population increased ($r = 0.706$, $n = 9$) at the Low and High study areas in Scotland (Jenkins et al. 1964). Further, the number of red grouse found killed by raptors increased linearly as the population increased ($r = 0.746$, $n = 9$, Jenkins et al. 1964).

Predators probably change the size of their territories as grouse numbers change, but the spacing of predators should still result in relatively constant overwinter natural mortality regardless of the size of posthunting populations. Possibly at extremely high harvest rates with few grouse remaining, predators may move to other areas or switch to other food sources, and then the natural winter mortality could be partly compensatory.

The control of hunting should involve removing a sufficient number of birds to ensure that hunting losses, plus a constant and predictable natural loss over winter, will provide optimum spring spacing (distances between birds) for high breeding success. Also, maximum spacing of advertising males and nesting females in the safest sites will decrease density-dependent mortality from predation during the breeding season. The optimum hunting pressure for maximum compensatory reproduction and survival when birds are spaced will be specific for each population, depending upon the kinds and number of winter predators, as well as the abundance of nest predators. Grouse populations with large numbers of nest predators, especially canids, should show the greatest positive response to heavy hunting removals. As the proportion of the habitat that is hunted increases in the future, one can predict more and more examples of hunting reducing the size of subsequent spring populations.

16.4 Control of food

One of Leopold's (1933) decimating factors was starvation, and one of his welfare factors was food. Poor food reduced productivity indirectly by decreasing the breeding rate and weakening defenses against starvation. Lack (1954) felt that birds were limited by winter food because (1) predators and disease appeared to be ruled out as limiting factors, (2) birds were more numerous where food was abundant, (3) related species ate different foods, and (4) there was fighting among birds for food in winter. Lack was not deterred that no one had found starving birds.

It must seem obvious to biologists that more food translates into more birds. Since Leopold wrote *Game Management*, more research has been conducted on food than on any other ecological factor. Nor is much letup in sight: 13 of 69 (19%) articles on grouse published between 1964–72 in the *Journal of Wildlife Management* were on food, and in the past 13 years 12% of the articles were food related (Table 16.1). The sophistication of analysis has become more complex; measurements of food *quantity* have been replaced by measurements of food *quality* (Linden 1984, Remington & Braun 1985). Trace elements were once in vogue, but recently we have embarked on chemical-warfare analysis, secondary compounds, and digestive limits (see review by Bryant & Kuropat 1980, Bryant et al. 1983). Few seem concerned that 30 years after Lack's assessment we still have not documented density-dependent starvation, even with the advent of radio-tracking. Johnsgard (1973, p. 309) said, "Dependable and nutritious winter food sources are critical to the survival of all grouse." True, but it does not necessarily follow that food is in short supply. The two species that are the best candidates for food shortage are ruffed grouse and prairie chickens. If these species are not limited by food, the other species, which have more abundant food, should not be limited.

16.4.1 Ruffed grouse and aspen buds

Two recent cyclic declines of ruffed grouse in northern Minnesota were associated with increased mortality of banded males (Fig. 14.26, Fig. 15.21, Gullion 1967, Gullion & Marshall 1968, and Little 1978). In both declines winter mortality of males was correlated with changes in spring counts of birds (1959–65, $r = -0.868$; 1971–74, $r = -0.718$). Little (1978, p. 106) speculated: "Svoboda and Gullion (1972) documented substantial variations in winter

Table 16.1. Subject content of articles published on grouse in the *Journal of Wildlife Management*, 1937 to 1985

Subject content	% total articles							
	1937– 1945	1946– 1954	1955– 1962	1963	1964– 1972	1973– 1981	1982– 1985	Total
Techniques								
Determining sex and age	12	8	15	11	13	12	11	12
Capture methods	0	8	19	3	7	2	0	6
Census methods	0	0	7	8	3	6	4	5
Other	6	0	0	0	3	12	7	5
Habitat studies								
Drumming sites	0	8	0	3	6	8	19	6
Food and diet	47	25	7	8	19	12	11	16
Other	0	0	0	11	13	12	11	9
Population dynamics								
Nesting studies	0	0	0	0	3	4	15	3
Hunting	0	0	0	13	4	4	4	4
Sex and age composition	6	17	0	3	1	4	0	3
Dispersal and movement	0	0	7	3	4	8	7	5
Disease	18	17	11	3	4	0	11	6
Predation	6	0	15	8	1	4	0	4
Status	6	8	4	16	1	2	0	5
General	0	8	15	13	16	10	0	11
Total articles	17	12	27	38	69	50	27	240

food utilization for these grouse, so fluctuations in food production combined with deteriorating snow conditions may determine the severity of individual winters for grouse." Gullion (1977a) has argued that a shortage of aspen buds can cause a decline in ruffed grouse—the large decline in 1971–72 and 1972–73 he attributed to shortages of aspen buds.

Aspen buds have also been counted from 1971 to 1974 at Cedar Creek, 120 km south of the area studied by Little and Gullion during the general decline of grouse in Minnesota. There was no shortage of aspen (Chap. 4, Table 4.6) even though aspen was much less abundant at Cedar Creek than farther north. Also, secondary foods were both available and acceptable (Chap. 4). The southern distribution of ruffed grouse does not coincide with aspen. There are viable populations of grouse living south of aspen in Oregon, Washington, Kentucky, and Virginia. I believe nesting success, rather than food, is the limiting factor, contrary to Gullion (1984). Huempfner radio-tracked grouse and found a gradual decline in the number of birds through the winter, from predation, not starvation (Huempfner pers. comm.). Svoboda and Gullion (1972) counted overwinter aspen buds for 8 years, but these counts were not correlated with mortality rates nor changes in population size (estimated from Gullion 1981; $r = -0.558$, $r = 0.166$, respectively). That ruffed grouse spend less than 5% of their time feeding (Table 4.2) implies that food per se is not limiting.

We have suggested that aspen is used not because it is necessary for nutrition, but because its characteristics allow optimal foraging with a reduced predation risk (Fig. 14.24). Gullion (1982) proposed that aspen had a defense mechanism that resulted in less use in some years. But another explanation is that aspen may be a risky place to feed under some snow conditions. Ruffed grouse may need suitable snow cover near aspen to escape goshawks by last-minute snow plunges (Fig. 14.24). Grouse fare well in some winters when they feed infrequently in aspen (cf. annual food supplies in Svoboda & Gullion 1972 vs. mortality rates in Gullion 1981); these data demonstrate that aspen buds are not a prerequisite for a healthy ruffed grouse population.

16.4.2 Prairie chickens and grain

Of all the grouse, prairie chickens are the most granivorous (Hamerstrom 1950). Snow should seriously limit the ability of chickens to locate food. Hamerstrom (1941) documented that captive birds lost weight on diets of buds alone. However, weight loss in winter may be typical and by itself is not evidence that food limits numbers of grouse.

The major evidence that food limits prairie chickens is that numbers increased with early settlement and the planting of cereal grains. Leopold (1931, p. 165) noted the correlation: "Here was an increase [in chickens] caused by, or at least associated with the introduction of settlements and grain feed." From that point on the argument snowballed. One can hardly find a thesis on prairie chickens that does not restate this association, accepted in the repeating as cause and effect. Chickens increased with more food. They "followed the plow"; but the hypothesis can be questioned. First, the argument is asymmetrical—the birds increased by "following the plow" but they decreased because of the "cow and the plow." More food resulted in more birds, but even more food but less cover resulted in declines. Second, a population can increase only when recruitment (m_x) is greater than mortality (q_x). Adult birds would show philopatry to the nests and lek ranges they selected as yearlings. For range expansion, breeding success would have had to exceed adult losses. The additional yearlings would push the frontier of the range forward (see Fig. 16.1). No one has explained why recruitment would have exceeded mortality because of more winter food.

Winter starvation of prairie chickens has not been documented. The two research teams that walked the winter landscapes for decades have not found starving birds (Fred and Fran Hamerstrom, Leo Kirsch, pers. comm.). When the birds were abundant in the 1870–90s, they also migrated from the northern states (Cooke 1888, Gross 1930, Schmidt 1936). This suggests that even when they were abundant, there was insufficient winter food on the range to hold them north. But we should not equate insufficient food to remain north with insufficient food to maintain numbers. Sharp-tailed grouse also increased at approximately the same time chickens reached high numbers (Fig. 16.9). Sharp-tailed grouse do not require grain, and high populations have developed in the past, north of settlements and cultivated grains (Snyder 1935).

The most telling counter argument to the plow hypothesis is that the supposed increase in prairie chickens is *not* correlated with settlement and farming. Peak numbers were reached in Illinois and Indiana from 1860 to 1870 (Sparling 1979), before the native prairie was drained and tilled (Weaver 1954). The chickens must have erupted in numbers between 1870 and 1890. As many as 300,000 were shipped out of Nebraska in 1874 (Kobriger 1964 quoting Aughey 1878). At this time settlement hardly had a foothold in the more western ranges in the Dakotas and Nebraska. The fait accompli that Leo Kirsch has documented, using interviews and historical literature, including references by Teddy Roosevelt, James Audubon, and the Lewis and Clark expedition, is that birds were in the western prairies before settlement and that in fact they increased in areas like his home at Woodworth, North Dakota, about 1880–90 (Fig. 16.9), before the region was settled (Kirsch & Kruse 1973). The first homesteaders found the prairie chicken already common when they arrived. The native prairie was still not under plow and some buffalo (*Bison bison*) still roamed until approximately 1883 (Roe 1951). Yet the population erupted. This response could not have been to new food resources.

An alternative to the hypothesis of increased food is that prairie chickens followed the grass (Kirsch & Kruse 1973, Kirsch 1983). They did not dog the heels of the homesteaders, but instead they followed the buffalo hunter! The original herds of buffalo were almost beyond imagination. Seton (1909) estimated 40 million on the plains. At their peak it is thought that they could have numbered 60–70 million; probably no other continent, not even Africa, has ever produced wild game animals in such great numbers (Anonymous 1965). If grazing by domestic cows can nowadays adversely affect prairie grouse breeding success, what must have been the effect from this horde?

There are many statements of the impact of buffalo on the native herbage. "Hundreds of thousands of acres literally eaten to the turf by the immense herds of buffalo. . . Scarcely a blade of grass standing after the herd passed" (from Marlin 1967). "Prairie so completely trodden by buffalo next to impossible to walk" (Audubon 1960). Buffalo had eaten the grass until it was very short, making food scarce, and the lakes were polluted by their wastes (see Roe 1951, p. 362). "The United States Army found it difficult to find sufficient grass for their horses

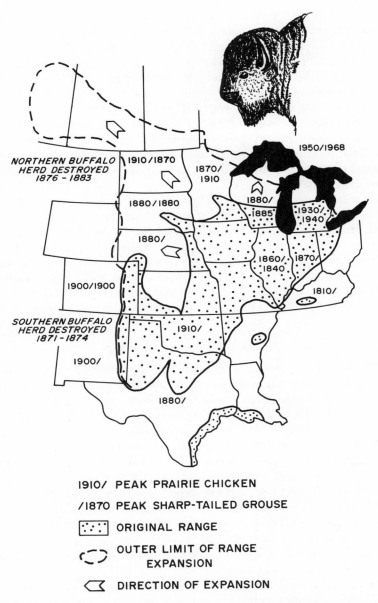

1910/ PEAK PRAIRIE CHICKEN

/1870 PEAK SHARP-TAILED GROUSE

ORIGINAL RANGE

OUTER LIMIT OF RANGE
EXPANSION

DIRECTION OF EXPANSION

Fig. 16.9. Original range of the prairie chicken and its range after expansion once the buffalo declined. Also shown are the reported dates of historical peak populations of sharp-tailed grouse and prairie chickens. (Data from Leopold 1931, Roe 1951, Sharpe 1968, Johnsgard & Wood 1968, Sparling 1979.)

and mules" (Roe 1951, p. 361). Reid and Gannon (1928) quote Alexander Henry, who on 15 February 1802 was in North Dakota: "Buffalo have destroyed the grass and our horses are starving" (other references in Kirsch & Kruse 1973).

Now imagine, incomprehensible as it may be, that the southern herd of buffalo (living south of the Platte River) was still 3 to 4 million in 1871 and that by the close of the hunting season in 1874 — just 4 years later — this herd had ceased to exist. It had been utterly annihilated (Hornaday *in* Roe 1951). Hunters then moved to the northern herd of about 1.5 million animals. Hornaday laments that "the hunting season which began in October 1882 and ended in February, 1883, finished the annihilation of the great northern herd and left but a few small bands of straggling numbers, only a very few thousand individuals all told" (Hornaday *in* Roe 1951, p. 458).

The grazers were gone in one decade. The wet years then occurred (Kiel et al. 1972, see also Will 1946), and the grasses flourished. There were as yet no serious predators; the wolf (*Canis lupus*) had been eliminated and the red fox and the skunk (*Mephitis* spp.) had hardly arrived (Seton 1953, Johnson & Sargeant 1977). Prairie chickens and sharp-tailed grouse must have erupted because of phenomenal nesting success, but they did so when most of the range was still prairie. Prairie chickens followed the grass, not the plow, and the high populations in the 1870–90s are not evidence that they were then or are now limited by food.

16.4.3 Food is not limiting

Food is generally not limiting for grouse. The major evidence is that grouse have not been reported starving in natural systems where predators are present. Grouse in several populations gained weight in the winter: sage grouse (*Centrocercus urophasianellus*) (Beck & Braun 1978); blue grouse (Redfield 1973b); white-tailed ptarmigan (May 1975); and willow ptarmigan (Fig. 10.26). Rock ptarmigan in Norway (65°40′N) maintain their weights in winter (Mortensen et al. 1985), and rock ptarmigan in Svalbard (78°N) put on fat in the autumn to tide them over 4 months without sunlight (Mortensen & Blix 1985, Steen & Unander 1985). Prairie chickens lost weight in several winters in Wisconsin (Fig. 16.10), but dead birds were not found and the declines in weight were not correlated with changes in numbers of birds (see Fig. 16.18). The spring weights of ruffed grouse were not correlated with prior snow conditions in Minnesota (Fig. 14.26) or British Columbia (Table 3.2). Grouse reach their lowest annual weight levels in the breeding season and not in the winter (Fig. 16.11).

Another line of evidence that food is not limiting is that grouse spend a very small fraction of their time feeding, whether they live in the arctic (Fig. 10.9) or in Minnesota and feed on aspen buds. Feeding is most vigorous during the short, morning and evening foraging bouts, when light intensity is low (Braun & Schmidt 1971; Svoboda & Gullion 1972; Figs. 4.7, 10.9). Vigilance and preda-

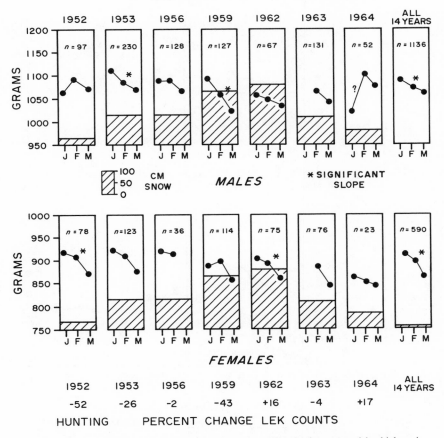

Fig. 16.10. Monthly mean weights of male (*top*) and female (*bottom*) prairie chickens in Wisconsin in relation to snow depth. The percent change in the number of total males counted on booming grounds from the previous spring is shown at *bottom* of figure. The large decrease in 1952 was a result of the hunting season in 1951. (Data from Hamerstrom & Hamerstrom 1973 and pers. comm.)

tion risk seem to be of major concern in the length of feeding, food abundance does not.

The actual amounts of food were measured in three studies in this volume when populations were high. In all cases food supplies remained, yet populations declined for other reasons (Table 4.6, Figs. 9.10, 10.4). Future studies of foraging and foods will need to consider predation risk as a major variable in feeding schedules and food preferences. Rock ptarmigan in Scotland, where there are no gyrfalcons, will eat heather, but in Iceland they take birch (*Betula* spp.) and willow (*Salix* spp.) (Gardarsson & Moss 1970). Birch and willow may well provide better cover from gyrfalcons than the shorter heather. Ptarmigan take birch in

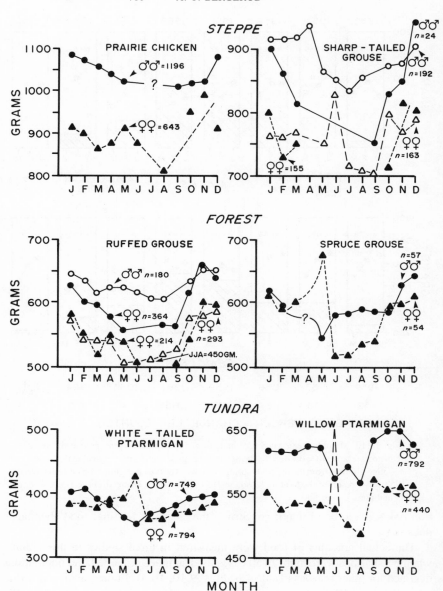

Fig. 16.11. Annual weight cycle for eight grouse populations. (Data from Bump et al. 1947, Keith 1962, West & Meng 1968, Hillman & Jackson 1973, May 1975, Ellison & Weeden 1979, Rusch et al. 1984, pers. comm. See also Szuba & Bendell 1984.)

preference to other species in Norway, but willow is preferred in North America (see Bryant & Kuropat 1980). Possibly these differences relate to resin levels (Bryant & Kuropat 1980), but I suspect that the ultimate value in species selection will be associated with characteristics of plant species that permit rapid ingestion of adequate food while providing suitable cover to escape predators.

16.5 Control of cover

Cover means vegetative or other shelter for grouse (Leopold 1933). But here I shall use it in a more restrictive sense—i.e., to enhance inconspicuousness or escape from predators. This definition excludes cover that is used to protect birds from weather. Substrates that can be considered as cover include: herbaceous vegetation, woody stems and logs, rocks, and snow which is used for snow-roosting and in which grouse may plunge. In addition, cover is provided by low clouds and fog and crepuscular light conditions. Gardarsson (Chap. 9) observed rock ptarmigan take cover from gyrfalcons in Iceland by flying to a fence and frequenting a human settlement. A ruffed grouse in flight from a Cooper's hawk (*Accipter cooperii*) approached Prawdzik (1963) and burrowed into the snow nearby. Steppe (Chap. 5) and tundra (Chap.10) grouse find cover by traveling in flocks. Some grouse populations have sufficient cover that birds can remain inconspicuous when they feed. Birds in conifer habitats have the highest annual survival rates (Fig. 15.4). I believe the reason is the protective "cover value" of these conifers.

Cover is commonly separated into that for nesting, brood rearing, roosting, and escape. A more appropriate classification might be breeding season and non-breeding season (winter) cover. Both males and females are prepared to compromise their own inconspicuousness to breed and to produce progeny. In winter their own inconspicuousness and survival are their primary concern. The argument has been made (Chap. 14) that fall movements are primarily the shift from cover that favors reproductive activities to that which provides maximum concealment in the absence of leaf cover and the presence of the new contrasting substrate, snow.

16.5.1 Cover during the breeding season

A primary management effort to increase the numbers of grouse should be to improve nesting success by enhancing nesting cover and reducing nest predation. With the exception of prairie grouse biologists, few workers have tried to manage grouse by improving nesting cover.

It is difficult to improve the nesting cover for ptarmigan in the Arctic, but there may be some opportunities. The order of density of ptarmigan in Newfoundland was: Brunette Island > the St. Shott's barrens > the Portugal Cove barrens (Mercer 1967, Bergerud & Huxter 1969b, Bergerud 1970a). There were no mammal predators on Brunette Island and grouse hens could successfully nest near each other. There was also more prostrate Krummholz, conifer cover at Brunette Island than at St. Shotts and Portugal Cove so that nesting females could remain concealed from corvids (*Corvus* spp.) and gulls (*Larus* spp.) (Fig. 16.12). The birds on the St. Shott's barrens were spaced closer together and had a higher breeding success than did the birds on the Portugal Cove barrens; pairs were closely associated with the presence of preferred nesting cover (Fig. 16.13; Bergerud & Huxter 1969a,b). Peters (1958) recommended burning these Newfoundland barrens to increase food supplies, but burning also destroyed the slow-growing, Krummholz nesting cover. The lower density of birds at Portugal Cove than at St. Shott's is in fact the result of prior fires that destroyed climax vegetation that serves as permanent nesting cover. This example illustrates that managers should not reduce nesting habitat to increase food supplies.

The forest grouse of North America illustrates a different problem for cover management. Hens use more open canopies with herbaceous growth to conceal nests, but males generally advertise in more protected, shade-tolerant cover to escape raptors. At present, cover management for these species takes the form of improving forest composition for displaying males (Kubisiak et al. 1980, Gullion 1982, Schulz 1982). This may result in shifting males about and decreasing the proportion of silent males, but it cannot result in a substantial increase in the population; breeding success of females drives numbers (Chap. 15, Fig. 15.41). In fact, such management to improve advertising locations for males could increase mortality of females. Females should seek the best available nest cover. If males are at great distances, females will need to compromise their inconspicuousness to move farther to breed. Here is where edge and interspersion of cover play a role. By increasing the interface between the cover type needs of males and females, mobility can be reduced along with predation risk.

Cover management for forest and steppe grouse must be directed at improving the concealment of nests and hens. One male can breed several females, and a population with a sex ratio weighted to females would have a higher potential rate-of-increase than a population with a balanced proportion of males and females. Males and females have different cover needs and this distinction must be clearly recognized in habitat manipulation.

Nest-brood cover has always been considered the crux of factors limiting prairie grouse (Hamerstrom et al. 1957, Kirsch 1974). Biologists have long noted that prairie grouse, especially prairie chickens, declined during periods of drought, especially in the 1930s and 1950s and when nesting cover was reduced by overgrazing. There have been cycles of wet and dry years for the past 500 years (Will 1946). The breeding success of several widely spaced populations of prairie grouse on the great plains is significantly correlated (Fig. 16.14). This broad synchronization is probably a result of annual variations in soil moisture being in phase over large areas of the grassland. When the soil bank program was in-

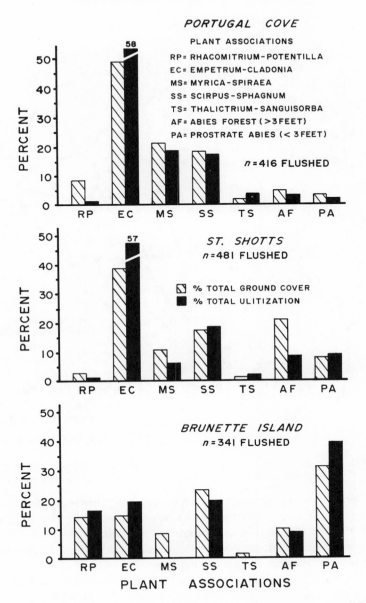

Fig. 16.12. Comparison of nesting and brood-rearing utilization and cover availability among three ptarmigan barrens (Mercer 1967, Bergerud & Huxter 1969a).

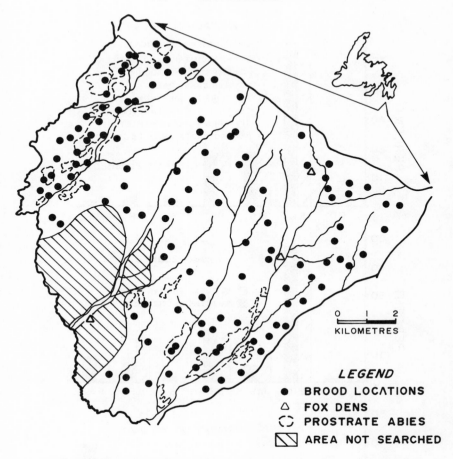

Fig. 16.13. Locations of ptarmigan pairs on the St. Shott's Barrens, Newfoundland, 1959, in relation to the abundance of nesting cover – prostrate *Abies-Picea* (Bergerud unpubl. data).

itiated, prairie grouse increased (Kirsch et al. 1973). However, there was also evidence of declines in populations when grasslands were idled for long periods (Kirsch 1974). Kirsch argued that the *quality* of grasslands for prairie chickens was not well understood, but that residual cover should average 52 cm in height and be sufficiently dense to hide nesting hens.

Nesting success should be the key variable to evaluate the quality of grasslands. In prairie grouse, there is more annual variability in nesting success than in brood size. The understanding of the *quality* of grassland cover will be unraveled when we know more about searching techniques of predators for nests, as affected by cover characteristics.

Nesting hens generally need dense cover, whereas young chicks need open-

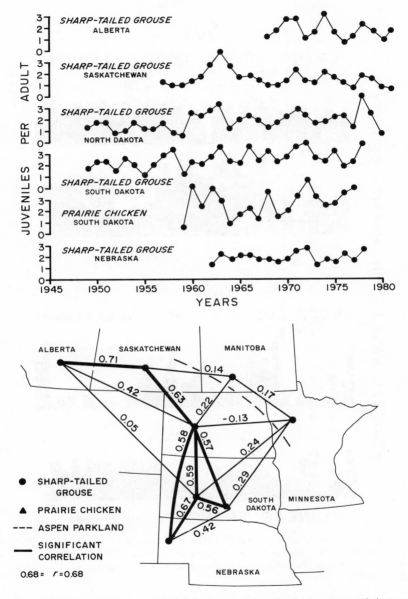

Fig. 16.14. Breeding success of birds in widely scattered prairie grouse populations on the Great Plains is correlated, suggesting wet and dry cycles of moisture occurring over large geographical areas. (Data from Mevel 1973, Robertson 1979, Kobriger 1975, 1981, Sisson 1976, Berg 1977, 1979, Linde et al. 1978, Hilton & Wishart 1981, Manitoba Game Records, S. R. Barber pers. comm.)

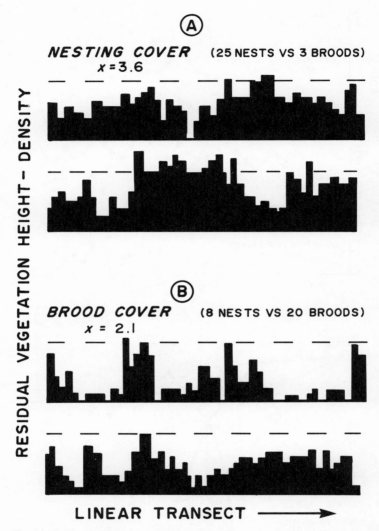

Fig. 16.15. Visual obstruction readings (VOR) from 100 sites along transects in 1977 in each of two fields in North Dakota that were burned in 1975 and planted with the same seed mixture. The nests are those of dabbling ducks, and the broods are sharp-tailed grouse. (Data from Leo Kirsch pers. comm.)

ness, insects, and warmth—these are different requirements (Fig. 16.15). The syntax "nest-brood cover" is inappropriate. Prairie chickens in Minnesota had high nesting success, but low chick survival (Chap. 6). Admittedly, some habitats may provide both cover and openness. Bunchgrasses in Illinois provide tall clumps to hide eggs and hens, yet they also provide interspaces for chicks seeking insects without hinderance of vegetation (Yeatter 1963). The juxtaposition of nest cover and brood foraging habitat may be one component of high-quality grassland cover. However, they are not one and the same at the microhabitat level.

Bunchgrasses may eventually be seen as another key to grassland quality. The greater prairie chicken now nests in many areas in sod grass, such as *Poa pratensis*. But hens are, and were, commonly killed on the nest in Minnesota (Svedarsky 1979), Michigan (Ammann 1957), Wisconsin (Gross 1930), and Kansas (Bowen 1971), most frequently by canids which rely on vision (cf. Wells & Lehner 1978). In contrast there are no reports of lesser prairie chickens or Attwater's prairie chickens being killed on the nest (Horkel et al. 1978, Riley 1978, pers. comm., Sell 1979, Lehmann 1941). These two races still nest in bunchgrasses, and use these with considerable preference to sod grasses (Table 16.2) (Bent 1932, Jones 1963, Copelin 1963, Horkel et al. 1978, Riley 1978, Davis et al. 1979, Sell 1979, Wilson 1982). Bunchgrasses in Texas did not significantly differ from sod grasses in cover density (VOR readings) or height (Table 16.2). By nesting in bunch-grasses, hens may have secure cover yet sufficient visibility to detect the approach of predators in time to decide escape tactics. That sage grouse hens are rarely killed on the nest and that the growth form of sagebrush is most similar to that of bunchgrasses is consistent with this hypothesis. Greater prairie chickens that nest in sod grasses often do so within 1 m of openings created by mowing (Westemeier 1973). Prairie chickens do well in tame, sod grasses (Hamerstrom et al. 1957, Westemeier 1973, Hamerstrom & Hamerstrom 1973), but to be "lost" in a field of exotic bluegrass (cf. photo in Hamerstrom et al. 1957, p. 39) may

Table 16.2. Attwater's prairie chicken use of bunch and sod grasses, visual obstruction reading, and height of these grass growthforms (data from Cogar et al. 1977)

Parameters	Clumped, bunch grasses	Unclumped, sod grasses	Difference, bunch vs. sod
% area	34	18	16
Visual obstruction readings (VOR)			
Spring	2.22	2.02	0.20
Summer	2.47	2.21	0.26
Height (cm)			
Spring	49.2	52.0	2.8
Summer	42.9	48.8	5.9
% nests ($n = 19$)	68	32	36
% observations ($n = 633$)	76	16	60

not be the same as to be lost in a sea of clumps of big bluestem (*Andropogon gerardi*), and may cost some hens their lives.

When the dry years come, as they must, or the buffalo—or nowadays the cow—not only are the height and density of grasses reduced but the species composition changes. Bunchgrasses are generally the warm-season species and are less resistant to grazing and drought. The sod grasses are the cool-season grasses and are more resistant to grazing and drought (Weaver 1954). Prairie chickens need bunchgrasses that grow in the *summer* and provide residual cover for *early* nesting the next spring, to give that added margin of time to renest. Bunchgrasses also have space between clumps, which allows chick movement, and are associated more often with less litter than are sod grasses. They thus may support fewer mice, possibly fewer insects, and hence probably fewer foxes and skunks. Bunchgrasses are needed for high-quality nesting habitats.

16.5.2 Cover during winter

Grouse generally leave the breeding range when they become conspicuous with leaf fall and snow cover. Blue and spruce grouse seek the safe conifer habitats, and the ruffed grouse may snow roost to escape predator detection. The ptarmigan and prairie grouse use shrubs for winter cover, also snow burrow, and use the advantages of large flocks, as do sage grouse. These tundra and steppe grouse also hide by using the crepuscular periods. The primary management aim for manipulation of winter habitat should be to prevent predators from obtaining advantages in particular predator-cover complexes. Managers should try to understand how grouse use the available cover to successfully cope with resident predators. Biologists must avoid altering habitat in such a fashion that the advantages are passed to predators. For example, in the past, prairie chickens made long migrations that may have been particularly advantageous if they were able to shift south of wintering goshawks. Today, however, with cultivated grains the close interspersion of winter and breeding cover in many prairie chicken areas has resulted in reduced movement and increased mortality of chickens when goshawks move south after hare (*Lepus americanus*) declines.

16.6 Predator control

The controversy about increasing game stocks through predator reduction is forever debated by naturalists and hunters. In earlier times raptors and nest predators were considered vermin, and control programs were generally aimed to reduce these predators. Then the Errington view began to prevail that predators took the surplus and that control would have little effect on prey numbers. Now predator control, which we call predator management for a ring of respectability, is again being suggested, but this time the control is directed at nest predators, primarily mammals, and not at raptors which principally hunt adult birds. Few advocates in these times are prepared to decimate the hawks and owls, even if it should mean more grouse.

16.6.1 Predator-control arguments

The evidence is generally without exception that if nest predators are substantially reduced the number of nests that hatch will increase. One confounding influence, however, in evaluating these data, is that there may be predator exchange—if one species is removed, another may, in the absence of the first, increase its predation. Nesting success of grouse increased following the reductions of predators in New York and Texas (Edminster 1939, Lawrence & Silvy 1981). Waterfowl enjoy increased hatching success following predator control or when they nest on islands, as have members of the phasianinae (Stoddard 1931, Chesness et al. 1968, Schranck 1972, Duebbert & Kantrud 1974, Trautman et al. 1974, Potts 1980, Duebbert 1982, Lokemoen et al. 1984, Sargeant et al. 1984). If we are prepared to reduce mammalian nest predators, we can have more grouse, both in the fall and the next spring, because breeding success is the primary force in population change.

Still, some biologists feel that it is unethical to reduce predators of nests. But ethics are an individual matter. Aldo Leopold, a philosopher in conservation ethics, did not view predator reduction as unethical and said (Leopold 1931, p. 225), "The fox question is not so much of whether foxes do more harm than good, but rather a question of what density of fox population affords the best balance between harm and good." Some would view as unethical a food pyramid too top-heavy in predators with a reduced herbivore stratum and a largely underutilized plant base.

Another argument is that there is a balance of nature and that predator reduction is an unjustified intrusion. Charles Elton, the father of ecology, would not agree, having said (1930, pp. 16–17) that "it is assumed that an undisturbed animal community lives in a certain harmony, the 'balance of nature.' The picture has the advantage of being an intelligible and apparently logical result of natural selection in producing the best possible world for each species. It has the disadvantage of being untrue." Connell and Sousa (1983) in their extensive review of the stability and persistence of a wide variety of animal populations, from protozoans to rodents, concluded that the evidence in the past 50 years upholds Elton's description. It is only our limited perspective of evolutionary time that persuades us to believe that the whole is greater than the parts and that stability exists.

The composition of predators of the steppe and forest is greatly changed from that of 100 years ago. Wolves have been eliminated and coyote (*Canis latrans*) populations have expanded north and east. The red fox was introduced and expanded south and west. Skunks, raccoons, (*Procyon lotor*), and opossum (*Didelphis virginiana*) moved north. Crows expanded across the prairies with increased nesting sites. Kalmback (1938) reported a 69% nesting success of waterfowl in

North Dakota 50 years ago. But now nesting success for many dabbling ducks is often less than 50%. The dynamics of the predator-prey adaptive race are always in a state of flux. The past is not a guide for the future.

In addition, humans have completely upset the interactions between predators and grouse in the steppe and forest. Populations of some predators have shifted, and others have increased. Road-kills and domestic animals provide alternative foods for foxes and skunks (Fig. 16.16). Cover for nesting grouse has been reduced or altered. Ambush sites and vantage lookouts for raptors have been provided. All is changed and changing, and the balance-of-nature concept has no special relevance to the real world of dynamic populations.

The proportion of males and females in several grouse populations is unbalanced because of differential rates of predation. Prairie chickens and ruffed grouse generally have more males than females (Table 15.8, Fig. 16.17), and this is partly a result of increased mortality of females during nesting and raising broods. The differential mortality of males and females has occurred because of an increased abundance and success of ground predators since settlement. Southern ptarmigan populations also have more males than females. These males may have a higher survival rate than females because of fewer raptors in the south (cf. Chap. 9). Populations with an excess of males will have lower potential rates-of-increase compared with populations, such as sage grouse, where females predominate.

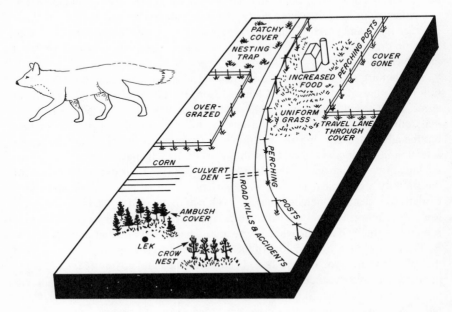

Fig. 16.16. Some examples of how human activities have upset predator-prey interactions.

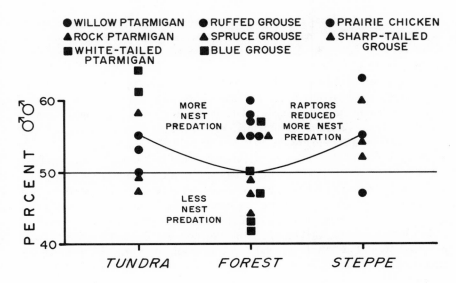

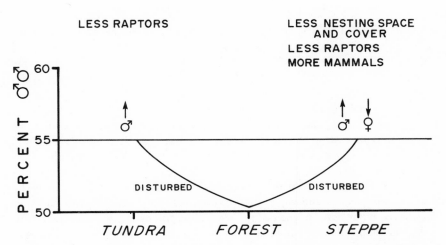

Fig. 16.17. In steppe and tundra populations, there are commonly more males than fe-males. In the steppe, human disturbance has reduced nesting space and cover, reduced raptor numbers, and increased mammalian nest predators. These disturbances are selective in favor-ing the differential survival of males. In the tundra, raptors have been reduced, again favoring male rather than female survival. (Data from Table 15.8.)

The view that a strong habitat is the best defense against excessive predation has merit, especially if "habitat" includes space as well as cover. Still, predator populations can be so abundant that habitat alone will not suffice to permit a population to increase.

The story of the Attwater's prairie chicken is a case in point. This race of prairie chicken is now reduced to fewer than 2,500 birds and restricted to about 120,000 ha along the Texas coast (Lawrence & Silvy 1980). Nesting success for Attwater's hens is terrible. Commonly, less than 25% are successful and most hens lose their clutches to predators (Brownlee 1971–74, Horkel et al. 1978). The sex ratio is heavily biased to males (Horkel & Silvy 1980). The population faces extinction because of high levels of predation. Large sums have been spent to purchase land. Additional land has been donated to the Aransas Refuge, but it is in small blocks which act as predator magnets. Money should now be spent to reduce or at least experiment with reducing nest predation by fencing predators out of key nesting habitat, and on predator reduction programs. This grouse could be saved. Why buy more land and invest in artificial rearing—a "hanging-on" strategy—when the key to recovery is to reduce skunks, armadillos (*Dasypus novemcinctus*), raccoons, and opossums? Habitat alone does not assure that grouse populations can cope with today's predator populations in today's space.

16.6.2 The return of prairie chickens in Wisconsin

A success story in which habitat management efforts can be partly evaluated against changes in predator abundance is the prairie chicken population in central Wisconsin. Prairie chickens in Wisconsin are probably the most intensively managed grouse in North America. In the late 1970s this population staged a spectacular recovery (Fig. 16.18).

Frederick and Fran Hamerstrom began watching these chickens in the 1930s and still do so today. They have devoted many years of their lives to saving this population (Hamerstrom 1939, Hamerstrom & Hamerstrom 1949, 1955, 1973, Hamerstrom et al. 1957); one might say their work was "strictly for the chickens" (Hamerstrom 1980). Bird buffs—"the boomers"—came from the cities to watch the dawn rise over the displaying males performing their ancient rituals. The Hamerstroms coaxed and cajoled the "concerned" for funds to purchase land. They saved many acres of the central Wisconsin grasslands, the necessary template, and the day did *not* come, as it had on Martha's Vineyard, Massachusetts, when a solitary heath hen (*T. c. cupido*) male boomed alone in the springs of 1929 and 1930; he was the last of his race.

But the fluctuations of prairie chickens in Wisconsin are not totally explained by alterations in the extent of their grassland habitat. The population at Buena Vista generally declined from 1950 to 1967–69, and recovered after 1970 (Fig. 16.18). The decline between 1953 and 1969 was 70%, yet through management efforts of the Hamerstroms and others the grassland acreages were held constant,

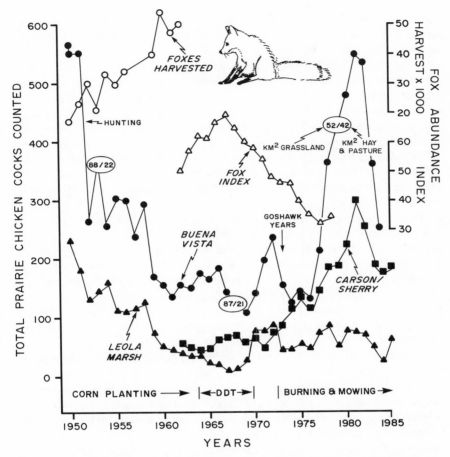

Fig. 16.18. Number of male prairie chickens counted on leks in central Wisconsin, 1950–82. Also shown are two indexes to the abundance of red foxes, and the extent of grasslands in 1953, 1969, and 1979. (Data from Hamerstrom & Hamerstrom 1973, Anonymous 1976, Burke 1979, Pils et al. 1981, R. K. Anderson pers. comm.)

88 km^2 in 1953 and 87 km^2 in 1969 (Hamerstrom & Hamerstrom 1973). The population increased to approximately 550 males by 1981 (a 400% increase), yet grassland acres were only 52 km^2 in 1980, a 40% decline (Burke 1979).

Nor did the dynamics of this population correspond to an increase in food. The sowing of corn in food patches began in the 1950s and was expanded in the 1960s, yet the population continued to decline. The numbers of birds on the Carson-Sherry marsh increased in 1975, similar to those at Buena Vista, but little or no corn was planted at Carson-Sherry. The marsh with the most corn, Leola, is the one area that showed the least recovery (B. Gruthoft pers. comm. to M. Gratson,

Fig. 16.18). It is apparent that food was not a problem for these populations. Changes in the number of birds were not correlated with snow statistics or winter weights (Figs. 16.10, 16.18).

In the mid-1960s DDT was sprayed on the marshes (Fig. 16.18) and may have affected insect abundance and thus directed predation at nests. However, the population was declining long before this spraying program was under way.

In summer 1972 a new program of burning and mowing these grasslands began upon the urging of J. Toepfer and R. Anderson. The goal was to open up rank grasslands and improve brood habitat. These practices were directed to Buena Vista and Leola marshes. Some mowing occurred at Carson-Sherry but the marsh was not burned (B. Gruthoft pers. comm. to M. Gratson). However, the populations that increased after 1975 were those at Buena Vista and Carson-Sherry (Fig. 16.18).

These management practices may have improved breeding success, especially in view of the dwindling acreage in grasslands. Although burning was initiated to enhance brood survival, it may have had a greater influence on nesting success. Variations in brood size between prairie grouse populations show less variation than does nesting success (Chap. 15). In both North Dakota and Minnesota, nesting success of prairie grouse was greater in burned or disturbed habitats than in those that were undisturbed (Kirsch & Kruse 1973, Chap. 6). Westemeier (1973), in Illinois, also showed an increase in the density of prairie chickens 2–4 years after burning.

Disturbing grassland sods could have several effects that would reduce predation. Early in secondary succession new grasses in a burned area may be dense enough to hide nesting hens, yet also in some areas sparse enough for feeding by young chicks – the ultimate interspersion (Fig. 16.19). Burning also provides vigorous, upright culms that resist snow loads better than older stems, improving residual nest cover (Ramharter 1976). Burning and mowing may reduce the diversity of plant species, reduce litter, and reduce alternative prey (Tester & Marshall 1961, Halvorsen 1981). With less litter to attract insects and mice, and fewer other alternative prey (small birds), predators may seek more diversified habitats elsewhere. Young, succulent plant stages and less litter could provide less scent for predators. Some burning may also make grasslands more homogeneous, providing fewer clues to predators on where to search. Only by radio-tracking predators hunting in burned, mowed, and undisturbed habitats can these hypotheses be tested.

An alternative to the explanation that habitat-manipulation practices have directly resulted in the recovery of chickens in Wisconsin is that nest predation has varied in response to fox numbers. The red fox population increased and spread north in Wisconsin in the 1940–50s (Richards & Hine 1953). The number of prairie chicken males on the Buena Vista and Leola marshes declined at the same time. The correlation between the number of booming males and the num-

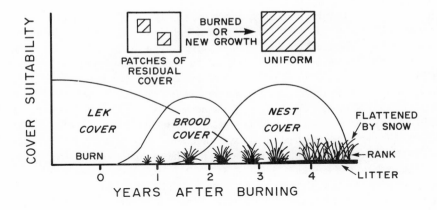

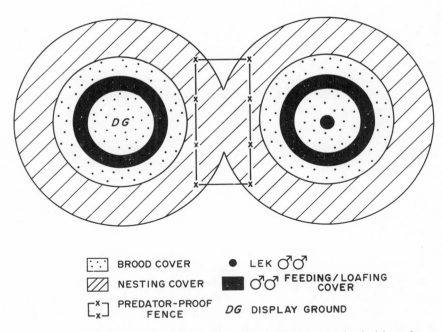

Fig. 16.19. Grass succession following burning (*top*). Nesting cover for the lek species should be halfway between leks (*bottom*), where it may be fenced to keep out nest predators. Hens need space and cover for nesting that are adjacent to more open habitat used by broods. (Adapted from Gratson 1983.)

ber of red foxes trapped in Wisconsin between 1950 and 1963 is significant ($r = -0.848$, $P < 0.01$; Fig. 16.18). The fox population remained high during the low years for chickens, the 1960s, then started down in about 1968 (Pils et al. 1981), possibly because coyotes were increasing (O. Rongstad pers. comm.). Chickens began to increase in 1970, and the correlation between total males (Buena Vista, Leola, and Carson-Sherry) and fox numbers between 1962 and 1978, using Pil's index, was again significant ($r = -0.782$, $n = 17$, $P < 0.01$; Fig. 16.18). Nesting success in 1984 was extremely high (78%, $n = 9$ nests, pers. files). The independent variation in fox numbers may have been more instrumental in the dynamics of this prairie chicken population than were the many years of manipulation of habitat.

Prairie chickens in Minnesota also increased in the late 1970s (Fig. 16.1) and this increase was correlated with the price of fox furs (Chap. 6, Fig. 6.18). Sargeant et al. (1984) reported the density of fox in North Dakota as one family/5.7 km^2 in 1964, decreasing to one family/20 km^2 in 1969, then increasing to one family/7.0 km^2 in 1973. The population then declines 1973 to 1977, then again increases. The expansion of the prairie chicken population in Minnesota into surrounding habitats is consistent with the view that the increase resulted from improved breeding success, and that the habitat had not been limiting. The point is that birds can utilize habitats less intrinsically secure when there are fewer predators. The *predator-cover complex* is what managers should strive to understand, and the requirement of a "strong habitat" should be viewed with the predator-grouse interaction in mind.

16.7 Control of space

The "control of space" in the discussion that follows means the use and manipulation of area (space), to mitigate unfavorable predator-cover complexes so that nesting success can improve. This space concept is not synonymous with the concept of a "space-factor", as outlined by Hamerstrom et al. (1957). These biologists have shown that prairie chickens select habitats with wide, unobstructed views of the horizon. Prairie chickens are granivorous and feed on the ground in the open. To escape raptors they often need a long lead time, and obstructed views would reduce the effectiveness of their breeding and wintering tactics.

Kupa (1966), on the frontispiece of his thesis, wrote: "The female ruffed grouse on her nest—key to population." But his advice was not heeded. Instead, grouse biologists, and especially students of the ruffed grouse, have concentrated on improving the habitat for advertising males. Between 1937 and 1985, there have been 15 articles in the *Journal of Wildlife Management* on the vegetative characteristics of where ruffed grouse males drum, and only eight on nesting studies, *for all nine grouse species* (8 of 240 articles, or 3%) (Table 16.1). The principal means of improving grouse numbers is to increase nesting success, not the survival of males (Chap. 15). *Space*, in which grouse may disperse their nests, is the key concept of successful management.

16.7.1 Size and uniformity of space

Spatial considerations in the literature have been specified only for the steppe grouse. Kirsch (1974) recommended blocks of 160 acres (65 ha) of nesting cover to maintain prairie chicken populations. Arthaud (1968) thought 60 acres (24 ha) were needed in Missouri. Hamerstrom et al. (1957) recommended a patterning of 80-acre (32-ha) parcels of nest-brood cover interspersed with other habitat types. But there seems to be nothing magic about these sizes. There should be no fixed space; what is desired is an area of sufficient size that hens can maximize nesting success in the face of the predator-cover complex they must contend with.

The size of the space will vary with the quality of the cover and with the predators. All hens could nest near each other on an island, such as Pelee Island, without predators, and management of cover would hardly be needed. A large space would not suffice for sage grouse if the individual sagebrush plants (*Artemisia* spp.) that hens nest under were sufficiently rare that coyotes could economically search in a plant-to-plant pattern for nests. The inconspicuousness in space of dummy clutches in sage grouse habitat and the nests of prairie chickens were compromised when workers marked the nests with conspicuous poles that attracted corvids (Bowen 1971, Autenrieth 1981). Uniformity is needed between selected and nonselected nest sites. There should be hundreds of tree bases from which to choose a nest site for spruce grouse, countless scattered stumps and logs for blue grouse hens to evaluate, and numerous rock fields where white-tailed females can make their choices. Such "likeness" means that predators cannot take advantage of the heterogeneity of cover to narrow their search. The hens are lost in a sea of potential sites.

Wildlife managers can actually create nesting "traps" by improving habitat heterogeneity (see Sugden & Beyersbergen 1986). The best and a large-scale example is the creation of refuges for waterfowl. The refuges serve as a respite for ducks from hunters but also as a magnet for nest predators. The Horicon Marsh in Wisconsin is one such trap; nesting waterfowl concentrate there but have an extremely low nesting success (see Livezey 1981, McCabe 1985). If managers create and maintain cover at the expense of space, they should consider fencing the cover to exclude predators. If grouse are given no choice between space and restricted cover, they will compromise space for cover, therein facilitating the searching effort of predators.

16.7.2 Females space away from males

Females of the lekking grouse do not nest near the display grounds of males as the older literature suggests; in fact they do the converse, they nest away from males. Nesting females should avoid males that are interested in breeding and whose unwanted attention can compromise inconspicuousness in space. When nests are located by radiotelemetry rather than by a biased search near leks, the locations of nests are normally distributed between leks, with the modal distance equal to one-half the distance between leks (Fig. 13.10; see also Davis et al. 1979, Autenrieth 1981). Most females also avoid nesting in the areas regularly visited by males when the latter are feeding or roosting away from the lek (Chap. 5, see Rothenmaier 1979).

Nesting cover for steppe species should be provided midway between leks (Fig. 16.19). If nesting cover is planted near leks, it will receive little use. If it is utilized because of a cover-space trade-off — i.e., there is no other cover — birds may show reduced nesting success. The mean distance of successful prairie chicken nests in Minnesota from nearest leks was $1,171 \pm 103$ m ($n = 20$), whereas unsuccessful nests were closer (975 ± 149 m, $n = 10$) (Table 6.4). Christenson (1970) found successful, sharp-tailed grouse nests $1,210 \pm 180$ m ($n = 11$) from leks and unsuccessful nests 740 ± 100 m ($n = 10$, $P < 0.05$) from leks. Sharp-tailed grouse in Saskatchewan were also more successful when they nested long distances from displaying males (Pepper 1972). Mammalian predators may frequently visit leks. Prospecting females should improve their chances by avoiding areas where predator routes converge. Females leave their nests during crepuscular periods (Table 14.5) — the same times when males move to leks and are most interested in locating females. Hens can thus avoid males at these predictable locations. Nesting cover should be created in places where the inconspicuousness of females will not be compromised by conspicuous males.

16.7.3 The big new space

If a large block of homogenous new habitat is suddenly created, colonizing birds may enjoy a high, initial nesting success because they can nest far apart. In addition, the new space may often lack alternative prey and seldom be frequented by predators. Large-scale examples of this big space should have been the midgrass prairies between the 1870s and 1890s, when the buffalo were suddenly gone. Nesting cover must have appeared in large blocks during wet cycles, and there were still few foxes, skunks, and crows on the plains during this period.

Large spaces have occurred on Vancouver Island when fires created new habitats for blue grouse (Redfield et al. 1970, Bendell 1974). The expansions that occurred in these blue grouse populations were measured by counting advertising males, but the growth of these populations would have arisen because *females* initially could nest far apart from each other. Their progeny then recruited to the habitat. Males were *then* attracted to these areas because of the presence of females. Initially there was little vegetative cover for males or females in these new burns (see Zwickel & Bendell 1967, Plate I), and space must have compensated for this lack of cover.

Another example is the response of ruffed grouse to logging. Populations were high in both Minnesota and Wisconsin in the early 1900s (Leopold 1931, King 1937, Grange 1948, Keith 1963). Large nesting areas were created by forest fires and the clearing of coniferous forests, releasing herbaceous and shrub growth. Females could reach high nesting densities in these new spaces before density-dependent predation dampened population increase.

16.7.4 Space and grouse introductions

At the 15th Prairie Grouse Technical Conference there was interest in reestablishing new populations of prairie grouse. A common reintroduction technique for steppe grouse has been to identify a likely lek location in some general habitat — low cover with wide horizons — and release males and females at the location in the presence of "dummy" males and taped vocalizations of advertising males. These procedures should generally fail because nesting females are the basic spacing unit. Males do not visit leks to be with other males; nor do females select nesting sites to be near males.

The priority in these introductions should be first to locate or create prime nesting cover. Then prospective lek locations can be created *away from* the nesting habitat — at a distance of at least 1 km. Females should have their best cover one-half the distance between proposed leks (Fig. 16.19). One could place yearling females in cages in April at the proposed lek location. Yearling males should then be released nearby. The males should display to the penned females (Toepfer 1979). Adults should not be used because they would scatter, attempting to return to where they had nested and advertised previously. After the males are firmly established, displaying near females, the females should be released. They should scatter to the nesting cover provided but return to breed. Once copulations have occurred, the reintroduction should be in place.

Another way to increase the numbers or distribution of grouse is to transplant birds to a new space where they cannot leave, such as an island. If the island is without predators the population should quickly expand. The best examples of this technique are the introductions of pheasants on Protection Island and Peele Island, Washington (Einarsen 1945, Stokes 1954). The highest density of sharp-tailed grouse reported in the literature was on Drummond Island, Michigan (Ammann 1957).

Ammann (1957) documented another factor in introductions of sharp-tailed grouse that directly relates to space. Introductions were more successful when the Michigan transplanted stock came from populations that were increasing. More of these founders from increasing populations would be the density-tolerant phenotypes that should produce young that are more viable than if founders were taken from declining populations, in which the density-intolerant morphs would be frequent and their offspring less viable.

16.8 Successful management

The highest densities of grouse over a considerable area are the red grouse populations on managed moors in the British Isles. Numbers in the spring commonly exceed 100 birds/km². These high densities result from intensive management; favorable nesting success has resulted from improved nesting cover owing to burning practices and the control of nest predators, particularly crows, foxes (Hewson 1984), and stoats (*Mustela* spp.). This system has now been in place for over 130 years (Lovat 1911, Leopold & Ball 1931), and was well established before intense research began in 1956 (Jenkins et al. 1963). Unfortunately, many biologists have not used the red grouse story to understand how to increase numbers of grouse, but instead have used the Scottish studies as an example of how natural populations are regulated. These Scottish populations have been intensively managed; food and nest cover have been increased, predators have been reduced, and hunting mortality is heavy and additive; thus current research findings are generally inappropriate for systems that are more natural (Lack 1965, 1966, Angelstam 1983, Bergerud et al. 1985).

The unmanaged red grouse populations in Ireland provide a control such that we can evaluate the management success in Scotland. The nesting success of Irish grouse is about 60%, whereas success in Scotland is over 80% (Table 16.3). Birds in both populations have similar clutch sizes, but mortality is much higher in Scotland, indicating additive hunting mortality (Fig. 16.8). The Irish grouse exist at low densities in which the summer rate-of-increase declines with increased numbers (Table 16.3). They are not living in marginal habitat as argued by Watson and O'Hare (1979); they live in unmanaged habitats where their more

Table 16.3. Comparison of the demographic parameters of unmanaged population of red grouse in Ireland and managed population in Scotland

Parameters	Unmanaged[a]	Managed[b]
Spring breeding density (birds/km²)	5.0	84.4
Clutch size	7.4 (13)[c]	7.0 (395)
Nesting success (%)	69 (13)	83 (395)
Chicks per adult in August	0.8	1.6
Adult annual mortality rate (%)	≈45–50	67–71
Regression breeding success on spring densities	$r = 0.989$ (4)	$r = -0.125$ (27)
Regression proportional change Spring numbers between years on prior breeding success	$r = 0.900$ (3)	$r = 0.594$ (22)

[a] Data from Ireland (Watson and O'Hare 1979).

[b] Data from Scotland—Glen Esk, Glen Muick, and Corndavon moors—all heavily hunted (Jenkins et al. 1963, 1967).

[c] Sample size in parentheses.

typical nesting success has resulted in nesting hens being well spaced, and hence at low densities.

The management of red grouse developed by landowners clearly shows how to increase the numbers of grouse. Improve nesting habitat and reduce predators and nesting success will improve. This should result in a stabilizing density, in which recruitment (m_x) = mortality (q_x), that is higher than in unmanaged populations. This is the oldest, managed grouse system, and the most successful.

Fossils of grouse date to the Miocene (review in Johnsgard 1973). The oldest remains have been located in North America. If grouse arose in the Americas, they had ancestors in common with the phasianinae. The phasianinae occupied the south and came to depend on seeds. Grouse expanded north and adapted to steppe-forest interfaces (Short 1967); possibly the prairie chicken secondarily invaded the south and adopted a granivorous diet.

The greatest advance for grouse may have occurred when they evolved their bill and the digestive physiology that permitted them to eat the needles, leaves, and buds of the dominant cover species. *Their home became their food.* They could remain in their cover to feed, and could stay north in the winter. They adapted long ago to eat northern plant species that are superabundant. Grouse have no food problems. Yet, biologists forever expect to find that grouse are food-limited. That most major plant species act as both food and cover is confounding, but plant species are selected more often for their cover value than for their food value. We must turn our emphasis away from food; not only does food not limit, it does not even set breeding densities. To the contrary, grouse could not perfectly adapt to predators as they had to food because predators were coevolving at equal rates with grouse. The key to increasing the numbers of grouse is to increase their nesting success—more space and cover, and/or fewer nest predators. There is no other practical way to have more grouse.

16.9 Summary

This chapter opens with a discussion of the mechanisms that determine the density of grouse. Evidence indicates that grouse females space their nests to reduce predation risk and that the prelaying ranges they search increase in size with increased nest losses. Males space themselves to be near nesting females. Sufficient space and cover for successful nesting are factors that influence the densities of populations. Each population has its own stabilizing density, determined by the predator-cover complex it inhabits. Hunting mortality is additive to natural mortality over winter, but may be partly compensatory to natural mortality during breeding periods. Also, reduced spring densities, brought about by hunting mortality, may provide inverse rate-of-gains if nests are far apart and difficult for predators to locate. Food supplies of adults neither limit population fluctuations nor determine mean densities. Control of space and cover for nesting and control of nest predators are the major management tools available to increase the nesting success of hens and thus increase the numbers of grouse.

References

References

Adamcik, R. S., A. W. Todd, and L. B. Keith. 1978. Demographic and dietary responses of great horned owls during a snowshoe hare cycle. Can. Field Nat. 92:156–66.

Alison, R. M. 1976. Female ptarmigan reoccupying nest site. Auk 73:657.

Allee, W. C., N. E. Collias, and C. Z. Lutherman. 1939. Modification of the social order in flocks of hens by the injection of testosterone propionate. Physiol. Zool. 12:412–40.

Allen, A. A. 1934. Breeding season behaviour of the ruffed grouse. Trans. Am. Game Conf. 20:311–22.

Allen, D. L. 1954. Our wildlife legacy. Funk and Wagnalls, New York. 422 pp.

Allen, H. M. and H. Parker. 1977. Willow ptarmigan remove broken eggs from the nest. Auk 94:612–13.

Allison, D. G. 1963. Basic features of the New Hampshire ruffed grouse census. J. Wildl. Manage. 27:614–16.

Allred, W. J. 1942. Predation and the sage grouse. Wyo. Wildl. 7:3–4.

Alway, J. H. and D. A. Boag. 1979. Behaviour of captive spruce grouse at the time broods break up and juveniles disperse. Can. J. Zool. 57:1311–17.

Ammann, G. A. 1944. Determining age of pinnated and sharp-tailed grouse. J. Wildl. Manage. 8:170–71.

Ammann, G. A. 1950. A ten year comparison of the ruffed grouse kill in Michigan, Minnesota and Wisconsin. Mich. Dep. Conserv. Game Div. Rep. 1096. 2 pp.

Ammann, G. A. 1957. The prairie grouse of Michigan. Mich. Dep. Conserv. Game Div. Fed. Aid in Wildl. Restoration Proj. 5-R, 37-R, 70-R. 200 pp.

Anderson, L. J. 1973. Habitat use, behavior, territoriality, and movements of the male spruce grouse of northern Minnesota. M.S. thesis. Univ. Minnesota, St. Paul.

Anderson, R. K. 1969. Prairie chicken responses to changing booming-ground cover type and height. J. Wildl. Manage. 33:636–43.

Anderson, W. W. and J. Arnold. 1983. Density-regulated selection with genotypic interactions. Am. Nat. 121:649–55.

Andersson, M. and C. G. Wiklund. 1978. Clumping versus spacing out: experiments on nest predation in Fieldfares (*Turdus pilaris*). Anim. Behav. 26:1207–12.

Andersson, M., C. G. Wiklund, and H. Rundgren. 1980. Parental defense of offspring: a model and an example. Anim. Behav. 28:536–42.

Andrewartha, H. G. and L. C. Birch. 1954. The distribution and abundance of animals. Univ. Chicago Press, Chicago. 782 pp.

Angelstam, P. 1983. Population dynamics of Tetraonids, especially the black grouse *Tetrao tetrix* L., in boreal forests. Ph.D. thesis. Uppsala Univ., Sweden.

Angelstam, P. 1984. Sexual and seasoned differences in mortality of black grouse *Tetrao tetrix* in boreal Sweden. Ornis Scand. 15:123–34.

Angelstam, P., E. Lindstrom, and P. Widen. 1984. Role of predation in short-term population fluctuations of some birds and mammals in Fennoscandia. Oecologia 63:199–208.

Angelstam, P., E. Lindstrom, and P. Widen. 1985. Synchronous short-term population fluctuations of some birds and mammals in Fennoscandia — occurrence and distribution. Holarctic Ecol. 8:285–98.

Anonymous. 1965. American buffalo. U.S. Dep. Conserv. Note 12. U.S. Dep. Inter.

Anonymous. 1976. Wisconsin game and fur harvests. Wis. Dep. Nat. Resour. 25 pp.

Anonymous. 1980. Saskatchewan game bird management objectives and strategies for the 80's. Sask. Dep. Tourism and Renewable Resour. 78 pp.

Archibald, H. L. 1973. Spring drumming activity and space use of ruffed grouse. Ph.D. thesis. Univ. Minnesota, St. Paul.

Archibald, H. L. 1974. Directional differences in the sound intensity of ruffed grouse drumming. Auk 91:517–21.

Archibald, H. L. 1975. Temporal patterns of spring space use by ruffed grouse. J. Wildl. Manage. 39:472–81.

Archibald, H. L. 1976a. Spatial relationships of neighboring male ruffed grouse in spring. J. Wildl. Manage. 40:750–60.

Archibald, H. L. 1976b. Spring drumming patterns of ruffed grouse. Auk 93:808–29.

Armleder, H. M. 1980. Habitat use and movements of hens and broods in relation to the demography of blue grouse. M.Sc. Thesis. Univ. Toronto, Toronto.

Arnold, S. J. 1983. Sexual selection: the interface of theory and empiricism. Pp. 67–107 in P. Bateson, ed. Mate choice. Cambridge Univ. Press, Cambridge.

Arthaud, F. L. 1968. Populations and movements of the prairie chicken related to land use in southwestern Missouri. M.A. thesis. Univ. Missouri, Columbia.

Artmann, J. W. 1970. Spring and summer ecology of the sharp-tailed grouse. Ph.D. thesis. Univ. Minnesota, St. Paul.

Aschoff, J. 1966. Circadian activity pattern with two peaks. Ecology 47:657–62.

Ash, A. N. 1979. The effect of urea fertilizer on the habitat, population dynamics, and local distribution of blue grouse. Ph.D. thesis. Univ. Toronto, Toronto.

Aubin, A. E. 1970. Territory and territorial behavior of male ruffed grouse in southwestern Alberta. M.Sc. thesis. Univ. Alberta, Edmonton.

Aubin, A. E. 1972. Aural communication in ruffed grouse. Can. J. Zool. 50:1225–29.

Audubon, M. R. 1960. Audubon and his journals. Dover Press, New York, Vol. 1, 532 pp. Vol. 2, 554 pp.

Aughey, S. 1878. Some facts and considerations concerning the beneficial work of birds. U.S. Entomol. Comm. Annu. Rep. 1877:338–50.

Austad, S. N. 1984. A classification of attentive reproductive behaviours and methods of field-testing ESS models. Am. Zool. 24:309–19.

Autenrieth, R. E. 1969. Impact of strip spray on vegetation and sage grouse use on summer habitat. Proc. West. States Sage Grouse Workshop 6:147–57.

Autenrieth, R. E. 1981. Sage grouse management in Idaho. Idaho Dep. Fish and Game, Wildl. Bull. 9. 238 pp.

Bailey, W. J., W. M. Sharp, R. B. Hazel, and G. Davis. 1955. Food habit trends of ruffed grouse in the Centre County "Barrens." Pennsylvania State Univ., Agric. Exp. Sta. Bull. 604. 18 pp.

Baker, M. F. 1952. The ecology and management of prairie chickens in Kansas. Ph.D. thesis. Univ. Kansas, Lawrence.

Baker, M. F. 1953. Prairie chickens of Kansas. State Biol. Survey, Univ. Kans. Misc. Publ. 5. 68 pp.

Baker, R. R. and G. A. Parker. 1979. The evolution of bird coloration. Philos. Trans. of the Royal Society of London, Ser. B. 287:63–120.

Bakke, E. L. 1980. Movements and habitat use of ruffed grouse in the Turtle Mountains, North Dakota. M.S. thesis. Univ. North Dakota, Grand Forks.

Balser, D. S., H. H. Dill, and H. K. Nelson. 1968. Effect of predator reduction on waterfowl nesting success. J. Wildl. Manage. 32:669–82.

Banasiak, C. F. 1951. Ruffed grouse, *Bonasa umbellus umbellus* (Linne), populations and cover use on two areas in central Massachusetts. M.S. thesis. Univ. Massachusetts, Amherst.

Barichello, N. 1983. Gyrfalcon nest site selection. M.Sc. thesis. Univ. British Columbia, Vancouver.

Barichello, N. and D. Mossop. 1983. Productivity of gyrfalcons as a response to changes in ptarmigan abundance. 34th. Alaska Sci. Conf., Whitehorse, Yukon Territ. (abstract)

Barrett, R. W. 1970. Behavior of ruffed grouse during the breeding and early brood rearing periods. Ph.D. thesis. Univ. Minnesota, St. Paul.

Bateman, A. J. 1948. Intra-sexual selection in *Drosophila*. Heredity 2: 349–68.

Bateson, P. (ed.). 1983. Mate choice. Cambridge Univ. Press, Cambridge. 462 pp.

Batterson, W. M. and W. B. Morse. 1948. Oregon state grouse. Oreg. State Game Comm. Fauna Ser. 1. 29 pp.

Beasom, S. L. 1974. Intensive short-term predator removal as a game management tool. Trans. N. Am. Wildl. Nat. Resour. Conf. 39:230–40.

Beck, A. M. and R. J. Vogl. 1972. The effects of spring burning on rodent populations in a brush prairie savanna. J. Mammal. 53:336–45.

Beck, T. D. I. 1975. Attributes of a wintering population of sage grouse, North Park, Colorado. M.S. thesis. Colorado State Univ., Fort Collins.

Beck, T. D. I. 1977. Sage grouse flock characteristics and habitat selection in winter. J. Wildl. Manage. 41:18–26.

Beck, T. D. I. and C. E. Braun. 1978. Weights of Colorado sage grouse. Condor 80:241–43.

Beck, T. D. I. and C. E. Braun. 1980. The strutting ground count: variation, traditionalism, management needs. Proc. West. Assoc. Fish and Wildl. Agencies 60:558–66.

Beckerton, P. R. and A. L. A. Middleton. 1982. Effects of dietary protein levels on ruffed grouse reproduction. J. Wildl. Manage. 46:569–79.

Beil, C. E. 1969. The plant associations of the Cariboo Aspen-Lodgepole pine – Douglas fir Parkland Zone. Ph.D. thesis. Univ. British Columbia, Vancouver.

Bendell, J. F. 1954. A study of the life history and population dynamics of the sooty grouse, *Dendragapus obscurus fuliginosus* (Ridgway). Ph.D. thesis. Univ. British Columbia, Vancouver.

Bendell, J. F. 1955a. Age, breeding behavior and migration of sooty grouse, *Dendragapus obscurus fuliginosus* (Ridgway). Trans. N. Am. Wildl. Conf. 20:367–81.

Bendell, J. F. 1955b. Disease as a control of a population of blue grouse, *Dendragapus obscurus fuliginosus* (Ridgway). Can. J. Zool. 33:195–223.

Bendell, J. F. 1972. Population dynamics and ecology of the Tetraonidae. Proc. Int. Ornithol. Congr. 15:81–89.

Bendell, J. F. 1974. Effects of fire on birds and mammals. Pp. 73–138 *in* T. T. Kozlowski and C. E. Ahlgren, eds. Fire and ecosystems. Academic Press, New York.

Bendell, J. F. and P. W. Elliott. 1966. Habitat selection in blue grouse. Condor 68:431–46.

Bendell, J. F. and P. W. Elliott. 1967. Behaviour and the regulation of numbers in blue grouse. Can. Wildl. Serv. Rep. Ser. 4. 76 pp.

Bendell, J. F., D. G. King, and D. H. Mossop. 1972. Removal and repopulation of blue grouse in a declining population. J. Wildl. Manage. 36:1153–65.

Bendell, J. F. and F. C. Zwickel. 1979. Problems in the abundance and distribution of blue, spruce, and ruffed grouse in North America. Pp. 48–63 *in* T. W. I. Lovel, ed. Woodland Grouse Symp. Culloden House, Inverness, Scotland.

Bengtson, S. A. 1971. Hunting methods and choice of prey of gyrfalcons *Falco rusticolus* at Myvatn in northeast Iceland. Ibis 113:468–76.

Bent, A. C. 1932. Life histories of North American Gallinaceous birds. U.S. Natl. Mus. Bull. 162. Wash., D. C. 490 pp.

Berg, W. E. 1975. Sharp-tailed grouse hunter check, northwestern Minnesota, 1974. Minn. Wildl. Res. Q. 35:94–100.

Berg, W. E. 1977. Sharp-tailed grouse hunter check, northwestern Minnesota, 1976. Minn. Wildl. Res. Q. 37:108–20.

Berg, W. E. 1979. Ruffed grouse drumming count, spring 1979. Minn. Wildl. Res. Job Progress Rep. 18 pp.

Berger, D. D., F. Hamerstrom, and F. N. Hamerstrom, Jr. 1963. The effect of raptors on prairie chickens on booming grounds. J. Wildl. Manage. 27:778–91.

Bergerud, A. T. 1970a. Population dynamics of the willow ptarmigan *Lagopus lagopus alleni* L. in Newfoundland 1955–1965. Oikos 21:299–325.

Bergerud, A. T. 1970b. Vulnerability of willow ptarmigan to hunting. J. Wildl. Manage. 34:282–85.

Bergerud, A. T. 1971. The past abundance of willow ptarmigan on the Avalon Peninsula of Newfoundland. Can. Field-Nat. 85:21–23.

Bergerud, A. T. 1972. Changes in the vulnerability of ptarmigan to hunting in Newfoundland. J. Wildl. Manage. 36:104–9.

Bergerud, A. T. and H. E. Butler. 1985. Aggressive and spacing behaviour of female blue grouse. Auk 102:313–22.

Bergerud, A. T. and H. D. Hemus. 1975. An experimental study of the behavior of blue grouse (*Dendragapus obscurus*). I. Differences between the founders from three populations. Can. J. Zool. 53:1222–37.

Bergerud, A. T. and D. S. Huxter. 1969a. Breeding season habitat utilization and movement of Newfoundland willow ptarmigan. J. Wildl. Manage. 33:967–74.

Bergerud, A. T. and D. S. Huxter. 1969b. Effects of hunting on willow ptarmigan in Newfoundland. J. Wildl. Manage. 33:866–70.

Bergerud, A. T. and W. E. Mercer. 1966. Census of the willow ptarmigan in Newfoundland. J. Wildl. Manage. 30:101–13.

Bergerud, A. T. and W. E. Mercer. 1972. Spring foods of willow ptarmigan *Lagopus lagopus alleni* in southeastern Newfoundland. Oikos 23:213–17.

Bergerud, A. T. and D. H. Mossop. 1985. The pair bond in ptarmigan. Can. J. Zool. 62:2129–41.

Bergerud, A. T., D. H. Mossop, and S. Myrberget. 1985. A critique of the mechanics of annual changes in ptarmigan numbers. Can. J. Zool. 63: 2240–48.

Bergerud, A. T., S. S. Peters, and R. McGrath. 1963. Determining sex and age of willow ptarmigan in Newfoundland. J. Wildl. Manage. 27:700–711.

Berner, A. and L. W. Gysel. 1969. Habitat analysis and management considerations for ruffed grouse for a multiple use area in Michigan. J. Wildl. Manage. 33:769–78.

Bernhoft, L. S. 1969. Reproductive ecology of female sharp-tailed grouse and food habits of broods in southwestern North Dakota. M.S. thesis. Univ. North Dakota, Grand Forks.

Berry, J. D. and R. L. Eng. 1985. Interseasonal movements and fidelity to seasonal use areas by female sage grouse. J. Wildl. Manage. 49:237–40.

Berry, R. J. and P. E. Davis. 1970. Polymorphism and behaviour of arctic skua, *Stercorarius parasiticus*. Proc. Royal Society London, Ser. B 175:225–67.

Beyer, C., K. Larsson, and M. L. Cruz. 1979. Neural mechanisms probably related to the effects of steroids on sexual behavior. *in* C. Beyer, ed. Endocrine control of sexual behaviour. Raven Press, New York.

Blackford, J. L. 1963. Further observations on the breeding behavior of a blue grouse population in Montana. Condor 65:485–513.

Blake, C. S. 1970. The response of sage grouse populations to precipitation trends and habitat quality in south central Idaho. Proc. West. Assoc. State Game and Fish Comm. 50:452–62.

Blom, R. 1980. Spring foods of the willow grouse *Lagopus l. lagopus* on Tranøy, northern Norway. Cand. Real. thesis. Univ. Bergen, Norway.

Blom, R. and S. Myrberget. 1978. Experiments on shooting territorial willow grouse *Lagopus lagopus*. Cinclus 1:29–33.

Blus, L. J. and J. A. Walker. 1966. Progress report on the prairie grouse nesting study in the Nebraska sandhills. Nebr. Bird Rev. 34:23–30.

Boag, D. A. 1965. Indicators of sex, age, and breeding phenology in blue grouse. J. Wildl. Manage. 29:103–8.

Boag, D. A. 1966. Population attributes of blue grouse in southwestern Alberta. Can. J. Zool. 44:799–814.

Boag, D. A. 1976a. The effect of shrub removal on occupancy of ruffed grouse drumming sites. J. Wildl. Manage. 40:105–10.

Boag, D. A. 1976b. Influence of changing grouse density and forest attributes on the occupancy of a series of potential territories by male ruffed grouse. Can. J. Zool. 54:1727–36.

Boag, D. A. and J. H. Alway. 1980. Effect of social environment within the brood on dominance rank in gallinaceous birds (Tetraonidae and Phasianidae). Can. J. Zool. 58:44–49.

Boag, D. A. and J. H. Alway. 1981. Heritability of dominance status among Japanese quail: a preliminary report. Can. J. Zool. 59:441–44.

Boag, D. A., K. H. McCourt, P. W. Herzog, and J. H. Alway. 1979. Population regulation in spruce grouse: a working hypothesis. Can. J. Zool. 57: 2275–84.

Boag, D. A., S. G. Reebs, and M. A. Schroeder. 1983. Egg loss among spruce grouse inhabiting lodgepole pine forests. Can. J. Zool. 62:1034–37.

Boag, D.A. and K. M. Sumanik. 1969. Characteristics of drumming sites selected by ruffed grouse in Alberta. J. Wildl. Manage. 33:621–28.

Boggs, C. E., E. Norris, and J. B. Steen. 1977. Behavioural and physiological temperature regulation in young chicks of the willow grouse (*Lagopus lagopus*). Comp. Biochem. Physiol. 58(A):371–72.

Borgia, G. 1979. Sexual selection and the evolution of mating systems. Pp. 19–80 *in* M. S. Blum and N. A. Blum, eds. Sexual selection and reproductive competition in insects. Academic Press, New York.

Bowen, D. E., Jr. 1971. A study of dummy nests and greater prairie chicken (*Tympanuchus cupido pinnatus*) nests in northeastern Kansas with notes on female nesting behavior. M.S. thesis. Kansas State Univ., Manhattan.

Bowman, T. J. and R. J. Robel. 1977. Brood break-up, dispersal, mobility, and mortality of juvenile prairie chickens. J. Wildl. Manage. 41:27–34.

Boyd, H. 1981. Prairie dabbling ducks. Can. Wildl. Serv. Prog. Note 119. 9 pp.

Bradbury, J. W. 1981. The evolution of leks. Pp. 138–169 *in* R. D. Alexander and D. W. Tinkle, eds. Natural selection and social behavior. Chiron Press, New York.

Bradbury, J. W. and R. M. Gibson. 1983. Leks and mate choice. Pp. 109–38 *in* P. Bateson, ed. Mate choice. Cambridge Univ. Press, Cambridge.

Bradbury, W. C. 1915. Notes on the nesting of the white-tailed ptarmigan in Colorado. Condor 17:214–22.

Braestrup, F. W. 1941. A study on the arctic fox in Greenland. Immigrations, fluctuations in numbers based mainly on trading statistics. Medd. om Grøland, 13:1–101.

Brander, R. B. 1965. Factors affecting dispersion of ruffed grouse during late winter and spring on the Cloquet Forest Research Center, Minnesota. Ph.D. thesis. Univ. Minnesota, St. Paul.

Brander, R. B. 1967. Movements of female ruffed grouse during the mating season. Wilson Bull. 79:28–36.

Braun, C.E. 1969. Population dynamics, habitat, and movements of white-tailed ptarmigan in Colorado. Ph.D. thesis. Colorado State Univ., Fort Collins.

Braun, C. E. 1979. Evolution of the effects of changes in hunting regulations on sage grouse populations. Colo. Div. Wildl., Game Res. Rep. Proj. W-37-R-32, Job 9a. Pp. 11–35.

Braun, C. E., T. Britt, and R. O. Wallestad. 1977. Guidelines for maintenance of sage grouse habitats. Wildl. Soc. Bull. 5:99–106.

Braun, C. E. and D. M. Hoffman. 1979. Vulnerability and population characteristics of sage grouse in Moffat County. Colo. Div. Wildl., Game Res. Rep. Proj. W-37-R-32, Job 11. Pp. 163–99.

Braun, C. E., R. W. Hoffman, and G. E. Rogers. 1976. Wintering areas and winter ecology of white-tailed ptarmigan in Colorado. Colo. Div. Game, Fish and Parks, Spec. Rep. 38. 38 pp.

Braun, C. E. and G. E. Rogers. 1971. The white-tailed ptarmigan in Colorado. Colo. Div. Game, Fish and Parks, Tech. Publ. 27. 80 pp.

Braun, C. E. and R. K. Schmidt. 1971. Effects of snow and wind on wintering populations of white-tailed ptarmigan in Colorado. Pp. 238–250 in A. O. Haugen, ed. Proc. Snow and Ice Symp. Iowa Coop. Wildl. Res. Unit, Iowa State Univ., Ames.

Braun, C. E., R. K. Schmidt, and G. E. Rogers. 1973. Census of Colorado white-tailed ptarmigan with tape recorded calls. J. Wildl. Manage. 37:90–93.

Brewer, L. W. 1980. The ruffed grouse in western Washington. Wash. State Dep. Game, Biol. Bull. 16. 102 pp.

Brewer, R. and K. L. Harrison. 1975. The time of habitat selection in birds. Ibis. 117:521–22.

Brittas, R. and V. Marcstrom. 1982. Studies in willow grouse Lagopus lagopus of some possible measures of condition in birds. Ornis Fenn. 59:157–69.

Brown, C. P. 1946. Food of Maine ruffed grouse by seasons and cover types. J. Wildl. Manage. 10:17–28.

Brown, J. L. 1964. The evolution of diversity in avian territorial systems. Wilson Bull. 76:160–69.

Brown, J. L. 1969. Territorial behavior and population regulation in birds: a review and re-evaluation. Wilson Bull. 81:293–329.

Brown, R. L. 1966a. Response of sharptail breeding populations to annual changes in residual grassland cover. Proc. Annu. Conf. Western Assoc. State Game and Fish Comm. 46:219–22.

Brown, R. L. 1966b. Sharptail grouse population study. Mont. Dep. Fish and Game. Proj. W-91-R-6 and W-91-R-7. 23 pp.

Brown, R. L. 1967. Sharptail grouse population study. Mont. Dep. Fish and Game. Proj. 91-R-8, Job II-E. 16 pp.

Brown, R. L. 1968a. Effects of land-use practices on sharptail grouse. Mont. Dep. Fish and Game. Proj. W-91-R-9, Job II-F. 11 pp.

Brown, R. L. 1968b. Sharptail grouse population study. Mont. Dep. Fish and Game. Proj. W-91-R-9. Job II-E. 18 pp.

Brownlee, W. C. 1971–74. Seasonal territorial ranges of Attwater's prairie chicken. Texas Parks and Wildl. Dep. Proj. W-100-R-Z, 3, 4, and 5. 13 pp.

Bryant, J. P. and P. J. Kuropat. 1980. Selection of winter forage by subarctic browsing vertebrates: the role of plant chemistry. Annu. Rev. Ecol. Syst. 11:261–85.

Buehler, D. A. and L. B. Keith. 1982. Snowshoe hare distribution and habitat use in Wisconsin. Can. Field-Nat. 96:19–29.

Bump, G., R. W. Darrow, F. C. Edminster, and W. F. Crissey. 1947. The ruffed grouse: life history, propagation, management. N.Y. State Conserv. Dep., Holling Press, Buffalo. 915 pp.

Burke, C. J. 1979. Effect of prey and land use on mating systems of harriers. M.S. thesis. Univ. Wisconsin, Stevens Point.

Byrkjedal, I. 1980. Nest predation in relation to snow-cover—a possible factor influencing the start of breeding in shorebirds. Ornis Scand. 11:249–52.

Cade, T. J. 1960. Ecology of the peregrine and gyrfalcon populations in Alaska. Univ. Calif. Publ. Zool. 63:151–290.

Cade, W. H. 1981. Alternative mating strategies: Genetic difference in crickets. Science 212:563–64.

Cade, W. H. 1984. Genetic variation underlying sexual behavior and reproduction. Am. Zool. 24:355–66.

Caldwell, J. P. 1982. Disruptive selection: a tail color polymorphism in *Acris* tadpoles in response to differential predation. Can. J. Zool. 60:2818–27.

Caldwell, P. J. 1976. Energetic and population considerations of the sharp-tailed grouse in the aspen parkland of Canada. Ph.D. thesis. Kansas State Univ., Manhattan.

Campbell, H. 1972. A population study of lesser prairie chickens in New Mexico. J. Wildl. Manage. 36:689–99.

Cancelado, R. and T. R. Yonke. 1970. Effect of prairie burning on insect populations. J. Kans. Society 43:274–81.

Cannon, R. W. and F. L. Knopf. 1979. Lesser prairie chicken responses to range fires at the booming ground. Wildl. Society Bull. 7:44–46.

Cannon, R. W. and F. L. Knopf. 1981. Lek numbers as a trend index to prairie grouse populations. J. Wildl. Manage. 45:776–78.

Capanna, E., M. Corti, D. Mainardi, S. Parmigiani, and P. F. Brain. 1984. Karyotype and intermale aggression in wild house mice: ecology and speciation. Beh. Genet. 14:195–208.

Caraco, T., S. Martindale, and H. R. Pullion. 1980. Avian flocking in the presence of a predator. Nature (London) 285:400–401.

Carr, H. D. 1967. Effects of sage brush spraying on abundance, distribution and movements of sage grouse. M.S. thesis. Colorado State Univ., Fort Collins.

Carrick, R. 1963. Ecological significance of territory in the Australian magpie, *Gymnorhina tibicen*. Proc. Int. Ornithol. Congr. 13:740–53.

Carrick, R. and M. D. Murray. 1964. Social factors in population regulation of the silver gull *Larus novaehollandiae*. C.S.I.R.O. Wildl. Res. 9:189–99.

Cartwright, B. W. 1944. The "crash" decline in sharp-tailed grouse and hungarian partridge in western Canada and the role of the predator. Trans. N. Am. Wildl. Conf. 9:324–30.

Cebula, J. J. 1966. Radio-telemetry as a technique used in greater prairie chicken (*Tympanuchus cupido pinnatus*) mobility studies. M.S. thesis. Kansas State Univ., Manhattan.

Charlesworth, B. 1971. Selection in density-regulated populations. Ecology 52:469–74.

Charlesworth, B. and J. T. Giesel. 1972. Selection in populations with overlapping generations. II. Relationship between gene frequency and demographic variables. Am. Nat. 106:388–401.

Charnov, E. L. and J. P. Finerty. 1980. Vole population cycles: a case for kin-selection? Oecologia 45:1–2.

Charnov, E. L. and J. R. Krebs. 1974. On clutch size and fitness. Ibis 116:217–19.

Chesness, R. A., M. M. Nelson, and W. H. Longley. 1968. The effect of predator removal on pheasant reproductive success. J. Wildl. Manage. 32:683–97.

Chitty, D. 1958. Self-regulation of numbers through changes in viability. Cold Spring Harbor Symp. Quant. Biol. 22:277–80.

Chitty, D. 1960. Population processes in the vole and their relevance to general theory. Can. J. Zool. 38:99–113.

Chitty, D. 1964. Animal numbers and behavior. Pp. 41–53 *in* J. R. Dymond, ed. Fish and wildlife. A memorial to W. J. K. Harkness. Honyman Press, Canada.

Chitty, D. 1967. The natural selection of self-regulatory behaviour in animal populations. Proc. Ecol. Society Aust. 2:51–78.

Chitty, D. 1970. Variation and population density. Symp. Zool. Society London 26:327–33.

Chitty, D. and E. Phipps. 1966. Seasonal changes in survival in mixed populations of two species of vole. J. Anim. Ecol. 35:313–31.

Choate, T. S. 1960. Observations on the reproductive activities of white-tailed ptarmigan (*Lagopus leucurus*) in Glacier Park, Montana. M.S. thesis. Montana State Univ., Missoula.

Choate, T. S. 1963a. Ecology and population dynamics of white-tailed ptarmigan (*Lagopus leucurus*) in Glacier National Park, Montana. Ph.D. thesis. Montana State Univ., Missoula.

Choate, T. S. 1963b. Habitat and population dynamics of white-tailed ptarmigan in Montana. J. Wildl. Manage. 27:684–99.

Christensen, K. and H. Pedersen. 1982. Variation in chromosome number in the blue fox (*Alopex lagopus*) and its effect on fertility. Hereditas 97:211–15.

Christenson, C. D. 1970. Nesting and brooding characteristics of sharp-tailed grouse (*Pedioecetes phasianellus jamesi* Lincoln) in southwestern North Dakota. M.S. thesis. Univ. North Dakota, Grand Forks.

Christisen, D. M. 1969. National status and management of the greater prairie chicken. Trans. N. Am. Wildl. and Nat. Resour. Conf. 34:207–17.

Cody, M. L. 1966. A general theory of clutch size. Evolution 20:174–84.

Cogar, V. F., J. D. Horkel, and N. J. Silvy. 1977. Vegetation type preferences of Attwater's prairie chicken in coastal prairie. Proc. Annu. Conf. Southeast. Assoc. Fish and Wildl. Agencies 31:41–50.

Cole, L. C. 1954. Some features of random population cycles. J. Wildl. Manage. 18:2–24.

Collias, N. E. 1950. Hormones and behavior with special reference to birds and mammals and the mechanism of hormone action. *in* E. S. Gordon, ed. A symposium of steroid hormones. Univ. Wisconsin Press, Madison.

Comins, H. N., W. D. Hamilton, and R. M. May. 1980. Evolutionarily stable dispersal strategies. J. Theor. Biol. 82:205–30.

Connell, J. H. and W. P. Sousa. 1983. On the evidence needed to judge ecological stability or persistence. Am. Nat. 121:789–824.

Connelly, J. W., Jr. 1982. An ecological study of sage grouse in southeastern Idaho. Ph.D. thesis. Washington State Univ., Pullman.

Cooke, F. and F. G. Cooch. 1968. The genetics of polymorphism in the snow goose *Anser caoerulescens*. Evolution 22:289–300.

Cooke, F. and P. J. Mirsky. 1972. A genetic analysis of lesser snow goose families. Auk 89:863–71.

Cooke, W. W. 1888. Report on bird migration in the Mississippi Valley in the years 1884 and 1885. U.S. Dep. Agric. Div. Econ. Ornithol. Bull. 2.

Cooper, C. R. 1977. Differences in behaviour between populations of captive blue grouse. M.Sc. thesis. Univ. Toronto, Toronto.

Copelin, F. F. 1963. The lesser prairie chicken in Oklahoma. Okla. Wildl. Conserv. Dep. Tech. Bull. 6. 58 pp.

Cowardin, L. M., D. S. Gilmer, and C. W. Shaiffer, 1985. Mallard recruitment in the agricultural environment of North Dakota. Wildl. Monog. 92. 37 pp.

Craig, J. V., L. C. Ortman, and A. M. Gull. 1965. Genetic selection for social dominance ability in chickens. Anim. Behav. 13:114–31.

Cramp, S., et al. 1980. Handbook of the birds of Europe, the Middle East and North Africa. The birds of the western Palearctic. Vol. 2. Hawks to bustards. Oxford Univ. Press, Oxford. 695 pp.

Cringan, A. T. 1970. Reproductive biology of ruffed grouse in southern Ontario, 1964–1969. J. Wildl. Manage. 34:756–61.

Crook, J. H. 1965. The adaptive significance of avian social organisations. Symp. Zool. Society London 14:181–218.

Croze, H. 1970. Searching image in carron crows. Z. Tierpsychol. 5:1–35.

Curio, E. 1975. The functional organization of antipredator behaviour in the pied flycatcher: a study of avian visual perceptions. Anim. Behav. 23:1–115.

Curio, E. 1976. The ethology of predation. Springer-Verlag, Berlin. 250 pp.

Curtis, J. T. 1959. The vegetation of Wisconsin. Univ. Wisconsin Press, Madison. 657 pp.

Dalke, P. D., D. B. Pyrah, D. C. Stanton, J. E. Crawford, and E. F. Schlatter. 1960. Seasonal movements and breeding behavior of sage grouse in Idaho. Trans. N. Am. Wildl. Conf. 25:396–407.

Dalke, P. D., D. B. Pyrah, D. C. Stanton, J. E. Crawford, and E. F. Schlatter. 1963. Ecology, productivity, and management of sage grouse in Idaho. J. Wildl. Manage. 27:810–41.

Dapkus, D. C. 1976. Differential survival involving the Burnsi phenotype in the northern leopard frog *Rana pipiens*. Herpetology 32:325–27.

Dargan, L. and R. J. Keller. 1940. Survey of 1940: North Park, Jackson County, Colo. Colo. Dept. Game and Fish. Sage grouse survey, Vol. 2. 28 pp.

Darwin, C. 1871. The descent of man and selection in relation to sex. John Murray Press, London. 490 pp.

Davies, N. B. 1978. Ecological questions about territorial behaviour. Pp. 317–50 *in* J. R. Krebs and N. B. Davies, eds. Behavioural ecology. Blackwell Sci. Publ., London.

Davies, N. B. and T. R. Halliday. 1979. Competitive mate searching in male common toads, *Bufo bufo*. Anim. Behav. 27:1235–67.

Davies, R. G. 1973. A study of demography and behaviour of ruffed grouse in British Columbia. M.S. thesis, Univ. Victoria, Victoria.

Davis, C. A., T. Z. Riley, R. A. Smith, H. R. Suminski, and M. J. Wisdom. 1979. Habitat evaluation of lesser prairie chickens in eastern Chaves County, New Mexico. Dep. Fish. and Wildl. Sci., New Mexico State Univ., Agric. Exp. Station, Las Cruces. 141 pp.

Davis, D. E. 1957. The existence of cycles. Ecology 38:163–64.

Davis, J. A. and R. J. Stoll, Jr. 1973. Ruffed grouse age and sex ratios in Ohio. J. Wildl. Manage. 37:133–41.

Dawkins, R. 1980. Good strategy or evolutionary stable strategy? Pp. 337–70 *in* G. W. Barlow and J. Silvererg, eds. Sociobiology: beyond nature/nurture. Westville Press, Boulder, Colo.

Dawkins, R. and T. R. Carlisle. 1976. Parental investment, male desertion and a fallacy. Nature 262:131–33.

DeStefano, S. and D. H. Rusch. 1982. Some historical aspects of ruffed grouse harvests and hunting regulations in Wisconsin. Wis. Acad. Trans. 70:27–35.

De Vos, G. J. 1979. Adaptedness of arena behaviour in black grouse (*Tetrao tetrix*) and other grouse species (Tetraoninae). Behaviour 68:277–314.

De Vos, G. J. 1983. Social behaviour of black grouse, an observational and experimental field study. Ardea 71:1–103.

Dixon, J. 1927. Contribution to the life history of the Alaska willow ptarmigan. Condor 29:213–23.

Dixson, A. F. 1980. Androgens and aggressive behavior in primates: a review. J. Aggress. Behav. 6:37–67.

Doerr, P. D., L. B. Keith, and D. H. Rusch. 1971. Effects of fire on a ruffed grouse population. Proc. Annu. Tall Timbers Fire Ecol. Conf. 10:25–46.

Doerr, P. D., L. B. Keith, D. H. Rusch, and C. A. Fischer. 1974. Characteristics of winter feeding aggregations of ruffed grouse in Alberta. J. Wildl. Manage. 38:601–15.

Dominey, W. J. 1984. Alternative mating tactics and evolutionary stable strategies. Am. Zool. 24:385–96.

Donaldson, J. L. and A. T. Bergerud. 1974. Behaviour and habitat selection of an insular population of blue grouse. Syesis 7:115–27.

Dorney, R. S. 1959. Relationship of ruffed grouse to forest cover types in Wisconsin. Wis. Conserv. Dep. Tech. Bull. 18. 32 pp.

Dorney, R. S. 1963. Sex and age structure of Wisconsin ruffed grouse populations. J. Wildl. Manage. 27:599–603.

Dorney, R. S. 1966. A new method for sexing ruffed grouse in late summer. J. Wildl. Manage. 30:623–25.

Dorney, R. S. and C. Kabat. 1960. Relation of weather, parasitic disease, and hunting to Wisconsin ruffed grouse populations. Wis. Conserv. Dep. Tech. Bull. 20. 64 pp.

Drobney, R. D. and R. D. Sparrowe. 1977. Land use relationships and movements of greater prairie chickens in Missouri. Trans. Mo. Acad. Sci. 10,11:146–60.

Duebbert, H. F. 1982. Nesting of waterfowl on islands in Lake Aububon, North Dakota. Wildl. Soc. Bull. 10:232–37.

Duebbert, H. F. and H. A. Kantrud. 1974. Upland duck nesting related to land use and predator reduction. J. Wildl. Manage. 38:257–65.

Dumke, R. T. and C. M. Pils. 1973. Mortality of radio-tagged pheasants on the Waterloo Wildlife Area. Wis. Dep. Nat. Resour. Tech. Bull. 72. 52 pp.

Dumke, R. T. and C. M. Pils. 1979. Renesting and dynamics of nest site selection by Wisconsin pheasants. J. Wildl. Manage. 43:705–16.

Dunn, P. O. and C. E. Braun. 1985. Natal dispersal and lek fidelity of sage grouse. Auk 102:621–27.

Edminster, F. C. 1939. The effect of predator control on ruffed grouse populations in New York. J. Wildl. Manage. 3:345–52.

Edminster, F. C. 1947. The ruffed grouse, its life story, ecology and management. Macmillan, New York. 385 pp.

Edminster, F. C. 1954. American game birds of fields and forest; their habits, ecology and management. Charles Scribner's Sons, New York. 490 pp.

Edmonds, M. 1974. Defence in animals. Longman, N.Y. 357 pp.

Einarsen, A. S. 1945. Some factors affecting ring-necked pheasant population density. The Murrelet 26:29,39–44.

Elliot, C. A. 1979. Insect availability as a food source for spruce grouse chicks. B.Sc. thesis. Univ. New Brunswick, Fredericton.

Elliott, P. W. 1965. Factors affecting the local distribution of blue grouse on a breeding range. M.Sc. thesis. Univ. British Columbia, Vancouver.

Ellison, L. N. 1967. Spring movements and behavior of territorial and non-territorial male Alaskan spruce grouse. Abst. Wildl. Society Northwest Sect. Annu. Conf. 18 pp.

Ellison, L. N. 1971. Territoriality in Alaskan spruce grouse. Auk 88:652–64.

Ellison, L. N. 1972. Role of winter food in regulating numbers of Alaskan spruce grouse. Ph.D. thesis. Univ. California, Berkeley.

Ellison, L. N. 1973. Seasonal social organization and movements of spruce grouse. Condor 75:375–85.

Ellison, L. N. 1974. Population characteristics of Alaskan spruce grouse. J. Wildl. Manage. 38:383–95.

Ellison, L. N. and R. B. Weeden. 1966. Small game and furbearers investigations. Alaska Dep. Fish and Game Proj. W-13-R-1, Work Plan B. (mimeogr.).

Ellison, L. N. and R. B. Weeden. 1979. Seasonal and local weights of Alaska spruce grouse. J. Wildl. Manage. 43:176–83.

Elton, C. 1930. Animal ecology and evolution. Clarendon Press, Oxford. 96 pp.

Elton, C. S. 1942. Voles, mice and lemmings. Clarendon Press, Oxford. 496 pp.

Emlen, S. T. and L. W. Oring. 1977. Ecology, sexual selection and the evolution of mating systems. Science 197:215–23.

Emmons, S. R. 1980. Lek attendance of male sage grouse in North Park, Colorado. M.S. thesis. Colorado State Univ., Fort Collins.

Emmons, S. R. and C. E. Braun. 1984. Lek attendance of male sage grouse. J. Wildl. Manage. 48:1023–28.

Eng, R. L. 1959. A study of the ecology of male ruffed grouse (*Bonasa umbellus* L.), on the Cloquet Forest Research Center, Minnesota. Ph.D. thesis. Univ. Minnesota, St. Paul.

Eng, R. L. 1963. Observations on the breeding biology of male sage grouse. J. Wildl. Manage. 27:841–46.

Eng, R. L. and G. W. Gullion. 1962. The predation of goshawks upon ruffed grouse on the Cloquet Forest Research Center, Minnesota. Wilson Bull. 74:227–42.

Eng, R. L., E. J. Pitcher, S. J. Scott, and R. J. Greene. 1979. Minimizing the effect of surface coal mining on a sage grouse population by a directed shift of breeding activities. Pp. 464–68 *in* G. A. Swanson, ed. The mitigation symposium. Gen. Tech. Rep. RM-65, Rocky Mt. For. Range Exp. Stn., Ft. Collins, Colo.

Eng, R. L. and P. Schladweiler. 1972. Sage grouse winter movements and habitat use in central Montana. J. Wildl. Manage. 36:141–46.

Erikstad, K. E. 1978. Relations between survival of chicks, brood movements and habitat utilization in willow grouse. Cand. Real. thesis. Univ. Bergen, Norway.

Erikstad, K. E. 1979. Effects of radio packages on reproductive success of willow grouse. J. Wildl. Manage. 43:170–75.

Erikstad, K. E. 1982. Effekten ar kaldt og fuktig vaer på lirypekyllingenes naering sadferd og over-lerelse. Pp. 207–25 in E. Østbye and I. Mysterud, eds. Høyfjelløkologisk Forskningsstasjon, Finse. Univ. Bergen and Oslo.

Erikstad, K. E. 1985a. Growth and survival of willow grouse chicks in relation to home range size, brood movements and habitat selection. Ornis Scand. 16:181–90.

Erikstad, K. E. 1985b. Territorial breakdown and brood movements in willow grouse Lagopus l. lagopus. Ornis Scand. 16:95–98.

Erikstad, K. E. 1985c. Clutch size and egg size variation in willow grouse Lagopus l. lagopus. Ornis Scand. 16:88–94.

Erikstad, K. E. and R. Andersen. 1983. The effect of weather on survival, growth rate and feeding time in different sized willow grouse broods. Ornis Scand. 14:249–52.

Erikstad, K. E., R. Blom, and S. Myrberget. 1981. Territorial hooded crows as predators of willow ptarmigan nests. J. Wildl. Manage. 46:109–14.

Erikstad, K. E. and T. K. Spidsø. 1982. The influence of weather on food intake, insect prey selection and feeding behaviour in willow grouse chicks in northern Norway. Ornis Scand. 13:176–82.

Errington, P. L. 1935. The 1934 drought and southern Iowa bobwhite. Iowa Bird Life 5:18–21.

Errington, P. L. 1937a. Food habits of Iowa red foxes during a drought summer. Ecology 18:53–62.

Errington, P. L. 1937b. Winter carrying capacity of marginal ruffed grouse environment in north-central United States. Can. Field-Nat. 51:31–34.

Errington, P. L. 1945. Some contributions of a fifteen-year local study of the northern bobwhite to a knowledge of population phenomena. Ecol. Monogr. 15:1–34.

Errington, P. L. 1951. Concerning fluctuations in populations of the prolific and widely distributed muskrat. Am. Nat. 85:273–92.

Errington, P. L., F. Hamerstrom, and F. N. Hamerstrom, Jr. 1940. The great horned owl and its prey in north central United States. Iowa State College. Agri. Exp. Stn. Bull. 277:757–850.

Evans, R. M. 1961. Courtship and mating behavior of sharp-tailed grouse (Pedioecetes phasianellus jamesi, Lincoln). M.S. thesis. Univ. Alberta, Edmonton.

Evans, R. M. 1969. Territorial stability in sharp-tailed grouse. Wilson Bull. 81:75–78.

Ewing, J. 1924. Plant successions of the brush-prairie in northwestern Minnesota. J. Ecol. 12:238–66.

Fairchild, L. 1984. Male reproductive tactics in an explosive breeding toad population. Am. Zool. 24:407–18.

Falconer, D. S. 1960. Introduction to quantitative genetics. Oliver and Boyd Press, Edinburgh. 365 pp.

Fallis, A. M. and C. E. Hope. 1950. Observations of ruffed grouse in southern Ontario with a discussion on cycles. Can. Field-Nat. 64:82–85.

Falls, J. B. and M. K. McNicholl. 1979. Neighbor-stranger discrimination by song in male blue grouse. Can. J. Zool. 57:457–62.

Farmes, R. E. and G. H. Maertens. 1973. The status of the prairie chicken in Minnesota: What now? Pp. 92–94 in W. D. Svedarsky and T. Wolfe, eds. Proc. The prairie chicken in Minnesota. Univ. Minn., Crookston.

Feyerherm, A. M., L. D. Bark, and W. C. Burrows. 1966. Probabilities of sequences of wet and dry days in Minnesota. Kans. Tech. Bull. 139j. Manhattan. 55 pp.

Ficken, R. W., M. S. Ficken, and J. P. Hailman. 1978. Differential aggression in genetically different morphs of the white-throated sparrow (Zonotrichia albicollis). Z. Tierpsychol. 46:43–57.

Fischer, C. A. and L. B. Keith. 1974. Population responses of central Alberta ruffed grouse to hunting. J. Wildl. Manage. 38:585–600.

Fisher, L. W. 1939. Studies of the eastern ruffed grouse in Michigan (*Bonasa umbellus umbellus*). Mich. Agric. Exp. Station, East Lansing. Tech. Bull. 166. 46 pp.

Fisher, R. A. 1930. The genetical theory of natural selection. Clarendon Press, Oxford.

Fisher, R. A. 1958. The genetical theory of natural selection. 2nd ed. Dover Press, New York.

Fleming, T. H. 1973. Numbers of mammal species in North and Central American forest communities. Ecology 55:555–63.

Fogleman, J. C., P. S. Corn, and D. Pettus. 1980. The genetic basis of a dorsal color polymorphism in *Rana pipiens*. J. Hered. 71:439–40.

Foster, M. S. 1983. Disruption, dispersion, and dominance in lek-breeding birds. Am. Nat. 122:53–72.

Fowle, C. D. 1944. The sooty grouse, *Dendragapus fuliginous fuliginous* (Ridgway), on its summer range. M.Sc. thesis. Univ. British Columbia, Vancouver.

Fowle, C. D. 1960. A study of the blue grouse (*Dendragapus obscurus*), on Vancouver Island, British Columbia. Can. J. Zool. 38:701–13.

Frandsen, D. H. 1980. Density, habitat, and behaviour of blue grouse. M.Sc. thesis. Univ. Toronto, Toronto.

French, N. R., T. Y. Tagami and P. Hayden. 1968. Dispersal in a population of desert rodents. J. Mammal. 49:272–80.

Fretwell, S. D. 1972. Populations in a seasonal environment. Princeton Univ. Press, Princeton, N.J. 217 pp.

Fretwell, S. D. and H. L. Lucas, Jr. 1969. On territorial behavior and other factors influencing habitat distribution in birds. I. Theoretical development. Acta Biotheoretica 19:16–36.

Gadgil, M. 1971. Dispersal: population consequences and evolution. Ecology 52:253–61.

Gadgil, M. and W. H. Bossert. 1970. Life history consequences of natural selection. Am. Nat. 104:1–24.

Gandelman, R. and B. Svare. 1974. Mice: pregnancy termination, lactation and aggression. Horm. Behav. 5:397–405.

Gardarsson, A. 1971. Food ecology and spacing behavior of rock ptarmigan (*Lagopus mutus*) in Iceland. Ph.D. thesis. Univ. California, Berkeley.

Gardarsson, A. 1979. Waterfowl populations of Lake Myvatn and recent changes in numbers and food habits. Oikos 32:250–70.

Gardarsson, A. and R. Moss. 1970. Selection of food by Icelandic ptarmigan in relation to its availability and nutritive value. Pp. 47–71 *in* A. Watson, ed. Animal populations in relation to their food resources. Blackwell Sci. Publ., Oxford and Edinburgh.

Gates, J. M. 1971. The ecology of a Wisconsin pheasant population. Ph.D. thesis. Univ. Wisconsin, Madison.

Gates, J. M. and J. B. Hale. 1974. Seasonal movement, winter habitat use and population distribution of an east central Wisconsin pheasant population. Wis. Dep. Nat. Resour. Tech. Bull. 76. 55 pp.

Gates, J. M. and J. B. Hale. 1975. Reproduction of an east central Wisconsin pheasant population. Wis. Dep. Nat. Resour. Tech. Bull. 85. 70 pp.

Gates, R. J. 1985. Observations on the formation of a sage grouse lek. Wilson Bull. 97:219–21.

Gershenson, S. 1945. Evolutionary studies on the distribution and dynamics of melanism in the hamster (*Cricetus cricetus* L.). Genetics 30:207–51.

Gibson, R. M. and J. W. Bradbury. 1985. Sexual selection in lekking sage grouse: phenotypic correlates of male mating success. Behav. Ecol. Sociobiol. 18:117–23.

Giesel, J. T. 1974. Fitness and polymorphism for net fecundity distribution in iteroparous populations. Am. Nat. 108:321–31.

Giesen, K. M. 1977. Mortality and dispersal of juvenile white-tailed ptarmigan. M.S. thesis. Colorado State Univ., Fort Collins.

Giesen, K. M. and C. E. Braun. 1976. Renesting of white-tailed ptarmigan in Colorado. Colorado-Wyoming Acad. Sci. J. 8:71–72.

Giesen, K. M. and C. E. Braun. 1979a. Nesting behavior of female white-tailed ptarmigan in Colorado. Condor 81:215–17.

Giesen, K. M. and C. E. Braun. 1979b. Renesting of white-tailed ptarmigan in Colorado. Condor 81:217–18.

Giesen, K. M., C. E. Braun, and T. A. May. 1980. Reproduction and nest-site selection by white-tailed ptarmigan in Colorado. Wilson Bull. 92:188–99.

Gill, R. B. 1965. Distribution and abundance of a population of sage grouse in North Park, Colorado. M.S. thesis. Colorado State Univ., Fort Collins.

Gillespie, J. 1974. Polymorphism in patchy environments. Am. Nat. 108:145–51.

Gjesdal, A. 1977. Social rank, mating and egg fertilization in willow ptarmigan (*Lagopus lagopus lagopus*). Poultry Science 56:41–44.

Gladfelter, H. L. and R. S. McBurney. 1971. Mating activity of ruffed grouse. Auk 88:176–77.

Gleason, H. A. and A. Cronquist. 1963. Manual of vascular plants of northeastern United States and adjacent Canada. Van Nostrand Reinhold, New York. 810 pp.

Godfrey, G. A. 1967. Summer and fall movements and behavior of immature ruffed grouse (*Bonasa umbellus* [L]). M.S. thesis. Univ. Minnesota, St. Paul.

Godfrey, G. A. 1970. Snow roosting behavior of immature ruffed grouse. Auk 87:578–79.

Godfrey, G. A. 1975. Home range characteristics of ruffed grouse broods in Minnesota. J. Wildl. Manage 39:287–98.

Godfrey, G. A. and W. H. Marshall. 1969. Brood break-up and dispersal of ruffed grouse. J. Wildl. Manage. 33:609–20.

Gower, W. C. 1939. The use of the bursa of Fabricius as an indication of age in game birds. Trans. N. Am. Wildl. Conf. 4:426–30.

Grange, W. B. 1948. Wisconsin grouse problems. Wis. Conserv. Dep. Publ. 328. 318 pp.

Gratson, M. W. 1981. Goshawks prey on radio-tagged sharp-tailed grouse. J. Field Ornith. 53:55–56.

Gratson, M. W. 1983. Habitat, mobility, and social patterns of sharp-tailed grouse in Wisconsin. M.S. thesis. Univ. Wisconsin, Stevens Point.

Grondahl, C. R. 1956. Predation studies using artificial pheasant nests. N.D. Game and Fish Dep. Fed. Aid Wildl. Restoration Proj. W-35-R-3. 14 pp.

Gross, A. O. 1928. The heath hen. Mem. Boston Society Nat. Hist. 6:491–588.

Gross, A. O. 1930. Progress report of the Wisconsin prairie chicken investigation. Wisc. Conserv. Comm., Madison. 112 pp.

Gudmundsson, F. 1960. Some reflections on ptarmigan cycles in Iceland. Proc. Int. Ornithol. Congr. 12:259–65.

Gullion, G. W. 1963. Populations of grouse. Minn. Div. Game and Fish Quart. Rept. 23:77–113.

Gullion, G. W. 1964. Evaluation of food, cover and other grouse management practices. Minn. Div. Game and Fish. Proj. C-35-R-8. 71 pp. (mimeogr.).

Gullion, G. W. 1965. Improvements in methods for trapping and marking ruffed grouse. J. Wildl. Manage. 29:109–16.

Gullion, G. W. 1966a. A viewpoint concerning the significance of studies of game bird food habits. Condor 68:372–76.

Gullion, G. W. 1966b. The use of drumming behavior in ruffed grouse population studies. J. Wildl. Manage. 30:717–29.

Gullion, G. W. 1967. Selection and use of drumming sites by male ruffed grouse. Auk. 84:87–112.

Gullion, G. W. 1970a. Factors affecting ruffed grouse populations in the boreal forests of northern Minnesota, USA. Finnish Game Res. 30:103–17.

Gullion, G. W. 1970b. Factors influencing ruffed grouse populations. Trans. N. Am. Wildl. Conf. 35:93–105.

Gullion, G. W. 1970c. The ruffed grouse in northern Minnesota. Univ. Minnesota For. Wildl. Relations Proj. Revisal FW67. No. 49. 37 pp.

Gullion, G. W. 1973. Grouse cycles: are they real? Minn. Sci. 29:6–7,10–11.

Gullion, G. W. 1977a. Forest manipulation for ruffed grouse. Trans. N. Am. Wildl. and Nat. Resour. Conf. 42:449–58.

Gullion, G. W. 1977b. Maintenance of the aspen ecosystem as a primary wildlife habitat. Proc. Int. Congr. Game Biol. 13:256–65.

Gullion, G. W. 1981. Non-drumming males in ruffed grouse population. Wilson Bull. 93:372–82.

Gullion, G. W. 1982. Rejuvenation and maintenance of forest habitats for the American ruffed grouse. Pp. 11–29 in T. W. I. Lovel, ed. Proc. 2nd Internatl. Symp. on Grouse. World Pheasant Assoc., Exning, England.

Gullion, G. W. 1984a. Managing northern forests for wildlife. The Ruffed Grouse Society, Coraopolis, Pa. 72 pp.

Gullion, G. W. 1984b. Grouse of the North Shore. Willow Creek Press, Oshkosh, Wis. 136 pp.

Gullion, G. W., R. T. King, and W. H. Marshall. 1962. Male ruffed grouse and thirty years of forest management on the Cloquet Forest Research Center, Minnesota. J. For. 60:617–22.

Gullion, G. W. and W. H. Marshall. 1968. Survival of ruffed grouse in a boreal forest. Living Bird 7:117–67.

Gwadz, R. W. 1970. Monofactorial inheritance of early sexual receptivity in the mosquito, *Aedes atropelus*. Anim. Behav. 18:358–61.

Gyllensten, U. 1984. Biochemical genetic variation, intraspecific genetic structure and postglacial evolution of select North European vertebrate species. Ph.D. thesis. Stockholm, Sweden.

Gyllensten, U. 1985. Temporal allozyme frequency changes in density fluctuating populations of willow grouse (*Lagopus lagopus L.*). Evolution 39:115–21.

Haas, G. F. 1974. Habitat selection, reproduction, and movements in female spruce grouse. Ph.D. thesis. Univ. Minnesota, St. Paul.

Hagen, Y. 1935. Ringmerking av lirype i Rauland og Tinn. Nytt. Mag. Naturv. 75:243–88.

Hagen, Y. 1952a. The gyrfalcon (*Falco r. rusticolus*) in Dovre, Norway. Some breeding records and food studies. Det Norske Videnskaps—Akademi i Oslo Mat. Naturv. Klassa 4:1–37.

Hagen, Y. 1952b. Rovfuglene og Viltpleien. Oslo (Gyldendal). 603 pp.

Hager, D. C., Jr. 1954. Ruffed grouse, *Bonasa umbellus umbellus* (L.), populations on two areas in central Massachusetts. M.S. thesis. Univ. Massachusetts, Amherst.

Hale, J. B. and R. S. Dorney. 1963. Seasonal movements of ruffed grouse in Wisconsin. J. Wildl. Manage. 27:648–56.

Hale, J. B. and R. F. Wendt. 1951. Ruffed grouse hatching dates in Wisconsin. J. Wildl. Manage. 15:195–99.

Halliday, W. E. D. 1937. A forest classification of Canada. Can. Dep. Mines, Resour., For. Serv. Bull. 89 pp.

Halvorsen, H. H. 1981. An evaluation of grassland management practices for wildlife in central Wisconsin. M.S. thesis. Univ. Wisconsin, Stevens Point.

Hamerstrom, F. 1950. Range, habits and food requirements of prairie chicken. Wis. Conserv. Bull. 15:9–11.

Hamerstrom, F. 1980. Strictly for the chickens. Iowa State Univ. Press, Ames. 174 pp.

Hamerstrom, F., D. D. Berger, and F. N. Hamerstrom, Jr. 1965. The effect of mammals on prairie chickens on booming grounds. J. Wildl. Manage. 29:536–42.

Hamerstrom, F. N., Jr. 1936. A study of the nesting habitats of the ring-necked pheasant in northern Iowa. Iowa State Coll. J. Sci. 10:173–203.

Hamerstrom, F. N., Jr. 1939. A study of Wisconsin prairie chicken and sharp-tailed grouse. Wilson Bull. 51:105–20.

Hamerstrom, F. N., Jr. 1941. A study of Wisconsin prairie grouse: breeding habits, winter foods, endoparasites, and movements. Ph.D. thesis. Univ. Wisconsin, Madison.

Hamerstrom, F. N., Jr. 1963. Sharptail brood habitat in Wisconsin's northern pine barrens. J. Wildl. Manage. 27:793–802.

Hamerstrom, F.N., Jr. 1981. Do prairie chicken cocks move from exterior to interior territories as they grow older? Proc. Prairie Grouse Tech. Counc. 14:16.

Hamerstrom, F. N. Jr. and F. Hamerstrom. 1949. Daily and seasonal movements of Wisconsin prairie chickens. Auk 66:312–37.

Hamerstrom, F. N., Jr. and F. Hamerstrom. 1951. Mobility of the sharp-tailed grouse in relation to its ecology and distribution. Am. Midl. Nat. 46:174–226.

Hamerstrom, F. N., Jr. and F. Hamerstrom. 1955. Population density and behavior in Wisconsin prairie chickens (*Tympanuchus cupido pinnatus*). Proc. Int. Ornithol. Congr. 11:459–66.

Hamerstrom, F. N., Jr. and F. Hamerstrom. 1961. Status and problems of North American grouse. Wilson Bull. 73:284–94.

Hamerstrom, F. N., Jr. and F. Hamerstrom. 1973. The prairie chicken in Wisconsin. Wis. Dep. Nat. Resour. Tech. Bull. 64. 52 pp.

Hamerstrom, F. N., Jr., F. Hopkins, and A. J. Rinzel. 1941. An experimental study of browse as a winter diet for prairie chickens. Wilson Bull. 53:185–95.

Hamerstrom, F. N., Jr., O. E. Mattson, and F. Hamerstrom. 1957. A guide to prairie chicken management. Wis. Conserv. Dep. Tech. Wildl. Bull. 15. 128 pp.

Hamilton, W. D. 1971. Geometry for the selfish herd. J. Theor. Biol. 31:295–311.

Hannon, S. J. 1978. The reproductive cycle, movements, and pre-nesting behavior of adult and yearling females in a population of blue grouse. M.Sc. thesis. Univ. Alberta, Edmonton.

Hannon, S. J. 1980. The cackle call of female blue grouse; does it have a mating or aggressive function? Auk 97:404–7.

Hannon, S. J. 1982. Female aggressiveness, breeding density, and monogamy in willow ptarmigan. Ph.D. thesis. Univ. British Columbia, Vancouver.

Hannon, S. J. 1983. Spacing and breeding density of willow ptarmigan in response to an experimental alteration of sex ratio. J. Anim. Ecol. 52:807–20.

Hannon, S. J. 1984. Factors limiting polygyny in the willow ptarmigan. Anim. Behav. 32:153–61.

Hannon, S. J., B. R. Smard, F. C. Zwickel, and J. F. Bendell. 1979. Differences in the gonadal cycles of adult and yearling blue grouse. Can. J. Zool. 57:1283–89.

Hannon, S. J. and J. N. M. Smith. 1984. Factors influencing age-related reproductive success in willow ptarmigan. Auk 101:848–54.

Hannon, S. J., L. G. Sopuck, and F. C. Zwickel. 1982. Spring movements of female blue grouse; evidence for socially induced delayed breeding in yearlings. Auk 99:687–94.

Hannon, S. J. and F. C. Zwickel. 1979. Probable non-breeders among female blue grouse. Condor 81:78–82.

Hanson, H. C. 1953. Muskeg as sharp-tailed grouse habitat. Wilson Bull. 65:235–41.

Hanssen, I., H. J. Grav, J. B. Steen, and H. Lysnes. 1979. Vitamin C deficiency in growing willow ptarmigan (*Lagopus lagopus lagopus*). J. Nutr. 109:2260–76.

Hanssen, I. and J. Ness. 1982. Chick nutrition and mortality in captive willow ptarmigan (*Lagopus l. lagopus*). Acta Vet. Scand. 23:456–65.

Hanssen, I., J. Ness, and J. B. Steen. 1982. Parental nutrition and chick production in captive willow ptarmigan (*Lagopus l. lagopus*). Acta Vet. Scand. 23:528–38.

Hanssen, I. and F. Utne. 1985. Spring phenology, egg quality and chick production in willow ptarmigan *Lagopus l. lagopus* in northern Norway. Fauna norv. Ser. C., Cinclus 8:77–81.

Hansson, L. 1982. Food as a limiting factor for small rodent numbers. Oecologia 37:297–314.

Hardy, F. C. 1950. Ruffed grouse studies in eastern Kentucky. Ky. Div. Fish and Game, Fed. Aid Unit. Proj. 18-R. 25 pp.

Harpending, H. C. 1979. The population genetics of interactions. Am. Nat. 113:622–30.

Harper, J. L. 1977. Population biology of plants. Academic Press, London.

Hart, C. M., O. S. Lee, and J. B. Low. 1950. The sharp-tailed grouse in Utah: its life history, status and management. Utah State Dep. Fish and Game. Fed. Aid Div. Publ. 3. 79 pp.

Hartzler, J. E. 1972. An analysis of sage grouse lek behavior. Ph.D. thesis. Univ. Montana, Missoula.

Hartzler, J. E. 1974. Predation and the daily timing of sage grouse leks. Auk 91:532–36.

Harvey, M. F. and R. W. Barbour. 1965. Home range of *Microtus ochrogaster* as determined by a modified minimum area method. J. Mammal. 46:398–402.

Haukioja, E. and T. Hakala. 1975. Herbivore cycles and periodic outbreaks. Formulation of a general hypothesis. Rep. Kevo Subarctic Res. Station 12:1–9.

Haukioja, E., K. Kapiainen, P. Niemela, and J. Tuomi. 1983. Plant availability hypothesis and other explanations of herbivore cycles: complementary or exclusive alternatives? Oikos 40:419–32.

Healy, M. C. 1967. Aggression and self-regulation of population size in deer mice. Ecology 48:377–92.

Hedberg, J. 1980. Habitat selection by spruce grouse in eastern Maine. M.S. thesis. Univ. Maine, Orono.

Hedrick, P. W., M. E. Ginevan, and E. P. Ewing. 1976. Genetic polymorphism in heterogeneous environments. Ann. Rev. Ecol. Syst. 7:1–32.

Heisler, I. L. 1985. Quantitative genetic models of female choice based on "arbitrary" male characters. Heredity 55:187–98.

Henderson, B. A. 1977. The genetics and demography of a high and low density of red grouse *Lagopus l. scoticus*. J. Anim. Ecol. 46:581–92.

Henderson, F. R., R. W. Brooks, R. E. Wood, and R. B. Dahlgren. 1967. Sexing of prairie grouse by crown feather patterns. J. Wildl. Manage. 31:764–69.

Henderson, F. R. and W. W. Jackson. 1967. History of selected dancing grounds in South Dakota. Proc. 7th Prairie Grouse Tech. Counc. (abstract.)

Herzog, P. W. 1977a. Dispersion and mobility in a local population of spruce grouse (*Canachites canadensis Franklinii*). M.Sc. thesis. Univ. Alberta, Edmonton.

Herzog, P. W. 1977b. Summer habitat use by white-tailed ptarmigan in southwestern Alberta. Can. Field-Nat. 91:367–71.

Herzog, P. W. 1978. Food selection by female spruce grouse during incubation. J. Wildl. Manage. 42:632–35.

Herzog, P. W. 1979. Effects of radio-marking on behavior, movements, and survival of spruce grouse. J. Wildl. Manage. 43:316–23.

Herzog, P. W. 1980. Winter habitat use by white-tailed ptarmigan in southwestern Alberta. Can. Field-Nat. 94:159–62.

Herzog, P. W. and D. A. Boag. 1977. Seasonal changes in aggressive behavior of female spruce grouse. Can. J. Zool. 55:1734–39.

Herzog, P. W. and D. A. Boag. 1978. Dispersion and mobility in a local population of spruce grouse. J. Wildl. Manage. 42:853–65.

Herzog, P. W. and D. M. Keppie. 1980. Migration in a local population of spruce grouse. Condor 82:366–72.

Hess, E. H. 1972. Imprinting in a natural laboratory. Sci. Am. 227:24–31.

Hewson, R. 1984. Changes in the numbers of foxes (*Vulpes vulpes*) in Scotland. J. Zool. Lond. 204:561–69.

Hickey, J. J. 1955. Some American population research on gallinaceous birds. Pp. 326–396 *in* A. Wolfson, ed. Recent studies in avian biology. Univ. Illinois Press, Urbana.

Higgins, K. F., L. M. Kirsch, H. F. Duebbert, A. T. Klett, J. T. Lokemoen, H. W. Miller, and A. D. Kruse. 1977. Construction and operation of cable-chain drag for nest searches. Wildl. Leafl. 512. U.S. Fish and Wildl. Serv., Wash., D.C. 14 pp.

Hillman, C. N. and W. W. Jackson. 1973. The sharp-tailed grouse in South Dakota. S.D. Dep. Game, Fish and Parks. Tech. Bull. 3. 64 pp.

Hilton, M. and W. Wishart. 1981. A summary of the Camp Wainwright grouse season September 5, 7–12, 1981. Alberta Energy and Natl. Resour. Fish and Wildl. Div. 9 pp.

Hines, J. E. 1986a. Recruitment of young in a declining population of blue grouse. Ph.D. thesis. Univ. of Alberta, Edmonton.

Hines, J. E. 1986b. Survival and reproduction of dispersing blue grouse. Condor 88:43–49.

Hjorth, I. 1967. Fortplantninsbetweenden inom honsfagelfamilien Tetraonidae. Var. Fågelvarld 26:193–241.

Hjorth, I. 1968. Significance of light in the initiation of morning display of the black grouse (*Lyrurus tetrix* L.). Viltrevy 5:39–94.

Hjorth, I. 1970. Reproductive behaviour in Tetraonidae with special reference to males. Viltrevy 7:183–596.

Hoffman, R. S. 1961. The quality of the winter food of blue grouse. J. Wildl. Manage. 25:209–10.

Hoffman, R. W. 1979. Population dynamics and habitat relationships of blue grouse. Colo. Div. Wildl., Game Res. Rep. Proj. W-37-R-32, Job 5. Pp. 201–44.

Hoffman, R. W. and C. E. Braun. 1975. Migration of a wintering population of white-tailed ptarmigan in Colorado. J. Wildl. Manage. 39:485–90.

Hofslund, P. B. 1973. An invasion of goshawks. Raptor Res. 7:107–8.

Hogen-Warburg, A. J. 1966. Social behaviour of the ruff (*Philomachus pugnax*). Ardea 55:109–299.

Hoglund, N. H. 1964. Fright moulting in Tetraonids. Viltrevy 2:419–25.

Hoglund, N. H. 1980. Studies on the winter ecology of the willow grouse (*Lagopus lagopus lagopus* L.). Viltrevy 11:249–70.

Horak, G. J. 1974. Population dynamics of prairie chicken in grassland and cropland areas. Kans. For., Fish and Game Comm., Final Rep. Proj. W-23-R, Job D-3. 98 pp.

Horkel, J. D. 1979. Cover and space requirements for Attwater's prairie chicken (*Tympanuchus cupido attwateri*) in Refugio County, Texas. Ph.D. thesis. Texas A&M Univ., College Station.

Horkel, J. D., R. S. Lutz, and N. J. Silvy. 1978. The influence of environmental parameters on nesting success of upland game birds. Proc. Annu. Conf. Southeast. Assoc. Fish and Wildl. Agencies 32:234–41.

Horkel, J. D. and N. J. Silvy. 1980. Evolutionary considerations in creating artificial leks for Attwater's prairie chicken. Pp. 42–47 in P. A. Vohs, Jr. and F. L. Knopf, eds. Proc. Prairie Grouse Symp., Oklahoma State Univ., Stillwater.

Horn, H. S. 1968. The adaptive significance of colonial nesting in the Brewer's blackbird *Euphagus cyanocephalus*. Ecology 49:682–94.

Hornocker, M. C. 1969. Winter territoriality in mountain lions. J. Wildl. Manage. 33:457–64.

Howard, R. D. 1984. Alternative mating behaviors of young male bullfrogs. Amer. Zool. 24:397–406.

Hudson, P. J. 1986. The effect of a parasitic nematode on the breeding production of red grouse. J. Anim. Ecol. 55:85–92.

Hudson, P. J., A. P. Dobson, and D. Newborn. 1985. Cyclic and noncyclic populations of red grouse: a role for parasitism? Pp. 79–89 in D. Rollinson and R. M. Anderson, eds. Ecology and genetics of host-parasite interactions. Academic Press, London.

Huempfner, R. A. 1981. Winter arboreal feeding behavior of ruffed grouse in east-central Minnesota. M.S. thesis. Univ. Minnesota, St. Paul.

Huempfner, R. A. and G. J. Erickson. 1975. A designation of plant communities on part of the Cedar Creek Natural History Area, Benthel, Minnesota. In-house plant community key and maps available at Cedar Creek, Univ. Minnesota. 25 pp.

Huempfner, R. A., S. J. Maxson, G. J. Erickson, and R. J. Schuster. 1975. Recapturing radio-tagged ruffed grouse by nightlighting and snow-burrow netting. J. Wildl. Manage. 39:821–23.

Huff, D. E. 1970. A study of selected nutrients in browse available to the ruffed grouse. M.S. thesis. Univ. Minnesota, St. Paul.

Huff, D. E. 1973. A preliminary study of ruffed grouse-aspen nutrient relationships. Ph.D. thesis. Univ. Minnesota, St. Paul.

Hungerford, K. E. 1951. Ruffed grouse populations and cover use in northern Idaho. Trans. N. A. Wildl. Conf. 16:216–24.

Hunt, F. 1982. Regulation of population cycles by genetic feedback: existence of periodic solutions of a mathematical model. J. Math. Biol. 13:271–82.

Hurst, G. A. 1970. The effects of controlled burning on arthropod denstiy and biomass in relation to bobwhite quail (*Colinus virginianus*) brood habitat. Ph.D. thesis. Mississippi State Univ.

Hussell, D. J. T. 1972. Factors affecting clutch size in Arctic passerines. Ecol. Monogr. 42:317–64.

Huxley, J. S. 1938. Threat and warning colouration in birds with a general discussion of the biological functions of colour. Zool. Society, London. Pp. 430–55.

Innes, D. J. and L. E. Haley. 1977. Inheritance of a shell-color polymorphism in the mussel. J. Hered. 68:203–4.

Irving, L., G. C. West, and L. J. Peyton. 1967a. Winter feeding program of Alaska willow ptarmigan shown by crop contents. Condor 69:69–77.

Irving, L., G. C. West, L. J. Peyton, and S. Paneak. 1967b. Migration of willow ptarmigan in arctic Alaska. Arctic 20:77–85.

Jacobs, J. 1981. How heritable is innate behaviour? Z. Tierpsychol. 55:1–18.

Jamieson, I. G. 1982. Spatial patterns and behavior of yearling blue grouse and their relation to recruitment into the breeding population. M.Sc. thesis. Univ. Alberta, Edmonton.

Jamieson, I. G. 1983. Seasonal changes in spatial patterns and behavior of yearling blue grouse on the breeding range. Can. J. Zool. 61:2777–80.

Jamieson, I. G. and F. C. Zwickel. 1983. Spatial patterns of yearling male blue grouse and their relation to recruitment into the breeding population. Auk 100:653–57.

Janson, R. G. 1951. Prairie grouse population trends in South Dakota. Midwest Wildl. Conf. Pp. 52–59.

Janson, R. G. 1955. Prairie grouse brood studies. 1953–1954. S.D. Dep. Game, Fish and Parks, Fed. Aid in Wildl. Restoration. Proj. W-17-R-8. 8 pp.

Jenkins, D. and A. Watson. 1962. Fluctuations in a red grouse (*Lagopus scoticus*) population 1956–59. Pp. 96–117 *in* E. D. LeCren and M. Holdgate, eds. The exploitation of natural animal populations. Blackwell Sci. Publ., Oxford. 399 pp.

Jenkins, D. and A. Watson. 1970. Population studies on red grouse, *Lagopus lagopus scoticus*. Trans Int. Congr. Union Game Biol. 7:121–41.

Jenkins, D., A. Watson, and G. R. Miller. 1963. Population studies on red grouse, *Lagopus lagopus scoticus* (Lath.) in north-east Scotland. J. Anim. Ecol. 32:317–76.

Jenkins, D., A. Watson, and G. R. Miller. 1964. Predation and red grouse populations. J. Appl. Ecol. 1:183–95.

Jenkins, D., A. Watson, and G. R. Miller. 1967. Population fluctuations in the red grouse *Lagopus lagopus scoticus*. J. Anim. Ecol. 36:97–122.

Jenkins, D., A. Watson, and N. Picozzi. 1965. Red grouse chick survival in captivity and in the wild. Trans. Int. Congr. Game Biol. 6:63–70.

Jenni, D. A. and J. E. Hartzler. 1978. Attendance at a sage grouse lek: implications for spring censuses. J. Wildl. Manage. 42:46–52.

Jensen, L. and R. A. Ryder. 1965. Breeding behavior of the white-tailed ptarmigan near Aspen, Colorado. Colorado-Wyoming Acad. Sci. J. 5:52–53.

Johns, J. E. and E. W. Pfeiffer. 1963. Testosterone induced incubation patches of phalaopes. Science 140:1225–26.

Johnsgard, P. A. 1973. Grouse and quails of North America. Univ. Nebraska Press, Lincoln. 553 pp.

Johnsgard, P. A. 1983. The grouse of the world. Univ. Nebraska Press, Lincoln 413 pp.

Johnsgard, P. A. and R. E. Wood. 1968. Distributional changes and interaction between prairie chickens and sharp-tailed grouse in the midwest. Wilson Bull. 80:173–88.

Johnson, D. H. and A. B. Sargeant. 1977. Impact of red fox predation on the sex ratio of prairie mallards. U.S. Dep. Inter. Fish and Wildl. Serv. Wild. Res. Rep. 6. 56 pp.

Johnson, M. D. 1964. Feathers from the prairie. N.D. Dep. Game and Fish, Proj. W-67-R-5. 240 pp.

Jones, D. M. and J. B. Theberge. 1982. Summer home range and habitat utilisation of the red fox (*Vulpes vulpes*) in a tundra habitat, northwest British Columbia. Can. J. Zool. 60:807–12.

Jones, R. E. 1963. Identification and analysis of lesser and greater prairie chicken habitat. J. Wildl. Manage. 27:757–78.

Jørgensen, E. and A. S. Blix, 1985. Effects of climate and nutrition on growth and survival of willow ptarmigan chicks. Ornis Scand. 16:99–107.

Jørgenson, J. P. 1977. Pinnated grouse (*Tympanuchus cupido pinnatus*) movements and habitat utilization in the northern Great Plains. M.S. thesis Univ. North Dakota, Grand Forks.

Jurries, R. W. 1981. Requirements of Attwater's prairie chicken. Texas Fed. Aid in Wildl. Restoration Act, Final Rep. Proj. W-108-R-4, Job 13. 3 pp.

Kalela, O. 1962. On the fluctuations in the numbers of arctic and boreal small rodents as a problem of production biology. Ann. Acad. Sci. Fenn. Ser. A, 4 Biol. 66:1–38.

Kalmbach, E. R. 1938. A comparative study of nesting waterfowl on the Lower Souris Refuge. 1936–1937. Trans. N. Am. Wildl. Conf. 3:610–23.

Kaufman, J. H. 1983. On the definitions and functions of dominance and territoriality. Biol. Rev. Cambridge Philosophical Soc. 58:1–20.

Keith, L. B. 1962. Fall and winter weights of Hungarian partridges and sharp-tailed grouse from Alberta. J. Wildl. Manage. 26:336–37.

Keith, L. B. 1963. Wildlife's ten-year cycle. Univ. Wisconsin Press, Madison. 201 pp.

Keith, L. B. 1974. Some features of population dynamics in mammals. Trans. Int. Congr. Game Biol. 11:17–58.

Keith, L. B., A. W. Todd, C. J. Brand, R. S. Adamcik, and D. H. Rusch. 1977. An analysis of predation during a cyclic fluctuation of snowshoe hares. Trans Int. Congr. Game Biol. 13:151–75.

Keith, L. B. and L. A. Windberg. 1978. A demographic analysis of the snowshoe hare cycle. Wildl. Monogr. 58. 70 pp.

Keller, B. and C. J. Krebs. 1970. Microtus population biology. III. Reproductive changes in fluctuating populations of *M. ochrogaster* and *M. pennsylvanicus* in southern Indiana, 1965–67. Ecol. Monogr. 40:263–94.

Keller, R. J., H. R. Sheperd, and R. N. Randall. 1941. Survey of 1941: North Park, Jackson County, Moffat County, including comparative data of previous seasons. Colo. Dep. Game and Fish, Sage Grouse Survey. Vol. 3. 31 pp.

Kelsall, J. P., E. S. W. Telfer, and R. D. Wright. 1977. The effects of fire on the ecology of the boreal forest with particular reference to the Canadian North: a review and selected bibliography. Can Wildl. Serv. Occas. Pap. No. 32, 58 pp.

Keppie, D. M. 1975a. Clutch size of the spruce grouse, *Canachites canadensis franklinii*, in southwest Alberta. Condor 77:91–92.

Keppie, D. M. 1975b. Dispersal, overwinter mortality and population size of spruce grouse (*Canachites canadensis franklinii*). Ph.D. thesis. Univ. Alberta, Edmonton.

Keppie, D. M. 1977a. Inter-brood movements of juvenile spruce grouse. Wilson Bull. 89:67–72.

Keppie, D. M. 1977b. Snow cover and the use of trees by spruce grouse in autumn. Condor 79:382–84.

Keppie, D. M. 1979. Dispersal, overwinter mortality, and recruitment of spruce grouse. J. Wildl. Manage. 43:717–27.

Keppie, D. M. 1980. Similarity of dispersal among siblings male spruce grouse. Can. J. Zool. 58:2102–4.

Keppie, D. M. 1982. A difference in production and associated events in two races of spruce grouse. Can. J. Zool. 60:2116–23.

Keppie, D. M. and P. W. Herzog. 1978. Nest site characteristics and nest success of spruce grouse. J. Wildl. Manage. 42:628–32.

Kermott, L. H., III. 1982. Breeding behavior in the sharp-tailed grouse. Ph.D. thesis. Univ. Minnesota, St. Paul.

Kermott, L. H. and L. W. Oring. 1975. Acoustical communication of male sharp-tailed grouse (*Pedioecetes phasianellus*) on a North Dakota dancing ground. Anim. Behav. 23:315-86.

Kessler, W. B. 1977. Availability and use of Attwater's greater prairie chicken habitat. Proc. Prairie Grouse Tech. Counc. 12:13-14.

Kettlewell, H. B. D. 1973. The evolution of melanism. Clarendon Press, Oxford. 423 pp.

Kiel, W. H., A. S. Hawkins, and N. G. Perret. 1972. Waterfowl habitat trends in the aspen parkland of Manitoba. Can. Wildl. Serv. Rep. Ser. 18. 63 pp.

King, D. G. 1971. The ecology and population dynamics of blue grouse in the sub-alpine. M.S. thesis. Univ. British Columbia, Vancouver.

King, J. A. 1955. Social behavior, social organization and population dynamics of a black-tailed prairie dog town in the Black Hills of South Dakota. Univ. Michigan, Contrib. Lab. Vertebr. Biol. 67:1-123.

King, R. T. 1937. Ruffed grouse management. J. For. 35:523-32.

Kirkpatrick, M. 1982. Sexual selection and the evolution of female choice. Evolution 36:1-12.

Kirkpatrick, M. 1985. Evolution of female choice and male parental investment in polygynous species: the demise of the "sexy son." Am. Nat. 125:788-810.

Kirkpatrick, M. 1986. The handicap mechanism of sexual selection does not work. Am. Nat. 127:222-40.

Kirsch, L. M. 1956. Spring prairie grouse census and habitat inventory methods. Wildl. Leafl. 13. U.S. Fish and Wildl. Serv., Wash., D.C. 7 pp.

Kirsch, L. M. 1969. Waterfowl production in relation to grazing. J. Wildl. Manage. 33:821-28.

Kirsch, L. M. 1974. Habitat management considerations for prairie chickens. Wildl. Soc. Bull. 2:124-29.

Kirsch, L. M. 1983. Historical ecological records of great plains grasslands workshop: management of public lands in the northern great plains, Bismarck, North Dakota. 3 pp.

Kirsch, L. M., A. T. Klett, and H. W. Miller. 1973. Land use and prairie grouse population relationships in North Dakota. J. Wildl. Manage. 37:449-53.

Kirsch, L. M. and A. D. Kruse. 1973. Prairie fires and wildlife. Proc. Annu. Tall Timbers Fire Ecol. Conf. 12:289-303.

Klebenow, D. A. 1968. Nesting and brood habitat of sage grouse. Ph.D. thesis. Univ. Idaho, Moscow. 61 pp.

Klebenow, D. A. 1969. Sage grouse nesting and brood habitat in Idaho. J. Wildl. Manage. 33:649-62.

Klett, A. T. and D. H. Johnson. 1982. Variability in nest survival rates and implications to nesting studies. Auk 99:77-87.

Klimstra, W. D. and J. L. Roseberry. 1975. Nesting ecology of the bobwhite in southern Illinois. Wildl. Mongr. 41. 37 pp.

Klomp, H. 1970. The determination of clutch-size in birds: a review. Ardea 58:1-124.

Kluyver, H. M. and L. Tinbergen. 1953. Territory and regulation of density in titmice. Arch. Neerl. Zool. 10:265-86.

Knapp, A. K. 1984. Water relations and growth of three grasses during wet and drought years in a tallgrass prairie. Oecologia 65:35-43.

Kobriger, G. D. 1965. Status, movements, habitats, and foods of prairie grouse on a sandhills refuge. J. Wildl. Manage. 29:788-800.

Kobriger, G. D. 1975. Correlation of sharp-tailed grouse population parameters. N.D. Outdoors 38(5):10-13.

Kobriger, G. D. 1981. Prairie grouse population data. N.D. State Game and Fish Dep. Rep. B-318, Proj. W-67-R-21, Jobs B-V-1-5. 30 pp.

Koertge, N. 1979. The problem of appraising scientific theories. Pp. 228-251 *in* P. D. Asquith and

H. E. Kyburg, Jr., eds. Current research in the philosophy of science. Philos. Sci. Assoc., East Lansing, Mich. 533 pp.

Kohn, S. C. 1976. Sharp-tailed grouse nesting and brooding habitat in southwestern North Dakota. M.S. thesis. South Dakota State Univ., Brookings.

Korschgen, L. J. 1962. Food habits of greater prairie chicken in Missouri. Am. Midl. Nat. 68:307–18.

Korschgen, L. J. 1966. Foods and nutrition of ruffed grouse in Missouri. J. Wildl. Manage. 30:86–100.

Koskimies, J. 1957. Flocking behaviour in capercaillie, *Tetrao urogallus* (L.), and blackgame, *Lyrurus tetrix* (L.). Finnish Game Res. 18:1–32.

Krajina, V. J., ed. 1965. Biogeoclimatic zones and biogeocoenoses of British Columbia. Ecology of western North America. Dep. of Bot. Univ. British Columbia, Vancouver. 112 pp.

Krebs, C. J. 1966. Demographic changes in fluctuating populations of *Microtus californicus*. Ecol. monogr. 36:239–73.

Krebs, C. J. 1978a. A review of the Chitty hypothesis of population regulation. Can. J. Zool. 56:2463–80.

Krebs, C. J. 1978b. The experimental analysis of distribution and abundance. 2nd ed. Harper and Row, New York.

Krebs, C. J. 1985. Do changes in spacing behaviour drive population cycles in small mammals? Pp. 295–312 *in* R. M. Sibley and R. H. Smith, eds. Behavioural ecology. Blackwell Sci Publ., Oxford.

Krebs, C. J., M. S. Gaines, B. L. Keller, J. H. Myers, and R. H. Tamarin. 1973. Population cycles in small rodents. Science 179:35–41.

Krebs, C. J. and J. H. Myers. 1974. Population cycles in small mammals. Adv. Ecol. Res. 8:267–399.

Krebs, C. J., I. Wingate, J. Leduc, J. A. Redfield, M. Taitt, and R. Hilborn. 1976. *Microtus* population biology: dispersal in fluctuating populations of *M. townsendii*. Can. J. Zool. 54:79–95.

Krebs, J. R. 1971. Territory and breeding density in the great tit, *Parus major* L. Ecology 52:2–22.

Krebs, J. R. 1973. Behavioural aspects of predation. Pp. 73–111 *in* P. P. G. Bateson and P. H. Klopfer eds. Perspectives in ethology. Plenum Press, New York.

Krebs, J. R. 1974. Colonial nesting and social feeding as strategies for exploiting food resources in the Great Blue Heron (*Ardea herodias*). Behaviour 52:99–131.

Krebs, J. R., M. H. Roberts, and J. M. Culen. 1972. Flocking and feeding in the great tit, *Parus major* L. – an experimental study. Ibis 114:507–30.

Kristensen, J. 1973. Distraction display in female blue grouse. B.Sc. honours thesis, Univ. Alberta, Edmonton.

Kristoffersen, S. 1937. Undersokelser over lirypens forplantinings forhold. Tromso Museums rypenndersokelser, Nytt Mag. Naturv. 77:141–94.

Kruijt, J. P., G. J. De Vos and I. Bossema. 1972. The arena system of black grouse. Proc. Int. Ornithol. Congr. 15:399–423.

Kruijt, J. P. and H. A. Hogan. 1967. Social behaviour on the lek in the black grouse *Lyrurus tetrix tetrix* (L.). Ardea 55:203–20.

Kubisiak, J. F. 1982. The impact of hunting on ruffed grouse populations. Paper presented at Ruffed Grouse Workshop, Oct. 7, Traverse City, Mich. 18 pp.

Kubisiak, J. F., J. C. Moulton, and K. R. McCaffery. 1980. Ruffed grouse density and habitat relationships in Wisconsin. Wis. Dep. Nat. Resour. Tech. Bull. 118. 16 pp.

Kuhn, T. S. 1962. The structure of scientific revolutions. Univ. Chicago Press, Chicago. 172 pp.

Kuhn, T. S. 1965. Logic of discovery or psychology of research? Pp. 231–78 *in* I. Lakatos and A. Musgrave, eds. Criticism and the growth of knowledge. Cambridge Univ. Press, Cambridge.

Kupa, J. J. 1966. Ecological studies of the female ruffed grouse (*Bonasa umbellus* L.) at the Cloquet Forest Research Center, Minnesota. Ph.D. thesis. Univ. Minnesota, St. Paul.

Lack D. 1939. The display of the black cock. British Birds 32:290–303.

Lack, D. 1947. The significance of clutch sizes. Ibis 89:302–52.

Lack, D. 1954. The natural regulation of animal numbers. Clarendon Press, Oxford. 343 pp.

Lack, D. 1965. Evolutionary ecology. J. Anim. Ecol. 34:223–31.

Lack, D. 1966. Population studies of birds. Clarendon Press, Oxford. 341 pp.

Lack, D. 1968. Ecological adaptations for breeding in birds. Methuen Press, London. 409 pp.

Laine, K. and H. Henttonen. 1983. The role of plant production in microtine cycles in northern Fennoscandia. Oikos 40:407–18.

Lakatos, I. 1965. Falsification and the methodology of scientific research programmes. Pp. 91–196 in I. Lakatos and A. Musgrave, eds. Criticism and the growth of knowledge. Cambridge Univ. Press, Cambridge.

Lakatos, I. and A. Musgrave. 1965. Criticism and the growth of knowledge. Cambridge Univ. Press, Cambridge. 282 pp.

Lake, P. E. 1975. Gamete production and the fertile period with particular reference to domestic birds. Symp. Zool. Lond. No. 35:225–44.

Lance, A. N. 1967. A telemetry study of dispersion and breeding biology in blue grouse. M.Sc. thesis. Univ. British Columbia, Vancouver.

Lance, A. N. 1970. Movements of blue grouse on the summer range. Condor 72:437–44.

Lance, A. N. 1978a. Survival and recruitment success of individual young cock red grouse *Lagopus L. scoticus* tracked by radio-telemetry. Ibis 120:369–78.

Lance, A. N. 1978b. Territories and the food plant of individual red grouse. II. Territory size compared with an index of nutrient supply in heather. J. Anim. Ecol. 47:307–13.

Lance, A. N. 1983. Selection of feeding sites by hen red grouse *Lagopus lagopus scoticus* during breeding. Ornis Scand. 14:78–80.

Lande, R. 1981. Models of speciation by sexual selection on polygenic traits. Proc. Nat. Acad. Sci., USA 78:3721–25.

Langvatn, R. 1977. Characteristics and relative occurrence of remnants of prey found at nesting places of gyrfalcon *Falco rusticolus*. Ornis Scand. 8:113–25.

Larsen, J. A. and J. F. Lahey. 1958. Influence of weather upon a ruffed grouse population. J. Wildl. Manage. 22:63–70.

Latham, R. M. 1947. Differential ability of male and female game birds to withstand starvation and climatic extremes. J. Wildl. Manage. 11:139–49.

Lawrence, J. S. and N. J. Silvy. 1980. Status of the Attwater's prairie chicken—an update. Pp. 29–33 in P. A. Vohs, Jr. and F. L. Knopf, eds. Proc. Prairie Grouse Symp., Oklahoma State Univ., Stillwater.

Lawrence, J. S. and N. J. Silvy. 1981. Effect of predator reduction on reproductive success of Attwater's prairie chicken. Proc. Prairie Grouse Tech. Counc. 14:8–9.

Lazarus, J. 1972. Natural selection and the functions of flocking in birds: a reply to Murton. Ibis 111:556–58.

Lee, L. 1950. Kill analyses for the lesser prairie chicken in New Mexico, 1949. J. Wildl. Manage. 14:475–77.

Lehmann, V. W. 1941. Attwater's prairie chicken: its life history and management. U.S. Fish and Wildl. Serv., N. Am. Fauna Ser. 57. 63 pp.

Leslie, P. H. 1959. The properties of certain lag type of population growth and the influence of an external random factor on a number of such populations. Physiol. Zool. 32:151–59.

Leopold, A. 1931. Report on a game survey of the north central states. Sporting Arms and Ammunition Manufacturers' Inst., Madison, Wis. 299 pp.

Leopold, A. 1933. Game management. Charles Scribner's Sons, New York and London. 481 pp.

Leopold, A. and J. N. Ball. 1931. British and American grouse management. Am. Game Mag. July–August. Sept.–Oct. Pp. 1–5.

Levins, R. 1968. Evolution in changing environments. Princeton Univ. Press, Princeton, N.J. 120 pp.

Lewis, E. 1904. The nesting habitats of the white-tailed ptarmigan in Colorado. Bird Lore 6:117–21.

Lewis, R. A. 1979. Suitability and selection of territorial sites used by male blue grouse. M.Sc. thesis. Univ. Alberta, Edmonton.

Lewis, R. A. 1981. Characteristics of persistent and transient territorial sites of male blue grouse. J. Wildl. Manage. 45:1048–51.

Lewis, R. A. 1984. Density movements and breeding success of female blue grouse in an area of reduced male density. Can. J. Zool. 62:1556–60.

Lewis, R. A. 1985. Do blue grouse form leks? Auk 102:180–83.

Lewis, R. A. and F. C. Zwickel. 1980. Removal and replacement of male blue grouse on persistent and transient territorial sites. Can. J. Zool. 58:1417–23.

Lewis, R. A. and F. C. Zwickel. 1981. Differential use of territorial sites by male blue grouse. Condor 83:171–76.

Lewis, R. A. and F. C. Zwickel. 1982. Survival and delayed breeding in male blue grouse. Can. J. Zool. 60:1881–84.

Linde, D. A., M. Muck, H. H. Pietz, and L. Roth. 1978. Grouse management surveys, 1978. S.D. Dep. Game, Fish and Parks. Game Rep. 80–6, Proj. W-95-R-13, Jobs 1-7. 24 pp.

Linder, R. L., L. David, L. Lyon, and C. P. Agee. 1960. An analysis of pheasant nesting in south central Nebraska. Trans. N. Am. Wildl. Conf. 25:214–30.

Lindroth, H. and L. Lindgren. 1950. On the significance for forestry of the capercaillie, *Tetrao urogallus* L., feeding on pine-needles. Suomen Rusta 4:60–81.

Lismann, H. W. 1932. Die Umwelt dws kampffishes (*Betta splendens* Regen). Cited in: P. R. Marler and W. J. Hamilton, 1966. Mechanisms of animal behavior. John C. Wiley & Sons, New York.

Little, T. W. 1978. Populations, distributions and habitat selection by drumming male ruffed grouse in central Minnesota prior to clearcutting. Ph.D. thesis. Univ. Minnesota, St. Paul.

Livezey, B. C. 1981. Duck nesting in retired croplands at Horicon National Wildlife Refuge, Wisconsin. J. Wildl. Manage. 45:27–37.

Lokemoen, J. T., H. F. Duebbert, and D. E. Sharp. 1984. Nest space, habitat selection and behavior of waterfowl on Miller Island, North Dakota. J. Wildl. Manage. 48:309–21.

Lomnicki, A. 1978. Individual differences between animals and the natural regulation of their numbers. J. Anim. Ecol. 47:461–75.

Lovat, Lord (ed.). 1911. The grouse in health and disease. 2 vols. Smith and Elder & Co., London.

Low, D. J. 1975. Qualities of individuals in a replacement stock of blue grouse. M.Sc. thesis. Univ. British Columbia, Vancouver.

Lumsden, H. G. 1965. Displays of the sharptail grouse. Ont. Dep. Lands and For., Res. Rep. 66. 68 pp.

Lumsden, H. G. 1968. The displays of the sage grouse. Ont. Dep. Lands and For., Res. Rep. 83. 94 pp.

Lumsden, H. G. 1970. The shoulder-spot display of grouse. Living Bird 9:65–74.

Lumsden, H. G. and R. B. Weeden. 1963. Notes on the harvest of spruce grouse. J. Wildl. Manage. 27:587–91.

Lutz, R. S. 1979. The response of Attwater's prairie chicken to petroleum development. M.Sc. thesis. Texas A&M Univ., College Station.

MacArthur, R. H. 1968. Selection for life tables in periodic environments. Am. Nat. 103:381–83.

MacDonald, S. D. 1968. The courtship and territorial behavior of Franklin's race of the spruce grouse. Living Bird 7:5–25.

MacDonald, S. D. 1970. The breeding behavior of the rock ptarmigan. Living Bird 9:195–238.

MacKenzie, J. M. D. 1952. Fluctuations in the numbers of British Tetraonids. J. Anim. Ecol. 21:128–53.

Marcstrom, V. and N. H. Hoglund. 1981. Factors affecting reproduction of willow grouse (*Lagopus lagopus*) in two highland areas of Sweden. Viltrevy 11:285–314.

Marler, P. 1955. Studies of fighting in chaffinches (2), the effect of dominance relations of disguising females as males. Br. J. Anim. Behav. 3:137–46.

Marlin, J. C. 1967. The grasslands of North America: prolegomena to its history with addenda and postscripts. Peter Smith, Gloucester, Mass.

Marr, J. W. 1961. Ecosystems of the east slope of the Front Range in Colorado. Univ. Colo. Serv. in Biol. 8. 132 pp.

Marshall, W. H. 1954. Ruffed grouse and snowshoe hare populations on the Cloquet Experimental Forest, Minnesota. J. Wildl. Manage. 18:109–12.

Marshall, W. H. 1965. Ruffed grouse behavior. Bioscience 15:92–94.

Marshall, W. H. and G. W. Gullion. 1963. A discussion of ruffed grouse populations. Cloquet Forest Research Center, Minnesota. Trans. Int. Union Game Biol. 6:93–100.

Marshall, W. H. and M. S. Jensen. 1937. Winter and spring studies of the sharp-tailed grouse in Utah. J. Wildl. Manage. 1:87–99.

Marshall, W. H. and J. J. Kupa. 1963. Development of radio-telemetry techniques for ruffed grouse studies. Trans. N. Am. Wildl. Conf. 28:443–56.

Martinka, R. R. 1972. Structural characteristics of blue grouse territories in southwestern Montana. J. Wildl. Manage. 36:498–510.

Martinson, R. K. 1963. The relationship of weather to productivity in upland game birds. N.D. State Game and Fish Dep. Proj. W-67-R-4, Job 17. 24 pp.

Martinson, R. K. and C. R. Grondahl. 1966. Weather and pheasant populations in southwestern North Dakota. J. Wildl. Manage. 30:74–81.

Maxson, S. J. 1974. Activity, home range, and habitat usage of female ruffed grouse during the egg-laying, incubation, and early brood periods as determined by radio telemetry. M.S. thesis. Univ. Minnesota, St. Paul.

Maxson, S. J. 1977. Activity patterns of female ruffed grouse during the breeding season. Wilson Bull. 89:439–55.

Maxson, S. J. 1978. Spring home range and habitat use by female ruffed grouse. J. Wildl. Manage. 42:61–71.

May, T. A. 1970. Effects of sagebrush control on distribution and abundance of sage grouse. Colo. Game Bird Survey. Proj. W-37-R-23, Job 8a. Pp. 115–38.

May, T. A. 1975. Physiological ecology of white-tailed ptarmigan in Colorado. Ph.D. thesis. Univ. Colorado, Boulder.

May, T. A. and C. E. Braun. 1972. Seasonal foods of adult white-tailed ptarmigan in Colorado. J. Wildl. Manage. 36:1180–86.

Maynard-Smith, J. 1958. The theory of evolution. Penguin Press, Harmondsworth. 320 pp.

Maynard-Smith, J. and C. R. Price. 1973. The logic of animal conflict. Nature 246:15–18.

McBride, G. 1958. The measurement of aggressiveness in the domestic hen. Anim. Behav. 6:87–91.

McCollom, R. E., P. B. Siegel, and H. P. Van Krey. 1974. Responses to androgens in lines of chickens selected for mating behavior. Horm. Behav. 2:31–42.

McCourt, K. H. 1969. Dispersion and dispersal of female and juvenile Franklin's grouse in south-western Alberta. M.S. thesis. Univ. Alberta, Edmonton.

McCourt, K. H., D. A. Boag, and D. M. Keppie. 1973. Female spruce grouse activities during laying and incubation. Auk 90:619–23.

McCoy, E. D. and E. F. Connor. 1980. Latitudinal gradients in the species diversity of North American mammals. Evolution 34:193–203.

McEwen, L. C., D. B. Knapp, and E. A. Hilliard. 1969. Propagation of prairie grouse in captivity. J. Wildl. Manage. 33:276–83.

McGowan, J. D. 1972. Population characteristics of rock ptarmigan. Alaska Dep. Fish and Game, Final Rep. Fed. Aid in Wildl. Restoration. 14 pp.

McLachlin, R. A. 1970. The spring and summer dispersion of male Franklin's grouse in lodgepole pine forest in southwestern Alberta. M.Sc. thesis. Univ. Alberta, Edmonton.

McNicholl, M. K. 1978. Behaviour and social organization in a population of blue grouse on Vancouver Island. Ph.D. thesis. Univ. Alberta, Edmonton.

McNicholl, M. K. 1979. Individual variation in behaviour among blue grouse. N. Am. Bird Bander 4:16–18.

Mercer, W. E. 1967. Ecology of an island population of Newfoundland willow ptarmigan. Newfoundland and Labrador Wildl. Sci. Tech. Bull. 2. 97 pp.

Merrell, D. J. and C. F. Rodell. 1968. Seasonal selection in the leopard frog *Rana pipiens*. Evolution 22:284–88.

Meslow, E. C. 1966. The drumming log and drumming log activity of male ruffed grouse. M.S. thesis. Univ. Minnesota, St. Paul.

Mevel, D. J. 1973. Sex and age ratios of sharp-tailed grouse and hungarian partridge. Sask. Dep. Tourism and Renewable Resour. 15 pp.

Miller, G. R., D. Jenkins, and A. Watson. 1966. Heather performance and red grouse populations. I. Visual estimates of heather performance. J. Appl. Ecol. 3:313–26.

Miller, G. R. and A. Watson. 1978. Territories and the food plant of individual red grouse. I. Territory size, number of mates, and brood size compared with the abundance, production and diversity of heather. J. Anim. Ecol. 47:293–305.

Miller, G. R., A. Watson, and D. Jenkins. 1970. Responses of red grouse populations to experimental improvement of their food. Pp. 323–35 *in* A. Watson, ed. Animal populations in relation to their food resources. Blackwell Sci. Publ., Oxford and Edinburgh.

Miller, H. W. and D. H. Johnson. 1978. Interpreting the results of nesting studies. J. Wildl. Manage. 42:471–76.

Mitchell, D. L. 1957. Dummy nest study. N.D. Dep. Game and Fish Fed. Aid Wildl. Rest. Proj. W-35-R-3. 9 pp.

Mitchell, J. and B. Vodehnal. 1982. Surveys and management of Prairie grouse. S.D. Fed. Aid Wildl. Rest. Proj W-15-R-38. 15 pp.

Mohr, C. O. 1947. Table of equivalent populations of North American small mammals. Am. Midl. Nat. 37:233–49.

Morse, D. H. 1970. Ecological aspects of some mixed species foraging flocks of birds. Ecol. Mongr. 40:119–68.

Mortensen, A. and A. S. Blix. 1985. Seasonal changes in the effects of starvation on metabolic rate and regulation of body weight in Svalbard ptarmigan. Ornis Scand. 16:20–24.

Mortensen, A., E. S. Nordøy, and A. S. Blix. 1985. Seasonal changes in the body composition of the Norwegian rock ptarmigan *Lagopus mutus*. Ornis Scand. 16:25–28.

Moss, R. 1972. Social organization of willow ptarmigan on their breeding grounds in interior Alaska. Condor 74:144–51.

Moss, R. 1973. The digestion and intake of winter foods by wild ptarmigan in Alaska. Condor 75:293–300.

Moss, R. 1983. Gut size, body weight, and digestion of winter foods by grouse and ptarmigan. Condor 85:185–93.

Moss, R. and I. Hanssen. 1980. Grouse nutrition. Nutrition abstracts and reviews, Ser. B. 50:555–67.

Moss, R. and J. Oswald. 1985. Population dynamics of Capercaillie in a north-east Scottish glen. Ornis Scand. 16:229–38.

Moss, R., P. Rothery, and I. B. Trenholm. 1985. The inheritance of social dominance rank in red grouse (*Lagopus lagopus scoticus*). Aggress. Behav. 11:253–59.

Moss, R. and A. Watson. 1980. Inherent changes in the aggressive behaviour of a fluctuating red grouse *Lagopus lagopus scoticus* population. Ardea 68:113–19.

Moss, R. and A. Watson. 1982. Heritability of egg size, hatch weight, body weight, and viability in red grouse (*Lagopus lagopus scoticus*). Auk 99:683–86.

Moss, R. and A. Watson. 1985. Adaptive value of spacing behaviour in population cycles of red grouse and other animals. Pp. 275–94 *in* R. M. Sibly and R. H. Smith, eds. Behavioural ecology. Blackwell, Oxford.

Moss, R., A. Watson, and J. Ollason. 1982a. Animal population dynamics. Chapman and Hall, London.

Moss, R., A. Watson, and R. Parr. 1974. A role of nutrition in the population dynamics of some game birds (Tetraonidae). Trans. Int. Congr. Game Biol. 11:193–201.

Moss, R., A. Watson, and R. Parr. 1975. Maternal nutrition and breeding success in red grouse (*Lagopus lagopus scoticus*). J. Anim. Ecol. 44:233–44.

Moss, R., A. Watson, R. A. Parr, D. Watt, and W. Glennie. 1978. Egg size and other factors in relation to early mortality in red grouse (*Lagopus lagopus scoticus*) chicks. Ibis 120:407.

Moss, R., A. Watson, and P. Rothery. 1984. Inherent changes in body size, viability and behaviour of a fluctuating red grouse (*Lagopus lagopus scoticus*) population. J. Anim. Ecol. 53:171–89.

Moss, R., A. Watson, P. Rothery, and W. W. Glennie. 1981. Clutch size, egg size, hatch weight and laying date in relation to early mortality in red grouse *Lagopus lagopus scoticus* chicks. Ibis 123:450–62.

Moss, R., A. Watson, P. Rothery, and W. Glennie. 1982b. Inheritance of dominance and aggressiveness in captive red grouse *Lagopus lagopus scoticus*. Aggress. Behav. 8:1–18.

Mossop, D. H. 1971. A relation between aggressive behavior and population dynamics in blue grouse. M.Sc. thesis. Univ. British Columbia, Vancouver.

Moyles, D. L. J. 1977. A study of territory establishment by and movements of male sharp-tailed grouse (*Pedioecetes phasianellus*) relative to the arena. M.Sc. thesis. Univ. Alberta, Edmonton.

Moyles, D. L. J. 1981. Seasonal and daily use of plant communities by sharp-tailed grouse (*Pedioecetes phasianellus*) in the parklands of Alberta. Can. Field-Nat. 95:287–91.

Moyles, D. L. J. and D. A. Boag. 1981. Where, when, and how male sharp-tailed grouse establish territories on arenas. Can. J. Zool. 59:1576–81.

Muehrcke, J. P. and C. M. Kirkpatrick. 1970. Observations of ecology and behavior of Indiana ruffed grouse. Proc. Indiana Acad. Sci. 79:177–86.

Mueller, H. C., D. D. Berger, and G. Allez. 1977. The periodic invasions of goshawks. Auk 94:652–63.

Murphy, G. I. 1968. Pattern in life history and the environment. Am. Nat. 102:391–403.

Mussehl, T. W. 1963. Blue grouse brood cover selection and land-use implications. J. Wildl. Manage. 27:546–55.

Mussehl, T. W. and P. Schladweiler. 1969. Forest grouse and experimental spruce budworm insecticide studies. Mont. Fish and Game Dep. Tech. Bull 4. 53 pp.

Myers, J. H. and C. J. Krebs. 1971. Genetic, behavioral, and reproductive attributes of dispersing field voles *Microtus pennsylvanicus* and *Microtus ochrogaster*. Ecol. Monogr. 41:53–78.

Myhre, K., M. Cabanac, and C. Myhre. 1975. Thermoregulatory behavior and body temperature in chicks of willow grouse (*Lagopus lagopus lagopus*). Poultry Sci. 54:1174–79.

Myrberget, S. 1970a. Fra et hønsehaukrede i Troms. Sterna 9:5–8.

Myrberget, S. 1970b. On the part played by predation in short-term variations in the population of willow grouse, *Lagopus lagopus*, in Norway. Trans. Int. Congr. Game Biol. 9:458–64.

Myrberget, S. 1970c. Reproductive success of young and old willow ptarmigan, *Lagopus lagopus lagopus*, in north Norway. Finnish Game Res. 30:169–72.

Myrberget, S. 1972. Fluctuations in a north Norwegian population of willow grouse. Proc. Int. Ornithol. Congr. 15:107–20.

Myrberget, S. 1974a. Vaeret som synkroniserende faktor for smågnagersvingninger. Medd. Stat. Viltunders. 2:1–16.

Myrberget, S. 1974b. Variations in the production of the willow grouse *Lagopus lagopus* (L.) in Norway, 1963–1972. Ornis Scand. 5:163–72.

Myrberget, S. 1975a. Vegetasjonskartlegging av Tranøy i Senja. Trondheim (DVF).

Myrberget, S. 1975b. Age distribution, mortality and migration of willow grouse, *Lagopus lagopus*, on Senja, north Norway. Astarte 8:29–35.

Myrberget, S. 1975c. Norske studier omkring 1930 over lirypas reproduksjon. Sterna 14:51–64.

Myrberget, S. 1975d. Gjenfangstrater ved to merkemetododer for lirype. Sterna 14:29–32.

Myrberget, S. 1976a. En censusmetode for hekkende ryper. Fauna 29:79–85.

Myrberget, S. 1976b. Hunting mortality, migration, and age composition of Norwegian willow grouse (*Lagopus lagopus*). Norwegian J. Zool. 24:47–52.

Myrberget, S. 1976c. Lirypas reirhabitat. Medd. norsk Viltforsk. 3:1–30.

Myrberget, S. 1977. Size and shape of eggs of willow grouse *Lagopus lagopus*. Ornis Scand. 8:39–46.

Myrberget, S. 1980. Eggpredasjon hos lirype på ei nord-norsk øy. Viltrapport 10:108–13.

Myrberget, S. 1981. Diet of willow grouse *Lagopus lagopus* chicks on a coastal island. Fauna norv. Ser. C, Cinclus 4:58–63.

Myrberget, S. 1982a. Bestandsvariasjoner hos lirype i Norge 1932–1971. Medd. norsk Viltforsk. 3:1–31.

Myrberget, S. 1982b. Fluctuations in microtine populations in an island area in northern Norway 1958–1981. Fauna norv. Ser. A 3:7–11.

Myrberget, S. 1982c. Kråkebestanden på ei nordnorsk øy 1960–1981. Fauna 35:8–10.

Myrberget, S. 1983a. Vacant habitats during a decline in a population of willow grouse *Lagopus lagopus*. Fauna norv. Ser. C, Cinclus 6:1–7.

Myrberget S. 1983b. Desertion of nests by willow grouse *Lagopus lagopus*. Fauna norv. Ser. C, Cinclus 6:109–13.

Myrberget, S. 1984a. Population cycles of willow grouse *Lagopus lagopus* on an island in northern Norway. Fauna norv. Ser. C, Cinclus 7:46–56.

Myrberget, S. 1984b. Population dynamics of willow grouse *Lagopus lagopus* on an island in Norway. Fauna norv. Ser. C, Cinclus 7:95–105.

Myrberget, S. 1985. Egg predation in an island population of willow grouse *Lagopus lagopus*. Fauna norv. Ser. C, Cinclus 8:82–87.

Myrberget, S. (in press). Cycles in an island population of willow grouse *Lagopus lagopus* 1960–1980.

Myrberget, S. and A. Aandahl. 1976. Jordugle og haukugle sompredatorer på lirype. Fauna 29:93–94.

Myrberget, S., K. E. Erikstad, R. Blom, and T. K. Spidsø. 1985. Estimation of nesting success and frequency of re-laying in willow grouse *Lagopus lagopus*. Ornis Fenn. 62:9–12.

Myrberget, S., K. E. Erikstad, and T. K. Spidsø. 1977. Variations from year to year in growth rates of willow grouse chicks. Astarte 10:9–14.

Myrberget, S., K. E. Erikstad, and T. K. Spidsø. 1982. Demography of a North Norwegian population of willow grouse. Trans. Int. Congr. Game Biol. 14:47–52.

Myrberget, S., P. Krigsvoll, and K. E. Erikstad. 1976. Et forsøk på å desimere en Kråkebestand. Sterna 15:127–32.

Myrberget, S., Ø. Olsvik, and T. Saether. 1981. On a "crash" in a population of willow grouse *Lagopus lagopus*. Fauna norv. Ser. C, Cinclus 4:64–68.

Myrberget, S. and H-J Skar. 1976. Fat and calorific content of willow grouse in autumn and winter. Norwegian J. Zool. 24:41–45.

National Academy of Sciences–National Research Council. 1982. Range research: basic problems and techniques. Publ. No. 890 NAS-NRC. Washington, D.C. 341 pp.

Neave, D. J. 1967. The population dynamics of ruffed grouse (*Bonasa umbellus* L.) in central New Brunswick. M.S. thesis. Univ. New Brunswick, Fredericton.

Neave, D. J. and B. S. Wright. 1969. The effects of weather and DDT spraying on a ruffed grouse population. J. Wildl. Manage. 33:1015–20.

Nelson, O. C. 1955. A field study of sage grouse in southeastern Oregon with special reference to reproduction and survival. M.S. thesis. Oregon State Coll., Corvallis.

Neu, C. W., C. R. Byers and J. M. Peek. 1974. A technique for analysis of utilization-availability data. J. Wildl. Manage. 38:541–45.

Newton, I. 1979. Population ecology of raptors. Buteo Books, Vermillion, S.D. 399 pp.

Nice, M. M. 1942. Analysis of losses in the nesting of birds (review). Bird Banding 13:90.

Nicholls, T. H. and D. W. Warner. 1972. Barred owl habitat use as determined by radio-telemetry. J. Wildl. Manage. 36:213–24.

Nicholson, A. J. 1933. The balance of animal populations. J. Anim. Ecol. 2:132–78.

Niebet, R. M. and W. S. C. Gurney. 1982. Modelling fluctuating populations. John Wiley and Sons, New York.

Nielsen, G. F. 1973. The status of prairie chicken in Minnesota: land acquisition programs. Pp. 86–88 in W. D. Svedarsky and T. Wolfe, eds. Proc. of the prairie chicken in Minnesota. Univ. Minnesota, Crookston.

Nielsen, L. S. and C. A. Yde. 1982. The effects of rest-rotation grazing on the distribution of sharp-tailed grouse. Pp. 147–65 in J. M. Peek and P. D. Dalke ed. Wildlife – Live stock relationships. Dept. Wildl. Res., College of Forestry, Wildlife and Range science, Univ. Idaho, Moscow, Idaho.

Noble, G. K. and W. Vogt. 1935. An experimental study of sex recognition in birds. Auk 52:278–86.

Nolan, V. 1963. Reproductive success of birds in a deciduous shrub habitat. Ecology 44:305–13.

Nugent, D. P. and D. A. Boag. 1982. Communication among territorial female spruce grouse. Can. J. Zool. 60:2624–32.

O'Donald, P. 1983. Sexual selection by female choice. Pp. 53–66 in P. Bateson, ed. Mate choice. Cambridge Univ. Press, Cambridge.

O'Donald, P. 1977. Mating preferences and sexual selection in the arctic skua. II. Behavioral mechanisms of the mating preferences. Heredity 39:111–29.

Olpinski, S. C. 1980. The significance of age differential courtship and aggression behaviour among male Canada spruce grouse Canachites canadensis canace (L.). B.Sc. honours thesis. Univ. New Brunswick, Fredericton.

Olstad, O. 1932. Undersøkelser over Lirypens Fortplantings for hold. Nytt Mag. Naturv. 51:1–71.

Olsvik, Ø. and O. Olsen. 1980. Ryper, bestandstetthet og eggtap. Jakt-Fiske-Friluftsliv 109:18–19.

O'Malley, B. W. 1977. Hormonal control of gene expression in reproductive tissue. in R. O. Greep and M. A. Koblinsky, eds. Frontiers in reproductive and fertility control. Part 2. MIT Press, Cambridge, Mass.

Orians, G. H. 1969. On the evolution of mating systems in birds and mammals. Am. Nat. 103:589–603.

Oring, L. W. 1982. Avian mating systems. Pp. 1–92 in D. S. Farner, J. R. King and K. C. Parkes, eds. Avian biology. Vol. 6. Chiron Press, New York.

Owen, R. E. and R. C. Plowright. 1980. Abdominal pile color dimorphism in the bumble bee, Bombus melanopygus. J. Hered. 71:241–47.

Page, G. W., L. E. Stenzei, D. W. Winkler, and C. W. Swarth. 1983. Spacing out at Mono Lake: breeding success, nest density, and predation in the snowy plover. Auk 100:13–24.

Palmer, R. S. 1949. Maine birds. Vol. 102. Mus. Comp. Biol. Bull. Cambridge, Mass. 656 pp.

Palmer, W. L. 1956. Ruffed grouse population studies on hunted and unhunted areas. Trans. N. Am. Wildl. Conf. 21:338–44.

Palmer, W. L. 1963. Ruffed grouse drumming sites in northern Michigan. J. Wildl. Manage. 37:656–63.

Parker, H. 1981a. Duration of fertility in willow ptarmigan hens after separation from the cock. Ornis Scand. 12:186–87.

Parker, H. 1981b. Renesting biology of Norwegian willow ptarmigan. J. Wildl. Manage. 45:858–64.

Parsons, P. A. 1983. The evolutionary biology of colonizing species. Cambridge University Press, Cambridge. 262 pp.

Partridge, L. 1980. Mate choice increases a component of offspring fitness in fruit flies. Nature 283:290–91.

Patterson, I. J. 1981. Territorial behaviour and the limitation of population density. Pp. 53–62 in H. Klomp and J. W. Woldendorp, eds. The integrated study of bird populations. North-Holland Publ., Amsterdam.

Patterson, R. L. 1952. The sage grouse in Wyoming. Sage Books, Denver. 341 pp.

Pearson, O. P. 1966. The prey of carnivores during one cycle of mouse abundance. J. Anim. Ecol. 35:217–33.

Pedersen, H. C. 1984. Territory size, mating status, and individual survival of males in a fluctuating population of willow ptarmigan. Ornis Scand. 15:197–203.

Pedersen, H. C. and J. B. Steen. 1979. Behavioural thermoregulation in willow ptarmigan chicks Lagopus lagopus. Ornis Scand. 10:17–21.

Pedersen, H. C. and J. B. Steen. 1985. Parental care and chick production in a fluctuating population of willow ptarmigan. Ornis Scand. 16:270–76.

Pedersen, H. C., J. B. Steen, and R. Andersen. 1983. Social organization and territorial behavior in a willow ptarmigan population. Ornis Scand. 14:263–72.

Pepper, G. W. 1972. The ecology of sharp-tailed grouse during spring and summer in the aspen parklands of Saskatchewan. Sask. Dep. Nat. Resour. Wildl. Rep. 1. 56 pp.

Perrins, C. M. 1977. The role of predation in the evolution of clutch size. Pp. 181–91 in B. Stonehouse and C. Perrins, eds. Evolutionary ecology. Univ. Park Press, Baltimore, Md.

Peters, S. S. 1958. Food habits of the Newfoundland willow ptarmigan. J. Wildl. Manage. 22:384–94.

Petersen, B. E. 1980. Breeding and nesting ecology of female sage grouse on North Park, Colorado. M.S. thesis. Colorado State Univ., Fort Collins.

Petersen, L. 1979. Ecology of great horned owls and red-tailed hawks in southeastern Wisconsin. Wis. Dep. Nat. Resour. Tech. Bull. 111. 63 pp.

Petraborg, W. H., E. G. Wellein, and V. E. Gunvalson. 1953. Roadside drumming counts—a spring census method for ruffed grouse. J. Wildl. Manage. 17:292–95.

Petrides, G. A. 1949. Viewpoints on the analysis of open season and age ratios. Trans. N. Am. Wildl. Conf. 14:391–410.

Phillips, J. and F. Aalerud. 1980. Rypas territoriale atferd. Jakt-Fiske-Friluftsliv 109:48–50.

Peilou, E. C. 1977. Mathematical ecology. John Wiley and Sons, New York. 385 pp.

Pietz, P. J. and J. R. Tester. 1979. Utilization of Minnesota peatland habitats by snowshoe hare, white-tailed deer, spruce grouse, and ruffed grouse. Final Tech. Rep., Minn. Dep. Nat. Resour. 80 pp.

Pietz, P. J. and J. R. Tester. 1982. Habitat selection by sympatric spruce and ruffed grouse in north central Minnesota. J. Wildl. Manage. 46:391–403.

Pils, C. M. and M. A. Martin. 1978. Population dynamics, predator-prey relationships and management of the red fox in Wisconsin. Wis. Dep. Nat. Resour. Tech. Bull. 105. 56 pp.

Pils, C. M., M. A. Martin, and E. L. Lange. 1981. Harvest, age structure, survivorship, and productivity of red foxes in Wisconsin, 1975–78. Wis. Dep. Nat. Resour. Tech. Bull. 125. 21 pp.

Pimentel, D. 1963. Natural population regulation and inter-species evolution. Proc. Int. Congr. Zool. 16:329–36.

Pitelka, F. A. 1958. Some aspects of population structure in the short-term cycle of the brown lemming in northern Alaska. Cold Spring Harbour Symp. Quant. Biol. 22:237–51.

Pitelka, F. A. and A. M. Schultz. 1964. The nutrient recovery hypothesis for arctic microtine cycles. Pp. 55–68 in D. Crisp, ed. Grazing in terrestrial and marine environments. Blackwell Sci. Publ., Oxford.

Platt, J. B. 1976. Winter activity of gyrfalcons at their nest sites in arctic Canada. Can. Field-Nat. 90:338–45.

Platt, J. B. and E. Tull. 1976. A study of wintering and nesting gyrfalcons on the Yukon north slope during 1975 with emphasis on their behavior during experimental overflights by helicopter. Chapter 2 *in* W. W. H. Gunn, R. E. Schweinsburg, C. E. Tull, and T. D. Wright, eds. Ornithological studies conducted in the area of the proposed gas pipeline route. Northwest Territory, Yukon and Alaska Arctic Gas Biol. Rep. Ser. Vol. 30.

Popper, K. R. 1959. The logic of scientific discovery. Basic Books, New York. 479 pp.

Popper, K. R. 1965. Normal science and its dangers. Pp. 51–58 *in* I. Lakatos and A. Musgrave, eds. Criticism and the growth of knowledge. Cambridge Univ. Press, Cambridge.

Porath, W. R. and P. A. Vohs, Jr. 1972. Population ecology of ruffed grouse in northeastern Iowa. J. Wildl. Manage. 36:793–802.

Porter, W. F. 1977. Home range dynamics of wild turkeys in southeastern Minnesota. J. Wildl. Manage. 41:434–37.

Pot, W., W. Van Delden, and J. P. Kruijt. 1980. Genetic differences in mating success and the maintainance of the alcohol dehydrogenase polymorphism in *Drosophila melanogaster*. Behav. Genet. 10:43–58.

Potts, G. R. 1980. The effects of modern agriculture, nest predation and game management on the population ecology of partridges (*Perdix perdix* and *Alectoris rufa*). Pp. 1–79 *in* A. MacFayden, ed. Advances in ecological research. Vol. 2. Academic Press, London.

Potts, G. R., S. C. Tapper, and P. J. Hudson. 1984. Population fluctuations in red grouse: analysis of bag records and a simulation model. J. Anim. Ecol. 53:21–36.

Poulsen, E. T. 1979. Model for population regulation with density and frequency dependent selection. J. Math. Biol. 13:305–24.

Powell, G. V. N. 1974. Experimental analysis of the social value of flockings by starlings (*Sturnus vulgaris*) in relation to predation and foraging. Anim. Behav. 22:501–5.

Powell, R. A. 1982. Evolution of black-tipped tails in weasels: predator confusion. Am. Nat. 119:126–31.

Prawdzik, T. R. 1963. Ruffed grouse escaping a cooper's hawk. J. Wildl. Manage. 27:639–42.

Prout, T. 1980. Some relationships between density-independent selection and density-dependent population growth. Pp. 1–68 *in* M. K. Hecht, W. C. Steele and B. Wallace, eds. Evolutionary biology. Vol. 13. Plenum, New York.

Pulliainen, E. 1975a. Choice of prey by a pair of gyrfalcons *Falco rusticolus* during the nesting period in Forest-Lapland. Ornis Fenn. 52:19–22.

Pulliainen, E. 1975b. Structure of two willow grouse (*Lagopus lagopus*) populations in Finnish Fjeld Lapland in the winters of 1972–1974. Ann. Zool. Fenn. 12:263–67.

Pulliainen, E. 1978. Behaviour of a willow grouse *Lagopus lagopus lagopus* at the nest. Ornis Fenn. 55:141–48.

Pulliam, H. R. and G. C. Millikan. 1982. Social organization in the nonreproductive season. Pp. 169–97 *in* D. S. Farner, J. R. King, and K. C. Parkes, eds. Avian biology. Vol. 6. Academic Press, New York.

Pyke, G. H., H. R. Pulliam, and E. L. Charnov. 1977. Optimal foraging: a selective review of theory and tests. Q. Rev. Biol. 52:137–54.

Quinn, N. W. S. and D. M. Keppie. 1981. Factors influencing growth of juvenile spruce grouse. Can. J. Zool. 59:1790–95.

Ramharter, B. G. 1976. Habitat selection and movements of sharp-tailed grouse (*Pedioecetes phasianellus*) hens during the nesting and brood rearing periods in a fire maintained brush prairie. Ph.D. thesis. Univ. Minnesota, St. Paul.

Rand, A. L. 1947. Clutch size in the spruce grouse and theoretical considerations of some factors affecting clutch size. Can. Field-Nat. 61:127–30.

Ransom, A. B. 1965. Observations of a ruffed grouse decline. Can. Field-Nat. 79:128–30.

Rasmussen, D. I. and L. A. Griner. 1938. Life history and management studies of the sage grouse in Utah, with special reference to nesting and feeding habits. Trans N. Am. Wildl. Conf. 3:852–64.

Redfield, J. A. 1972. Demography and genetics in colonizing populations of blue grouse (*Dendragapus obscurus*). Ph.D. thesis. Univ. Alberta, Edmonton.

Redfield, J. A. 1973a. Demography and genetics in colonizing populations of blue grouse (*Dendragapus obscurus*). Evolution 27:576–92.

Redfield, J. A. 1973b. Variations in weight of blue grouse (*Dendragapus obscurus*). Condor 75:312–21.

Redfield, J. A. 1974. Genetics and selection at the *Ng* locus in blue grouse (*Dendragapus obscurus*). Heredity 33:69–78.

Redfield, J. A. 1975. Comparative demography of increasing and stable populations of blue grouse (*Dendragapus obscurus*). Can. J. Zool. 53:1–11.

Redfield, J. A. 1978. Growth of juvenile blue grouse, *Dendragapus obscurus*. Ibis 120:55–61.

Redfield, J. A., F. C. Zwickel, and J. F. Bendell. 1970. Effects of fire on numbers of blue grouse. Proc. Annu. Tall Timbers Fire Ecol. Conf. 10:63–83.

Redfield, J. A., F. C. Zwickel, J. F. Bendell, and A. T. Bergerud. 1972. Temporal and spatial patterns of allele and genotype frequencies at the Ng locus in blue grouse (*Dendragapus obscurus*). Can. J. Zool. 50:1657–62.

Redmond, G. W., D. M. Keppie, and P. W. Herzog. 1982. Vegetative structure, concealment, and success at nests of two races of spruce grouse. Can. J. Zool. 60:670–75.

Reid, R. and C. G. Gannon. 1928. Natural history notes on the journals of Alexander Henry. N.D. Hist. Q. 2:168–201.

Reynolds, R. T., E. C. Meslow, and H. M. Wight. 1982. Nesting habitat of coexisting *Accipiter* in Oregon. J. Wildl. Manage. 46:124–38.

Rice, L. and A. Carter. 1975. Evaluation of South Dakota grassland management practices as they affect prairie chicken populations, 1973–74 and 1974–75. S.D. Dep. Game, Fish and Parks. Proj. W-75-R-16, 17, Jobs I–V. 16 pp.

Rice, L. and A. Carter. 1976. Evaluation of South Dakota grassland management practices as they affect prairie chicken populations, 1975–1976. S.D. Dep. Game, Fish and Parks. Proj. W-75-R-18. Jobs I–V. 17 pp.

Rice, L. and A. Carter. 1977. Evaluation of South Dakota grassland management practices as they affect prairie chicken populations 1976–77. S.D. Dep. Game, Fish and Parks. Proj. W-75-R-19, Jobs I–V. 16 pp.

Richards, S. H. and R. L. Hine. 1953. Wisconsin fox populations. Wis. Conserv. Dep. Final Rep., Tech. Wildl. Bull. 6. 78 pp.

Ricker, W. E. 1954. Effects of compensatory mortality upon population abundance. J. Wildl. Manage. 18:45–51.

Ricklefs, R. E. 1969. An analysis of nesting mortality in birds. Smithsonian Contrib. Zool. 9:1–48.

Ricklefs, R. E. 1970. Clutch size in birds: outcome of opposing predator and prey adaptations. Science 168:599–600.

Ricklefs, R. E. 1972. Breeding biology of birds. Pp. 366–435 *in* D. S. Farner, ed. Symposium on breeding behavior and reproductive physiology in birds. Natl. Acad. Sci., Washington, D.C.

Ricklefs, R. E. 1977. On the evolution of reproductive strategies in birds: reproductive effort. Am. Nat. 111:453–61.

Riewe, J. W. 1975. Mammalian carnivores. Pp. 493–501 *in* L. C. Bliss, ed. Truelove Lowland, Devon Island, Canada: a high arctic ecosystem. Univ. Alberta Press, Edmonton.

Riley, T. Z. 1978. Nesting and brood-rearing habitat of lesser prairie chickens. M.S. thesis. New Mexico State Univ., Las Cruces.

Rippin, A. B. and D. A. Boag. 1974a. Recruitment to populations of male sharp-tailed grouse. J. Wildl. Manage. 38:616–21.

Rippin, A. B. and D. A. Boag. 1974b. Spatial organization among male sharp-tailed grouse on arenas. Can. J. Zool. 52:591–97.

Ritcey, R. W. and R. Y. Edwards. 1963. Grouse abundance and June temperatures in Wells Gray Park, British Columbia. J. Wildl. Manage. 27:604–6.

Robel, R. J. 1964. Quantitative indices to activity and territoriality of booming *Tympanuchus cupido pinnatus* in Kansas. Trans. Kans. Acad. Sci. 67:702–12.

Robel, R. J. 1966. Booming territory size and mating success of the greater prairie chicken (*Tympanuchus cupido pinnatus*). Anim. Behav. 14:328–31.

Robel, R. J. 1970. Possible role of behavior in regulating greater prairie chicken populations. J. Wildl. Manage. 34:306–12.

Robel, R. J. 1972. Possible function of the lek in regulating tetraonid populations. Proc. Int. Ornithol. Congr. 15:121–33.

Robel, R. J. and W. B. Ballard, Jr. 1974. Lek social organization and reproductive success in the greater prairie chicken. Am. Zool. 14:121–28.

Robel, R. J., J. N. Briggs, J. J. Cebula, N. J. Silvy, C. E. Viers, and P. G. Watt. 1970a. Greater prairie chicken ranges, movements, and habitat usage in Kansas. J. Wildl. Manage. 34:286–306.

Robel, R. J., J. N. Briggs, A. D. Dayton, and L. C. Hulbert. 1970b. Relationships between visual obstruction measurements and weight of grassland vegetation. J. Range Manage. 23:295–97.

Robel, R. J., F. R. Henderson, and W. W. Jackson. 1972. Some sharp-tailed grouse population statistics from South Dakota. J. Wildl. Manage. 36:87–98.

Robertson, K. 1979. Surveys and management of prairie grouse. Nebr. Game and Parks Comm. Proj. W-15-R-35, Work Plan E-78. 53 pp.

Robinson, W. L. 1969. Habitat selection by spruce grouse in northern Michigan. J. Wildl. Manage. 33:113–20.

Robinson, W. L. 1980. Fool hen: the spruce grouse on the yellow dog plains. Univ. Wisconsin Press, Madison. 221 pp.

Rodgers, R. D. 1980. Ecological relationships of ruffed grouse in southwestern Wisconsin. Wis. Acad. Sci., Arts, and Letters. 68:97–105.

Roe, F. G. 1951. The North American buffalo. Univ. Toronto Press, Toronto. 957 pp.

Roff, D. A. 1974. Spatial heterogeneity and the persistence of populations. Oecologia 15:245–58.

Roff, D. A. 1975. Population stability and the evolution of dispersal in a heterogeneous environment. Oecologia 15:259–75.

Rogers, G. E. 1964. Sage grouse investigations in Colorado. Colo. Game, Fish and Parks Dep. Tech. Publ. 16. 132 pp.

Rohwer, S., S. D. Fretwell, and D. M. Niles. 1980. Delayed maturation in passerine plumages and the deceptive acquisition of resources. Am. Nat. 115:400–437.

Romesburg, H. C. 1981. Wildlife science: gaining reliable knowledge. J. Wildl. Manage. 45:293–313.

Rose, M. R., M. L. Dorey, A. M. Coye, and P. M. Service. 1984. The morphology of postponed senescence in *Drosophila melanogaster*. Can. J. Zool. 62:1576–80.

Rothenmaier, D. 1979. Sage grouse reproductive ecology: breeding season movements, strutting ground attendance and site characteristics, and nesting. M.S. thesis. Univ. Wyoming, Laramie.

Roughgarden, J. 1971. Density-dependent natural selection. Ecology 52:453–68.

Rubenstein, D. I. 1980. On the evolution of alternative mating strategies. Pp. 65–100. *in* J. E. R. Staddon, ed. Limits to action: the allocation of individual behavior. Academic Press, New York.

Rusch, D. H. 1976. The wildlife cycle in Manitoba. Manit. Dep. Mines, Resour. and Wildl. Manage. Wildl. Branch Inf. Ser. 11. 14 pp.

Rusch, D. H., M. M. Gillespie, and D. I. McKay. 1978. Decline of a ruffed grouse population in Manitoba. Can. Field-Nat. 92:123–27.

Rusch, D. H. and L. B. Keith. 1971a. Ruffed grouse-vegetation relationships in central Alberta. J. Wildl. Manage. 35:417–29.

Rusch, D. H. and L. B. Keith. 1971b. Seasonal and annual trends in numbers of Alberta ruffed grouse. J. Wildl. Manage. 35:803–22.

Rusch, D. H., L. B. Keith, P. D. Doerr, and C. A. Fischer. 1984. Demography of a ruffed grouse population in central Alberta. Unpubl. report, Dept. of Wildlife Ecology, Univ. Wisconsin, Madison.

Rusch, D. H., E. C. Meslow, P. D. Doerr, and L. B. Keith. 1972. Response of great horned owl populations to changing prey densities. J. Wildl. Manage. 36:282–296.

Sadlier, R. M. F. S. 1965. The relationship between agonistic behavior and population changes in the deer mouse, *Peromyscus maniculatus* (Wagner). J. Anim. Ecol. 34:331–52.

Safriel, U. N. 1975. On the significance of clutch size in nidifugous birds. Ecology 56:703–8.

Salmon, W. C. 1979. Informal analytical approaches to the philosophy of science. Pp. 3–15 *in* Current research in philosophy of science. Edwards Bros., Ann Arbor, Mich.

Salo, L. J. 1978. Characteristics of ruffed grouse drumming sites in western Washington and their relevance to management. Ann. Zool. Fenn. 15:261–78.

Salomonsen, F. 1939. Moults and sequence of plumages in the rock ptarmigan (*Lagopus mutus* [Montin]). Videnskabelige Meddelelser Fra Dansk Naturhistorisk Forening 103:1–491.

Salomonsen, F. 1972. Presidential address: zoogeographical and ecological problems in arctic birds. Proc. Int. Ornithol. Congr. 15:25–77.

Sargeant, A. B. 1972. Red fox spatial characteristics in relation to waterfowl predation. J. Wildl. Manage. 36:225–36.

Sargeant, A. B. 1983. A case history of a dynamic resource—the red fox. Pp. 127–37 *in* G. C. Sanderson, ed. Midwest Furbearer Manage. Symp. The Wildl. Society.

Sargeant, A. B., S. H. Allen, and R. T. Eberhardt. 1984. Red fox predation of breeding ducks in midcontinent, North America. Wildl. Mongr. 89. 41 pp.

Sargeant, A. B. and L. E. Eberhardt. 1975. Death feigning by ducks in response to red foxes (*Vulpes fulva*) Am. Midl. Nat. 94:108–19.

Sassaman, C. and R. Garthwaite. 1980. Genetics of a pigment polymorphism in the isopod *Porcellio dilatatus*. J. Hered. 71:158–60.

Savory, C. J. 1975. Seasonal variation in the food intake of captive red grouse. Br. Poult. Sci. 16:471–79.

Savory, C. J. 1977. The food of red grouse chicks *Lagopus l. scoticus*. Ibis 119:1–9.

Savory, C. J. 1978. Food consumption of red grouse in relation to age and productivity of heather. J. Anim. Ecol. 47:269–82.

Schemnitz, S. D. 1970. Fall and winter feeding activities and behavior of ruffed grouse in Maine. Proc. Northeast Sect. Wildl. Society Annu. Conf. 27:127–40.

Schilcher, F. V. 1977. A mutation which changes courtship song in *Drosophila melanogaster*. Behav. Genet. 7:251–59.

Schiller, R. J. 1973. Reproductive ecology of female sharp-tailed grouse (*Pedioecetes phasianellus*) and its relationship to early plant succession in northwestern Minnesota. Ph.D. thesis. Univ. Minnesota, St. Paul.

Schladweiler, P. 1965. Movements and activities of ruffed grouse, *Bonasa umbellus* (L.), during the summer period. Ph.D. thesis. Univ. Minnesota, St. Paul.

Schladweiler, P. 1968. Feeding behavior of incubating ruffed grouse females. J. Wildl. Manage. 32:426–28.

Schmidt, F. J. W. 1936. Winter food of the sharp-tailed grouse and pinnated grouse in Wisconsin. Wilson Bull. 48:186–230.

Schmidt, R. K., Jr. 1969. Behavior of white-tailed ptarmigan in Colorado. M.S. thesis. Colorado State Univ., Fort Collins.

Schofield, R. D. 1960. A thousand miles of fox trails in Michigan's ruffed grouse range. J. Wildl. Manage. 24:432–34.

Schorger, A. W. 1944. The prairie chicken and sharp-tailed grouse in early Wisconsin. Trans. Wis. Acad. Sci., Arts and Letters 35:1–59.

Schorger, A. W. 1945. The ruffed grouse in early Wisconsin. Trans. Wis. Acad. Sci., Arts and Letters 37:35–90.

Schranck, B. W. 1972. Waterfowl nest cover and some predation relationships. J. Wildl. Manage. 36:182–86.

Schroeder, M. A. 1985. Behavioral differences of female spruce grouse undertaking short and long migrations. Condor 87:281–86.

Schultz, A. M. 1964. The nutrient-recovery hypothesis for arctic microtine cycles. II. Pp. 57–68 in D. Crisp, ed. Grazing in terrestrial and marine environments. Blackwell Sci. Publ., Oxford.

Schulz, J. W. 1981. Ruffed grouse population data. N.D. State Game and Fish Dep. Proj. W-67-R-21, Jobs B-XI-1, 2, 3. 15 pp.

Schulz, J. W. 1982. Examination of ruffed grouse populations and habitat requirements on the Turtle Mountains. N.D. State Game and Fish Dep. Proj. W-67-R-22, Jobs B-XIV-2, 3. 22 pp.

Schulz, J. W. 1983. Ruffed grouse population data. N.D. State Game and Fish Dep. Proj. W-67-R-23, Jobs B-XI-1, 2, 3, 4. 19 pp.

Schwartz, C. W. 1944. The prairie chicken in Missouri. Mo. Conserv. Comm. 179 pp.

Schwartz, C. W. 1945. The ecology of the prairie chicken in Missouri. Univ. Mo. Studies 20:1–99.

Scott, J. W. 1942. Mating behavior of sage grouse. Auk 59:477–98.

Scott, T. G. ed. 1981. Fisheries and wildlife research 191. U.S. Fish and Wildl. Serv. Denver, Colo. 191 pp.

Scott, W. E. 1956. The wildlife resources of Wisconsin. The Natural Resources of Wisconsin, December. Pp. 32–34.

Searcy, W. A. and K. Yasukawa. 1981. Does the "sexy son" hypothesis apply to mate choice in red-winged blackbirds? Am. Nat. 117:343–48.

Seiskari, P. 1962. On the winter ecology of the capercaillie, *Tetrao urogallus*, and the black grouse, *Lyrurus tetrix*, in Finland. Pap. on Game Res. 22:1–119.

Selander, R. K. 1965. On mating systems and sexual selection. Am. Nat. 99:129–41.

Selander, R. K. 1972. Sexual selection and dimorphism in birds. Pp. 180–230 in B. Campbell, ed. Sexual selection and the descent of man. 1871–1971. Aldine Press, Chicago.

Sell, D. L. 1979. Spring and summer movements and habitat use by lesser prairie chicken females in Yoakum County, Texas. M.S. thesis. Texas Tech. Univ., Lubbock.

Seton, E. T. 1953. Lives of game animals. Vol. 3. Charles T. Branford, Boston (first published in 1904). 780 pp.

Severson, R. 1982. Ninety years of weather reporting in northwest Minnesota. Minn. Rep. 1892–1982. Agric. Exp. Station, Univ. Minn., St. Paul. 46 pp.

Sexton, D. A. and M. M. Gillespie. 1979. Effects of fire on the location of a sharp-tailed grouse arena. Can. Field-Nat. 93:74–76.

Sharpe, R. S. 1968. The evolutionary relationships and comparative behavior of prairie chickens. Ph.D. thesis. Univ. Nebraska, Lincoln.

Short, L. L., Jr. 1967. A review of the genera of grouse (Aves, Tetraoninae). Am. Mus. Novitates 2289. 39 pp.

Siivonen, L. 1957. The problem of the short-term fluctuations in numbers of tetraonids in Europe. Pap. on Game Res. 19:1–44.

Silver, R., M. O'Connell, and R. Saad. 1979. Effect of androgens on the behavior of birds. Pp. 223–78 in C. Beyer, ed. Endocrine control of sexual behavior. Raven Press, New York.

Silvy, N. J. 1968. Movements, monthly ranges, reproductive behavior, and mortality of radio-tagged greater prairie chickens (*Tympanuchus cupido pinnatus*). M.S. thesis. Kansas State Univ., Manhattan.

Silvy, N. J. and R. S. Lutz. 1978. Attwater's prairie chicken response to petroleum development. Caesar Kleberg Res. Program in Wildl. Ecol., Coll. Agric., Texas A&M Univ., College Station. 69 pp.

Simmons, K. E. L. 1955. The nature of the predator-reaction of waders towards humans with special reference to the role of the aggressive-escape and brooding drives. Behaviour 8:130–73.

Sisson, L. 1976. The sharp-tailed grouse in Nebraska. Nebr. Game and Parks Comm., Lincoln. 88 pp.

Skinner, R. M. 1977. A comparison of grassland structure and prairie chicken use in Missouri. Proc. Prairie Grouse Tech. Counc. 12:12.

Skutch, A. F. 1949. Do tropical birds rear as many young as they can nourish? Ibis 91:430–55.

Slagsvold, T. 1975. Production of young by the willow grouse (*Lagopus lagopus* (L.) in Norway in relation to temperature. Norwegian J. Zool. 23:269–75.

Slagsvold, T. 1984. Clutch size variation of birds in relation to nest predation and the cost of reproduction. J. Anim. Ecol. 53:945–53.

Slatkin, M. 1979. Frequency and density dependent selection in a quantitative character. Genetics 93:755–71.

Smith, H. M., C. T. Garten, Jr., and P. R. Ramsey. 1975. Genetic heterozygosity and population dynamics in small mammals. Pp. 85–102 *in* C. L. Markert, ed. Isozymes IV. Genetics and evolution. Academic Press, New York.

Smith, S. M. 1967. Seasonal changes in the survival of the black capped chickadee. Condor 69:344–59.

Smouse, P. E. 1976. The implications of density-dependent population growth for frequency- and density-dependent selection. Am. Nat. 110:849–60.

Smyth, K. E. and D. A. Boag. 1984. Production in spruce grouse and its relationship to environmental factors and population parameters. Can. J. Zool. 62:2250–57.

Snyder, L. L. 1935. A study of sharp-tailed grouse. Univ. Toronto Studies Biol. Ser. 40. 66 pp.

Soikiro, T., S. Nobuo, and S. Chiba. 1969. On territory of Japanese ptarmigan (*Lagopus mutus japonicus* Clark) in the Murodo area, Taeyama, Japan Alps, in 1967 and 1968. Misc. Rep. of the Nat'l Park for Nature Study. 1:14–18.

Sokal, R. R. and F. J. Rohlf. 1969. Biometry. W. H. Freeman and C., San Francisco. 776 pp.

Sonerud, G. A. 1985. Brood movements in grouse and waders as defense against win-stay search in their predators. Oikos 44:287–300.

Sopuck, L. G. 1979. Movements and breeding biology of blue grouse in relation to recruitment, reproductive success, and migration. M.Sc. thesis. Univ. Alberta, Edmonton.

Sopuck, L. G. and F. C. Zwickel. 1983. Renesting in adult and yearling blue grouse. Can. J. Zool. 61:289–91.

Southwick, C. H. 1955. Regulatory mechanisms of house mouse populations: social behavior affecting litter survival. Ecology 36:627–34.

Southwood, T. R. E. 1977. Habitat, the templet for ecological strategies? J. Anim. Ecol. 46:337–65.

Southwood, T. R. E. and D. J. Cross. 1969. The ecology of the partridge. III. Breeding success and the abundance of insects in natural habitats. J. Anim. Ecol. 38:497–509.

Sparling, D. W., Jr. 1979. Reproductive isolating mechanisms and communication in greater prairie chickens (*Tympanuchus cupido*) and sharp-tailed grouse (*Pedioecetes phasianellus*). Ph.D. thesis. Univ. North Dakota, Grand Forks.

Sparling, D. W. 1981. Communication in prairie grouse. I. information content and intraspecific functions of principal vocalizations. Behav. Neurol. Biol. 32:463–86.

Sparling, D. W. 1983. Quantitative analysis of prairie grouse vocalizations. Condor 85:30–42.

Sparling, D. W., Jr. and W. D. Svedarsky. 1978. Responses of prairie grouse to avian and mammalian visitors on display grounds in northwestern Minnesota. Prairie Nat. 10:17–22.

Spidsø, T. K. 1980. Food selection by willow grouse *Lagopus lagopus* chicks in northern Norway. Ornis Scand. 11:99–105.

Stanton, D. C. 1958. A study of breeding and reproduction in a sage grouse population in southeastern Idaho. M.S. thesis. Univ. Idaho, Moscow.

Steen, J. B. 1978. Rypeboka. Oslo (Gyldendal). 231 pp.

Steen, J. B., H. C. Pedersen, K. E. Erikstad, K. B. Hansen, K. Høydal, and A. Størdal. 1985. The significance of cock territories in willow ptarmigan. Ornis Scand. 16:277–82.

Steen, J. B. and S. Unander. 1985. Breeding biology of the Svalbard rock ptarmigan *Lagopus mutus hyperboreus*. Ornis Scand. 16:191–97.

Stenseth, N. C. 1978. Demographic strategies in fluctuating populations of small rodents. Oecologia 33:149–72.

Stewart, P. A. 1967. Hooting of sitka blue grouse in relation to weather, season, and time of day. J. Wildl. Manage. 31:28–34.

Stewart, R. E. 1975. Breeding birds of North Dakota. Trinity Coll. Center for Environ. Studies. Fargo, N.D. 295 pp.

Stirling, I. G. 1965. Studies of the holding, behaviour and nutrition of captive blue grouse. M.Sc. thesis. Univ. British Columbia, Vancouver.

Stirling, I. 1968. Aggressive behavior and the dispersion of female blue grouse. Can. J. Zool. 46:405–8.

Stirling, I. and J. F. Bendell. 1970. The reproductive behaviour of blue grouse. Syesis 3:161–71.

Stoddard, H. L. 1931. The bobwhite quail: its habits, preservation and increase. Charles Scribner's Sons, New York. 559 pp.

Stokes, A. W. 1954. Population studies on the ring-necked pheasant on Pelee Island, Ontario. Ont. Dep. Lands and For. Tech. Bull. Wildl. Ser. 4. 154 pp.

Stokkan, K-A. 1979a. The effect of permanent short days and castration on plumage and comb growth in male willow ptarmigan (*Lagopus lagopus*). Auk 96:682–87.

Stokkan, K-A. 1979b. Testosterone and daylength-dependent development of comb size and breeding plumage of male willow ptarmigan (*Lagopus lagopus lagopus*). Auk 96:106–15.

Stoneberg, R. P. 1967. A preliminary study of the breeding biology of the spruce grouse in north-western Montana. M.S. thesis. Montana State Univ., Missoula.

Sugden, L. G. and G. W. Beyersbergen. 1986. Effect of density and concealment on American crow predation of simulated duck nests. J. Wildl. Manage. 50:9–14.

Svedarsky, W. D. 1979. Spring and summer ecology of female greater prairie chickens in north-western Minnesota. Ph.D. thesis. Univ. North Dakota, Grand Forks.

Svedarsky, W. D. 1980. Juvenile prairie chicken predation by marsh hawk. Raptor Research 14:31–32.

Svedarsky, W. D., R. J. Oehlenschlager, and T. D. Tonsager. 1982. A remnant flock of greater prairie chickens in north central Minnesota. Agr. Exp. Station, Univ. of Minnesota, No. 1802, 13 pp.

Svedarsky, W. D. and T. D. Tonsager. 1981. A remnant flock of greater prairie chickens in north central Minnesota. Univ. of Minnesota, Crookston.

Svoboda, F. J. 1972. Instructions for site selection, plot establishment and catkin production measurements of preferred ruffed grouse winter foods. Univ. Minnesota Forestry Center, Cloquet. Misc. Note 9 pp.

Svoboda, F. J. and G. W. Gullion. 1972. Preferential use of aspen by ruffed grouse in northern Minnesota. J. Wildl. Manage. 36:1166–80.

Swanson, G. A. and M. I. Meyer. 1973. The role of invertebrates in the feeding ecology of Anatinae during the breeding season. Pp. 143–85 *in* Proc. Waterfowl Habitat Management Symposium. 1973. Moncton, New Brunswick.

Swenson, J. E. 1985. Seasonal habitat use by sharp-tailed grouse, *Tympanuchus phasianellus*, on a mixed-grass prairie in Montana. Can. Field-Nat. 99:40–46.

Szuba, K. J. and J. F. Bendell. 1982. Population densities and habitats of spruce grouse in Ontario. Pp. 199–213 *in* R. W. Wein, R. R. Riewe, I. R. Methuen, eds. Resources and dynamics of the boreal forest. Association of Canadian Universities for Northern Studies, Ottawa.

Szuba, K. J. and J. F. Bendell. 1984. Weights of Ontario spruce grouse by sex, age, and breeding success. Can. J. Zool. 62:788–92.

Tanner, W. D. 1948. A population study of the ruffed grouse (*Bonasa umbellus monticola*) in Pennsylvania at the low of the cycle. M.S. thesis. Pennsylvania State Univ., State College.

Tast, J. and O. Kalela. 1971. Comparison between rodent cycles and plant production in Finnish Lapland. Ann. Acad. Sci. Fenn., Ser. A, 4 Biol. 186:1–14.

Tate, J., Jr., M. S. Boyce, and T. R. Smith. 1979. Response of sage grouse to artificially created display ground. Pp. 459–63 *in* The Mitigation Symposium. Gen. Tech. Rep. RM-65, Rocky Mt. For. Range Exp. Stn., Fort Collins, Colo.

Taylor, D. A. 1976. An analysis of some physical characteristics of ruffed grouse (*Bonasa umbellus*) drumming sites and logs in middle and eastern Tennessee. Tenn. Wildl. Resour. Agency Tech. Rept. 15–25. 72 pp.

Taylor, J. 1976. The advantage of spacing out. J. Theor. Biol. 59:485–90.

Taylor, L. R. and J. Taylor. 1977. Aggregation, migration and population mechanics. Nature 365:415–20.

Taylor, M. A. 1979. Lesser prairie chicken use of man-made leks. Southwest. Nat. 24:706–7.

Taylor, M. A. and F. S. Guthery. 1980. Status, ecology, and management of the lesser prairie chicken. U.S. Dep. Agric. For. Serv. Gen. Tech. Rep. RM-77. Rocky Mountain For. and Range Exp. Station, Fort Collins, Colo. 15 pp.

Taylor, P. D. and G. C. Williams. 1982. The lek paradox is not resolved. Theor. Pop. Biol. 22:392–409.

Tester, J. R. and W. H. Marshall. 1961. A study of certain plant and animal interrelations on a native prairie in northwestern Minnesota. Minn. Mus. Nat. Hist., Univ. Minn. Occasional Pap. 8:1–51.

Tester, J. R. and W. H. Marshall. 1962. Minnesota prairie management techniques and their wildlife implications. Trans. N. Am. Wildl. Nat. Resour. Conf. 27:267–87.

Theberge, J. B. 1971. Population fluctuation and changes in the quality of rock ptarmigan in Alaska. Ph.D. thesis. Univ. British Columbia, Vancouver.

Theberge, J. B. and J. F. Bendell. 1980. Differences in survival and behaviour of rock ptarmigan (*Lagopus mutus*) chicks among years in Alaska. Can. J. Zool. 58:1638–42.

Theberge, J. B. and D. A. Gauthier. 1982. Factors influencing densities of territorial male ruffed grouse, Algonquin Park, Ontario. J. Wildl. Manage. 46:263–68.

Theberge, J. B. and G. C. West. 1973. Significance of brooding to the energy demands of Alaskan rock ptarmigan chicks. Arctic 26:138–48.

Thomas, V. G. 1982. Energetic reserves of Hudson Bay willow ptarmigan during winter and spring. Can. J. Zool. 60:1618–23.

Thompson, D. R. and J. C. Moulton. 1981. An evaluation of Wisconsin ruffed grouse surveys. Wis. Dep. Nat. Resour. Tech. Bull. 123. 13 pp.

Thorneycroft, H. B. 1975. A cytogenetic study of the white-throated sparrow, *Zonotrichia albicollis* (Gimelin). Evolution 29:611–21.

Tinbergen, N. 1951. The study of instinct. Oxford Univ. Press, London. 228 pp.

Tinbergen, N. 1959. Comparative studies of the behavior of gulls (*Laridae*): a progress report. Behaviour 15:1–70.

Tinbergen, N., M. Imperkoven and D. Franck. 1967. An experiment on spacing out as defence against predators. Behavior 28:307–21.

Titus, K. and J. A. Mosher. 1981. Nest-site habitat selected by woodland hawks in the Central Appalachians. Auk. 98:270–81.

Todd, A. W., L. B. Keith, and C. A. Fischer. 1981. Population ecology of coyotes during a fluctuation of snowshoe hares. J. Wildl. Manage. 45:629–40.

Toepfer, J. E. 1973. Movements and habitat use of greater prairie chickens in central Wisconsin. College of Nat. Resour., Univ. Wisconsin, Stevens Point. 2 pp. (mimeogr.)

Toepfer, J. E. 1976. Reintroduction of prairie chickens into the Crex Meadows Wildlife Area, Burnett County, Wisconsin. 5 pp. (mimeogr.)

Toepfer, J. E. 1979. Reintroduction of prairie chickens into the Crex Meadows Wildlife Area Burnett County, Wisconsin, Proc. Prairie Grouse Tech. Counc. 13, 12–14.

Tompa, F. S. 1964. Factors determining the numbers of song sparrows, *Melospiza melodia* (Wilson) on Mandarte Island, B. C., Canada. Acta Zool. Fenn. 109:1–73.

Trautman, L. G., L. F. Fredrickson, and A. V. Carter. 1974. Relationships of red foxes and other predators to populations of ring-necked pheasants and other prey. Trans. N. Am. Wildl. Nat. Resour. Conf. 39:24–52.

Treisman, M. 1975. Predation and the evolution of gregariousness. I. Models for concealment and evasion. Anim. Behav. 23:779–800.

Triver, R. L. 1972. Parental imvestment and sexual selection. Pp. 136–79 *in* B. G. Campbell, ed. Sexual selection and the descent of man. 1871–1971. Aldine Press, Chicago.

Triver, R. L. 1974. Parent-offspring conflict. Am. Zool. 14:249–64.

Trobec, R. J. and L. W. Oring. 1972. Effect of testosterone proprionate implantation on lek behavior of sharp-tailed grouse. Am. Midl. Nat. 87:531–36.

Unander, S. and J. B. Steen. 1985. Behaviour and social structure in Svalbard rock ptarmigan *Lagopus mutus hyperboreus*. Ornis Scand. 16:198–204.

Vakkari, P. 1980. Polymorphism in *Simyra albovenosa (Lepidoptera, Nocturidae). I.* Genetic control of the melanic forms. Hereditas 93:181–84.

Van Amburg, G. L., J. A. Swaby, and R. H. Pemble. 1981. Response of arthropods to a spring burn of tall grass prairie in northwestern Minnesota. Pp. 240–43 *in* R. L. Stuckey and K. J. Reese, eds. The prairie peninsula – in the "shadow" of Transeau. Proc. 6th N. Am. Prairie Conf. Ohio State Univ., Columbus.

Vance, D. R. and R. L. Westemeier. 1979. Interactions of pheasants and prairie chickens in Illinois. Wildl. Soc. Bull. 7:221–25.

Vanderschaegen, P. V. 1970. Food habits of ruffed grouse at the Cloquet Forest Research Center, Minnesota. M.S. thesis Univ. Minnesota, St. Paul.

Varley, G. C. and G. R. Gradwell. 1970. Recent advances in insect population dynamics. Annu. Rev. Entomol. 15:1–24.

Veen, J. 1977. Functional and causal aspects of nest distribution in colonies of the sandwich tern (*Sternas sandvicensis* Lath.). Behav. Supplement. 193 pp.

Viers, C. E., Jr. 1967. Home range and movements of the greater prairie chicken(*Tympanuchus cupido pinnatus*) with note on activities. M.S. thesis. Kansas State Univ., Manhattan.

Vine, I. 1973. Detection of prey flocks by predators. J. Theor. Biol. 40:207–10.

Vogl, R. J. 1964. Vegetational history of Crex Meadows, a prairie savanna in northwestern Wisconsin. Am. Midl. Nat. 72:157–75.

Voronin, R. N. 1978. Belaya kuropatka Bol'shezemel'skoy tundry. Leningrad (NAUKA).

Wagner, F. H. 1957. Late-summer mortality in the pheasant hen. Trans. N. Am. Wildl. Conf. 22:301–15.

Wagner, F. H., C. D. Besadny, and C. Kabat. 1965. Population ecology and management of Wisconsin pheasants. Wis. Conserv. Dep. Tech. Bull. 34. 168 pp.

Wagner, G. C., L. J. Beuving, and R. R. Hutchinson. 1979. Androgen dependency of aggressive target-biting and paired fighting in male mice. Physiol. Behav. 22:43–46.

Wallestad, R. O. 1971. Summer movements and habitat use by sage grouse broods in central Montana. J. Wildl. Manage. 35:129–36.

Wallestad, R. O. 1975a. Male sage grouse responses to sagebrush treatment. J. Wildl. Manage. 39:482–84.

Wallestad, R. O. 1975b. Life history and habitat requirements of sage grouse in central Montana. Mont. Dep. Fish and Game. 66 pp.

Wallestad, R. O. and D. Pyrah. 1974. Movement and nesting of sage grouse hens in central Montana. J. Wildl. Manage. 38:630–33.

Wallestad, R. O. and P. Schladweiler. 1974. Breeding season movements and habitat selection of male sage grouse. J. Wildl. Manage. 38:634–37.

Wallestad, R. O. and R. C. Watts. 1972. Factors effecting annual sage grouse productivity in central Montana. Mont. Fish and Game Dep. Proj. 120-R-3, Job GB-2.01. 23 pp.

Ward, P. and A. Zahavi. 1973. The importance of certain assemblages of birds as information centers for finding food. Ibis 115:517–34.

Waser, P. M. and R. H. Wiley. 1979. Mechanisms and evolution of spacing in animals. Pp. 159–223 *in* P. Marler and J. G. Vandenbergh, eds. Handbook of behavioral neurobiology. Vol. 3. Social Behavior and Communication. Plenum Press, New York and London.

Watson, A. 1964. Aggression and population regulation in red grouse. Nature 202:506–7.

Watson, A. 1965. A population study of ptarmigan (*Lagopus mutus* in Scotland. J. Anim. Ecol. 34:135–72.

Watson, A. 1967a. Population control by territorial behaviour in red grouse. Nature 215:1274–75.

Watson, A. 1967b. Social status and population regulation in the red grouse (*Lagopus lagopus scoticus*). Proc. Royal Society Pop. Study Group 2:22–30.

Watson, A. 1970. Territorial and reproductive behaviour of red grouse. J. Reprod. Fert., Suppl. 11:3–14.

Watson, A. 1972. The behaviour of the ptarmigans. Br. Birds 65:43–117.

Watson, A. 1973. Moults of wild Scottish ptarmigan, *Lagopus mutus*, in relation to sex, climate and status. J. Zool. 171:207–23.

Watson, A. 1985. Social class, socially-induced loss, recruitment and breeding of red grouse. Oecologia 67:493–98.

Watson, A., R. Hewson, D. Jenkins, and P. Parr. 1973. Population densities of mountain hares compared with red grouse on Scottish moors. Oikos 24:225–30.

Watson, A. and D. Jenkins. 1964. Notes on the behaviour of the red grouse. Br. Birds 57:137–70.

Watson, A. and D. Jenkins. 1968. Experiments on population control by territorial behavior in red grouse. J. Anim. Ecol. 37:595–614.

Watson, A. and G. R. Miller. 1971. Territory size and aggression in a fluctuating red grouse population. J. Anim. Ecol. 40:367–83.

Watson, A. and R. Moss. 1970. Dominance, spacing behaviour and aggression in relation to population limitation in vertebrates. Pp. 167–220. *in* A. Watson, ed. Animal populations in relation to their food resources. Blackwell Sci. Publ., Oxford and Edinburgh.

Watson, A. and R. Moss. 1972. A current model of population dynamics in red grouse. Proc. Int. Ornithol. Congr. 15:134–49.

Watson, A. and R. Moss. 1979. Population cycles in the Tetraonidae. Ornis Fenn. 56:87–109.

Watson, A. and R. Moss. 1980. Advances in our understanding of the population dynamics of red grouse from a recent fluctuation in numbers. Ardea 68:103–11.

Watson, A. and R. Moss. 1982. Heritability of egg size, hatch weight, body weight, and viability in red grouse (*Lagopus lagopus scoticus*). Auk 99:683–86.

Watson, A., R. Moss, and R. Parr. 1984a. Effects of food enrichment on numbers and spacing behaviour of red grouse. J. Anim. Ecol. 53:663–78.

Watson, A., R. Moss, P. Rothery, and R. Parr. 1984b. Demographic causes and predictive models of population fluctuations in red grouse. J. Anim. Ecol. 53:639–62.

Watson, A. and P. J. O'Hare. 1979. Red grouse populations on experimentally treated and untreated Irish bog. J. Appl. Ecol. 16:433–52.

Watson, A. and R. Parr. 1981. Hormone implants affecting territory size and aggressive and sexual behavior in red grouse. Ornis Scand. 12:55–61.

Watt, P. G. 1969. Mobility patterns, habitat relationships and reproductive success of greater prairie chickens (*Tympanuchus cupido pinnatus*) in northeastern Kansas. M.S. thesis. Kansas State Univ., Manhattan.

Wayne, P. and G. F. Jolly. 1958. Notes on the breeding of the Iceland gyrfalcon. Br. Birds 51:285–290.

Weatherhead, P. J. and R. J. Robertson. 1979. Offspring quality and the polygyny threshold: "the sexy son hypothesis." Am. Nat. 113:201–8.

Weatherhead, P. J. and R. J. Robertson. 1981. In defence of the "sexy son" hypothesis. Am. Nat. 117:349–56.

Weaver, J. E. 1954. North American prairie. Johnsen Publ. Co., Lincoln, Nebr. 348 pp.

Weber, D. A. 1975. Blue grouse ecology, habitat requirements and response to habitat manipulation in north central Utah. Utah Coop. Wildl. Res. Unit. Special Rep. 33. 66pp.

Weeden, R. B. 1959a. Ptarmigan ecology and distribution of ptarmigan in western North America. Ph.D. thesis. Univ. British Columbia, Vancouver.

Weeden, R. B. 1959b. Ptarmigan research report. Arctic Inst. N. Am. Final Rep. 176 pp.

Weeden, R. B. 1963. Management of ptarmigan in North America. J. Wildl. Manage. 27:672–83.

Weeden, R. B. 1964. Spatial separation of sexes in rock and willow ptarmigan in winter. Auk 81:534–41.

Weeden, R. B. 1965a. Breeding density, reproductive success, and mortality of rock ptarmigan at Eagle Creek, Central Alaska, from 1960 to 1964. Trans. N. Am. Wildl. and Nat. Res. Conf. 30:336–48.

Weeden, R. B. 1965b. Grouse and ptarmigan in Alaska. P.R. project W-6-R-5 Vol. 5. Alaska Dept. of Fish and Game, Juneau, Alaska. 110 pp.

Weeden, R. B. 1969. Foods of rock and willow ptarmigan in central Alaska with comments on interspecific competition. Auk 86:271–81.

Weeden, R. B. and J. B. Theberge. 1972. The dynamics of a fluctuating population of ptarmigan in Alaska. Proc. Int. Ornithol. Congr. 15:90–106.

Weeden, R. B. and A. Watson. 1967. Determining the age of rock ptarmigan in Alaska and Scotland. J. Wildl. Manage. 31:825–26.

Wegge, P. 1980. Distorted sex ratio among small broods in a declining Capercaillie population. Ornis Scand. 11:106–9.

Wegge, P. and B. B. Larsen. 1987. Spacing of adult and juvenile capercaillie, *Tetrao urogallus* L., cocks during the breeding season. Auk (in press).

Weigand, J. P. 1977. The biology and ecology of Hungarian (European gray) partridge (*Perdix perdix* L.) in north central Montana. Mont. Dep. Fish and Game. Proj. W-91-R-12, W-120-R-1 through 8, Study GB-16.1, Job 1, Final Rep. 338 pp.

Weise, C. M. and J. R. Meyer. 1979. Juvenile dispersal and development of site-fidelity in the black-capped chickadee. Auk 96:40–55.

Weller, M. W. 1979. Density and habitat relationships of blue-winged teal nesting in northwestern Iowa. J. Wildl. Manage. 43:367–74.

Wells, D. G. 1981. Utilization of a northern Minnesota peatland by sharp-tailed grouse. M.S. Plan B Paper. Univ. Minnesota.

Wells, K. D. 1977. The social behaviour of anuran amphibians. Anim. Behav. 25:666–93.

Wells, M. C. and P. N. Lehner. 1978. The relative importance of the distance senses in coyote predatory behaviour. Anim. Behav. 26:257–58.

West, G. C. 1968. Bioenergertics of captive willow ptarmigan under natural conditions. Ecology 49:1035–45.

West, G. C. and M. S. Meng. 1966. Nutrition of willow ptarmigan in northern Alaska. Auk. 83:603–15.

West, G. C. and M. S. Meng. 1968. Seasonal changes in body weight and fat and the relation of fatty acid composition to diet in the willow ptarmigan. Wilson Bull. 80:426–41.

Westemeier, R. L. 1971a. Fourth annual report of the prairie grouse committee. Illinois Chapter—The Nature Conservancy. Ill. Nat. Hist. Survey, Urbana. 25 pp.

Westemeier, R. L. 1971b. The history and ecology of prairie chickens in central Wisconsin. Univ. of Wis., Col. of Agric. and Life Sciences. Res. Bull. 281. 61 pp.

Westemeier, R. L. 1973. Prescribed burning in grassland management for prairie chickens in Illinois. Proc. Tall Timbers Fire Ecol. Conf. 12:317–38.

Westemeier, R. L. and D. R. Vance. 1975. Eighth annual report of the prairie grouse committee. Illinois Chapter–The Nature Conservancy. Ill. Nat. Hist. Survey, Urbana. 27 pp.

Westerskov, K. 1956. Age determination and dating nesting events in the willow ptarmigan. J. Wildl. Manage. 20:274–79.

White, T. C. R. 1978. The importance of a relative shortage of food in animal ecology. Oecologia 33:71–86.

Wiens, J. A. 1974. Climatic instability and the "ecological saturation" of bird communities in North American grasslands. Condor 76:385–400.

Wiens, J. A. 1976. Population responses to patchy environments. Annu. Rev. Ecol. Syst. 7:81–120.

Wiger, R. 1982. Role of self-regulation mechanisms in cyclic populations of *Clethrionomys* with special reference to *C. glareolus*: a hypothesis. Oikos 38:60–71.

Wiley, R. H. 1973a. The strut display of male sage grouse: a "fixed" action pattern. Behaviour 47:129–52.

Wiley, R. H. 1973b. Territoriality and non-random mating in sage grouse *Centrocercus urophasianus*. Anim. Behav. Monogr. 6:85–169.

Wiley, R. H. 1974. Evolution of social organization and life history patterns among grouse (Aves:Tetraonidae). Q. Rev. Biol. 49:201–27.

Wiley, R. H. 1978. The lek mating system of the sage grouse. Sci. Am. 238:114–25.

Will, G. F. 1946. Tree ring studies in North Dakota. Agric. Exp. Station, N.D. Agric. Coll. Fargo, N.D. Bull. 338. 24 pp.

Williams, G. C. 1966a. Adaptation and natural selection: a critique of some current evolutionary thought. Princeton Univ. Press, Princeton, N.J. 307 pp.

Williams, G. C. 1966b. Natural selection, the costs of reproduction, and a refinement of Lack's principle. Am. Nat. 100:687–90.

Williams, G. C. 1975. Sex and evolution. Princeton Univ. Press. Princeton, N.J. 200 pp.

Williams, G. D. V. and G. W. Robertson. 1965. Estimating most probable prairie wheat production from precipitation data. Can. J. Plant Sci. 45:34–47.

Williams, J. B., D. Best, and C. Warford. 1980. Foraging ecology of ptarmigan at Meade River, Alaska. Wilson Bull. 92:341–51.

Williams, J. C. 1974. Mathematical analysis of red grouse populations. B.Sc. thesis. Univ. York, Toronto, Ontario.

Wilson, D. L. 1982. Nesting habitat of lesser prairie chickens in Roosevelt and Lea Counties, New Mexico. M.S. thesis. New Mexico State Univ., Las Cruces.

Wilson, E. O. 1975. Sociobiology: the new synthesis. Belknap Press, Cambridge, Mass., and London. 697 pp.

Wilson, J. W. III. 1974. Analytical zoogeography of North American mammals. Evolution 28:124–40.

Wise, D. R. 1982. Nutrition of wild red grouse (*Lagopus lagopus scoticus*). J. World Pheasant Assoc. 7:36–41.

Wittenberger, J. F. 1978. The evolution of mating systems in grouse. Condor 80:126–37.

Wittenberger, J. F. 1979. The evolution of mating systems in birds and mammals. Pp. 271–349 *in* P. Marler and J. G. Vandenbergh, eds. Handbook of behavioral neurobiology. Vol. 3. Social behavior and communication. Plenum Press, New York and London.

Wittenberger, J. F. 1981a. Animal social behavior. Duxbury Press, Boston, Mass. 722 pp.

Wittenberger, J. F. 1981b. Male quality and polygyny: "the sexy son" hypothesis revisited. Am. Nat. 117:329–42.

Wittenberger, J. F. and R. L. Tilson. 1980. The evolution of monogamy: hypotheses and evidence. Annu. Rev. Ecol. Syst. 11:197–232.

Woehr, J. R. 1974. Winter and spring shelter and food selection by ruffed grouse in central New York. M.S. thesis. State Univ. of New York.

Wolff, J. O. 1980. The role of habitat patchiness in the population dynamics of snowshoe hares. Ecol. Monogr. 50:111–30.

Wrangham, R. W. 1980. Female choice of least costly males; a possible factor in the evolution of leks. Z. Tierpsychol. 54:357–67.

Wright, S. 1968. The theory of gene frequencies. Vol. 2. Univ. Chicago Press, Chicago. 511 pp.

Wydoski, R. S. 1964. Seasonal changes in the color of starling bills. Auk 81:542–50.

Wynne-Edwards, V. C. 1962. Animal dispersion in relation to social behaviour. Oliver and Boyd, Edinburgh. 653 pp.

Wynne-Edwards, V. C. 1966. Regulation of numbers as a homeostatic process involving social behavior. Proc. Royal Society Pop. Study Group 1967. 2:7–12.

Yeatter, R. E. 1943. The prairie chicken in Illinois. Ill. Nat. Hist. Survey Bull. 22:377–416.

Yeatter, R. E. 1963. Population responses of prairie chickens to land-use changes in Illinois. J. Wildl. Manage. 27:739–57.

Zedja, J. 1966. Litter size in *Clethrionomys glareolus*. Zool. Listy 16:193–206.

Zweifel, R. G. 1981. Genetics of color pattern polymorphism in the California kingsnake. J. Hered. 72:238–44.

Zwickel, F. C. 1965. Early mortality and the numbers of blue grouse. Ph.D. thesis. Univ. British Columbia, Vancouver.

Zwickel, F. C. 1967. Some observations of weather and brood behavior in blue grouse. J. Wildl. Manage. 31:563–68.

Zwickel, F. C. 1972. Removal and repopulation of blue grouse in an increasing population. J. Wildl. Manage. 36:1141–52.

Zwickel, F. C. 1973. Dispersion of female blue grouse during the brood season. Condor 75:114–19.

Zwickel, F. C. 1975. Nesting parameters of blue grouse and their relevance to populations. Condor 77:423–30.

Zwickel, F. C. 1977. Local variations in the time of breeding of female blue grouse. Condor 79:185–91.

Zwickel, F. C. 1980. Surplus yearlings and the regulation of breeding density in blue grouse. Can. J. Zool. 58:896–905.

Zwickel, F. C. 1982. Demographic composition of hunter-harvested blue grouse in east central Vancouver Island, British Columbia. J. Wildl. Manage. 46:1057–61.

Zwickel, F. C. 1983. Factors affecting the return of young blue grouse to breeding range. Can. J. Zool. 61:1128–32.

Zwickel, F. C. and J. F. Bendell. 1967. Early mortality and the regulation of numbers in blue grouse. Can. J. Zool. 45:817–51.

Zwickel, F. C. and J. F. Bendell. 1972. Blue grouse, habitat, and populations. Proc. Int. Ornithol. Congr. 15:150–69.

Zwickel, F. C., J. F. Bendell, and A. N. Ash. 1983. Population regulation in blue grouse. Pp. 212–25 *in* F. L. Bunnell, D. S. Eastman, and J. M. Peek, eds. Proc. 14th Natural Regulation of Wildlife Populations Symp. For., Wildl. and Range Exp. Station, Univ. Idaho, Moscow.

Zwickel, F. C. and J. H. Brigham. 1970. Autumn sex and age ratios of spruce grouse in north-central Washington. J. Wildl. Manage. 34:218–19.

Zwickel, F. C., J. H. Brigham, and I. O. Buss. 1975. Autumn structure of blue grouse populations in north-central Washington. J. Wildl. Manage. 39:461–67.

Zwickel, F. C., I. O. Buss, and J. H. Brigham. 1968. Autumn movements of blue grouse and their relevance to populations and management. J. Wildl. Manage. 32:456–68.

Zwickel, F. C. and R. G. Carveth. 1978. Desertion of nests by blue grouse. Condor 80:109–11.

Zwickel, F. C. and A. N. Lance. 1965. Renesting in blue grouse. J. Wildl. Manage. 29:402–4.

Zwickel, F. C. and A. N. Lance. 1966. Determining the age of young blue grouse. J. Wildl. Manage. 30:712–17.

Zwickel, F. C., J. A. Redfield, and J. Kristensen. 1977. Demography, behavior, and genetics of a colonizing population of blue grouse. Can. J. Zool. 55:1948–57.

Index

Index

Prairie Chicken (cont'd.)

incubation, 202, 212, 228, 518, 519, 524, 576

introductions, 727

inversity, 605–609, 693, 694

latitude, 443, 496, 582–584, 592, 594, 628, 657, 658, 672–676, 680

laying, 202, 215, 228, 515–519, 524, 576, 588–589, 640, 677

"least-costly male" hypothesis, 465–472, 627, 628

lek, 201, 204, 205, 211, 216–220, 226, 227, 465–472, 476, 477, 483–485, 493, 498, 502–504, 515, 574, 671, 687, 688, 727, 728

limiting factors, 236–239, 679–686, 696–731

longevity, 532, 574, 575, 586–592 (*see also* mortality)

management, 225, 236–239, 644, 686–731

mate, 465–472, 666–672, 677, 679, 683–685

mate choice, 465–472, 474, 533–537, 576, 666–672, 677, 679, 683–685, 691

mating system, 226, 227, 439, 440, 465–472, 665–672

microtines, 681, 682

migration, 550–555, 576, 641–643, 670, 718

mortality, 206–209, 211, 232–235, 238, 239, 532, 537–548, 550–560, 574–579, 581, 586–592, 609–636, 642, 645, 647, 649, 650, 652, 656, 660, 662, 665–669, 672–676, 678, 679, 680, 683–686, 691, 693–696, 703, 720, 721, 730, 731 (*see also* survival)

movements, 197, 211–220, 226, 227, 230–232, 235, 236, 238, 239, 528, 529, 537–540, 545, 546, 550–556, 614, 641–643, 670, 704 (*see also* dispersal, migration)

natural selection, 473, 495

nest, 193, 201–207, 211–213, 215–224, 229, 230, 238, 239, 441–443, 465–472, 503–533, 578, 588–609, 617, 618, 627–629, 647, 659, 661, 662, 672–696, 719, 722, 724, 725, 729, 730, 731

nesting behavior, 193, 201–207, 211–213, 215–224, 229, 230, 238, 239, 441–443, 472, 474, 483–488, 503–533, 555, 567,

575, 576, 578–583, 614, 622–624, 666, 687, 688, 704, 711–718, 724–729

nonbreeding, 475, 534, 578–583, 635, 640–642, 644

numbers, 193, 236–239, 531, 532, 567–731

nutrition, 514–517, 581–584, 614, 640, 641, 644, 677, 681, 682 (*see also* food)

parental investment, 439–440, 477, 533, 596, 624

phenotypes, 567–577, 659, 664–672, 677, 683–685

philopatry, 204–206, 476, 477, 505, 517, 526, 527, 553, 555, 575, 705

plumage, 548, 549

polymorphism, 567–577, 643, 659, 664

population dynamics, 236–239, 578–685

population size, 193, 236–239, 531, 532, 567–731

predation, 203, 204, 207–209, 211, 212, 229, 234–239, 440–443, 465, 472, 527, 530–533, 540, 546–549, 557–560, 576, 581, 584–615, 626–630, 634–636, 637–640, 642, 666, 672–686, 693–695, 704, 711, 720–722, 728, 729, 731

predator control, 718–726, 730, 731

predator-cover complex, 587, 588, 619–624, 656, 680–686, 693, 711–726, 731

"predator switch-over" hypothesis, 635, 637–640, 681, 682

predators, 203, 204, 207–209, 211, 229, 234, 235, 441–443, 465–467, 472, 473, 481, 506, 518–520, 525, 527, 540, 546–549, 557–560, 562–565, 576, 587–589, 592–596, 606, 607, 610–616, 619–622, 626–630, 637–640, 656, 670–679, 680, 681, 683–685, 689, 690, 693, 696, 702, 703, 708, 712, 718–726, 730, 731

productivity, 203–209, 229, 236–239, 495, 503, 578, 579, 602–615, 618, 626–629, 635, 636, 645–673, 677, 679–686, 705, 730, 731 (*see also* brood, chicks, nest)

promiscuity, 439, 440, 465–472 (*see also* mating system)

renesting, 201, 203, 204, 215, 229, 230, 238, 239, 505, 506, 511, 512, 527, 530–533, 576, 595, 597–599, 659

reproduction, 193, 225, 226, 439, 440, 465–555, 575–577, 622, 702 (*see also* breeding behavior, brood-rearing behavior, nesting behavior)

Arthur T. Bergerud is an adjunct full-professor in the department of biology at the University of Victoria, British Columbia, where he has taught since 1967. Previously, he served as director of management for the Newfoundland Government's Wildlife division. Bergerud received his master's degree from the University of British Columbia. Some of the jounals to which he contributes are *Journal of Wildlife Management, Canadian Journal of Zoology, Arctic, Auk, Oikos,* and *Oecologia.*

Michael W. Gratson is currently working on his Ph.D. in zoology at the University of Victoria. He received his bachelor's and master's degrees in wildlife and biology from the University of Wisconsin, Stevens Point, in 1983.